PUBLIC OPINION IN EARLY MODERN SCOTLAND, C.1560–1707

In early modern Scotland, religious and constitutional tensions created by Protestant reform and regal union stimulated the expression and regulation of opinion at large. Karin Bowie explores the rising prominence and changing dynamics of Scottish opinion politics in this tumultuous period. Assessing protestations, petitions, oaths, and oral and written modes of public communication, she addresses major debates on the fitness of the Habermasian model of the public sphere. This study provides a historicised understanding of early modern public opinion, investigating how the crown and its opponents sought to shape opinion at large; the forms and language in which collective opinions were represented; and the difference this made to political outcomes. Focusing on modes of persuasive communication, it reveals the reworking of traditional vehicles into powerful tools for public resistance, allowing contemporaries to recognise collective opinion outside authorised assemblies and encouraging state efforts to control seemingly dangerous opinions.

KARIN BOWIE is Senior Lecturer in the School of Humanities at the University of Glasgow and a Fellow of the Royal Historical Society where she received the David Berry prize in 2015. She is the author of *Scottish Public Opinion in the Anglo-Scottish Union, 1699–1707* (2007) and articles in *Scottish Affairs, Journal of British Studies, Journal of Scottish Historical Studies* and the *Scotsman*.

CAMBRIDGE STUDIES IN EARLY MODERN BRITISH HISTORY

Series Editors
MICHAEL BRADDICK
Professor of History, University of Sheffield

ETHAN SHAGAN
Professor of History, University of California–Berkeley

ALEXANDRA SHEPARD
Professor of Gender History, University of Glasgow

ALEXANDRA WALSHAM
Professor of Modern History, University of Cambridge

This is a series of monographs and studies covering many aspects of the history of the British Isles between the late fifteenth century and the early eighteenth century. It includes the work of established scholars and pioneering work by a new generation of scholars. It includes both reviews and revisions of major topics and books which open up new historical terrain or which reveal startling new perspectives on familiar subjects. All the volumes set detailed research within broader perspectives, and the books are intended for the use of students as well as of their teachers.

For a list of titles in the series go to
www.cambridge.org/earlymodernbritishhistory

PUBLIC OPINION IN EARLY MODERN SCOTLAND, C.1560–1707

KARIN BOWIE
University of Glasgow

CAMBRIDGE
UNIVERSITY PRESS

University Printing House, Cambridge CB2 8BS, United Kingdom

One Liberty Plaza, 20th Floor, New York, NY 10006, USA

477 Williamstown Road, Port Melbourne, VIC 3207, Australia

314–321, 3rd Floor, Plot 3, Splendor Forum, Jasola District Centre, New Delhi – 110025, India

79 Anson Road, #06–04/06, Singapore 079906

Cambridge University Press is part of the University of Cambridge.

It furthers the University's mission by disseminating knowledge in the pursuit of education, learning, and research at the highest international levels of excellence.

www.cambridge.org
Information on this title: www.cambridge.org/9781108843478
DOI: 10.1017/9781108918787

© Karin Bowie 2020

This publication is in copyright. Subject to statutory exception and to the provisions of relevant collective licensing agreements, no reproduction of any part may take place without the written permission of Cambridge University Press.

First published 2020

A catalogue record for this publication is available from the British Library.

Library of Congress Cataloging-in-Publication Data
Names: Bowie, Karin, author.
TITLE: Public opinion in early modern Scotland, c.1560–1707 / Karin Bowie, University of Glasgow.
DESCRIPTION: First edition. | New York : Cambridge University Press, 2020. | Series: Cambridge studies in early modern British history | Includes bibliographical references and index.
IDENTIFIERS: LCCN 2020023803 (print) | LCCN 2020023804 (ebook) | ISBN 9781108843478 (hardback) | ISBN 9781108825184 (paperback) | ISBN 9781108918787 (epub)
SUBJECTS: LCSH: Public opinion–Scotland–History–16th century. | Public opinion–Scotland–History–17th century. | Scotland–Politics and government–16th century | Scotland–Politics and government–17th century. | Scotland–History–16th century. | Scotland–History–17th century.
CLASSIFICATION: LCC DA800 .B68 2020 (print) | LCC DA800 (ebook) | DDC 941.106–dc23
LC record available at https://lccn.loc.gov/2020023803
LC ebook record available at https://lccn.loc.gov/2020023804

ISBN 978-1-108-84347-8 Hardback

Cambridge University Press has no responsibility for the persistence or accuracy of URLs for external or third-party internet websites referred to in this publication and does not guarantee that any content on such websites is, or will remain, accurate or appropriate.

Contents

Acknowledgements	*page* vi	
List of Abbreviations	vii	
Introduction	1	
1 Protestations	21	
2 Petitions	50	
3 Oaths	89	
4 Public Communications	137	
5 The Inclinations of the People	185	
6 The Sense of the Nation	211	
Conclusions	239	
Bibliography	247	
Index	286	

Acknowledgements

At my viva in 2004, Dr Lionel Glassey asked me about the origins of the public sphere that, in typically narrow doctoral fashion, I had identified in Scotland in the decade before the Union of 1707. I thank him for this question and for the feedback he and others in the warm-hearted Early Modern Work in Progress seminar series at the University of Glasgow, chaired by my much-esteemed colleague Thomas Munck, have provided to my evolving efforts to answer this question. With funding from the Royal Society of Edinburgh, Thomas and I hosted a pair of workshops on early modern petitioning in 2017. I am grateful to the workshop participants for their inspiring contributions; Catherine Fergusson, then clerk to the Public Petitions Committee at the Scottish Parliament, for serving as our knowledge exchange partner; and Laura Doak for her able work as our project assistant. Special thanks are owed to John Young who shepherded our papers into a dedicated issue of *Parliaments, Estates and Representation* shortly after recovering from a serious illness. I thank the History subject area and Scottish history endowments at the University of Glasgow for funding conference and research travel relating to this project and the staff of the National Records of Scotland and the National Library of Scotland for their untiring aid. Thanks are also due to the series editors, Alasdair Raffe, Scott Spurlock, Neil McIntyre, Jamie Reid Baxter, Roger Mason, Ted Vallance, Laura Stewart, Callum Brown and all my wonderful colleagues in Scottish History at Glasgow for their advice and encouragement. I am deeply grateful to my doctoral students Laura Doak, Andrew Lind, Rebecca Mason, Jamie McDougall and Edwin Sheffield. Their research and publications have informed and stimulated this project immeasurably and it has given me great pleasure to be able to cite their exceptional work in this book. Lastly, but most importantly, I thank Jonathan, Emily and Lucy for recognising the importance of this project to me and supporting my efforts to carve out time for it.

Abbreviations

AGA	*Acts of the General Assembly of the Church of Scotland, 1638–1842* (Edinburgh: Church Law Society, 1843)
APGA	*Acts and Proceedings of the General Assemblies of the Kirk of Scotland*, ed. T. Thomson, 3 vols. (Edinburgh: Bannatyne Club, 1839–45)
CSP Scot	*Calendar of State Papers Relating to Scotland and Mary, Queen of Scots, 1543–1603*, ed. Joseph Bain and William K. Boyd, 12 vols. (Edinburgh: HMSO, 1898–1969)
DOST	'Dictionary of the Older Scottish Tongue' in *Dictionary of the Scots Language* (Glasgow, 2018), www.dsl.ac.uk
ERBG	*Extracts from the Records of the Burgh of Glasgow*, ed. Sir J. D. Marwick and Robert Renwick, 5 vols. (Glasgow: Scottish Burgh Records Society, 1876–916)
MPESE	Manuscript Pamphleteering in Early Stuart England, www.mpese.ac.uk
NLS	National Library of Scotland
NRS	National Records of Scotland
OED	*Oxford English Dictionary*
RCGA	*The Records of the Commissions of the General Assemblies of the Church of Scotland*, ed. Alexander F. Mitchell and James Christie, 2 vols. (Edinburgh: Scottish History Society, 1892–6)
RPCS	*The Register of the Privy Council of Scotland*, 3 series, 36 vols., ed. John Hill Burton, David Masson, P. Hume Brown, Henry Paton and Robert Kerr Hannay (Edinburgh: HM General Register House, 1877–1933; Burlington: Tanner Ritchie, 2004)
RPS	*Records of the Parliaments of Scotland to 1707*, ed. K. Brown (St Andrews, 2007–19), www.rps.ac.uk

viii *List of Abbreviations*

SND   'Scottish National Dictionary' in *Dictionary of the Scots Language* (Glasgow, 2018), www.dsl.ac.uk

TSP   *Tudor and Stuart Proclamations, 1485–1714, Vol. II Scotland and Ireland*, ed. Robert Steele (Oxford: Clarendon Press, 1910)

Introduction

In November 1706, as the Scottish Parliament debated a treaty of incorporating union between the Scottish and English kingdoms, the Scottish clergyman Robert Wylie published a pamphlet in Edinburgh arguing against this union. Wylie stated that 'the General Declared Sense and Sentiment of the Nation, runs so mightily against this Proposed Scheme of an Union; that the very Fears of it are like to cause a most dreadful Convulsion!' For the union to succeed, Wylie asserted, the 'Minds of the People' needed to be reassured and 'the Reasonable Part of the Nation' had to be persuaded that 'the Terms of Incorporating with England, are Honourable, Advantageous and Safe'.[1] These quotes suggest that at this time in Scotland, it was possible to imagine a collective body of individuals outside the Scottish parliament holding informed opinions on national affairs and, more importantly, that claims about their collective opinions could be presented in public discourse to influence political decisions. Wylie's argument, that the people's fears needed to be calmed and the nation's rational concerns assuaged before the government could achieve its union, would have made no sense if contemporaries did not acknowledge the existence and relevance of opinion at large.

Wylie's language is difficult to explain with current paradigms. The rise of authoritative, even sovereign, public opinion is seen as a crucial marker of modern Western democracy. For the past several decades, this phenomenon has been associated with the development of a structural public sphere, understood as an extra-institutional social space for the rational discussion of printed information by a male urban middle class. Through the public sphere, public opinion was created. But how could public opinion be formed in early modern polities like Scotland that lacked the large metropolitan print markets, clusters of coffee houses and burgeoning bourgeoisie so essential to the formation of this public sphere? The poor fit

---

[1] [Wylie], *The Insecurity of a Printed Overture for an Act for the Church's Security*, 6.

2   Public Opinion in Early Modern Scotland, c.1560–1707

of this structural model suggests that nothing should be happening with public opinion in early modern Scotland, yet the evidence tells another story.

To explain the Scottish case, this book offers a new approach that places public opinion at the centre of the analysis. Scholars have no agreed definition for public opinion, but it involves 'the formation, communication, and measurement of citizens' attitudes toward public affairs'.[2] Public opinion can be historicised by taking into account the political, social and technological context of governed human societies in specific times and places. Any person, male or female, elite or plebeian, might form and express an opinion through their perception and experience of governance, possibly enhanced by persuasive communications; and the opinions of collective groups of people might be invoked and represented to influence political decisions, though these representations may not be based on direct or accurate measurement. Public opinion could form in response to local or national governance, though this book will focus on national affairs.

This contrasts with alternative approaches that tie public opinion to the modern era in much more restrictive terms. In France on the eve of the Revolution, public opinion was seen by contemporaries as a modern invention, a product of stadial progress.[3] A similar spirit continues to inform histories of the public sphere and modern democratic public opinion. In investigating 'the rise of public opinion', Hans Speier defined public opinion as 'opinions on matters of concern to the nation freely and publicly expressed by men outside the government who claim as a right that their opinions should influence or determine the actions, personnel, or structure of their government.'[4] The rooting of Speier's definition in male rights–based citizenship inevitably led him to find the origins of public opinion in the birth of modern representative democracies. This suggests that public opinion cannot exist outside the modern moment. This book instead proposes to 'distinguish historical practice and outcomes from modern ideals' by investigating public opinion in early modern Scotland, providing a template for the investigation of public opinion in historical time.[5]

---

[2] Glynn et al., *Public Opinion*, 13. In some historical contexts, the notion of 'citizen' may be too restrictive.
[3] Baker, 'Politics and public opinion under the Old Regime: some reflections', 241.
[4] Speier, 'The rise of public opinion', 26–46.
[5] Bowie, 'Newspapers, the early modern public sphere and the 1704–05 *Worcester* affair', 10.

Introduction   3

The key questions to ask about public opinion are, how engaged were governed people in political affairs; how did they express their opinions; and what difference could these expressions make? These questions assess the formation and communication of collective opinions and their influence on political events. Historical study of public opinion needs to grapple with the problem that actual opinions may not have been equivalent to represented opinions. Unless a means of direct measurement such as polling or consultation was pursued, it may be difficult to recover actual opinion from the available sources. In other words, Wylie's assertions about widespread opposition to incorporating union do not provide conclusive evidence for opinion at large, though confidence might be improved through corroboration with other sources. This problem leads to the study of 'opinion politics', focusing on the courting and manifestation of opinions for political advantage and the vocabulary, authority and effect of these representations rather than a hindsight evaluation of the balance of actual opinions (though opinion formation can be considered as far as surviving sources allow).[6] This recognises that leaders, whether authorised or oppositional, might seek 'a power base in public opinion' and sees the resulting representations of collective opinion as 'constructed artefacts of a political process' encompassing 'opinion formation, expression and impact'.[7]

This study focuses on four modes of engagement and communication that were significant in the early modern Scottish context: protestations, petitions, oaths and public communications in oral, written and printed forms. These offered ways to record dissent (protestations), make complaints (petitions), create commitments (oaths) or speak to wide audiences (through a range of channels including proclamations, sermons, political poetry and pamphlets). By looking beyond the consumption of print, this approach will show how traditional devices like the protestation and petition were reworked into new tools for the making of public arguments on behalf of groups; how oaths were used in new ways to shape the opinions of large numbers of men and women; and how a range of communications was used by the crown and its opponents to inform and influence audiences, generating new ways of talking and thinking about extra-institutional opinions. Though crowds are not presented as a separate factor, the analysis will consider the involvement of related crowds

---

[6] Jon Cowans has called this 'the politics of public opinion'. Cowans, *To Speak for the People: Public Opinion and the Problem of Legitimacy in the French Revolution*, 6–8.
[7] Bowie, *Scottish Public Opinion and the Anglo-Scottish Union, 1699–1707*, 1.

(for example, the gathering of a crowd to present a petition) and how early modern representations of public opinion borrowed strength from a threat of collective disorder and violence.

The book will relate these activities to the political context of early modern Scotland, showing how the 1560 Protestant Reformation and the 1603 union of the Scottish and English crowns created situations in which oppositional groups found it useful to mobilise opinion at large and the crown found it necessary to devote effort to the management of opinions. It also will relate these activities to Scotland's social and cultural context, showing how rising literacy and religiosity made it easier to stimulate political views among ordinary men and women and at the same time made it harder to control their opinions. This will take account of linguistic differences between Scots and Gaelic-speaking regions in assessing the social reach of political communications and the inclusiveness of representations of national opinion.

This approach will yield a historicised portrait of public opinion in early modern Scotland, capturing subtle but substantive shifts that explain why Wylie could speak meaningfully of the sense of the nation and the minds of the people by 1706. These findings will enhance the political history of early modern Scotland and the composite British monarchy by systematically revealing the forms, rhetoric and political significance of public opinion in Scottish political affairs from the Reformation to the 1707 Union. In turn, by providing an analysis of what public opinion could mean in one early modern polity, the book outlines a method for the study of public opinion in any place and time without recourse to programmatic models.

***

This approach has been informed by the rich and diverse body of scholarship on the public sphere that has appeared since the 1990s and earlier works providing a history of public opinion in the modern era. Writing in 1989, J. A. W. Gunn provided an intellectual history of the concept of public opinion, seeking to identify 'at what points awareness of the sentiments of others matured into a formula similar to our modern notion'. Focusing on France and England, Gunn identified precursor language for what would become public opinion and dated the coining of 'public opinion' in English to the 1730s.[8] In the same year, however,

---

[8] Gunn, 'Public opinion', 246, 249–50.

Introduction

the publication of an English translation of Jürgen Habermas' neo-Marxist structural study of the making and decline of the modern public sphere provided early modernists with a compelling new way to investigate the rise of public opinion.[9] Habermas' emphasis on the reading and discussion of printed newspapers by a literate urban bourgeoisie in England complemented long-standing interest in the periodical press, more recent work on the 'print revolution' and, among historians of England, a shift in attention to extra-parliamentary politics in the Stuart and Hanoverian periods.[10] From the 1990s, as research proliferated on early modern news, pamphleteering and petitioning, early modern England, France and England's American colonies came to be seen as hotbeds for the development of a modern public sphere fed by political print, allowing 'public opinion' – a product of the public sphere that remained less well defined than its structural context – to become authoritative in Western politics and cultural life by the eighteenth century.[11]

As this work progressed, the Habermasian framework came under critique and scholars sought to refine its terms.[12] Tim Blanning aimed to strip any 'Marxist residue' from his 2002 account of the public sphere in eighteenth-century Britain, France and the Holy Roman Empire by recognising that the public sphere was both 'socially heterogeneous' and 'politically multi-directional', created by nobles, officials and clergy as well as burghers for state as well as private interests.[13] For Blanning and James Van Horn Melton, writing in 2004 on 'the public' in Enlightenment Europe, Habermas' public sphere appeared too late and his emphasis on the middle class was too limited.[14] While accepting 'the public sphere' and 'the public' as appropriate objects of study, these scholars sought to

---

[9] Habermas, *The Structural Transformation of the Public Sphere*.

[10] Cowan, 'Geoffrey Holmes and the public sphere: Augustan historiography from post-Namierite to post-Habermasian'; Lake and Pincus, 'Rethinking the public sphere in early modern England', 271–2. An example of eclipsed work on public opinion includes Downie, *Robert Harley and the Press: Propaganda and Public Opinion in the Age of Swift and Defoe*.

[11] Cust, 'News and politics in early seventeenth-century England'; Raymond, *The Invention of the Newspaper: English Newsbooks, 1641–49*; Raymond, *Pamphlets and Pamphleteering in Early Modern Britain*; Zaret, *Origins of Democratic Culture: Printing, Petitions and the Public Sphere in Early-Modern England*; Sawyer, *Printed Poison: Pamphlet Propaganda, Faction Politics and the Public Sphere in Early Seventeenth-Century France*; Warner, *The Letters of the Republic: Publication and the Public Sphere in Eighteenth-Century America*; Gunn, *Queen of the World: Opinion in the Public Life of France from the Renaissance to the Revolution*; Blanning, *The Culture of Power and the Power of Culture: Old Regime Europe 1660–1789*; Wilson, *The Sense of the People: Politics, Culture and Imperialism in England, 1715–1785*.

[12] Rospocher, 'Beyond the public sphere: a historiographical transition'.

[13] Blanning, *The Culture of Power*, 5–14.

[14] Melton, *The Rise of the Public in Enlightenment Europe*, 10–13.

6   Public Opinion in Early Modern Scotland, c.1560–1707

accommodate these concepts more closely to their eighteenth-century evidence. In 2006, Peter Lake and Steven Pincus offered an assessment of the changing contours of the public sphere in early modern England, seeking to refine Habermas' analytical concept by fitting it more closely to the English context. For Lake and Pincus, the notion of a public sphere helped to resolve historiographical disputes in English Civil War studies by integrating accounts of 'what actually happened' with 'contemporary perceptions and claims about what happened'.[15] In other countries where the Habermasian model did not fit so well, scholars described the public sphere as ephemeral or episodic, advancing and retreating with fluctuating print outputs, as in the 'evanescent' public sphere of sixteenth-century Venice.[16] In eras before the invention of print, researchers challenged Habermas' notion of a feudal public sphere monopolised by elite representations of power by identifying handwritten or oral forms of communication exchanged between ordinary people in social spaces. David Rollinson, for example, pointed to 'the emergence of public opinion' in thirteenth-century England, as a new middle class read handwritten bills.[17]

Other scholars, especially in historical literary studies, identified 'publics' and 'counter-publics', defined as the audiences and interest groups that formed around texts or discourses.[18] By challenging the idea that the public sphere created a unified, male, bourgeois public, this approach drew attention to the reception of texts by a range of readers, including women and radicals. Though the constitution of a public remained defined by the consumption of texts, these texts could include manuscript works. Concurrently, the cultural turn stimulated researchers to link the study of the book trade, literacy and reading with political history through the concept of print culture. This evaded the strictures of the public sphere, though not the tendency to assume, as in histories of the public sphere, that print enabled a progressive 'march of literacy, enlightenment and democracy'.[19] Though print culture focuses on printed texts, scholars

---

[15]   Lake and Pincus, 'Rethinking the public sphere', 272.

[16]   Rospocher and Salzberg, 'An evanescent public sphere: voices, spaces and publics in Venice during the Italian wars'.

[17]   Rollinson, *The Commonwealth of the People: Popular Politics and England's Long Social Revolution, 1066–1649*, 5, 141–3.

[18]   Warner, 'Publics and counterpublics'; Wilson and Yachnin, 'Introduction'; Benchimol and Maley (eds.), *Spheres of Influence: Intellectual and Cultural Publics from Shakespeare to Habermas*. The 'counter' concept also has been applied to the public sphere, e.g. Mellor, 'Joanna Baillie and the counter-public sphere'.

[19]   Raven, '"Print culture" and the perils of practice'; Raven, 'New reading histories, print culture and the identification of change: the case of eighteenth-century England', 272.

Introduction 7

like Jason Peacey have integrated parliamentary lobbying and petitioning with the production, distribution and reception of texts.[20] Others, including Adam Fox, have sought to reduce the hegemony of print by stressing the continuing importance of oral and manuscript communications.[21] Historians of the Reformation have included a wide range of communication forms, extending to musical performance, in studying what Andrew Pettegree has called a 'culture of persuasion'.[22] Similarly, Dutch historians have described a 'culture of communication' encompassing printed and oral propaganda in the urbanised United Provinces.[23] A cultural approach also has informed Mark Knights' wide-ranging study of the representation of public opinion in late Stuart England, including petitions, parliamentary instructions, oaths of association and pamphlets.[24]

At the same time, social and cultural research on popular politics has drawn attention to the role of communications and propaganda in the construction of popular consent. In closing his 2002 study of early modern English popular politics with a critique of the Habermasian public sphere, Andy Wood noted that while the proliferation of printed communications might have been new, the reliance of early modern monarchs on the tacit consent of their subjects was not.[25] In a 2003 study, Ethan Shagan highlighted the importance of popular engagement and cooperation in the successful embedding of the Reformation in England, urging scholars to attend to the creation of compliance as well as resistance.[26] John Walter's work on English popular politics in the civil war era has sought to break down barriers between high and low politics by illuminating the wide variety of means by which ordinary people became engaged in parliamentary politics in the 1640s, ranging from word-of-mouth networks, sermons and public events to protestations, pamphlets, petitions and oaths.[27] Noah Millstone's study of early Stuart manuscript pamphleteering has considered how these sources helped to create 'political

---

[20] Peacey, *Print and Public Politics in the English Revolution*; Peacey, 'The print culture of Parliament, 1600–1800'.
[21] Fox, *Oral and Literate Culture in England, 1500–1700*; Love, *Scribal Publication in Seventeenth-Century England*.
[22] Pettegree, *Reformation and the Culture of Persuasion*.
[23] Pollmann and Spicer (eds.), *Public Opinion and Changing Identities in the Early Modern Netherlands*.
[24] Knights, *Representation and Misrepresentation in Later Stuart Britain: Partisanship and Political Culture*.
[25] Wood, *Riot, Rebellion and Popular Politics in Early Modern England*, 186.
[26] Shagan, *Popular Politics and the English Reformation*.
[27] Walter, *Covenanting Citizens: The Protestation Oath and Popular Political Culture in the English Revolution*; Walter, *Understanding Popular Violence in the English Revolution: The Colchester Plunderers*.

8   Public Opinion in Early Modern Scotland, c.1560–1707

awareness' beyond high political circles, with a focus on practice and impact as well as text.[28] Tim Harris has shown how Charles II saw his father's wars with his three kingdoms as a failure in public relations, stimulating greater efforts to hold the hearts of his subjects in all three British kingdoms. Though Charles' efforts were facilitated by print technology, Harris has argued that the press 'is not the right place to start', because print provides a restricted view of popular politicisation by downplaying the formation of opinions through the experience of government.[29] A 2017 collection of papers organised by Laura Stewart on public and political participation in early modern Britain indicates a desire to integrate research on the public sphere and popular politics.[30]

Historians of Scotland have struggled to apply a model of the public sphere to the pre-Union era, in part because Alastair Mann's research on the Scottish book trade has confirmed the smallness of the domestic print market.[31] In a 2007 monograph, I used the concept of an emerging public sphere to explain the formation and expression of Scottish public opinion on Anglo-Scottish union in the period 1699–1707, but I had to stretch the Habermasian model to include petitions and crowd protests alongside printed texts. The resulting snapshot left open the question of what came before or after this episode.[32] In 2012, Alasdair Raffe described a 'culture of controversy' from the Restoration to the reign of Anne, arguing that the Habermasian public sphere could not explain early modern religious argument in Scotland because it could not accommodate the continuing authority of scripture over human reason and the relative paucity of printed discourse in Scotland. Raffe's cultural study incorporated a broad range of communications to describe religious disputation, including sermons, crowds and pamphlets.[33] Though these arguments overlapped with political affairs, the 'culture of controversy' framework reflected ecclesiastical debates and could not replace the public sphere as a model for political discourse. Laura Stewart turned to the notion of 'the public' in her 2015 study of the making of a Covenanted public from 1637 to 1651,

---

[28] Millstone, *Manuscript Circulation*.
[29] Harris, 'Publics and participation in the three kingdoms: was there such a thing as "British public opinion" in the seventeenth century?', 736.
[30] Stewart (ed.), *Publics and Participation in Early Modern Britain*.
[31] Mann, *The Scottish Book Trade 1500–1720: Print Commerce and Print Control in Early Modern Scotland*.
[32] Bowie, *Scottish Public Opinion*.
[33] Raffe, *The Culture of Controversy: Religious Arguments in Scotland, 1660–1714*.

Introduction 9

incorporating protestations, petitions, covenant oaths and pamphlets with attention to oral and manuscript delivery.[34]

Together these studies invite a longitudinal project to explain early modern public opinion in terms that fit the Scottish context. Groundwork for this book has been provided by recent publications on forms of popular political participation in Scotland. In a 2017 jointly-authored paper, Alasdair Raffe and I argued that 'new opportunities for public participation and political collectivity also developed from older modes of protest, complaint, association, and consultation' and identified protestations as an important mode of collective resistance in seventeenth-century Scotland.[35] The following year, a pair of workshops funded by the Royal Society of Edinburgh produced analyses of petitioning in legal, ecclesiastical and parliamentary contexts in early modern Scotland; and my volume of transcribed petitions from the 1706 to 1707 parliamentary session on Anglo-Scottish union included a discussion of participative petitioning and addressing in the century before the Union.[36]

In drawing attention to public opinion, this book follows Joad Raymond's 2007 call for 'a new model of something like a public sphere, built upon the categories of the actors who participated in it'.[37] But instead of offering a new model, it offers an approach for historicising public opinion in any given time and place that focuses on recovering the language, forms and impact of public opinion. David Coast's recent paper on public opinion in early modern England has confirmed the utility of this approach by showing how the voice of the people was constructed in early seventeenth-century complaint literature.[38] Keeping James Raven's warning against a 'teleological chronicle of progress' in mind, this study will not return to a search for the origins of modern public opinion.[39] Instead, it aims to overturn what Arlette Farge has identified as the 'facile anachronism' seen when historians take public opinion in the past for granted.[40] By identifying early modern public opinion in Scotland, the

---

[34] Stewart, *Rethinking the Scottish Revolution: Covenanted Scotland, 1637–1651*.
[35] Bowie and Raffe, 'Politics, the people, and extra-institutional participation in Scotland, c. 1603–1712'.
[36] Bowie and Munck (eds.), *Early Modern Political Petitioning and Public Engagement in Scotland, Britain and Scandinavia, c.1550–1795*; Bowie (ed.), *Addresses*.
[37] Raymond, 'Perfect speech: the public sphere and communication in seventeenth-century England', 49. On the problem of applying modern concepts to the past, see Kidd, 'Identity before identities: ethnicity, nationalism and the historian'.
[38] Coast, 'Speaking for the people in early modern England'.
[39] Raven, 'New reading histories, print culture and the identification of change', 272.
[40] Farge, *Subversive Words: Public Opinion in Eighteenth-Century France*, 2–3.

10   Public Opinion in Early Modern Scotland, c.1560–1707

book's findings can be compared to later forms of public opinion, informing current debates on the authority of extra-institutional opinion (a pressing example being the use of referenda to resolve contentious political questions).

***

To introduce the study of public opinion in early modern Scotland, the following will consider what is already known about public opinion in this era, incorporating a brief sketch of the meaning of the words 'public' and 'opinion' in seventeenth- and early eighteenth-century England, France and Scotland. 'The public' and 'public opinion' have been identified as neologisms in early modern England and France. 'The public' derived from the humanist term *res publica*, meaning the state or the commonweal.[41] In the sixteenth century, 'the public' commonly referred to public affairs and the public offices managed by appointees on behalf of the crown, but, Geoff Baldwin has argued, England's civil wars required a linguistic shift as parliament took charge of the commonweal.[42] The 'public' came to refer to 'an aggregate of particular persons' whose collective needs, known as the 'public interest', were served by the government.[43] By the Restoration, English writers routinely referred to their readers as 'the public', suggesting a national body of readers at large, while a 1696 dictionary defined the public as 'the Generality of Fellow-Citizens or People'.[44] Knights has agreed that the idea of an English public emerged in the 1640s and 'came of age' by the late seventeenth century, allowing public opinion to emerge alongside this new sense of the public, though the actual phrase 'public opinion' did not become prominent in political discourse until the 1730s.[45] Lexical evidence suggests that 'public opinion' in English or French (*l'opinion publique*) at first meant any opinions expressed in public, but by the early eighteenth century the phrase had attained the sense of widely held, collective opinions.[46] As Kathleen Wilson has shown, terms like 'the voice of the people' and 'the sense of the nation' were ubiquitous in Hanoverian political culture.[47] Public

---

[41] Gunn, 'Public interest'; Gunn, 'Public opinion'; Baldwin, 'The "public" as a rhetorical community in early modern England'; Withington, *Society in Early Modern England: The Vernacular Origins of Some Powerful Ideas*, 146, 166.

[42] Baldwin, 'The "public" as a rhetorical community in early modern England', 201–6.

[43] Gunn, 'Public interest', 198.

[44] Baldwin, 'The "public" as a rhetorical community in early modern England', 209.

[45] Knights, *Representation and Misrepresentation*, 94–5; Gunn, 'Public opinion', 249–50.

[46] 'Public, adj. and n.', *OED*; Gunn, 'Public opinion', 249.   [47] Wilson, *The Sense of the People*.

Introduction   11

opinion could be discerned from various sources, including printed materials, coffeehouse talk and collective petitions. As Knights has shown, public opinion in early modern England became increasingly contested, with competing representations seeking to speak for localities and the nation at large.[48]

The term 'opinion' could carry negative associations. Gunn has suggested that the neo-Latin *opinio* was 'a philosophical term to describe a product of the imagination' rather than 'the more reliable judgments derived from reason'.[49] The French maxim that opinion was 'the queen of the world' reflected a jaundiced view of 'common', 'vulgar' or 'general' opinion, considered to be ill-informed and unreliable. More positively, Rollinson has identified a literary and political language of 'commune opinioun' in England from the thirteenth century that could refer to the shared views of a community.[50] In the seventeenth century, Baldwin and Knights have argued, theories of popular sovereignty and the English system of representative parliamentary government allowed public opinion to be considered authoritative in a general sense, although any particular representation of public opinion could be attacked as partisan, ill-informed or unreasonable.[51]

Public opinion in early modern Scotland shared some cultural and linguistic elements with England and France. As in England, 'public' ('publick', 'publict', 'publique') derived from *res publica* and was used as a shorthand for the public weal, public affairs or the public purse.[52] In a sermon delivered at the coronation of Charles II in January 1651, the cleric Robert Douglas urged the new king to 'care more for the publick, then his owne interest', contrasting the needs of the commonweal with selfish personal desires.[53] In the same year, a manuscript declaration made in the name of the 'poor oprest Commons of Scotland' referred to 'the publique' in a way that could be interpreted as a body of taxpayers or, more indirectly, as the treasury, funded by taxpayers at large.[54] Scottish writers recognised their readers as an aggregate of individuals with opinions, but explicit references to them as a 'public' appeared more slowly

---

[48] Knights, *Representation and Misrepresentation.*   [49] Gunn, 'Public opinion', 248.

[50] Speier, 'The rise of public opinion', 30–31; Gunn, *Queen of the World*, 13–14; Rollinson, *The Commonwealth of the People*, 136–43.

[51] Baldwin, 'The "public" as a rhetorical community in early modern England', 209–11; Knights, *Representation and Misrepresentation*, esp. 34–37, 95–96.

[52] 'Public wele', *DOST.*

[53] Douglas, *The Form and Order of the Coronation of Charles the Second*, 33.

[54] Stevenson, 'Reactions to ruin, 1648-51. A declaration and vindication of the poore opprest commons of Scotland, and other pamphlets', 261.

12   Public Opinion in Early Modern Scotland, c.1560–1707

than in England, probably indicating the adoption of an English idiom. In his 1597 legal reference work *De Verborum Significatione*, the lawyer Sir John Skene expressed a conventional fear of the judgement of readers: 'I am affrayed of all Readers, for ilk man hes his awin Judgement and opinion, quhairof their is als mony contrarieties, as diversities of persons'.[55] Writing a century later in 1700, the Aberdeenshire laird William Seton of Pitmedden still used 'the Publick' to refer to the public interest or commonweal, rather than a public of critical readers.[56] In 1711, however, Patrick Abercromby reflected a newer sense of the public in his statement that as an author he aimed to 'court the Publick into a good Opinion of my self'.[57]

In Scottish sources, 'opinion' tended to indicate an informed view, with positive or negative connotations depending on the context.[58] In the records of the early modern Scottish parliament, 'opinions' are mentioned in relation to consultations. In 1630, the estates were told that Charles I wished to hear their 'opinions' on tithes, the economy, the law and taxation.[59] For Sir John Skene, an opinion was a reasoned argument supported with evidence, offered as a viewpoint rather than a known truth.[60] In religious matters, God's revealed truth served as the benchmark against which opinions were judged. In sending a paper on predestination to a friend, the minister Robert Baillie asked him to 'shew me your opinion of the trueth of my arguments.'[61] Seeing the diversity of opinion on religious matters as a threat to the hegemony of God's truth, a 1627 pamphlet bemoaned the 'singularitie of Opinion' found among apparently pious people.[62] In 1621, a proclamation by James VI ordered dissident clerics to leave Edinburgh because they were encouraging 'badd opinions' among the people. A subsequent supplication by the ministers refuted the idea that their views, which they considered to be true, should be called mere 'opinions'.[63] These clerics did not agree that their views were 'badd', though they agreed that 'opinions' could be wrong or misguided.

Like 'opinion', 'common opinion' could have positive or negative implications. John Ford has shown that in Scotland's legal and learned

---

[55] 'To the Reader', in Skene, *De Verborum Significatione: The Exposition of the Termes and Difficill Wordes, Conteined in the Foure Buikes of Regiam Majestatem, and Uthers.*
[56] Seton of Pitmedden, *The Interest of Scotland in Three Essays*, 79.
[57] Abercromby, *The Martial Achievements of the Scots Nation*, i, 1.   [58] 'Opinioun, n.', *DOST.*
[59] *RPS* A1630/7/2, 28 July 1630.   [60] Skene, *De Verborum Significatione*, sig. B2v.
[61] Laing (ed.), *The Letters and Journals of Robert Baillie*, 8.
[62] Hay, *An Advertisement to the Subjects of Scotland*, 3.
[63] Calderwood, *The History of the Kirk of Scotland*, vii, 465, 473.

Introduction 13

spheres, 'common opinion' referred to the collective or majority views of experts, tested by disputation in academic settings or issued by courts as judgements.[64] More generally, the term indicated impressions generated by gossip and hearsay. A 1643 remonstrance to the Scottish parliament equated 'common opinion' with 'conceatt' and rejected both in favour of 'particular and distinct knowledge'.[65] 'The opinion of the world' acknowledged an even more general sense of reputation, going beyond national boundaries. Demonstrating a contemporary awareness of what now would be called public relations, in 1646 a lawyer warned that charges of treason brought against his client were contrary to the law of nations and would not be viewed as fair 'in the opinion of the warld'.[66]

Though public opinion has not been a common topic of investigation in early modern Scottish history, the study of counsel and consent indicates traditional channels for the expression of elite political opinions. Emphasising the importance of counsel in Scotland's personal monarchy, Roger Mason, Alan MacDonald and Jacqueline Rose have argued that the eclipsing of typical patterns of conciliar government and personal access to the monarch after the 1603 union stimulated the 1637–41 Covenanting revolution, with its assertion of constitutional limits on monarchical powers and desire for improved dialogue between Scotland and London.[67] Before 1603, parliaments and conventions of the estates were called frequently by the adult James VI, achieving what MacDonald has called an 'unprecedented level of formal consultation' that made the falling away of meetings after 1603 all the more painful.[68] Existing tensions, especially in relation to unresolved disputes over the security of the reformed church, were exacerbated by the monarch's greater distance. As Mason has stated, a 'perceived sidelining of Scottish voices and Scottish grievances reflected the apparent malfunctioning of counsel under an absentee ruler'.[69]

This sidelining was manifested not just with a reduction in the frequency of parliamentary meetings, but also through the exertion of greater crown control over parliament when it met, limiting the ability of members to express considered opinions on legislation and policies. From 1587,

---

[64] Ford, *Law and Opinion in Scotland During the Seventeenth Century*, 8–9, 25.

[65] *RPS* 1643/6/21, 6 July 1643. [66] *RPS* 1646/11/113, 10 January 1646.

[67] MacDonald, 'Consultation and consent under James VI'; MacDonald, 'Consultation, counsel and the "early Stuart period in Scotland"'; Mason, 'Counsel and covenant: aristocratic conciliarism and the Scottish Revolution'; Rose, 'Councils, counsel and the seventeenth-century composite state'.

[68] MacDonald, 'Consultation, counsel and the "early Stuart period in Scotland"', 196.

[69] Rose, 'Councils, counsel and the seventeenth-century composite state', 273.

14 Public Opinion in Early Modern Scotland, c.1560–1707

Scotland's unicameral assembly of estates consisted of individually invited peers, commissioners elected from a small pool of lesser nobles from each shire, commissioners selected by burgh councils to represent chartered royal burghs and, in 1600–38 and 1662–89, bishops from the reformed church.[70] As the King's head court for his tenants-in-chief, the Scottish parliament did not offer direct representation for 'the commons'; instead, the interests of rural tenants and urban inhabitants were represented by their landlords and burgh commissioners. Though parliament, as a result, was socially narrow, members were expected to serve the commonweal by presenting local grievances, hearing petitions and debating and voting on laws proposed by the crown. After 1603, however, debate increasingly was restricted to the Lords of the Articles, a committee for the preparation of legislation with strong royal influence over the selection of members. Under Charles I, after the Articles committee reviewed proposed legislation and petitions, acts were aggregated and presented for the simple assent of the estates.[71]

A similar trend towards the restriction of meetings and debate can be identified in the General Assembly of the reformed Kirk (Church) of Scotland. By the late sixteenth century, this assembly consisted of clerical commissioners from presbyteries (regional church courts encompassing 12 to 20 parishes) and the universities.[72] Some lay elders also attended, with more appearing during periods of contention. The general assembly voted on acts relating to the activity, government and worship practices of the church, while parliament gave civil sanction to the national kirk's confession, constitution and laws relating to moral behaviour and worship. As with parliament, the general assembly met regularly before 1603 and far less often after the 1603 Union. In 1592, the monarch's power to convene the assembly was ratified and after 1596 James VI established a compliant executive committee and restored bishops as a parliamentary estate.

---

[70] The barons attended parliament intermittently in the medieval period. After 1587, baron representatives were elected from each shire. The church estate after the 1560 Reformation included bishops and lay commendators. After a period of controversy over the presence of bishops in parliament, crown-appointed bishops were reinstated in parliament from 1600. McAlister and Tanner, 'The first estate: parliament and the church'; Brown, 'The second estate: parliament and the nobility'.

[71] MacDonald, 'Voting in the Scottish parliament before 1639'; Wells, 'Constitutional conflict after the union of the crowns: contention and continuity in the parliaments of 1612 and 1621'; Goodare, The Scottish parliament of 1621'; Goodare, 'The Scottish convention of estates of 1630'; Young, 'Charles I and the 1633 parliament'; Koenigsberger, 'The power of deputies in sixteenth-century assemblies'. Restrictions on petitioning to parliament will be discussed in chapter 2.

[72] For a map of parishes and presbyteries in 1607, see McNeill and MacQueen (eds.), An Atlas of Scottish History to 1707, 390.

Introduction 15

Between 1603 and 1618, only six meetings of the general assembly were held, with none in the following two decades. These meetings were much more managed, with greater use made of a 'privie conference' for preparing acts (like the Lords of the Articles) to minimise open debate.[73]

In the absence of satisfactory meetings, dissidents found ways to organise and express extra-institutional opinions in the name of the nation and the kirk, while the crown devoted varying levels of effort to wooing and containing opinion at large. This book will provide the first systematic study of the expression of extra-institutional opinions in Scotland across two phases. In the first phase, from the 1560 Reformation to the eve of the 1688–90 Revolution, traditional devices like protestations, petitions and oaths were re-engineered to increase their reach and impact while rising literacy and print production made written and printed information more accessible alongside oral communications. In the language of public opinion, claims about the actual opinions of subjects at large began to be made alongside abstract representations of the realm and its commonweal. These claims and representations were set in opposition to royal policy as dissidents demanded unfettered meetings of parliament and the general assembly. In response, the crown sought to contain adversarial expressions of opinion, using laws designed to suppress sedition, while also deploying public communications to inform and persuade. Both sides employed oaths to stimulate, shape and contain opinion in targeted groups or, more ambitiously, the entire population. In the second phase, from the 1688-90 Revolution to the making of the United Kingdom in 1707, the Scottish parliament and general assembly met regularly, and petitioning and printing were less constrained. In these new circumstances, the crown's management methods were not always able to maintain control of parliament as discontent with the royal policy was expressed more freely in the name of the people and the nation. Because the Revolution had removed prelacy on the grounds that the people preferred presbyterian church government, the inclinations of the people became a focus of public discourse. The sense of the nation came to the fore as King William made a series of missteps in the management of Scottish opinion at large and Queen Anne twice proposed an incorporating union of Scotland and England. Tools honed under previous reigns were deployed in large-scale petitioning efforts, high-profile protestations and fierce pamphlet attacks as opponents attempted to counter royal policy with public opinion.

---

[73] MacDonald, *The Jacobean Kirk 1567–1625: Sovereignty, Polity and Liturgy*, chs 2–6; *APGA*, iii, 1152, 1154–6.

16 Public Opinion in Early Modern Scotland, c.1560–1707

A striking element of these activities was their potential to include women. Women heard oral communications and increasingly received the necessary education, especially in godly households, to read written or printed papers, pamphlets and books. As members of the kirk, women could be included in national confessional oaths from 1581 and certainly were included in the very widespread swearing of covenant oaths from 1638. Men typically signed protestations, petitions and oaths on behalf of their communities, but for each category, a few examples survive with female hands. Women participated in events relating to these devices, as planners, strategists, rioters and members of demonstrating crowds. When their husbands were constrained by judicial penalties, the wives of clerical dissidents produced manuscript polemic and staged female-led petitioning events. In the late Restoration, women died for treason because they would not recant their views. The engagement of women in Scottish opinion politics meant that, by 1706, a commentator calling for a referendum on the question of union could argue that this should include not just male freeholders but their female relatives.

At the same time, opinion politics in Scotland faced limitations. Sheer distance from Edinburgh to the west and north, including the Hebrides, Orkney and Shetland, acted as a constraint, requiring greater travel time for communications and people. Language also provided a significant barrier. In this period, the business of kirk and crown was conducted in Scots, yet most of the population to the north and west spoke vernacular Gaelic. Though multilingual elites in Gaelic-speaking regions, including clan chiefs, gentry, clerics and bards, could translate and mediate, this complicated the engagement of opinions at large. Moreover, the Highlands occupied a cultural blind spot for many Lowlanders, making it easy for Scotland's sylvan regions to be overlooked in the making of claims about the nation or the people. As Martin MacGregor has shown, Lowland literati recognised the Gaelic roots of the Scottish realm but saw contemporaneous Gaels as barbarous and uncivil. As a result, Gaels tended to be 'present in the past, absent in the present'.[74] In 1621, for example, the Presbyterian minister David Calderwood asked if any other Reformation had spread the true gospel 'so universally', forgetting that the reformed church faced real difficulties in providing sufficient Gaelic-speaking ministers to Highland parishes.[75] Historians of early modern Ireland have rejected a narrow view of the Irish public sphere in which 'Gaelic Ireland

[74] MacGregor, 'Gaelic barbarity and Scottish identity in the later Middle Ages', 47.
[75] Calderwood, *Quaeres Concerning the State of the Church of Scotland*, 3.

Introduction 17

is presumed to be too illiterate and impoverished to form anything resembling public opinion'. Instead, they have emphasised forms of communication beyond printed English, stretching the Habermasian framework to fit Ireland's bilingual and colonial context.[76] This book will consider how grassroots opinion formation was facilitated in Scottish Gaeldom through a range of practices, though further research is required to pursue this topic more fully. While protestations, petitions and pamphlets printed or written in Scots may have had a less immediate social reach and impact, oral modes of engagement facilitated by Gaelic-speaking elites included the taking of covenant oaths and the hearing of Gaelic political poetry in meaningful community settings.

The long time frame of this book will capture tensions arising from the Scottish Reformation, the 1603 union, the Covenanting revolution and British Civil Wars, the creation of a British commonwealth in 1652, the restoration of the monarchy and episcopacy in 1660-62, the accession of the Catholic James VII and II in 1685 and a subsequent revolution in 1688–90. The first four chapters will consider how traditional tools for the engineering of consent and the expression of collective grievances came to be used more proactively and forcefully, making opinion at large more prominent in Scottish political discourse and more significant in political events. Chapter 1 will show how the protestation, a standard juridical device used across Europe to defend legal rights, was adapted to deliver public statements of dissent in extra-institutional settings, allowing contemporaries to imagine public opinion as something existing outside of authorised assemblies. This will indicate how contemporary notions of Christian testimony and the collection of signatures added weight to these opinions. Chapter 2 will show how humble petitions were turned into adversarial demands for change, supported by reasoned arguments and large numbers of signatures in increasingly specialised forms, including remonstrances, representations and addresses. As with protestations, this chapter will show how large-scale petitioning created popular engagement and provided public representations of extra-institutional opinions. Chapter 3 will show how the opinions of subjects were stimulated and corralled as confessional oaths and feudal bands were synthesised into powerful new covenant oaths that engendered religious and political opinions and facilitated claims about the conscientious commitments of the laity at large. When the politicisation

---

[76] Hamrick, 'The public sphere and eighteenth-century Ireland', 87–100.

forged by these oaths stimulated civil disobedience, the crown sought to regain control of its subjects through oaths of obedience, allegiance and abjuration and, briefly, the abandonment of religious oaths in 1687. Chapter 4 will consider how far and in what terms persuasive arguments were directed in oral, written and printed forms to an increasingly literate nation. Contemporary rationales for publication will be traced, showing how negative ideas about the limited capacity of the multitude were moderated by an increasing expectation that subjects should be addressed with reasoned arguments. This chapter will explore also a shift in contemporary rhetoric for the representation of public opinion from allegorical figures to direct statements on behalf of extra-institutional communities and groups.

The last two chapters will assess the application of these tools and terms in the period from the Revolution of 1688–90 to the Union of 1707. Chapter 5 will consider how the 'inclinations of the generality of the people' came to appear in the 1689 Claim of Right and what contemporaries meant by this phrase. By bringing popular preferences to the forefront of political discourse, this unusual formulation stimulated attempts to measure the actual opinions of the people through polls and petitions. Chapter 6 will consider the crown's difficulties in managing parliament after the Revolution and how an aggressive 'Country' opposition party sought to shape and capitalise on 'the sense of the nation'. This will show how Queen Anne's proposals for incorporating union stimulated the question of whether the sense of the nation was to be measured by an elected parliament or other means. The conclusion will consider the political significance of this story of public opinion for Scottish and British history, looking beyond 1707 to see how the articulation of Scottish national opinion before the Union helped to shape British political culture thereafter.

As Phil Withington has observed, early modernists have wavered between diachronic searches for the origins of modernity and synchronic analyses of words, behaviours and ideas, but 'a growing number of studies show that it is possible for social historians to reconcile the possibilities of historicism with an appreciation of change over time'.[77] In this book, a series of synchronic snapshots, assessing the meaning of words and actions in particular episodes, will yield a diachronic sense of change across one and a half centuries. Space will not allow a close

---

[77] Withington, *Society in Early Modern England*, 6.

Introduction 19

account of every petition, protestation or pamphlet produced in this period, but significant and typical texts from formative events will be interpreted with close attention to context. This will draw on methodologies from the history of ideas in which texts are interpreted in a wide and deep discursive context and incremental changes are understood to be stimulated by the demands placed on actors by events and circumstances.[78] Plenty of space will remain for further and deeper research, especially to probe differences between Scots and Gaelic-speaking regions, the participation of women and the impact of particular genres of communication.

The sources consulted for this book have in the past been used to speculate about what opinions the nation held at key moments, from the 1560 Reformation to the 1707 Union. But this study does not wish to answer these over-generalised and often fruitless questions. Instead, it seeks to understand how opinion at large was stimulated and expressed and what impact this had. This will require consultation of a very wide range of primary sources with the aid of relevant secondary literature, including protestations, declarations, testimonies, petitions, supplications, remonstrances, representations, addresses, bands, oaths, covenants, pamphlets, proclamations, pasquils, poems and ballads. To contextualise these sources and show how the government responded to them, council records, assembly minutes, legislation and letters will be consulted. While this source base will include archival discoveries, the originality of this study primarily will be created by asking new questions of a new combination of sources.

By identifying the language and dynamics of public opinion in early modern Scotland – a place that was not meant to have a public opinion because it had no public sphere – this book outlines a new approach that sidesteps the determinism of structural models, advocating instead an empirical analysis of language and cultural forms specific to a political context. This analysis can shed light on questions presently addressed by studies of the public sphere. It will show how public opinion became more salient in early modern Scottish political culture, contributing to the prominence and authority of public opinion in modern British political culture, without relying on a vigorous print market or urban coffeehouses. Moreover, by providing the first survey of Scottish public opinion from the Reformation to the Union, it will illuminate a political phenomenon only

---

[78] Tully, 'The pen is a mighty sword: Quentin Skinner's analysis of politics', 7–25.

glancingly identified in current Scottish historiography, cutting across more typical lines of inquiry defined by reigns, institutions or distinctive elements such as the Covenanters. It does not aim to provide a prescriptive model; instead, it invites further research to develop its approach, allowing historians to compare early modern Scottish public opinion to public opinion in other polities and eras.

CHAPTER I

Protestations

A Protestatione is the most ordinarie, humble and legall way for obviating any prejudice may redound to any legall act, and of preserving our right, permitted to the meanest subjects in the highest Courts of Assemblie and Parliament, whensoever they are not fully heard, or, being heard, are grieved by any iniquitie in the sentence; which is grounded on the law of nature and nationes, that it is the perpetuall custom of this kingdome, even upon this reason, to protest, as it wer in favour of all persons interested.

Reasons for a Protestation, 1638[1]

We distinguish therefore, between a Declaring of a Hostil War and Martial Insurrection, and Declaring a War of Contradiction and Opposition by Testimonies.

James Renwick and Alexander Shields, *Informatory Vindication*, 1687[2]

This book begins with a surprisingly obscure device for registering a dissent in a court or assembly: the protestation. Protestations appear in episodes of political conflict in early modern Europe but have attracted little systematic analysis as a mode of resistance. A very significant early modern protestation was recorded in the legislative assembly of the Holy Roman Empire in Speyer in 1529. Faced with the likely passage of an edict designed to limit the spread of religious reform, a group of princes and representatives of imperial cities made a formal protestation against the ratification of the edict, citing law and conscience as grounds for their dissent. From this, they and their co-religionists became known as 'Protestants'.[3] In Scotland too, protestation was available as a means of dissent. Sir David Lindsay imagined a situation opposite that of Speyer in his 1552 play, *Ane Satyre of the Thrie Estaits*. When the Scottish estates

---

[1] Leslie, A *Relation of Proceedings Concerning the Affairs of the Kirk of Scotland, from August 1637 to July 1638*, 119.
[2] [Renwick and Shields], *Informatory Vindication*, 68.   [3] Wolgast, 'Speyer, Protestation of'.

22   Public Opinion in Early Modern Scotland, c.1560–1707

proposed an act to reduce corruption in Scotland's consistory courts, Spiritualie, a character embodying the ecclesiastical estate, made a protestation. Stating 'Till all your acts plainly I dissent', Spiritualitie asked a scribe to prepare an 'instrument' recording his protest.[4]

Reformers and dissenters in Scotland transformed the protestation into a vehicle for collective public protest. While authorised assemblies (such as the parliamentary estates) normally were considered to embody the nation, oppositional groups could express conscientious opinions with public protestations. These could be made in an assembly or out of doors, and signatures could be collected to demonstrate adherence. Moreover, protestations on religious issues could be linked to the Christian notion of testimony, making protestation a means of witnessing for God's cause. This helped to overcome strong cultural norms valuing consensus and discouraging disruptive dissent.

The phenomenon of political protestation remains largely unexplored. Alan MacDonald has noted the recording of formal protestations in the early modern Scottish parliament and Alasdair Raffe and I have outlined the function of the protestation in Scottish courts and suggested the significance of this device as a mode for popular political participation.[5] Historians have examined a handful of prominent protestations in early modern England and its dependencies. The 1641 Protestation, ordered by the English parliament to be subscribed as a 'protestation, vow and promise' by all adult males, has been recognised as a key instrument in the escalation of conflict between parliament and Charles I and the politicisation of ordinary people by subscriptional association. But though the function of this protestation as an oath and vow has been examined, its meaning as a 'protestation' has not attracted the same level of notice.[6] In the first book-length study of the 1641 Protestation, John Walter suggested that the label 'protestation' may have been designed to evade the question of whether the English parliament was authorised to promulgate oaths.[7] In his 2006 study of offices and oaths, Conal Condren took a

---

[4] Lyall (ed.), *Ane Satyre of the Thrie Estaits*, 112.
[5] MacDonald, 'Uncovering the legislative process in the parliaments of James VI', 606; Bowie and Raffe, 'Politics, the people and extra-institutional participation in Scotland, c. 1603–1712', 801–5.
[6] Cressy, 'The Protestation protested, 1641 and 1642', 255–6. See also Fletcher, *The Outbreak of the English Civil War*, 15–6; Walter, *Understanding Popular Violence in the English Revolution: The Colchester Plunderers*, 292–6; Vallance, 'Protestation, vow, covenant and engagement: swearing allegiance in the English Civil War'; Braddick, 'Prayer book and protestation: anti-popery, anti-puritanism and the outbreak of the English civil war', 131; Morrill, 'An Irish protestation? Oaths and the confederation of Kilkenny'.
[7] Walter, *Covenanting Citizens: The Protestation Oath and Popular Culture in the English Revolution*, 1 n.1.

Protestations 23

similar view, noting that in common usage 'protestation' could be synonymous with an oath, vow or promise but usually indicated a less rigorous assertory, rather than promissory, commitment.[8] The historian of a 1649 'Declaration and Protestation of the Governor and Inhabitants of Virginia' has suggested that this document reflected a 'popular mood', indicating that a 'protestation' could convey collective sentiments.[9]

This chapter will tease out the meaning and function of the protestation in Scotland to see how this was reworked into an early modern form of public opinion. The first section will explain the normative role of the protestation in late medieval Scottish courts, including practices of presentation, recording and subscription. Subsequent sections will indicate how concepts of testimony and conscience were infused into the protestation to overcome a cultural distaste for schism and produce a distinctive expression of collective public dissent in and beyond courts and assemblies. This will consider how the gathering of signatures stimulated opinion at large and allowed contemporaries to recognise the views of a body of people standing apart from authorised assemblies. Protestations will be explored from the Reformation of 1560 to the reign of James VII, focusing on protestations made against ecclesiastical innovations in the reign of James VI, the use of protestations in the Covenanting rebellion from 1637, the emergence of the 'Protesters' in 1650 and public protestations, testimonies and declarations made by militants in the Restoration period.

1.1 Protestation Practices

The protestation was a statement of dissent by which the action of a court might be voided, or its effect limited in certain circumstances. A set of concepts and customary practices relating to protestation can be identified across civil, criminal, parliamentary and church courts in early modern Scotland, though changes in procedure have made it rare in present-day legal practice.[10] The following description of protestation procedures will demonstrate the ubiquity of this device in the courts of Scotland. It will also show how a protestation could indicate a public declaration or affirmation synonymous with the Christian concept of testimony.

---

[8] Condren, *Argument and Authority in Early Modern England: The Presupposition of Oaths and Offices*, 233–5.

[9] McElligott, 'Atlantic royalism? Polemic, censorship and the "Declaration and Protestation of the Governour and Inhabitants of Virginia"', 227.

[10] I am grateful to Simon Bowie QC for his advice on this point. Watson (ed.), *Bell's Dictionary*, 870; Brodie-Innes, *Comparative Principles of the Courts and Procedure of England and Scotland*, 381–2, 441, 793; Godfrey, *Civil Justice in Renaissance Scotland: The Origins of a Central Court*, 35.

24   Public Opinion in Early Modern Scotland, c.1560–1707

These layered meanings gave the protestation a rich cultural script on which dissidents could draw.

In his 1681 procedural handbook *Modus Litigandi*, Sir James Dalrymple of Stair described the routine use of a protestation in the Court of Session, the highest court in Scotland's civil law system. If a person bringing a suit did not pursue their case by a designated day, a protestation could be presented by the summoned party to make 'null' any further action in the case 'till new Citation'. With the recording of this protestation by the clerk of court, a new summons would be required to allow the case to proceed.[11] Thereafter, the protestation could be suspended on payment of 'protestation money' to the court by the accuser. This was in effect a fine imposed for what had proved to be a frivolous summons.[12] Similar procedures can be found in the records of the Privy Council for criminal cases. For example, in 1593, the Privy Council admitted the protestation of Richard Gordon, a litster (cloth dyer) in Inverness. Gordon had come to court in response to a summons but found his accuser, one John McRannald, not present. Gordon's protestation halted the case, requiring McRannald to generate a new summons for Gordon to re-appear.[13]

Protestations also were used to preserve rights affected by a court decision. Dalrymple noted that if a motion to suspend a decreet (a final judgement in a case) was rejected by a judge, the pursuer could protest that this failure should not prejudice any attempt to secure a suspension by other arguments or procedures. Similarly, if a judge were to discount a particular claim on a property, a protestation could be used to preserve any other right to the property that the claimant might be able to assert.[14] A protestation also provided a vehicle by which cases could be appealed to a higher court. As the quote at the opening of this chapter shows, protestations could be made for those 'grieved by any iniquitie in the sentence'. More precisely, legal historians have shown how a 'protestation for remeid of law' could be used to refer a case from the Court of Session to the Scottish parliament as a supreme court in the event of procedural errors.[15]

---

[11] Dalrymple of Stair, *Modus Litigandi, or Form of Process, Observed before the Lords of Council and Session in Scotland*, 5, 7, 22; Hope, *Minor Practicks, or, A Treatise of the Scottish Law*, 5; Commissioners for Regulating the Judicatories, *Articles for Regulating of the Judicatories*, 10.

[12] Dalrymple of Stair, *The Institutions of the Law of Scotland*, 779; Hope, *Minor Practicks*, 228.

[13] *RPCS*, ser. 1, v, 81.   [14] Dalrymple of Stair, *Modus Litigandi*, 22.

[15] Ford, 'Protestations to parliament for remeid of law'; Godfrey, *Civil Justice in Renaissance Scotland*, 33–7.

Protestations 25

Scottish legal culture encouraged routine protestation to avoid indicating approval by silence. Even if a protestation did not have an immediate impact on the outcome of a case, or the opposing party registered a counter-protestation, it was important to make the protestation so that, as Dalrymple explained, 'it be not presumed those who protest do acquiesce by their silence'.[16] In his 1681 *Institutions of the Law of Scotland*, Dalrymple noted a case in which an heir had been unable to contest the terms of his inheritance because two years had passed before he raised his case.[17] The concept of silence had particular significance in the Scottish parliament where acts typically were passed by common assent if no member voiced an objection. Julian Goodare has noted a transition to majority voting in the seventeenth century, making dissenting minorities more visible.[18] With votes more often being counted, acts passed without a division were recorded as *nemine contradicte* or *nemine contradicente* (nobody dissenting).[19] In 1701, a dissenting minority on a contentious vote with a bare majority of 108 to 84 demanded that their names be recorded.[20]

Protestations had to be made before a court and recorded by the court clerk or a notarial instrument. 'Taking instruments' involved the documentation of the protestation by a notary public and the signing of the paper by the protester, witnesses and any adherents. In 1440, parliamentary records show that Alexander Seton, lord of Tullibody, made a protestation declaring void any contracts made in the past by his mother or grandfather that might have prejudiced him or his heirs. In reply, the Marischal of Scotland, Sir William Keith, counter-protested that Seton's protestation should not prejudice Keith's property rights. Both protestations were recorded by 'Henry Melville, priest of St Andrews diocese, master of arts, [and] notary public by imperial authority' and endorsed by several witnesses.[21]

Other examples from the records of parliament and the general assembly of the reformed church indicate protestations being presented by individuals to protect their rights in the context of new legislation or the

---

[16] Dalrymple of Stair, *Modus Litigandi*, 22.
[17] Dalrymple of Stair, *The Institutions of the Law of Scotland*, 149.
[18] Goodare, 'Parliament and politics', 265–7.
[19] MacDonald, 'Deliberative processes in parliament c. 1567–1639: multicameralism and the lords of the articles', 51; MacDonald, 'Voting in the Scottish parliament', 158. For examples, see *RPS* A1678/6/14, 4 July 1678; M1681/7/9, 18 August 1681.
[20] Bowie, 'Publicity, parties and patronage', 83; *RPS* 1700/10/179, 14 January 1701.
[21] *RPS* A1440/2/1, 20 February 1440.

26   Public Opinion in Early Modern Scotland, c.1560–1707

ratification of charters and gifts. In 1384, for example, a series of legal reforms passed by parliament under Robert II stimulated protestations from the earl of Fife and the lord of Galloway. Both promised to implement the king's new judicial procedures but protested to preserve the earl's rights as 'head of the law of Clan MacDuff' and the lord of Galloway's right to maintain local Galloway law. The protestations were attached to the registration of the new legislation in the parliamentary record, suggesting that they were accepted as conditions on the new law.[22] The ratification of charters or gifts could also stimulate protestations. In the 1569 general assembly, a parish minister attempted to protect assets gifted to him from the property of a man forfeited for moral crimes. Fearing that the man might be 'received to publick repentance' and restored to his estates, the cleric protested that this should not prejudice his rights to the gift.[23] In 1592, the bishop of Dunkeld protested to parliament that the ratification of a charter giving former church lands to a private individual should not be 'hurtful or prejudicial to the said bishop' and that he retained the right 'to propose his reasons and defences against the same'.[24] From 1594, an attempt was made to eliminate this type of blanket protestation in parliament by passing an act *salvo jure cujuslibet* (without prejudice to the right of each) at the end of each legislative session. This provided that any ratifications of private rights would not prejudice other rights, leaving the way open for the pursuit of civil cases to settle conflicting claims.[25] Another common type of protest in the Scottish parliament involved protestations for precedency in the calling of the rolls. Alan MacDonald has noted an attempt in the late sixteenth century to require these to be provided as written rather than oral protestations. This was designed to prevent duels arising from the voicing of protests and counterprotests in the parliamentary chamber.[26]

The protestation offered a potentially powerful means of expressing political, rather than judicial, dissent in courts and assemblies by groups as well as individuals, often as a last-ditch device after other forms of negotiation had failed. When in 1558 the regent Mary of Guise blocked the presentation of a petition to parliament from a group of lords in favour of Protestant worship, the lords turned to protestation. In his account of this event, the cleric John Knox explained that the protestation allowed the lords to avoid implying any acceptance of the government's position by

---

[22] *RPS* 1384/11/12–13, November 1584.   [23] *APGA*, i, 150.
[24] *RPS* 1592/4/175, 5 June 1592.   [25] *RPS* 1594/4/36, 8 June 1594.
[26] MacDonald, 'Voting in the Scottish parliament', 159–60.

Protestations

their silence. Citing conscience and the word of God, they protested to preserve their liberties and prevent any future prosecution of their practice of the reformed religion. The protestation was not admitted to the parliamentary register, but its presentation stimulated a soothing response from Mary of Guise, who needed to retain the support of these lords in parliament.[27]

More generally, the term 'protestation' could indicate a positive declaration made before witnesses and God as the ultimate judge, typically defending an action or rejecting an accusation. This sense of the word carried a strong association with the public communication of truth. When a group of Protestants stormed St Andrews Castle and killed Cardinal Beaton in 1546, the killer was reported to have made a verbal declaration to justify his actions. Stating 'heere, before my God, I protest', he explained that he acted because of Beaton's enmity to the reformed religion and not from greed or animosity.[28] In 1581, on being raised to the status of the earl of Arran, James Stewart wished to deny rumours that he intended to use his new title to claim a place in the line of succession to the Scottish throne. In parliament, he 'protestit' that 'all sic reportis to his prejudice sould be estemit to have bene spokin aganis the trewth'.[29] Stewart's action reflected the biblical example of David in Psalm 131 who, 'charged with ambition and greedy desire to reign, protesteth his humility and modesty before God'.[30] In 1580, at a time when James VI's commitment to the reformed church was being questioned in 'evill reports', the monarch used a meeting of the general assembly of the church 'to make protestation of his perseverance and soundness in religion'.[31] Again in 1582, James made a proclamation in which he 'protest[ed] solemnly' his adherence to the reformed kirk against 'maist fals and untrew bruites [rumours]' to the contrary.[32] In a 1599 book of advice for his son Prince Henry, *Basilikon Doron*, James used a protestation to warn his son to be a good king. If not, he wrote, 'I take the Great God to record, that this booke shall one day be a witness betwixte me and you; and shall procure to be ratified in heaven, the curse that in that case I here give unto you. For I protest before that great God, I had rather be not a Father and child-lesse, nor [than] a Father of wicked children'.[33]

In this context, James' protestation before God served as a public promise, like an assertory oath.[34] The binding power of the promise lay

---

[27] Knox, *The Works of John Knox*, i, 312–4.   [28] Calderwood, *History*, i, 223.
[29] *RPS* 1581/10/74, 29 Nov. 1581.   [30] Psalm 131:1, 1599 Geneva Bible.   [31] *APGA*, ii, 646.
[32] *RPCS*, ser. 1, iii, 492–4.   [33] James VI, *Basilikon Doron*, sig. B.
[34] Condren, *Argument and Authority*, 233.

28 Public Opinion in Early Modern Scotland, c.1560–1707

in the belief, expressed in Romans 2, that an omniscient God exercised justice through the conscience.[35] This is illustrated in vivid terms in a dream reported by the dissident minister Robert Bruce in 1605. Bruce had agreed not to preach for a time, but 'in his sleepe the Lord wakenned his conscience, and made his conscience accuse him'.[36] In 1570, the general assembly ruled that all clergy were to be required to 'protest solemnlie that they sall never leave their vocation any tyme therafter'. These public protestations, functioning as an oath rather than dissent, were to be recorded in local church court books.[37]

Protestation before God overlapped with concepts of religious testimony, witnessing and confession. Knox's view of religious testimony expressed in his *History* had strong parallels with the notion of protestation to avoid acquiescence by silence: 'By the plane Scriptures it was found, "That a lyvelie faith required a plane confessioun, when Christs trewth is oppugned; that not only ar thei gyltie that do evill, bot also thei that assent to evill."'[38] The idea that the godly must confess, witness and testify in support of what they saw as God's truth became a central tenet of Scottish Protestantism, rooted in the words of Matthew in the 1560 Scottish Confession of Faith: 'And these glad tidings of the kingdom shall be preached through the whole world for a witness unto all nations'. The 1560 confession also gave the church's general assembly a role in 'giving public confession of their faith'.[39] For the laity, a 1615 manuscript guide to the scriptures urged the study of biblical 'testimonies' to prove the 'veritie' of 'promises of graice and mearcie'.[40] Moreover, humanists saw religious testimony as the duty of the virtuous citizen as well as the godly subject. For the presbyterian laird David Hume of Godscroft, it was the 'public declaration of what seems right that really deserves to be rewarded', in contrast to self-interested courtiers who followed the maxim that 'silence is golden'.[41]

Public protestation became part of Scottish religious culture through a practice of national collective confession from 1581. Chapter 3 on oaths will explain in more detail how a confession of faith, known as the Negative or King's Confession, was ordered to be sworn by the king and people in 1581 and renewed for national subscription in 1590 and 1638. The 1581 national confession made three protestations emphasising the

---

[35] Romans 2: 14–5, 1599 Geneva Bible; Gray, *Oaths and the English Reformation*, 19–20, 45–6.
[36] Calderwood, *History*, vi, 279.   [37] *APGA*, i, 175–6.   [38] Knox, *Works*, i, 299
[39] *RPS* A1560/8/3, 17 August 1560.   [40] Forrester, 'The Paithe Way to Salvatione', 66.
[41] McGinnis and Williamson (trans and eds), *The British Union: A Critical Edition and Translation of David Hume of Godscroft's De Unione Insulae Britannicae*, 227.

Protestations 29

engagement of the swearer's conscience and placing the swearer in a body of fellow believers. The first formed the opening statement of the confession:

> We all and euerie one of vs underwritten protest, that after long and dewe examination of our owne Consciencis in maters of trew and fals Religioun, are now throughly resolved in the trueth, by the worde and the spirit of God. And therefore we beleve with our heartis, confesse with our mouthes, Subscryve with our hands, and constantly affirme before God and the whole worlde, that this onely is the true Christiane Faith and Religion[.]

After repudiating a list of Catholic beliefs, the confession made a second statement of conviction: 'We . . . protest and call the searcher of all hearts for witnes, that our minds and heartis doe fully agree with this our confession, promise, othe and Subscription'. A third protestation formed a final vow to defend the king on whom the security of the church and nation rested: 'we protest & promes with our heartis, under the same othe, hand writ, and panes, that we sal defend [the king's] persone and authoritie with our geir, bodeis, and lyves, in the defence of Christis Evangel'.[42] David Cressy has noted the likely influence of the 1638 National Covenant, containing the 1581 confession, on England's 1641 Protestation with its protest, vow and promise.[43] In turn, an English print described the National Covenant as a protestation in *The Profession of the True Protestant Religion, or the Protestation of the Kirk of Scotland* (1642).

Although protestations were omnipresent in Scottish legal and religious culture, minority voices could be considered self-interested, deluded, factional or schismatic. In 1605, the privy council characterised a group of dissident clerics as a 'little handful of discontented Spirits' and 'factious brethren'.[44] To strengthen a dissenting position, group protestations stressed the unanimity of their protest. In 1572, for example, the 'haill' (whole) general assembly 'in ane voyce' approved a protestation against the use of terms like 'archbishop' and 'dean' in a concordat submitted to them by the government.[45] In 1581, twenty-seven members of parliament dissented 'in ane voce' from proposals they considered unlawful.[46] Nevertheless, norms for consensus could make it very uncomfortable to

---

[42] James VI, *Ane Shorte and General Confession of the Trewe Christiane Fayth and Religion According to Godis Word*.

[43] Cressy, 'Protestation protested', 254. [44] Calderwood, *History*, vi, 333. [45] *APGA*, i, 246.

[46] *RPS* 1581/10/73, 29 November 1581.

30   Public Opinion in Early Modern Scotland, c.1560–1707

take up a minority position, especially in the church where schism was strongly discouraged. In a 1604 church meeting, 'manie' synodical representatives resented proposed restrictions on their meetings but because 'the greatest part' followed the new procedures, the rest complied 'least they sould seeme singular, or authors of schism'.[47]

The general assembly's emphasis in 1572 on speaking in one voice reflected the belief that an authorised assembly made collective decisions according to the common good of the community that it embodied. Consensus was preferred in decision-making, so when a vote was taken, the majority was expected to be substantial. A simple numerical majority (the greater part or *maior pars*) might be accepted, but a considerable majority of two-thirds carried more force. Alternatively, the views of the sounder or wiser sort (*sanior* or *valientor pars*) could be emphasised to give ballast to one side.[48] Scottish church councils typically weighted their membership in favour of clerical over lay voices, as seen in the general assembly of 1578 when votes by nobles were limited to fifteen, so that the greater part would be clerical.[49] In the Scottish parliament, the landowning nobles and barons could combine to outvote the burgh estate. The burghs argued that the approval of each estate, rather than an overall majority, should be required to pass an act of parliament, but these practices recognised landowners as the *valientor pars*.[50] A national assembly was itself considered a gathering of the *sanior et valientor pars* of the nation, giving their opinions more weight than those of their constituents.

Yet despite these conventions, minority positions could be justified. The notion of the weightier part could be used to undermine a majority decision, as seen in 1591 when the presbyterian cleric Andrew Melville commented that 'votes should be weighed, not counted'.[51] Dissidents could also claim that their position was justified by scripture and required as a duty of testimony and conscience. This strategy recalled the smallness of the early Christian church and the implications of Matthew 18:20 where it was said that Jesus would be found where two or three gathered in his name.[52]

---

[47] Calderwood, *History*, vi, 271.
[48] Monahan, *Consent, Coercion and Limit: The Medieval Origins of Parliamentary Democracy*.
[49] MacDonald, 'Voting in the Scottish parliament before 1639', 149.
[50] MacDonald, 'Voting in the Scottish parliament before 1639', 154; MacDonald, 'Deliberative processes in parliament c. 1567–1639', 31–2, 34.
[51] MacDonald, 'Voting in the Scottish parliament before 1639', 149.
[52] Calderwood, *History*, vi, 312.

Protestations

In the absence of a vote, signatures provided direct evidence of support for a protestation. As Dalrymple of Stair noted, in law 'consent may be adhibit by signes'.[53] Though a 1540 parliamentary act still expected shire and burgh officers to endorse letters with a signet, manual subscription of documents was becoming typical.[54] When a paper was circulated for subscription by presbyteries in November 1596, the clergy were asked to 'sett your hand writt and subscriptiouns therunto, for testifeing your approbatioun therof'.[55] The aim was to generate evidence for what the organisers wished to present as the collective opinion of the national kirk.[56] Signatures might be listed in hierarchical order to indicate social weight. For example, in organising a petition to parliament in 1706, the Ayrshire gentleman John Cochrane of Waterside judged his own hand was 'to[o] mean to begin sutch a work'.[57]

But signing a protestation could be dangerous. In March 1597, many clerics declined to adhere to a controversial protestation to the general assembly complaining, in the presence of James VI, that 'this present Assemblie was not ane frie Assembly'. The protestation was not admitted because it had no public adherents at the time of its presentation by the dissident minister John Davidson. The presbyterian historian David Calderwood reported that 'three or four score' brethren signed the protestation after the assembly, but the names later were cut off to avoid reprisals.[58]

In late sixteenth-century Scotland, a protestation could make a public statement to limit judicial actions, deny unfriendly accusations, assert a religious belief or dissent from a collective decision in church and civil courts and assemblies. The protestation gained legitimacy from the legal premise that silence indicated satisfaction and drew purpose from the practice of testifying to Christian truths, even though dissenters could be subject to accusations of schism. Augmented by the taking of signatures to indicate adherence, from the mid-sixteenth century the protestation was being refashioned by religious dissidents as a mode of public opposition.

---

[53] Dalrymple of Stair, *The Institutions of the Law of Scotland*, 120.
[54] *RPS* 1540/12/18, 10 December 1540; Sanderson, *A Kindly Place? Living in Sixteenth-Century Scotland*, 135.
[55] Calderwood, *History*, v, 461.   [56] MacDonald, *Jacobean Kirk*, 67.
[57] Bowie (ed.), *Addresses against Incorporating Union*, 282.
[58] *APGA*, iii, 947; Spottiswood, *History of the Church of Scotland*, iii, 71; Calderwood, *History*, v, 697–702, 709–10; Row, *The History of the Kirk of Scotland, from the Year 1558 to August 1637*, 191; MacDonald, *Jacobean Kirk*, 86–7.

32   Public Opinion in Early Modern Scotland, c.1560–1707

1.2   Protestations, 1560–1621

Building on the examples of post-Reformation protestations seen above, this section will consider more closely how the unsettled circumstances created by the 1560 Reformation encouraged political protestations. Examples of group protestations can be found in parliament, as in the 1581 protestation noted above, but the more significant trend in this period is the use of protestation by clerics to resist perceived encroachments by the crown on the rights of the kirk. Assertive extra-institutional protestations led by clerics became a feature of the Jacobean period, reflecting fears for the purity of the Scottish reformed church among those who wished bishops to have little or no role in the kirk.

A change in the ruling clique around James VI after the 1582 Ruthven Raid led to an unusual open-air protestation in Edinburgh. In 1584, a new regime aimed to increase the crown's control over the kirk by passing acts asserting the supremacy of the crown over ecclesiastical courts and augmenting the authority of bishops, among other measures.[59] During the parliamentary session, unhappy clerics sought to make an oral petition and then an 'open protestatoun' against the acts, but were prevented. When the acts were proclaimed on 25 May 1584, two clerics, Robert Pont and Walter Balcanquall, made a protestation against any prejudice to the rights and liberties of the kirk on behalf of themselves and their adherents. This was performed at Edinburgh's mercat (market) cross and recorded in a notarial instrument, setting an influential precedent for extra-institutional protestation by presbyterian opinion groups.[60]

Historians have debated how far James VI aimed to create congruent episcopal churches in Scotland and England after 1603, but it is clear that many in Scotland resented episcopalian and Erastian royal authority, seeing these as a threat to what they considered the best-reformed church in Christendom.[61] When the 1604 Scottish parliament agreed to a request from the king for negotiations with England on a closer union, the estates also ratified standing law in relation to the Scottish church and declared that the union negotiators could not 'do ony thing that in ony maner of way may be hurtfull or prejudiciall to the religioun presentlie professit in

---

[59] *RPS* 1584/5/7–15, 22 May 1584.

[60] Calderwood, *History*, iv, 62–5; MacDonald, 'Subscription crisis', 222–55. See chapter 3 for a subscription of obedience linked to the 1584 acts.

[61] Wormald, 'The headaches of monarchy: kingship and the kirk in the early seventeenth century'; Stewart, 'The political repercussions of the Five Articles of Perth: A reassessment of James VI and I's religious policies in Scotland'.

Protestations 33

Scotland'.[62] Calderwood interpreted this as a protestation against any prejudice to the rights of the church 'in discipline or doctrine'.[63] As the king pursued closer union, in conjunction with limitations on meetings of the general assembly and the elevation of episcopal authority, groups of dissident clergy brought forwards new collective protestations.

In negotiating the restoration of the clerical estate to parliament, James had agreed that prelatical representatives for the kirk should operate under the direction of the general assembly.[64] When the king postponed an assembly due to meet in July before the 1604 parliament, preventing clerical discussion of the union question, protestations were made to defend the right of the church to meet as planned. Gathering in Aberdeen at the time of the scheduled meeting, three ministers declared that the postponement went against 'the Word of God', the 'constitutiouns, and continuall custome of our kirk' and 'the laws of the realm' and described their protest as a 'necessar dutie' of testimony 'before God and his angels.'[65] After this event, it was reported to the king that ministers in the area were 'preiching maliciuslie agains the union of the kingdomes'.[66] When a larger group of ministers gathered in Aberdeen a year later to hold an unauthorised assembly in defiance of the king, a protestation 'in name of the brethrein' sought to defend the meeting as lawful, again according to the word of God, standing law and customary practice.[67]

In 1606, commissioners from several presbyteries were prevented from submitting to the parliament a protestation against an act restoring the Scottish bishops to their pre-Reformation rents and privileges, which the clerics felt would create 'papisticall bishops'.[68] They instead presented their protestation to each estate as they 'sat severallie' outside of the parliamentary session.[69] Their paper provided an extensive set of 'admonitions' against the proposed act and closed with an expansive protest in the name of the presbyteries and, notably, 'the kirk in generall'. Two further sets of manuscript 'Reasons' elaborated on these arguments, including the point that episcopacy was 'against the weale of all Scotishmen'. Subscribed by forty-two clerics, the protestation included a request that it be inserted in the parliamentary register. A final attempt by Andrew Melville to make a

---

[62] *RPS* 1604/4/21, 11 July 1604.   [63] Calderwood, *History*, vi, 263.
[64] MacDonald, *Jacobean Kirk*, ch. 4.
[65] Calderwood, *History*, vi, 264–8; Row, *History of the Kirk*, 224–5.
[66] Balfour (ed.), *Letters and State Papers During the Reign of King James the Sixth*, 60.
[67] Calderwood, *History*, vi, 279–84.   [68] *Ibid.*, 484.
[69] The estates met separately outside of the formal parliamentary session until this was curtailed in 1621 as part of heightened management practices. Goodare, 'The Scottish parliament of 1621', 34.

34   Public Opinion in Early Modern Scotland, c.1560–1707

protestation in parliament failed when he was removed from the chamber, though he managed to 'make all that saw and heard him understand his purpose'.[70]

In 1617, during a visit to Scotland by James VI, a group of clerics attempted again to protest 'in open parliament' against an act allowing the king to determine doctrine with the advice of his bishops rather than the general assembly. Recognising that this could be dangerous, fifty-five adherents signed a separate roll so that their individual names would not be revealed. The group hoped to present the protestation through the minister Peter Hewat, who sat in parliament as titular abbot of Crossraguel.[71] Calderwood reported that when Hewat showed the paper to John Spottiswood, archbishop of St Andrews, Spottiswood tore it up. Another copy was said to have been given by the minister of Dalkeith, Archibald Simson, to Clerk Register Sir George Hay for presentation, but the king refused to allow it to be read, stating that 'he thought it verie prejudiciall to his prerogative and power to be bound to take advise'.[72] In his 1599 *Basilikon Doron*, James had advised his son not to allow 'anie contradiction' to the judgements of royal courts, because this 'diminisheth the majestie of your authority'.[73]

The 1617 protestation escalated oppositional rhetoric by appropriating the nullifying power of a protestation to justify civil disobedience, attracting charges of sedition for the organisers. The text first asked that the intended act be set aside so that the adherents could avoid being brought 'to that poore and simple point of protestation, which, if remedie be not provydit, we must be forced to use for the freedome of our kirk and discharge of our conscience'. A concluding protest baldly stated the protesters' intention to disregard the act if it were to be passed. Though parliamentary opposition to the act led to its being dropped, Hewat, Simpson and Calderwood were pursued by the episcopal court for holding an unauthorised 'mutinous assemblie' to 'seditiouslie' procure signatures on the protestation. With the agreement of the king, all three were deprived of office, Hewat and Simson were imprisoned and Calderwood was banished.[74]

The Scottish bishops clearly recognised the disruptive danger presented by collective protestations, later denouncing the 1617 protestation as

---

[70] Calderwood, *History*, vi, 485–91, 494, 500–39.
[71] *Ibid.*, vii, 256; Row, *History of the Kirk*, 307–11; MacDonald, *Jacobean Kirk*, 159.
[72] Calderwood, *History*, vii, 253.   [73] James VI, *Basilikon Doron*, 139.
[74] Calderwood, *History*, vii, 257–71, quotes at 258; MacDonald, 'Voting in the Scottish parliament', 158; MacDonald, *Jacobean Kirk*, 159.

'treasonable and seditious'.[75] Attempts to make protestations in the 1606, 1610 and 1618 general assemblies were blocked by what the presbyterian historian John Row described as a combination of 'minassing' (menacing) and persuasion.[76] In the 1618 assembly at Perth, these methods allowed the bishops to push through five provocative alterations to Scotland's reformed practices, including a requirement to kneel rather than sit for communion.[77] The reported vote of eighty-four to forty-one achieved a two-thirds majority, but opponents argued that this was invalid because the assembly had not been free.[78]

Protestation offered a means of opposing the ratification of these disputed articles in the 1621 parliament. At the start of the 1621 diet, a group of about thirty ministers circulated 'Informations and Admonitions' for lobbying purposes while holding a protestation in reserve as a 'last remedie'. Citing the danger of silence, their protestation demanded that parliament defend the legal and customary forms of the Scottish reformed church and rejected the legitimacy of any ratification of the Perth articles in parliament. By adhering to the former protestations of 1606 and 1617, they indicated a new practice of recognising serial protestations.[79] As in 1617, the clergy were not allowed to submit their protestation to the estates. To avoid arrest and exile, unsubscribed 'coppies' were 'publictlie affixed upon the Parliament-house doore, upon the kirk doores, and upon the mercat-crosse', so that, as with an official proclamation, 'ignorance might not be pretended'.[80] To convey an impression of numbers, the text spoke in name of ministers 'conveened from all the quarters of the countrie' and 'in the name of the brethren of the ministrie professing the religion as it has been receaved and practiced since the first Reformation'.[81]

A divided parliament passed the Perth articles by a modest majority under heavy royal pressure, allowing dissidents to reject the vote as an inadequate measure of national consent.[82] A surviving division list shows a majority of 60 per cent (seventy-eight to fifty-one), slightly less than two-thirds. While the bishop of Aberdeen castigated opposing voters as 'singulare', Sir John Hamilton of Preston and others who voted against the king

---

[75] *APGA*, iii, 1159. [76] Row, *History*, 242, 279.

[77] Calderwood, *History*, vii, 258–60, 305–34; Stewart, *Urban Politics and British Civil Wars: Edinburgh, 1617–53*, 176–82.

[78] Laing, (ed.), *Original Letters Relating to the Ecclesiastical Affairs of Scotland*, ii, 576.

[79] Calderwood, *History*, vii, 474–87.

[80] Row, *History of the Kirk*, 329; Stewart, '"Brothers in treuth"', 166.

[81] Calderwood, *History*, vii, 485, 487.

[82] *RPS* 1621/6/13, 4 August 1621; Goodare, 'The Scottish parliament of 1621', 29–51.

36   Public Opinion in Early Modern Scotland, c.1560–1707

stated their obligation to 'beare witness to the treuth' to satisfy their consciences.[83] By providing a rationale for the substantial 'no' vote, the clerical protestation undermined the legitimacy of the ratification and encouraged widespread resistance to the articles by committed clergy and laity. As Stewart has shown, levels of non-conformity to the requirement to kneel at communion were significant.[84] A 1638 account characterised this disobedience as an act of adherence to the clergy's public protestation by both the greater and the weightier part of the church, described as 'the most part of the particular Congregations' and 'the most religious and judicious of the Ministerie'.[85]

By 1621, under James VI the protestation had become a vehicle for the public expression of resistance by clerics who claimed to represent like-minded brethren and the kirk at large. Though no court registered these out-of-doors protestations and few included signatures, campaigners recognised a chain of public protestations preserving the rights of the kirk and providing grounds for civil disobedience. By declaring dissenting opinions and using these to encourage non-conformity, these protestations stimulated and brought into focus the opinion of presbyterian clerics and laity at large, provocatively implying that authorised assemblies were unrepresentative of the kirk and nation.

1.3   Covenanting Protestations and the Protesters, 1637–1659

In the reign of Charles I (1625–49), protestation practices became more participative and assertive. Resistance by a broad coalition of clerics, nobles, gentry, burgesses and lawyers was stimulated by contentious ecclesiastical innovations, including new clerical vestments in 1633, a book of canons in 1636 and a liturgy in 1637, combined with the revocation of charters, raising of taxes, aggressive management of national assemblies and heavy-handed policing of opposition.[86] When a petitioning campaign against the 1637 liturgy (examined in the next chapter) was condemned in royal proclamations, protestations were made in response. Offering a direct challenge to royal authority in front of large crowds, the protestations aimed to nullify the king's commands. As Chapter 3 will show,

---

[83] Calderwood, *History*, vii, 491–501.   [84] Stewart, *Urban Politics*, 185–94.
[85] [Johnston of Wariston], *A Short Relation of the State of the Kirk of Scotland.*
[86] Macinnes, *Charles I and the Making of the Covenanting Movement 1625–1641*, chs 3–7; Wells, 'Constitutional conflict after the Union of Crowns: contention and continuity in the parliaments of 1612 and 1621'; Young, 'Charles I and the 1633 Parliament', 82–100; Goodare, 'The Scottish convention of estates of 1630', 29–51.

a confessional oath, the 1638 National Covenant, drew together a resistance movement against the king, reinforced by the 1643 Solemn League and Covenant. The resulting wars led to a tussle over the recruitment of 'malignants' into the army in 1650 to defend Scotland from English invasion. When hardline Covenanters registered a protestation against controversial resolutions agreed by the commission of the general assembly in December 1650 relating to the levy, they became known as the Protesters. The Protesters went on to make further statements against the legitimacy of general assembly meetings in 1651 and 1652, collecting the signatures of followers and claiming the adherence of Scotland's godly.

When a royal proclamation on 7 December 1637 stated that Charles would not respond to what he considered tumultuous petitioning against the new liturgy, his opponents turned to protestation. Characterising their actions as lawful, leaders negotiated with the privy council to resubmit their petitions and readied a protestation to demand, if they were refused, 'immediate recourse to their sacred Soveraigne for a redress of their just grievances'. This was drawn up according to 'ane paterne set down in Knoks [John Knox's] chronicle', indicating an awareness of recent historical practices of protestation on behalf of the reformed kirk.[87] The privy council agreed to renew their supplications to the king, preventing the protestation, but Charles again refused their petitions. When the supplicants became aware in February 1638 that a royal proclamation intended to charge attenders of unauthorised meetings with treason, the lawyer Archibald Johnston of Wariston prepared a protestation against the proclamation, again demanding access to the king and asserting the lawfulness of the petitioners' meetings.[88] Government officers were reported to have been 'stark mad' at this intended show of defiance. The proclamation was made a day early in Stirling instead of Edinburgh to prevent the protestation, but a tip-off allowed a small group of nobles to reach Stirling in time to read the protestation and take instruments 'at the crosse' after the royal proclamation.[89] Subsequent readings of the king's proclamation in Linlithgow on 21 February and in Edinburgh on 22 February were met with the protestation, with a considerable audience reported in Edinburgh.[90] The assertiveness of this act astonished observers, with a

---

[87] Paul et al. (eds.), *The Diary of Sir Archibald Johnston of Wariston*, i, 284; Leslie, *Relation*, 41.
[88] Leslie, *Relation*, 87.
[89] The protestation also was handed to a meeting of the privy council in Stirling. Paul et al. (eds.), *Diary*, i, 316–8; Leslie, *Relation*, 63, 86.
[90] Paul et al. (eds.), *Diary*, i, 318; Leslie, *Relation*, 86–9.

38   Public Opinion in Early Modern Scotland, c.1560–1707

contemporary noting that the bishops 'never once imagined that they durst have protested.'[91]

As in 1621, this protestation presumed to nullify the king's position. Having made what the presbyterian historian John Row described as a judicial protestation 'for remedie', the organisers assured their followers that they had 'legallie obviate[d]' the king's ban on their meetings.[92] 'Letters of advertisement' called 'all considerable persons' to Edinburgh regarding 'the most important bussines that ever concerned this natione'.[93] Adherents were asked to swear the National Covenant, a renewal of the 1581 confession with a 'Band, quherby al sould be linked together'.[94] From early March, a copy of the February protestation was circulated to burghs and leading nobles with the new covenant and 'Reasons' explaining why the king's proclamation against meetings should be considered null.[95]

Leaders continued to counter royal proclamations with protestations in May and June 1638, demanding a meeting of the nation's civil and ecclesiastical assemblies to consider the king's new liturgy.[96] The swearing of the National Covenant allowed them to claim to speak on behalf of a covenanted nation at large. A 4 July protestation, 'in name of all who adheres to the Confession of Faith and Covenant lately renewed', was made in front of 'great numbers' in Edinburgh, after which representatives from the gathered nobles, barons, burghs and clergy took instruments.[97] In justifying the movement's opposition to the king, the protestation argued that the supplicants should not be prejudged until the disputed issues had been considered by the general assembly and parliament, 'the onely proper judges to national causes and proceedings'.[98] In defiance of an order against unauthorised printing, the protestation was published as a pamphlet, making it even more public.[99]

Protestations allowed these dissidents to set their views in opposition to the king's judgement of the common good and demand the measurement of the nation's opinion in unrestricted assemblies. In response, Charles struck at the practice of protestation in September 1638 by excoriating those 'who held thameselves exeemed from censure and punishment' by

---

[91] Row, *History*, 488.   [92] Leslie, *Relation*, 65; Row, *History*, 488.   [93] Leslie, *Relation*, 67–8.
[94] Paul et al. (eds.), *Diary*, i, 319.   [95] Leslie, *Relation*, 82.   [96] *Ibid.*, 111.
[97] [Balcanquhall], *A Large Declaration Concerning the Late Tumults in Scotland*, 98–106; Paul et al. (eds.), *Diary*, i, 360.
[98] Paul et al. (eds.), *Diary*, i, 360. Stevenson, *The Scottish Revolution, 1637–1644: The Triumph of the Covenanters*, 97–8.
[99] [Henderson], *The Protestation of the Noblemen*; NRS GD406/1/966 Earl of Traquair to Marquis of Hamilton, 20 July 1638; Gordon, *History of Scots Affairs*, 32–4.

Protestations   39

their protestations. The Covenanters replied with a new protestation pointing out that while the king had named dates for meetings of the general assembly and parliament, he seemed to intend to force the promised assemblies to accept the contested liturgy. Citing scriptures to justify a further protestation on behalf of the church, the new protestation rejected any pre-limitation on the general assembly and parliament. As before, the protestation was made before enthusiastic crowds in Edinburgh and afterwards was circulated in print.[100] Duplicate protestations were made at mercat crosses elsewhere, though not always successfully. In Aberdeen, where clerics at the university had mounted a counter-campaign against the National Covenant (discussed in Chapter 4), the Marquis of Huntly reported that the king's proclamation was made to 'universall applause' while the Covenanters' protestation was read by a small group of nobles with 'so evill successe' that Huntly 'behoved to enterpose my self for preventing that the paper might not be torne out of theyr handes'.[101]

Archibald Johnston of Wariston recognised that these protestations flowed from a tradition of protest established by the supplicants' 'forfaythers'.[102] His September protestation described the supplicants as 'delighting to use no meanes but such as are legall, and have beene ordinarie in this Kirk since the reformation.'[103] He agreed that the 1621 protestation allowed the parliamentary ratification of the Perth articles to be disregarded.[104] Yet his protestations went beyond earlier precedents by speaking not just for the clergy and church but the nation at large. The mobilisation of secular support for the supplications and National Covenant allowed John Leslie, earl of Rothes to refer to crowds gathered in Edinburgh as 'the collective body of the kingdome ther[e] present for the good and defence of religione and the countrey'. Rothes stated that the protesters had decided not to 'obey whatsoever was enjoyned by these in the greatest places'; instead, 'they wer now resolved in this bussines to look only to the conveniencie and good of it'.[105] The Covenanters, not the king, would judge the best interests of the commonweal.

The 1638 general assembly became a battlefield for competing protestations as the Covenanters sought to ensure that the assembly followed their agenda.[106] Both the bishops and the king's commissioner, the marquis of Hamilton, protested in the meeting against the packing of

---

[100] [Balcanquhall], *Large Declaration*, 157–73; Paul et al. (eds.), *Diary*, i, 392–3.
[101] NRS GD406/1/450 [Marquis of Huntly] to [Marquis of Hamilton], [October 1638].
[102] Paul et al. (eds.), *Diary*, i, 379.   [103] [Balcanquhall], *Large Declaration*, 157.
[104] Leslie, *Relation*, 91.   [105] *Ibid.*, 113–14.
[106] Mason, 'The aristocracy, episcopacy and the revolution of 1638', 7–24.

40   Public Opinion in Early Modern Scotland, c.1560–1707

the assembly through the selection of presbyterial representatives, with the
prelates declaring the assembly 'voyde, and Null in Lawe'.[107] When copies
of the bishops' protestation were later printed in London and Aberdeen,
the Covenanters' Edinburgh press produced a refutation.[108] Hamilton left
the assembly on 28 November, refusing to hear a protestation prepared by
Johnston of Wariston defending the lawfulness of meeting in the absence
of the king's commissioner. Speaking on behalf of covenanted 'noblemen,
barons, gentlemen, borrows [burghs], ministers and commons', this
described the bishops as 'Disturbers of the Peace' for their protestation.
The assembly voted to adhere to Johnston's protestation, and it was read at
Glasgow's mercat cross on 29 November to refute a public order to
disperse. A further protestation was made on 18 December against a royal
proclamation that had rejected the proceedings of the unauthorised
assembly.[109]

The practice of collective protestation appeared also in the
1639 Scottish parliament when a protestation was read on 14 November
'in publict audience' in name of 'the kingdom which we do represent'. As
in the general assembly, this countered an attempt by crown officials to
prorogue the meeting. Claiming that prorogation was subject to parliamentary consent by 'the laws, liberties and perpetual practice of the
kingdom' and noting that the king had promised to remedy the realm's
affairs in parliament, the protestation declared the prorogation null and
void. It also authorised the parliament to appoint representatives to 'make
remonstrances to his majestie' based on the 'informationis and generall
declarationis of ane whole kingdome'.[110] In the following session of 1640,
the Covenanters' use of protestations to repel laws against unauthorised
meetings was confirmed with an act allowing meetings 'for maintenance
and preservation of the king's majesty, the religion, laws and liberties of the
kingdom, or for the public good, either of kirk or state'.[111]

Drawing on a pattern of protestation for the liberties of the kirk, the
protestations of 1638–9 allowed the Covenanting movement to defend the
lawfulness of their resistance and reject royal actions, claiming to do so on

---

[107] NRS GD406/1/674, bishops of Ross and Brechin to Marquis of Hamilton, 21 November 1638;
Archbishops and bishops of Scotland, *The Declinator and Protestation*.
[108] Johnston of Wariston, *The Declinatour and Protestation of the Some-times Pretended Bishops*.
[109] Paul et al. (eds.), *Diary*, i, 402; Row, *History of the Kirk*, 503–5; General Assembly, *The Protestation
of the Generall Assemblie of the Church of Scotland . . . Made in the High Kirk, and at the Mercate
Crosse of Glasgow, the 28 and 29 of November 1638*; General Assembly, *The Protestation of the
Generall Assembly of the Kirk of Scotland . . . Lately Made at the Mercat Crosse of Edinburgh the 18. of
December 1638*.
[110] *RPS* 1639/8/31/10 14 November 1639.   [111] *RPS* 1640/6/29, 6 June 1640.

Protestations

behalf of the nation. Protestations were defended by the earl of Rothes as a 'legall course' according to the 'perpetuall custom of this kingdome' and a 'Testimonie' to the nation's covenant.[112] When the 1647 Engagement created fractures in the covenanted consensus, protestations again appeared. In parliament, the marquis of Argyll made a protestation in March 1648 against preparations for war on behalf of the king and led at least forty members out of the chamber. In response, the estates refused to record his protestation and confirmed that their orders reflected 'the sense [of] parliament'.[113] A further split late in 1650 over a levy created the Protesters, a breakaway hardline group that gathered the signatures of clerics and laymen on protestations to prove that they spoke for the truly godly in the kirk and nation. While the 1638–9 protestations contested the judgement of the king and demanded meetings of national assemblies, these new protestations suggested that an authorised assembly might fail to represent opinion at large.

Following the January 1649 execution of Charles I in England, the Scottish regime proclaimed his son as Charles II and asked him to swear the covenants before acting as king. Though he eventually agreed, his obvious reluctance, combined with his association with supporters of the 1647 Engagement (known as 'malignants') and the reputed immorality of his entourage, encouraged doubts about his status as a truly covenanted king. Concerns were expressed in the Western Remonstrance, a message of dissent, later described as a 'testimonie', that was sent to the committee of estates in October 1650.[114] In December, supporters of this text provided a protestation to the commission of the general assembly objecting to a set of 'public resolutions' allowing the participation of former malignants in a general levy for the king. When the commission wrote to presbyteries urging them to support the levy, letters of dissension were sent to the commission from church courts sympathetic to the Protesters, including the presbyteries of Stirling, Glasgow, Paisley, Ayr, Irvine, Hamilton, Lanark, Peebles, Aberdeen and Deer and the Synod of Dumfries.[115]

---

[112] Leslie, *Relation*, 119.

[113] Stevenson, *Revolution and Counter-Revolution*, 87; *RPS* A1648/3/5, 17 March 1648. An act of 1643 prevented the clerk of parliament from recording any protestation without the express permission of the estates (with the exception of routine protests for precedency): *RPS* 1643/6/10, 26 June 1643.

[114] *RCGA* iii, 126–7. The practice of remonstrance is discussed in chapter 2.

[115] *RPS* A1650/11/16, 23 Dec. 1650; *RCGA*, iii, 159–60, 173–82, 196–9, 243–51, 255–8, 274–6, 276–9, 298–303, 304, 362–3, 390–2, 460–2, 468–71; Stevenson, *Revolution and Counter-Revolution*, 159, 162. See chapter 4 on the printing of a remonstrance from the presbytery of Stirling.

42   Public Opinion in Early Modern Scotland, c.1560–1707

Conversely, support for moderate 'Resolutioners' was indicated by letters of concurrence from the synods of Fife, Angus, Moray and Perth, the universities of St Andrews and Glasgow, the presbytery of Chanonry in the synod of Ross, the presbytery of Dumbarton and a dissenting group of brethren in the presbytery of Glasgow.[116]

In order to justify their opposition to the kirk's duly constituted executive body, Stirling and other presbyteries stressed the quality of reflection involved in the formation of their opinions and the strength and value of the opinions of the godly. This rhetoric presumed that the 'tender' consciences of the godly made them more susceptible to God's influence and better able to understand and act appropriately.[117] After 'pondering' and 'debating' the public resolutions, Stirling presbytery found that they could not 'finde clearnesse in our Judgements, nor satisfactions to our Consciences'. Their letter of dissent included a comprehensive list of 'Reasons' for their position, including the fear that the commission's new policy would alienate 'the Religious and Godly of the Land'. Suggesting that the weightier part of the clergy and laity deserved greater consideration, the presbytery warned against 'the vanitie of multitudes of men' and declared that 'a few whom God will countenance, are of more worth then many against whom he hath a controversie'.[118] In reply, an exhortation issued by the commission to be read from the pulpit called on 'all sortes, both of high and lowe degree' to consider themselves bound by the covenants to support the defence of the realm.[119]

The Protesters continued to oppose the view of the kirk as embodied in its general assembly. At the next meeting of the general assembly in St Andrews in July 1651, a general protestation argued that the meeting was illegitimate because Protester clerics were not permitted to be elected as representatives to the assembly.[120] Archibald Johnston of Wariston provided a paper justifying the protestation according to the historical practice of the kirk. For Wariston, 'these legal means of Protestation' had preserved the Scottish church 'from a total and universal back-sliding and breach of

---

[116] RCGA, iii,119–201, 379–81, 386–7, 412–4, 418–9, 429–31, 464–6, 466–8, 487–9, 490–2.

[117] Spurr, '"The strongest bond of conscience": oaths and the limits of tolerance in early modern England', 152.

[118] Presbytery of Stirling, The Remonstrance of the Presbyterie of Sterling against the Present Conjunction with the Malignant Party.

[119] RCGA, iii, 346–52.

[120] RCGA, iii, 445; [Guthrie], The Nullity of the Pretended-Assembly at Saint Andrews and Dundee, 1–5.

Covenant.'[121] After the assembly, the Protesters sought statements of adherence from synods in name of 'all the professors' in each province. These supplementary protestations aimed to invalidate the 1651 assembly by claiming that it had not represented the kirk at large. As stated by an extant manuscript from the synod of Merse and Teviotdale, the signatories felt 'bound to testifie and declare our adherence to the protestatatione', so that 'wee may not only be free off all the sin and guilt therof but alsoe that all thes proceedings may be void and null'.[122] The Protester campaign continued with another protestation against the 1652 general assembly as an incomplete representation of the church.[123] Presented by 'the Ministers, Elders and Professors undersubscribed for themselves, and in name of many others well-affected Ministers, Elders and People', this claimed to have 'the concurrence of the generality of the Godly in the Land'. A printed version listed the names of sixty-seven subscribing ministers and eighty-five 'Elders, Professors and Expectants', some of whom were said to have signed 'in Name of others from whom they were sent to the meeting', with many more being said to be ready to sign.[124]

The Protesters were met with counter-protests and tracts deploring schism and populism. In 1651, the synod of Glasgow and in 1652 the presbytery of Glasgow recorded dissenting protestations from Resolutioner minorities.[125] Tracts debating the legitimacy of these general assemblies continued to be published until the Cromwellian regime restricted access to the press and banned further meetings of the assembly.[126] Defenders of the meetings argued that protestations from synods and presbyteries overturned the church hierarchy. Calling the practice of protestation 'odious', one author argued that the requirements of the covenants for unity meant that the protestation had made an appalling schism. The Protesters' attempt to claim the backing of the godly was declared a 'strange assertion, and of dangerous consequence', for 'they seem to subject the Publick Ministeriall Authority to the People'. Instead, the author asserted, the protestation was the action of a 'pre-meditate[d] Faction'.[127]

---

[121] [Guthrie], *The Nullity of the Pretended Assembly*, 8–13.

[122] NRS GD157/1349, 'Copy of protestation by synod of Merse and Teviotdale', 1651.

[123] McCrie, *The Life of Robert Blair, Minister of St Andrews: Containing his Autobiography, from 1593 to 1636*, 296.

[124] Anon., *Representation, Propositions, and Protestation*, 15–9. The number of elders, professors and expectants is misstated as 95 in the text.

[125] Laing (ed.), *Robert Baillie*, iii, 194–5, 561–2.   [126] See Chapter 4.

[127] Anon., *The Protestation Given in by the Dissenting Brethren to the General Assembly, July 21 1652, Reviewed and Refuted*, 3–6, 20.

44   Public Opinion in Early Modern Scotland, c.1560–1707

During the Cromwellian Commonwealth and Protectorate (1652–9), the Protesters directed missives to the government in London in response to events, developing an expanded practice of declaration, testimony and protestation. Identifying past protestations with the practice of witnessing, Johnston of Wariston wrote that 'our waye of testimonyes' was a 'deutye, and the meane of keeping God in the land in the tyme of our forfaythers and our awen'.[128] In March 1653, the Protesters produced a manuscript 'Declaration or Testimonie' against the forced union of Scotland and England, describing the formation of the British Commonwealth as a betrayal of the 1643 Solemn League and Covenant. Another declaration was made a year later to 'testify their sense' of the 1653 Instrument of Government, which confirmed Anglo–Scottish union and toleration for Protestant worship 'without the free consent of the Nation'.[129] In October 1658, a group of eight Protester ministers provided a testimony against the principle of religious toleration affirmed in the Protectorate's 1657 Humble Petition and Advice. Printed as a *Testimony to the Truth of Jesus Christ*, this expressed a duty to 'bear witness to the truth' as established in 1581, sworn by 'persons of all ranks' in 1590, renewed in 1638 by 'almost the whole Land' and reinforced by the swearing of the Solemn League in 1643 by 'the whole body of Scotland from the highest to the lowest'. Affirming that they were 'perswaded in our Minds and convinced in our Consciences' of the rightness of the covenants, the Protesters urged their 'flocks' to stay true to their sworn commitments. A year later, another group of nine clerics affirmed this testimony with a signed and published letter attacking a petition presented in London for religious toleration in Scotland.[130]

From 1637 to 1659, the practice of political protestation saw several significant developments. Royal proclamations were countered by protestations, ostensibly nullifying their legal force and allowing a resistance movement to grow. While previous protestations spoke in the name of dissenting brethren and the kirk, these spoke for a covenanted nation, setting opinions at large in opposition to the judgement of the monarch and demanding free meetings of national assemblies to resolve the nation's concerns. From 1650, the Protesters' dispute with the commission of the general assembly and subsequent general assemblies pitted godly opinion against the kirk as they collected clerical and lay signatures as evidence of

---

[128] Paul et al. (eds.), *Diary*, ii, 223–4.
[129] Stephen (ed.), *Register of Consultations*, 13–36, 42–56; Mackenzie, *Solemn League*, 129.
[130] Anon., *A Testimony to the Truth of Jesus Christ*, 4, 7, 9, 11, 13, 34, 36.

Protestations 45

adherence and emphasised the weightiness of their views regardless of numbers. After 1653, the Protesters extended the concept of the protestation to make public testimonies and declarations on behalf of the true covenanted nation. The next section will show how this practice of protestation and testimony was taken up by a new generation of presbyterian dissenters after the 1660 Restoration to express oppositional opinions in the name of the true church and nation.

1.4 Protestation and Testimony, 1660–1687

By 1662, the restoration of Charles II to his British thrones had brought the return of episcopalian church government, the re-assertion of the royal supremacy over the church and the removal of legislative authority for the 1638 and 1643 covenants. From August 1660, the reconstituted privy council moved quickly to contain any dissent and in 1662 parliament condemned 'insolent and seditious protestations' alongside tumultuous petitions and unlawful covenants and meetings.[131] When crown agents broke up a meeting of the synod of Galloway where a petition was being prepared, the moderator made an oral protestation and took instruments against this encroachment of civil power on a church judicatory.[132] Other ministers preached against the return of prelacy, making public protestations for the rights of the kirk from the pulpit. John Blackadder declared, 'I as a member and minister of the gospel in the Church of Scotland, (though unworthy) do solemnly declare and enter my dissent in heaven against this dreadfull course of defection, and do protest, that I may be free of what grievous guilt is to be found therein'.[133] About a quarter of Scotland's ministers felt unwilling to betray their covenanted commitments and accept the authority of bishops, choosing instead to leave the church. Some began to hold illegal conventicles, especially in southwest and central areas where the Protesters had been strongest.[134] As government pressure for ecclesiastical conformity bore down on these communities, hardliners followed the example of earlier Covenanters and Protesters in offering public testimonies. These were staged by men and women from a network of extremists known as the Cameronians, for their association with the field preacher Richard Cameron, or, after they formed

---

[131] *RPS* 1662/5/20, 24 June 1662.
[132] Wodrow, *History*, i, appendix, 22. The intended petition included a protestation against any prejudice to the church.
[133] Quoted in Mullan, *Narratives of the Religious Self*, 57.
[134] Cowan, *The Scottish Covenanters, 1660–1688*, 50–63.

46   Public Opinion in Early Modern Scotland, c.1560–1707

a confederation of praying societies, the United Societies or Society people. From 1679, they appropriated public places to make open declarations of their opinions. Representing a small minority of mostly plebeian people, these claimed to speak for the true covenanted church and nation, however small.

In 1679, an assassination of the archbishop of St Andrews by hardliners stimulated an uprising. A handful of militants announced their intentions by reading and posting a written statement at the mercat cross in the royal burgh of Rutherglen south of Glasgow on 29 May (the anniversary of the Restoration and the birthday of Charles II). An armed group of about eighty men extinguished official bonfires marking the Restoration and burned copies of parliamentary acts disowning the covenants and re-establishing prelacy and the royal supremacy. A participant later explained that they felt a 'Duty to publish to the World their Testimony to the Truth and Cause which they owned, and against the Defections of the Times.' The declaration described itself as 'witnessing' for the covenanted cause, to 'add our Testimony to those of the Worthies who have gone before us'.[135] A few weeks later, a further manifesto was posted at the mercat cross in the burgh of Hamilton on 13 June 1679 and printed in Glasgow. This justified rebellion as a confirmation of 'all the Testimonies of our faithful sufferers for Truth in Scotland'.[136]

A year later, on the 22 June anniversary of the defeat of the uprising at Bothwell, a group of twenty-one armed men read a new declaration in the Dumfriesshire burgh of Sanquhar repudiating their allegiance to Charles II and protesting the future succession of his Catholic brother James, duke of York. The declaration was made at the mercat cross 'after a solemn procession and singing of psalmes', with copies posted on the cross and the church door.[137] The text declared that the king had forfeited his crown by 'his Perjury and Breach of Covenant' and 'his Tyranny and Breach of the very *leges regandi* in Matters Civil'. These protesters rejected the Hamilton declaration as insufficiently rigorous and affirmed the 'Testimony given at Rutherglen' along with all other testimonies of suffering. Speaking as 'representatives of the true Presbyterian and covenanted people of Scotland', these militant dissenters relied on a claim of truth rather than numbers, later describing themselves as 'the more faithful and better part'.[138] Their extraordinary testimony took the practice of protestation to extremes by refusing the authority of the monarch.

---

[135] Wodrow, *History*, ii, 43–4.
[136] Wodrow, *History*, ii, appendix, 23–4; Greaves, *Secrets of the Kingdom*, 61, 63–4.
[137] *RPCS*, ser. 3, vi, 481.
[138] Wodrow, *History*, ii, appendix, 47–51; [Renwick and Shields], *Informatory Vindication*, 37.

Protestations

These militants meant to declare war on the king, but not by a 'Martial Insurrection'. Instead, they intended something new, 'a War of Contradiction and Opposition by Testimonies'.[139] On 12 January 1682, another declaration in 'the forme of a proclamation' was made at the royal burgh of Lanark by forty armed men on horseback and twenty on foot. The 'Act and Apologetic Declaration of the True Presbyterians of the Church of Scotland' again spoke out against what these extremists saw as a misguided majority. Objectionable legislation was burned, including a 1681 test act and a succession act confirming the king's Catholic brother as his heir.[140] Responding to a crackdown on militancy, on 28 October 1684 an 'apologetical declaration' was issued warning that anyone helping the government to apprehend them would be 'dealt with as ye deal with us'. A high risk of arrest meant that no one read this paper publicly but copies appeared on mercat crosses and church doors across south-west Scotland.[141] When this stimulated the imposition of an abjuration oath to identify militants (as discussed in Chapter 3), the refusal of the oath, often leading to summary execution, was described as a 'Testimony'.[142]

The accession of James VII was marked with another public protestation at the royal burgh of Sanquhar on 28 May 1685. An organiser commented that James' accession 'could not pass without some Witness and Testimony', 'unless we had forgotten the Method of our worthy, zealous, and resolute Reformers'. Identifying themselves as 'a very small Remnant' of the true church, the protesters affirmed their former testimonies and, to 'exoner our Consciences', made a protestation against the illegal accession of a Catholic king and any prejudice arising to the reformed religion from his rule.[143]

Alongside these group declarations, individuals seized opportunities to make a public testimony to God's truth. In October 1681, Robert Garnock, a blacksmith arrested in May 1679 for attending an illegal conventicle, wrote and presented to the privy council a personal 'protestation and testimony against parliamenters'. As Laura Doak has shown, Garnock protested against the back-sliding of the 1681 parliament from covenanted commitments made by all ranks of people in Scotland at the 1651 coronation of Charles I.[144] Other individuals offered testimonies

---

[139] [Renwick and Shields], *Informatory Vindication*, 68.
[140] *RPCS* ser. 3, vii, 310–11, 329, 342; Wodrow, *History*, ii, 227; Greaves, *Secrets of the Kingdom*, 82. For the acts see, *RPS* 1681/7/29, 31 August 1681 and 1681/7/18, 13 August 1681.
[141] Wodrow, *History*, ii, 429–30.   [142] [Renwick and Shields], *Informatory Vindication*, 19.
[143] [Renwick and Shields], *Informatory Vindication*, 20, 191–204.
[144] Doak, 'Robert Garnock's protestation against the parlimenters'; Wodrow, *History*, ii, 188.

48   Public Opinion in Early Modern Scotland, c.1560–1707

before being executed, writing and voicing the seditious opinions for which they had been condemned. In her dying words, Marion Harvie, a young servant girl from Bo'ness, adhered to the Rutherglen and Sanquhar declarations and offered a protestation against the judicial pursuit of her fellow extremists.[145] Harvie's case confirms the participation of women in dissent and, as recent scholarship has emphasised, the importance of women in sustaining networks of conventiclers and extremists.[146] Prior to being banished from Scotland for refusing the oath of allegiance, twenty-two men and six women signed in August 1685 a 'testimony' against the Catholic James VII.[147]

The 1662 act against protestations, petitions and covenants stated that 'the rise and progress of the late troubles did, in a great measure, proceed from some treasonable and seditious positions infused into the people'.[148] Revulsion at what had become a plebeian movement is reflected in a 1680 letter from the Scottish privy council describing the perpetrators of the Sanquhar declaration as 'the scum of the people'.[149] Yet these men and women had, by necessity, invented a new form of collective grassroots resistance. Continuing the practice of declaration, testimony and protestation developed by presbyterians, Covenanters and Protesters, they replaced popular revolt with war by public testimony after the failure of the 1679 uprising. Drawing on a conscious sense of heritage, their protestations set the views of a small but true covenanted nation in opposition to the acts of an authorised parliament and the rule of Charles II and James VII.

1.5   Conclusions

On being tried for treason in 1661, the Protester minister James Guthrie argued that protestations did not challenge the king's authority, 'it being not Authority it self that is protested against, but only a particular Act of the Authority, against which Protestations in many Cases are ordinary.' Like Johnston of Wariston before him, Guthrie portrayed protestations as a normal judicial device and attempted to argue that political protestations by the Covenanters and Protesters were unexceptional. The 1661 Scottish

---

[145] Anon., *A Cloud of Witnesses*, 88–93.

[146] Doak, 'Militant women: the execution of Isabel Alison and Marion Harvie, 1681'; Raffe, 'Female authority and lay activism in Scottish presbyterianism, 1660–1714'.

[147] Anon., 'Banishment from Scotland, 1685'.   [148] *RPS* 1662/5/20, 24 June 1662.

[149] The group included sons of tenant farmers, a merchant and a servant to a laird. *RPCS*, ser. 3, vi, 481–2.

parliament found this unconvincing. The protestation was indeed ubiquitous in civil and ecclesiastical courts in Scotland and clerics like Guthrie, whose own lawyers praised him for his 'Exactness in our Scots Law', were familiar with them.[150] But Guthrie and others turned the protestation into something different, a vehicle for the presentation of collective opinions in opposition to the views of constituted authorities.

Normally, the consent of the nation at large was expressed by an authorised assembly, preferably with unanimity or a large majority. Political protestations challenged this norm by presenting opinions within and beyond these assemblies, at mercat crosses and on church doors, in the name of clerics, the church, the laity, the nation and the godly. By 1617, it was being said that a protestation could invalidate an act of parliament and justify disobedience. By 1638, protestations were being used in the name of a covenanted nation to defend unauthorised meetings in direct opposition to the crown and its officers. When the kirk split in 1650, Protesters gathered signatures on protestations to prove that they spoke for the godly in the church and nation, emphasising the greater weight of their opinions. After the Restoration, militants made public testimonies, expressing their views as the surviving remnant of the true covenanted church and nation. Plebeian supporters like Harvie proved willing to die for these declarations as the crown attempted to stamp out this new style of rebellion by testimony. As Raffe has emphasised, a perception of God's truth, as captured in the 1581 confession and subsequent covenants, remained the touchstone for these statements of opinion.[151] In this spirit, Harvie stated, 'I hate all opinions that are contrar to the found truths of God'.[152] Public protestations asserted the views of clerics and the laity, or a weightier part who had given the matter 'serious Consideration', with an insistence that their views be taken into account and their consciences satisfied.[153] Elided with the Christian concept of testimony, protestations challenged the power of the monarch or an assembly to judge the common good and drew attention to opinions held by ordinary men and women. The next chapter will show how subscriptional petitioning campaigns achieved a similar effect.

---

[150] Wodrow, *History*, i, 65–6.   [151] Raffe, *Culture of Controversy*, 12–9.
[152] Anon., *Cloud of Witnesses*, 90.   [153] Wodrow, *History*, i, appendix, 18.

CHAPTER 2

Petitions

[T]he humble desire of the supplication ... is the substance, life and quintessence of all petitions.

Defence for Lord Balmerino, 1634[1]

[T]he rise and progresse of the late troubles did, in a great measure, proceid from some treasonable and sedicious positions infused into the people ... [and] many wilde and rebellious courses wer taken and practised in pursueance thairof by unlawfull meitings and gatherings of the people [and] by mutinous and tumultuary petitions.

Act for preservation of his majesties' person, authoritie and government, 1662[2]

That it is the right of the subjects to petition the king and that all imprisonments and prosecutiones for such petitioning are contrary to law.

Claim of Right, 1689[3]

In the first quote above, lawyers for a Scottish nobleman, John Elphinstone, second Lord Balmerino, tried to protect their client from a death sentence by emphasising the apparent humility of petitioning. Capital charges of sedition had been brought against Balmerino for possessing a draft of a collective petition making assertive complaints against the behaviour and policies of Charles I. Balmerino's petition illustrates, and this chapter will explore, three shifts in early modern petitioning that helped to make extra-institutional opinion more visible in Scotland. The first was a rhetorical emphasis on petitioners' thoughts and opinions. While traditional petitioning emphasised the grief of the petitioner and humbly asked the recipient to exercise his judgement in coming to a solution, political petitions presented arguments and expressed an expectation that these would be satisfied. The second was the presentation of

[1] Howell (ed.), *A Complete Collection of State Trials, Vol. III*, 626.
[2] *RPS* 1662/5/20, 24 June 1662.   [3] *RPS* 1689/3/108, 11 April 1689.

50

Petitions 51

petitions in name of a group of people, such as the inhabitants of a parish or burgh, a body of dissenters or the laity at large, with signatures as evidence of adherence by members of this group. This contrasted with more typical practices of personal petitioning or, for a political body, endorsement by an authorised leader of the community. The third was a tactical move towards repeated petitioning on the same matter, disrupting the normal assumption that a petition's humble plea would be dropped if the recipient found it unacceptable. Together, these trends made petitioning more adversarial, pitting the assertive opinions of groups of people against the judgement of monarchs and national assemblies. Often backed by crowds of male and female supporters, adversarial petitioning stimulated efforts by the crown to subdue what it considered as a seditious and tumultuous activity.

In the historiography of early modern England, petitions have been recognised as an important element in the explosion of political debate seen from the 1640s. Studies of medieval petitioning confirm that aggrieved parties, including commoners, used petitions to bring political complaints and pleas to local and national authorities.[4] David Zaret has argued that the printing of petitions and counter-petitions during the 1640s marked the origins of a modern democratic public sphere involving 'rival appeals to public opinion in a marketplace of ideas'.[5] Mark Knights has agreed that petitioning 'helped to constitute public discourse' and that subscription campaigns made English politics more participatory from the 1640s onwards.[6] Numerous studies of petitioning in the civil war era have shown how these campaigns brought local voices to the centre and engaged women and men from outside the formal political nation through the collection of signatures.[7] Jason Peacey has indicated how deeply embedded the practice of petitioning was in English parliamentary culture and how, by the 1640s, even local or private petitions could trigger counter-petitions

---

[4] Hoyle, 'Petitioning as popular politics in early sixteenth-century England'.

[5] Zaret, 'Petitions and the "invention" of public opinion in the English Revolution', 1498; Zaret, *Origins of Democratic Culture: Printing, Petitions, and the Public Sphere in Early-Modern England*, 6–10.

[6] Knights, *Representation*, 110.

[7] Hopper et al. (eds.), *Civil War Petitions: Conflict, Welfare and Memory During and After the English Civil Wars, 1642–1710*; Whiting, *Women and Petitioning in the Seventeenth-Century English Revolution: Deference, Difference, and Dissent*; Lake, 'Puritans, popularity and petitions: local politics in national context, Cheshire, 1641'; Walter, 'Confessional politics in pre-civil war Essex: prayer books, profanations, and petitions'; Maltby, *Prayer Book and People in Elizabethan and Early Stuart England*, chs 3, 5.

52 Public Opinion in Early Modern Scotland, c.1560–1707

and an escalation from manuscript to print publication.[8] With the increasing presentation of partisan petitions, the loyal address emerged, as Ted Vallance has shown, when affirmative addresses were sent to Richard Cromwell after his father's death in September 1658. The loyal address was a type of petition designed to counter dissenting voices by making a public statement of adherence to a ruler, often through a message of congratulations. The loyal address still presented a partisan view, normally sympathetic to monarchical policy but with the potential to include veiled criticisms.[9] As illustrated by the exchange of petitions and addresses in England's 1679–81 exclusion crisis, these petitionary forms contributed to public contests in which each side claimed to speak for a consensual local or national community, backed with large numbers of signatures.[10] Knights has investigated the sophisticated debates that arose in English political culture stimulated by public petitioning on national affairs, including questions of representation (who speaks for the nation, parliament or petitioners?) and accountability (can members of parliament be instructed by petitioners?). Knights has also traced attempts to constrain parliamentary petitioning as it became more collective and assertive.[11]

In Scottish historiography, Laura Stewart has suggested that widespread petitioning in 1637 against a controversial new prayer book kickstarted the making of a covenanted public during the Covenanting Revolution (1637–41), while my study of petitioning in 1706–7 against incorporating union with England placed this activity within a nascent public sphere.[12] In 2018, deeper foundations for these unusual efforts were provided by a collection of papers on Scottish petitioning practices. These described everyday petitioning in Scotland's early modern parliament, church and civil courts and revealed a battle over the right to petition stimulated by the rise of more adversarial practices.[13] My volume of transcribed addresses on

---

[8] Peacey, *Print and Public Politics in the English Revolution*, 285–95. See also Dodd, *Justice and Grace* on the medieval roots of English petitioning practices.

[9] Vallance, '"From the hearts of the people": loyalty, addresses and the public sphere in the exclusion crisis'.

[10] Knights, *Representation*, 110; Knights, *Politics and Opinion in Crisis, 1678–81*, chs 8–9; Knights, 'London's "monster" petition of 1680'.

[11] Knights, *Representation*; Knights, '"The lowest degree of freedom": The right to petition parliament, 1640–1800'.

[12] Stewart, *Rethinking the Scottish Revolution: Covenanted Scotland, 1637–1651*, ch. 1; Bowie, *Scottish Public Opinion*, ch. 6.

[13] Bowie, 'From customary to constitutional right: the right to petition in Scotland before the 1707 Act of Union'; Finlay, 'The petition in the Court of Session in early modern Scotland'; MacDonald, 'Neither inside nor outside the corridors of power: prosaic petitioning and the royal burghs in early modern Scotland'; Raffe, 'Petitioning in the Scottish church courts, 1638–1707'.

the 1707 Union was contextualised with an initial survey of political petitioning in Scotland across the early modern era.[14]

This chapter will build on these insights by outlining typical petitioning concepts and practices and showing how these were extended and subverted in moments of political conflict from the 1560 Reformation to the eve of the 1688–90 Revolution. Providing a mode of negotiation and an assertive means of collective resistance, adversarial supplications and petitions brought forward grievances at key moments, presenting collective demands under the guise of humble entreaty. As the conditions of conflict created in Scotland by the Reformation and 1603 regal union encouraged tactical tweaks in language and presentation to highlight the opinions of petitioners, it became easier to imagine the subjects at large, rather than the monarch, parliament or general assembly, as the arbiters of the common good. This unwelcome challenge led to the increasing regulation of political petitioning as the crown sought to block or remove customary pathways for the hearing of petitions.

2.1   Petitioning Practices

As Lex Heerma van Voss has observed, petitioning was 'a common human experience' in medieval and early modern Europe.[15] Andreas Würgler has identified national forms in grievances, supplications, *Gravamina, Suppliken, Beschwerden, doléances, requêtes, représentations, gravami, petizioni, querele, clamores, greuges* and griefs.[16] The practice had ancient cultural roots in prayer to gods as well as social superiors. In the medieval era, cultural values of good lordship were affirmed in choreographed rituals for the presentation, hearing and answering of petitions.[17] These values required petitions to be submitted humbly and received graciously. A petition for a gift, favour or intercession was answered by the recipient to achieve justice, alleviate hardship or reward faithfulness. At the core of this exchange was 'the idea of public office as a *ministerium* whose moral responsibilities bound king or count more straitly than any accountability to public wishes.'[18] Lords were expected to hear and resolve the grievances

---

These papers arose from a pair of workshops funded by the Royal Society of Edinburgh and co-organised with Professor Thomas Munck. I am grateful to the RSE and Professor Munck.

[14] 'Introduction' in Bowie (ed.), *Addresses.*   [15] van Voss, 'Introduction', 1.

[16] Würgler, 'Voices from among the "silent masses"', 12.

[17] Ormrod, 'Murmur, clamour and noise: Voicing complaint and remedy in petitions to the English crown, c. 1300-c. 1460', 136–41; Lacey, '"Grace for the rebels": The role of the royal pardon in the Peasants' Revolt of 1381', 38–44.

[18] Koziol, *Begging Pardon and Favor: Ritual and Political Order in Early Medieval France,* 56.

54   Public Opinion in Early Modern Scotland, c.1560–1707

of subjects, from nobles to commons, not because their subjects could hold them to account but because God would. When James VI advised his son to 'wearie not to heare the complaintes of the oppressed', he endorsed a standard kingly virtue.[19]

By the late medieval period, petitioning had proliferated across a variety of administrative, judicial and political contexts and the petition had become a standard means of initiating a query, complaint, request, suit or case on behalf of an individual or group. Though still often read aloud, petitions increasingly were delivered in a written form to aid accurate recall and processing. In Scotland, the commission of the general assembly in 1596 noted that previous 'verball' arguments had been 'forgot and denied', while a 1625 convention of estates ordered that 'thair be no sollistatioun' of court of session judges 'bot be write'.[20] Writing also allowed the petitioner (or a literate agent) to sign the document to affirm the truth of the contents.

A petition presented a problem and the desired remedy. The Scots term 'petitioun' derived from the Latin *petitio*, meaning a request, demand or claim, while 'supplicatioun' (*supplicatio*) meant a prayer or entreaty.[21] In Scotland and England, the term 'supplication' was applied to requests to senior clergy, including the pope.[22] One of the best-studied types of petition in pre-Reformation Scotland is the papal supplication, painstakingly calendared by two generations of scholars.[23] A petition might be termed as a 'complaint and petition' to distinguish the grievance from the plea. This points to the more precise meaning for 'complaint' in a judicial setting as a formal statement of injury or wrong leading to an investigation. The use of petitions to bring cases to courts created a high degree of overlap between these terms. In the medieval Scottish parliament, a petition could be described as a 'bill of complaint'. In 1425, the parliament ordered that 'billis of complantis' relating to the 'colmon profyt [common profit] of the realme' should be handled by local justices, with appeals to the king.[24] In Scots, a 'bill' meant a legal or commercial document while 'bille', as Gwilym Dodd has shown, in fourteenth-century England meant

---

[19] James VI, *Basilikon Doron*, 111.
[20] Calderwood, *History*, v, 456; *RPS* A1625/10/55, 2 November 1625.
[21] 'Petitio', 'supplicatio', *Logeion*.
[22] Dodd, 'Kingship, parliament and the court: The emergence of 'high style' in petitions to the English crown, c.1350–1405', 528.
[23] Cowan et al. (eds.), *Calendar of Scottish Supplications to Rome, 1417–1492*.
[24] *RPS* 1425/3/25, 12 March 1425. In his early seventeenth-century *Minor Practicks*, Sir Thomas Hope used 'bill' to refer to written requests to law courts, including petitions.

Petitions

'a complaint for which the king or his ministers could provide a remedy'.[25] Alternative Scottish terms for a petition included 'grievances', 'grieves', 'griefs', 'desires' and 'suits'.

Other forms of communication served a similar petitionary function or could be linked to a petition. The 'remonstrance' was a formal statement of grievance on public affairs.[26] In 1630, a convention of estates ordered negotiators for a fishing treaty with England to 'make remonstrance' to the king in London on the taking of Scottish ships by privateers.[27] A 'representation' was a formal communication providing explanations and arguments to justify a desired outcome. In 1693, the 'present state of Glasgow as to its need of moe ministers' was 'humblie Represented' to the synod of Glasgow and Ayr.[28] Related to this was the 'information', which provided details to support a case at law. An example from 1700 illustrates some of these variations: a 'Petition' by the magistrates of Edinburgh to the Scottish parliament requesting a tax on animals brought to their 'Flesh Mercat' stimulated a dissenting 'Representation and Answers' from meat traders, to which the magistrates replied with an 'Information' and a second petition renewing their request.[29] Other forms that might be paired with a petition included the 'admonition', 'declaration' and 'memorial'. As noted above, the term 'address' or 'loyal address' was applied to acclamatory public statements of support in England from the late 1650s. In Scotland, 'address' acted more generally as a synonym for petition, encompassing but not limited to loyal addresses. It could also refer to the informational part of a petition, as in an 'address and petition'.[30] Over the early modern period, 'supplication' gave way to 'petition' and 'address' as more common terms.

Petitioners were expected to submit themselves humbly, expressing their respect for the power and dignity of the recipient. James VI noted that supplicants should speak 'reverentlie' to God and kings alike and complained of the 'indiscreit' behaviour of subjects who thrust petitions at him 'without reverence'.[31] To meet these expectations, written petitions used submissive language. Stereotyped phrases can be seen in petitions submitted to the Scottish parliament in 1700: the phrase, 'Humbly sheweth', meaning to exhibit or submit, was followed by an explanation of the

---

[25] 'Bill, n.', *DOST*; Dodd, 'Kingship, parliament and the court', 528.
[26] 'Remonstrance, n.', *OED*.   [27] *RPS* A1630/7/74, 12 November 1630.
[28] NLS Wodrow Folio 28, vol. 2, ff. 146–7
[29] NRS PA7/17/1/38, 'The petition of the magistrates of Edinburgh in behalf of their poor' (1700).
[30] Bowie, *Addresses*, 9–11.   [31] James VI, *Basilikon Doron*, 15; *RPCS* ser. 1, iii, 349.

56   Public Opinion in Early Modern Scotland, c.1560–1707

petitioner's problem.[32] 'May it therefore please [the recipient]' led to a statement of the desired remedy. The paper closed with a respectful 'And your petitioner shall ever pray'.[33] Submissive language signalled a petitioner's acceptance of the superior stature of the recipient and his judgement. Crucially, complainants were not meant to blame the petitioned authority for their problems. As Cecilia Nubola put it, '[l]aws, regulations and officials can be unjust and corrupt – never the prince.'[34] The standard trope of the evil counsellor served this norm by providing a scapegoat for royal failings.

Such measures maintained the position of the recipient as the decision-maker. Though petitioners clearly had views, as expressed in their representations and recommended remedies, the decision was meant to rest with the recipient, who would determine what was best for the common good as well as the petitioner. Because petitioned cases might involve overlapping rights or knotty problems, administrative procedures were developed to screen petitions and protect the ruler from unanswerable or obnoxious pleas. Savvy petitioners paid experts to pen their requests or asked senior officers to vet their petitions. Respect for the recipient required the humble acceptance of decisions without question and certainly without any repeat of the petition. These expectations indicate how shocking assertive petitioning could be, especially for the Scottish monarch after 1603 when, as David Stevenson has shown, the Stewarts developed a greater taste for pomp and majesty.[35]

The norms and tropes of petitioning would have been familiar to early modern Scots across the social scale. William Dunbar's late medieval petitionary poems indicate that Scottish elites found humour in his acknowledgement of the duplicity often lurking behind formulaic pleas.[36] A facility in petitioning was encouraged by the legal education received by many of Scotland's landed elites and reformed clergy by the late sixteenth century.[37] Ordinary people too were familiar with these forms. The concept of a formal complaint would have been widely understood through the operation of local barony and burgh courts, as seen in the 1640 complaint of a miller to the barony court of Ardrossan on tenants not

---

[32] 'S(c)haw, v.', *DOST*.   [33] *RPS* A1700/10/9–12, 27 November 1700.
[34] Nubola, 'Supplications between politics and justice', 37.
[35] Stevenson, 'The English devil of keeping state'.
[36] Hasler, *Court Poetry in Late Medieval England and Scotland*, ch. 3.
[37] Allan, *Philosophy and Politics in Later Stuart Scotland: Neo-Stoicism, Culture and Ideology in an Age of Crisis*, 19–23.

Petitions

paying his fees.[38] Petitions were used to make requests in burghs, as seen in a 1610 'supplicatioun' to the Glasgow burgh council from a group of 'nychtboris' asking the council to authorise the digging of a well, and on landed estates, as shown by Rab Houston's study of petitions from tenants to their landlords.[39] Women could submit private petitions, though political petitioning nearly always was restricted to male subjects.

Petitioning also was common within the Scottish parliament, though as Julian Goodare has noted, the topic 'demands further research'.[40] In the fourteenth century, petitions were heard by a committee for supplications and complaints (*supplicationes et querelas*) and in the fifteenth and early sixteenth century by lords auditors of causes and complaints (*auditores querelarum*).[41] Legal historians have shown that the consideration of judicial complaints and appeals gradually shifted to extraordinary sessions and the privy council in the 1400s and the newly constituted Court of Session from 1532, with a limited petition for remeid (remedy) of law allowed to parliament for procedural failure.[42] In the early modern period, most petitions to the Scottish parliament involved routine requests for ratifications or privileges, leading to private acts. In 1592, for example, a group of landowners, described as 'dyvers of the gentilmen duelland to landwart of the parochin of Sanctandrois', successfully petitioned for permission to build a new kirk outside the burgh.[43] During the disorders of the 1640s, a flood of private petitions to the estates on taxation and quartering can be compared to a similar phenomenon in England.[44]

Petitions on political affairs could be made to the estates, though there was no Scottish label equivalent to the 'common petitions' relating to public affairs that were distinguished from legal complaints in the fourteenth-century English parliament and no regularised mode for the submission of grievances from the estates like the *gravamina* of the Hessian diet.[45] Nor was petitioning from the Scottish parliament to the crown elaborated to the same extent as in Elizabethan England, where the Lords

---

[38] NRS GD3/10/22 Barony Court Book of Ardrossan, f.33.
[39] *ERBG*, i, 312; Houston, *Peasant Petitions.*   [40] Goodare, 'Parliament and politics', 252.
[41] *RPS* 1341/6, 24 Sept. 1341; 1466/2, 9 October 1466; 1492/2/23, 11 February 1492; 1526/6/4, 13 June 1526.
[42] Godfrey, *Civil Justice in Renaissance Scotland,* 7–12, 33–7; Ford, 'Protestations to parliament for remeid of law'.
[43] *RPS* 1592/4/38, 5 June 1592.
[44] Stewart, 'Petitioning in early seventeenth-century Scotland, 1625–51', 314–20; Hopper et al. (eds.), *Civil War Petitions.*
[45] Dodd, *Justice and Grace,* ch. 5; Kümin and Würgler, 'Petitions, *Gravamina* and the early modern state: local influence on central legislation in England and Germany', 41, 47–9.

58   Public Opinion in Early Modern Scotland, c.1560–1707

and Commons could petition the queen to highlight matters requiring crown attention.[46] Nevertheless, written grievances could be given to the clerk register before and during parliamentary sessions. As Alan MacDonald has shown, the collective views of the royal burghs were expressed to parliament through petitions from the Convention of Royal Burghs, an independent assembly that usually met before or during parliamentary sessions.[47]

However, though petitions could be submitted to parliament, before the Revolution of 1688–90 there was no guarantee that they would be read. The clerk register normally remitted petitions to a preparatory committee known as the Lords of the Articles, where legislation was drafted before being submitted to the full house for their approval.[48] In its review function, this committee can be compared to the *Tre Maggiori* of the medieval Florentine state, a vetting body that forwarded successful petitions for legislative ratification.[49] An attempt was made in 1594 to prevent the presentation of a 'confusit multitude of doubtfull and informall articles and supplicationis' to the Lords of the Articles by requiring prior inspection of petitions.[50] In keeping with the general constriction of consultation and tighter management of parliamentary affairs by the crown at this time, expectations for the receipt and review of petitions became more stringent over time, with proclamations in 1617, 1621 and 1633 ordering early submission of petitions for scrutiny.[51]

As John Watts has pointed out, 'displays of common dissatisfaction had some legitimacy' because a monarch's responsibility for justice and good government produced a duty to hear complaints.[52] Like the customary function of the protestation in reserving personal rights, traditional petitioning practices could provide an entry point for forceful arguments in supplicative sheep's clothing. Moreover, in the era of the Reformation, religious conflicts encouraged appeals to conscience and the authority of God's law, challenging the norms of subordination implicit in a petition.[53]

---

[46] Foster, 'Petitions and the Petition of Right', 27–9.

[47] MacDonald, 'Neither inside or outside the corridors of power'; MacDonald, 'The third estate: Parliament and the burghs', 109–10.

[48] Tanner, 'The Lords of the Articles before 1540: A reassessment'; MacDonald, 'Uncovering the legislative process', 3–6.

[49] Cohn, *Creating the Florentine State: Peasants and Rebellion, 1348–1434*, 172–3.

[50] *RPS* 1594/4/39, 8 June 1594; Mann, 'House rules: parliamentary procedures', 129; Goodare (ed.), 'Diary of the convention of estates, 1630', 91 n.27

[51] MacDonald, 'Legislative process', 606–8.

[52] Watts, 'Public or plebs: The changing meaning of "commons", 1381–1549', 243.

[53] van Nierop, 'A beggars' banquet: The compromise of the nobility and the politics of inversion', 419–25.

Petitions 59

This can be seen in a 1558 'oratioun' and 'petitioun' presented by a group of Protestant nobles known as the Lords of the Congregation to the regent Mary of Guise. This offered a complaint against the 'tyranny' of the 'Estate Ecclesiasticall' and petitioned for five points of reformation, including permission to worship and baptise in the vernacular.[54] By providing scriptural and patristic authorities in support of these requests, the petitioners highlighted their own informed opinions and set limits on the regent's judgement of their petition. During and after the successful 1559–60 Reformation rebellion, the religious opinions of Protestants continued to be emphasised. A large body of 'barons and freeholders' who did not normally attend the Scottish parliament petitioned for entry to the 1560 diet, arguing that they ought to 'ressoune and vote in all caussis [causes] concerning the commoune wele', including 'the caussis of trew religioune'.[55] In exercising the maxim from Roman law that what concerns all should be approved by all (*quod omnes tangit*), the barons' petition emphasised the validity of the opinions of these lesser nobles.

As these examples indicate, by the time of the 1560 Reformation, humble petitioning was being appropriated by interest groups as a mode of negotiation and pressure. While protestations were considered a last resort, petitions offered a more immediate tool for those seeking to influence policy. Because petitions offered a familiar means of complaint that authorities were expected to hear and answer, they could be adapted with an emphasis on collective judgements and consciences. This trend can be seen in December 1566 when the general assembly of the newly reformed kirk issued a robust 'supplicatioun' to the privy council asking that a restoration of powers to the archbishop of St Andrews be suspended because it contravened not only the 1560 Reformation parliament, 'ane lawfull and most frie parliament that ever was in this realme', but also the desires of 'the greatest part of the subjects of this realme'. In 'humblie' requesting 'ane reasonable ansuer', the kirk showed an expectation that its arguments would be taken seriously.[56] The next section will consider the development of adversarial petitioning during the adult reign of James VI, spurred by the conflict between those who supported a presbyterian form of church government and those who preferred stronger royal and episcopal control.

---

[54] Laing (ed.), *The Works of John Knox*, i, 301–6. [55] *RPS* A1560/8/2, 1 August 1560.
[56] *APGA*, i, 88–90.

60   Public Opinion in Early Modern Scotland, c.1560–1707

2.2 Jacobean Petitioning

After the 1560 Reformation, the general assembly of the reformed kirk routinely interacted with the government through petitions and supplications. As seen in Chapter 1, the Scottish Confession gave a responsibility to the general assembly to defend and promote the interests of the kirk, with silence being sinful. During the reign of James VI, petitions facilitated an active, ongoing and sometimes heated dialogue with the king. While simple petitions on minor matters were delivered to the king's master of requests, 'special grieves' and proposed remedies on national affairs were handed to the king in person by commissioners.[57] James provided answers in writing or by attending conferences or the assembly.[58] When tensions rose between kirk and crown, petitioning became more assertive. Unwelcome grievances were asserted repeatedly, and both clerical signatures and crowds of men and women were marshalled to demonstrate support for the kirk's position. This section will feature an episode of aggressive petitioning in 1596 which led the king to curtail dialogue with the assembly. As executive and episcopal control of the kirk increased after this event, dissidents began to use extra-institutional petitions to call for more frequent meetings of the general assembly, incorporating demands on behalf of the laity at large.

A period of intense debate between kirk leaders and the king in 1596 was stimulated by fears for the security of the Protestant Reformation. Anticipating the return from exile of Catholic lords at a time of Spanish aggression, the general assembly took a forthright tone with James in 'Grieves' and detailed 'Articles' presented in March 1596.[59] A committee of leading clerics pursued these concerns with the king after the assembly.[60] The indictment in October of a clergyman, David Black, for seditious sermons led these clerics to take the unusual step of signing a paper rejecting the jurisdiction of civil courts over clerical speech and beseeching the king to maintain the liberties of the kirk. Copies were circulated to Scotland's fifty-one regional presbyteries for their endorsement and parish ministers were urged to advertise the cause to their congregations.[61] Few presbytery records survive from this period, but extant examples suggest that subscriptions may have been widespread.[62] Kirk leaders saw this extraordinary endeavour as a means of expressing the

---

[57] *APGA*, ii, 561, 581.   [58] E.g. *APGA*, iii, 828–34, 990–1.
[59] *APGA*, iii, 875–8; Calderwood, *History*, v, 415–8.   [60] MacDonald, *Jacobean Kirk*, 64.
[61] Calderwood *History*, v, 454, 456–61.   [62] MacDonald, *Jacobean Kirk*, 67–8.

Petitions 61

kirk's consensual views, though the king saw it as 'tending to a direct mutiny'.[63] In early November they again 'shew[ed] his Majestie the greeves of the kirk', offering 'plaine replyes' to the king's answers, and in subsequent meetings they continued to 'deale earnestlie' with the king.[64] A proclamation to ban meetings by these clerics led them on 30 November to pen a 'humble Supplication and faithful Admonition' to James. Admitting that the 'libertie of our admonitiouns' put them in 'hazard', they asserted that 'silence' was impossible in the face of sin. The petition asked the king to remit Black's case from the civil courts to the next general assembly. A separate paper explaining the kirk's position asked the same in the name of 'the whole ministrie of Scotland'. As intense negotiations continued, the king was asked to satisfy not just the nation's ministry but 'the whole rest of [his] good subjects'.[65]

Events came to a head on 17 December 1596, centred on a new petition. Between 9 and 14 December, the king had ordered Black to be incarcerated and proposed that clergy sign a 'prooffe of obedience' before receiving their stipends.[66] Further commands to disperse the clerical committee and expel twenty-four sympathetic burgesses from Edinburgh stimulated open resistance.[67] Sermons marking the baptism of Princess Elizabeth on 28 November and fast days on 5 and 12 December had stimulated 'a mightie motioun amongst the people of God' against a perceived Catholic threat (including Catholics in the king's circle of advisors). Edinburgh's 'flockes' were warned that their pastors, like Black, might be arrested.[68] After an incendiary sermon on 17 December, activist clerics met with 'well-affected' nobles and burgesses who swore to defend the 'present state of religioun' and agreed to approach the king with a petition complaining of the evil influence of his Catholic counsellors. The delegation went to the king in the Edinburgh tolbooth (town hall), reportedly speaking in a 'humble and lamentable manner', but with confederates 'thronging unmannerly into the room'. When the king refused to answer their petition, an angry crowd nearly broke down the tolbooth door as they denounced the king's Catholic advisors. Rumours of danger to the kirk produced a 'hurlie burlie' in the street with nobles, gentlemen and burgesses in arms. Speaking on behalf of the king, the earl of Mar assured a delegation that 'any reasonable petition would be heard

---

[63] Calderwood, *History*, v, 461; Spottiswood, *History*, iii, 17.
[64] Calderwood, *History*, v, 439–41, 450–6, 463–5; Spottiswood, *History*, iii, 12–3.
[65] Calderwood, *History*, v, 470–97.   [66] *Ibid.*, 498–501. See chapter 3.   [67] *Ibid.*, 501, 510.
[68] Spottiswood *History*, iii, 9, 26; Calderwood, *History*, v, 500–1.

62   Public Opinion in Early Modern Scotland, c.1560–1707

and answered' if presented in a 'dutiful manner'. They responded with a three-point petition that the king referred to a meeting of the privy council that afternoon. The group drew up a fuller paper for that meeting but were discouraged from presenting it.[69] The event fizzled out when the king left Edinburgh the next morning and no magnate proved willing to take matters further.[70]

After this affront, James sought to increase the crown's control over the kirk by establishing a more compliant executive committee and rebuilding a crown-appointed episcopate.[71] In his 1599 *Basilikon Doron*, he made clear his frustration with presbyterian 'Puritans', 'pestes' in 'the Church and Common-weill of Scotland', and their notion of 'Paritie' in church government, 'which can not agree with a Monarchie'.[72] The 1603 union worsened the resulting constriction in petitionary dialogue. At the last general assembly before the regal union, James attended in person, answered a petition from the previous assembly and participated in a discussion on clerical stipends.[73] His subsequent departure for London created what MacDonald has described as 'the difficulties involved in communicating with a distant monarch through unreliable channels'.[74] Though James VI advised his son Henry to return to Scotland every three years to hear complaints, James only managed a single trip back in 1617 before his death in 1625.[75] At first, Scottish clerics were invited to attend conferences with the king in London, but English prelates were said to be shocked by the blunt tone taken by the Scots and these occasional meetings soon became more circumscribed.[76]

Meetings of the general assembly became less frequent after 1603, stimulating repeatedly unsuccessful petitions for church assemblies alongside the protestations noted in Chapter 1. '[A]ll maner of earnest supplicatioun' by church courts, including the synod of Fife and the presbytery of Edinburgh, were conveyed to London by clerics or nobles to no effect.[77] A petition sent by the synod of Lothian and Tweeddale with John Spottiswood, archbishop of Glasgow, reportedly never reached the king.[78] At a 1606 conference in London, James received a petition on behalf of ministers convicted of treason for holding an unauthorised assembly in

---

[69] Calderwood *History*, v, 512–3; Spottiswood *History*, iii, 28–32.
[70] *RPCS*, ser. 1, v, 349–52; Goodare, 'The attempted Scottish *coup* of 1596', 320–2.
[71] MacDonald, *Jacobean Kirk*, 68–73, 80–1.   [72] James VI, *Basilikon Doron*, 48–51.
[73] *APGA*, iii, 990–91; Spottiswood, *History*, iii, 104–5.   [74] MacDonald, *Jacobean Kirk*, 114.
[75] James VI, *Basilikon Doron*, 65; McNeill and McNeill, 'The Scottish progress of James VI, 1617'.
[76] MacDonald, *Jacobean Kirk*, 125; Calderwood, *History*, v, 505.
[77] Calderwood, *History*, vi, 315–7.   [78] MacDonald, *Jacobean Kirk*, 114.

Petitions 63

July 1605, but made no formal answer.[79] Unhappiness in the assembly still could generate petitions to the king, but in more restricted terms. When the king threatened to ban presbyterial meetings, a 'tightly controlled' 1610 assembly still managed to send 'a most humble Supplication'. This begged James to accept their compliance with other demands, including the ratification of an oath for new entrants acknowledging the royal supremacy, as sufficient evidence of their acquiescence to his authority.[80] In 1617, James confirmed that one of the purposes of the general assembly was 'to put up petitions to king and parliament' on behalf of the church.[81] Yet as episcopal control increased over synods and the general assembly, petitions became an orchestrated means of displaying episcopal and royal authority. In calling a general assembly in 1616, at which he intended to propose new canons and a liturgy, James noted that he had graciously licenced the meeting in response to the 'good advice and opinion' of the bishops expressed in a petition for a meeting.[82]

Increasing crown control of kirk meetings encouraged extra-institutional communications emphasising the dissenting opinions of clerics and laity at large. As noted in Chapter 1, in 1617 a group of clerics prepared a supplication and protestation asking the estates not to approve an act allowing the king to make policy without consulting the general assembly. When the supplication was submitted to the clerk register, James, who was present for the parliament, blocked its presentation. The ringleaders were accused of holding a seditious meeting.[83] Opponents of controversial liturgical reforms presented to the 1618 general assembly in Perth were unable to have their reasons against the proposed articles sent to the king for his answers.[84] They wrote a petition to the 1621 parliament against civil ratification of the articles, supplicating on behalf of 'wearied and broken-hearted brethren, ministers and people'. Parliament was begged to ask James for 'a safe libertie' to maintain Scottish worship according to law, free from 'novations'. The petition was signed by Andrew Duncan, minister at Crail, on behalf of other supplicants, prior experience having made it too dangerous to collect individual signatures. The clerk register was only 'with great difficulty' persuaded to take the petition, saying he 'doubted whether he wold exhibit it in parliament'.

---

[79] Spottiswood, *History*, iii, 176–82. Later the king rejected the petition by ordering the clerics to be banished.
[80] APGA, iii, 1098; MacDonald, *Jacobean Kirk*, 146.   [81] Calderwood, *History*, vii, 262.
[82] *APGA*, iii, 1115, 1128; MacDonald, *Jacobean Kirk*, 157.   [83] Calderwood *History*, vii, 257–71.
[84] *APGA*, iii, 1164.

64 Public Opinion in Early Modern Scotland, c.1560–1707

The petition was suppressed and Duncan was warded in Dumbarton castle.[85] The privy council also ordered all non-resident ministers to leave Edinburgh to stop them from making 'malignant aspersions' about the king's intentions to members of parliament.[86] Many obeyed, but left written 'Informations and Admonitions' offering arguments against the Perth articles on behalf of the 'ministers and professors of this kingdome'.[87]

In the early adult reign of James VI, petitioning provided a vehicle for dialogue between the king and the reformed kirk, sometimes in assertive forms reinforced with subscriptions and repeated presentation. In 1596, a spiralling exchange, exacerbated by anxious sermons and a dispute over the regulation of clerical speech, led to an explosive confrontation in Edinburgh. When James responded by enhancing royal and episcopal authority over the general assembly, dissident clerics turned to extra-institutional petitioning for meetings of the general assembly and against acts ratifying controversial changes to Scottish church government and worship, citing the opinions of clergy and laypeople at large. As the next section will show, James' son Charles I recognised the affront presented by these antagonistic practices. His decision to discourage petitioning while pursuing even more controversial policies only succeeded in storing up unresolved discontent.

2.3 Petitioning under Charles I, 1625–1636

In the first decade of his reign, Charles I launched a tranche of controversial reforms affecting all sectors of Scottish society while continuing to enhance episcopal authority. Clerical and lay complainants soon found the new king was averse to criticism. By providing a close study of Charles' handling of petitions, this section will find that the king paid too much attention to traditional judicial petitions, while refusing to hear political petitions that encroached on his dignity or prerogative. Though Charles acknowledged the principle that a monarch should hear petitioned grievances, laws against seditious speech were applied to Balmerino for possessing a draft of a sharply worded extra-institutional petition, forcing the king's opponents to escalate their methods of collective complaint.

In Charles' first convention of estates in 1625, his officers sought to constrain petitioning. Unhappy with the granting of baronet titles to Nova

---

[85] Calderwood, *History*, vii, 464–71; *RPCS* ser. 1, xii, 545–6.   [86] *RPCS* ser. 1, xii, 546–7.
[87] Calderwood, *History*, vii, 474–85.

Petitions

Scotia investors, elected commissioners for the shires had asked the rest of the estates to join them in petitioning Charles against this practice. Because the granting of titles did not require parliamentary consent, they were told that 'his majesties prerogative wald not admitt ony sort of oppositioun' in this matter. The barons in reply 'most humblie protestit that the least derogatioun of his majesties royall prerogative sould never enter in thair hairtis' and 'thair petitioun wes in no sort contrair to the same'. They merely wished to express their grievances and ask Charles not to include new titles in the plantation scheme.[88] Nevertheless, this was considered 'derogatorie' and the petition was rejected.[89]

Early in 1626, Charles sought to create a new judicatory, staffed by leading officers of state, to hear complaints and punish wrongdoers. Any officer, lawyer or clerk could be reported to this new court for corruption.[90] This might have been welcomed as an improvement on a narrower commission constituted by James VI in 1623 to hear complaints on monopolies, which also heard petitions on bureaucratic failings and abuses.[91] But the new commission on grievances also was empowered to police seditious speech, encompassing any private or public slander or misrepresentation of the actions of the king or his government. It could appoint informers in every shire, interrogate witnesses and fine or imprison offenders. Under this scheme, it was unclear where the line would be drawn between a humble complaint and a seditious slander. Contemporaries feared that this would be 'nothing els bot the star-chamber courte of England under ane other name'.[92] Indeed, at the same time as Charles announced his new commission, he also warned that anyone spreading evil talk about his deeply controversial scheme to revoke and regrant crown charters on former church lands would be pursued 'with all rigour' as 'seditious personis and enemies to his Majesties auctoritie'.[93] Not even the bishops were exempt from criticism: when in 1627 they pleaded that the revocation scheme was drawing the kirk into disrepute, the king upbraided them as 'timorous'.[94]

Opposition by leading nobles sank the proposed court, but Charles' attitude towards direct criticism was clear. As Peter Donald has observed, a

---

[88] *RPS* A1625/10/48, 2 November 1625.
[89] Rogers (ed.), *The Earl of Stirling's Register of Royal Letters*, i, 18.
[90] *RPCS*, ser. 2, i, 231–2, 263–5.
[91] *RPCS*, ser. 1, xiii, 219–23; Rogers (ed.), *The Earl of Stirling's Register of Royal Letters*, i, 20, 24.
[92] Haig (ed.), *The Historical Works of Sir James Balfour*, ii, 131.   [93] *RPCS*, ser. 2, i, 227–30.
[94] Haig (ed.), *The Historical Works of Sir James Balfour*, ii, 156.

66   Public Opinion in Early Modern Scotland, c.1560–1707

'remedy pushed from below was to his mind more aggravation than cure.'[95] In England, Charles sought to restrict access to his person and avoided contact with petitioners.[96] When he agreed to hear supplicants, Charles expected them to display 'the duetifulnes of loveing subjects' and the 'modestie of humble suppliants' according to strict standards of decorum and protocol.[97] In November 1626, a delegation carried to London a petition on the revocation scheme signed by several nobles and freeholders. The king 'storm'd at their petition, as of too heigh a straine for subiects and petitioners' and he refused to answer the petition until they begged pardon.[98] Charles eventually agreed to grant their request for a new commission to consider disputed revocation cases but he made the most of this concession by writing to subscribing nobles to emphasise his expectation of compliance.[99] A similar approach can be seen in Charles' efforts to enforce his father's provocative Perth articles. In 1628, the clergy of Edinburgh wrote a letter to the king in advance of the Easter communion 'beeseeching' him to allow them not to kneel at communion. '[E]xceeding offended', Charles refused to answer the letter and ordered the writers to be punished.[100]

At the same time, Charles and his master of requests, Sir James Galloway, could be overzealous in handling private petitions for justice.[101] As John Ford has shown, in the previous century Scottish monarchs had minimised their involvement in civil cases in Scotland's Court of Session.[102] Charles, by contrast, chose to intervene more often in response to petitions from litigants, urging the judges to hurry or delay cases or, more controversially, indicating a desired outcome.[103] In 1630, a convention of estates petitioned the king to send unresolved judicial cases back to the ordinary courts and arbitrate only on matters of 'delay or want of justice'.[104] Emphasising the unusual nature of Charles' micro-

---

[95] Donald, *An Uncounselled King: Charles I and the Scottish Troubles, 1637–1641*, i, 17.
[96] Richards, '"His nowe majestie" and the English monarchy: The kingship of Charles I before 1640', 77–81.
[97] Rogers (ed.), *The Earl of Stirling's Register of Royal Letters*, i, 109; Stevenson, 'The English devil of keeping state: Elite manners and the downfall of Charles I in Scotland'.
[98] Rogers (ed.), *The Earl of Stirling's Register of Royal Letters*, i, 109, 117, 119.
[99] Haig (ed.), *The Historical Works of Sir James Balfour*, ii, 152, 154–5; Rogers (ed.), *The Earl of Stirling's Register*, vol. 1, 117, 119.
[100] Row, *History*, 345–6; Rogers (ed.), *The Earl of Stirling's Register of Royal Letters*, i, 271–2.
[101] Haig (ed.), *The Historical Works of Sir James Balfour*, ii, 132.
[102] Ford, 'Epistolary control of the College of Justice in Scotland'. I am grateful to Mark Godfrey for bringing this paper to my attention.
[103] Rogers (ed.), *The Earl of Stirling's Register of Royal Letters*, i, 17, 19, 23, 37, 41, 43.
[104] *RPS* A1630/7/32, 2 August 1630.

Petitions

management, this request echoed the view of James VI that the monarch should hear complaints for justice but 'remitte eueyrything to the ordinarye judicatoure for eschewing of confusion'.[105]

Charles also sought to increase the scrutiny of petitions submitted to conventions and parliaments of the estates. Before the 1630 convention, Charles ordered that no petition be presented unless it had been approved by him or his 'principal adviser in Scottish affairs', William Graham, earl of Menteith.[106] Of the grievances submitted by the shire and burgh estates, three minor items were cut from the shire list.[107] More significantly, two petitions asking for relief from the enforcement of the Perth articles were rejected.[108] In July 1626, Charles had ordered his bishops to exact greater compliance with these articles by imposing an oath of conformity for new clergy.[109] When it was argued in the 1630 convention that a petition on the articles contravened no law and should be accepted, the earl of Menteith 'declaired oppinlie in presence of the haill estates' that 'he wald not admitt' it. A further petition was presented by Balmerino 'in name of the laick [lay] patrones'. This complained against the new oath of conformity, arguing that it was preventing patrons from filling vacancies and that it contravened a 1612 law establishing a different oath.[110] The lord advocate (the king's attorney) refused to take up the second point, in effect confirming that a royal edict could supersede standing law on ecclesiastical matters. Balmerino's petition was rejected after being 'long disputit'.[111] This intense controversy points to the significance in members' minds not just of the 1626 oath (discussed further in Chapter 3) and the constitutional question of the king's powers over the church but also the apparent endangerment of a customary liberty to petition for relief of grievances.

Control of petitions ratcheted higher in Charles' first Scottish parliament, held in June 1633 during a visit for his Scottish coronation.[112] As usual, petitions were invited for submission to the clerk register, Sir John

---

[105] James VI, *Basilikon Doron*, 111.

[106] Goodare (ed.), 'Diary of the convention', 92. In 1630, Menteith was the president of the privy council. Lee, 'Graham, William, first earl of Airth and seventh earl of Menteith'.

[107] *RPS* A1630/7/20, 29 June 1630, A1630/7/38–40, 2 August 1630; Goodare (ed.), 'Diary of the Convention', 110.

[108] *RPS* A1630/7/20, 29 June 1630; 'Diary of the Convention', 95–6.

[109] Haig (ed.), *The Historical Works of Sir James Balfour*, ii, 142–4. See chapter 3.

[110] Goodare (ed.), 'Diary of the Convention', 107–8; Donald, *Uncounselled King*, 28–9. The oath was ratified by the 1610 general assembly and 1612 parliament: *APGA*, iii, 1097; *RPS* 1612/10/8, 23 October 1612.

[111] Goodare (ed.), 'Diary of the Convention', 109.

[112] Airy (ed.), *Burnet's History of My Own Time*, i, 31.

68   Public Opinion in Early Modern Scotland, c.1560–1707

Hay of Landis, but the preparation of collective grievances by the estates was curtailed by the prohibition of separate meetings of the estates, a measure introduced at the 1621 parliament.[113] A deposed clergyman, Thomas Hogg, submitted 'just griuances and reasonable petitions' in the name of himself and 'others of the ministrie lykwayes greiued', taking a notarial instrument to confirm his submission. Hogg's petition outlined recent shifts in ecclesiastical policy, including the augmentation of the powers of bishops, the blocking of annual meetings of the general assembly, changes to sacramental forms and the exercise of civil authority over clerical speech. As in the 1630 convention, it was argued that the 1626 oath imposed on new entrants had no statutory basis. The petition contended that the enforcement of the Perth articles contravened 'the meining of the wotters [voters]' at the 1618 general assembly, who had not expected these alterations to be enforced. Hogg submitted a second supplication to Charles at Dalkeith asking him, 'in all humility', 'to be fauorable to our petitions, wich we have deliuered to the Clerck of Register' and hoping for 'a gratious anssuer'. Both petitions were ignored.[114] In the parliamentary session, a legislative programme prepared by the Lords of the Articles with the king's personal oversight was voted without debate, though some members made statements of opposition when called to express their vote.[115] Charles noted down the names of dissenting voters with expressions of 'spleene', an 'unseimly acte' said to have 'bred a grete hearte burning in many'.[116]

According to the presbyterian historian John Row, a group of parliamentarians intended to petition the king before the session concluded but did not manage it, leading them to consider an extra-parliamentary petition. After the session, a petition drafted by an advocate, William Haig, circulated among 'some noblemen and others', including Balmerino and John Leslie, sixth earl of Rothes.[117] Though described as a 'humble Supplication', the text was remarkably assertive, providing arguments

---

[113] Haig (ed.), *The Historical Works of Sir James Balfour*, ii, 205–6; *RPS* 1633/6/1, 18 June 1633; Young, 'Charles I and the 1633 parliament', 115–7, 126; Wells, 'Constitutional conflict after the union of the crowns', 99. Goodare (ed.), 'Diary of the convention', 90–1.

[114] Haig (ed.), *The Historical Works of Sir James Balfour*, ii, 207–16; Young, 'Charles I and the 1633 parliament', 116–7.

[115] Row, *History*, 364, 366–7; Airy (ed.), *Burnet's History*, i, 32.

[116] Haig (ed.), *The Historical Works of Sir James Balfour*, ii, 200. A substantial minority of fifteen nobles, forty-four burghs and 'some' barons voted against the acts. Fleming, *Scotland's Supplication and Complaint against the Book of Common Prayer (Otherwise Laud's Liturgy), the Book of Canons, and the Prelates, 18th October 1637*, 45–6.

[117] Row, *History*, 364–6, 375–82.

Petitions

against the king's legislation and closing with a confident expectation of his agreement. The petition complained about the disregard paid to the 'just and heavy Grievances' submitted to the 1625 and 1630 conventions and the suppression of supplications to the 1633 parliament. Invoking opinion at large, it stated that 'the minds of most of your good people' were in 'perplexity' over recent church innovations and warned the king that he was in danger of losing the affections of 'a great many of your good subjects' whose consciences were 'tender' in these 'points of novation'.[118]

When a copy of this text with edits in Balmerino's own hand was handed to the crown by archbishop Spottiswood of St Andrews and Balmerino failed to submit in public to the king's mercy, the nobleman was charged with leasing-making, a Scots term for *lèse-majesté* or seditious words.[119] Approved personally by Charles, his indictment characterised the supplication as 'a most scandalous, reproachful, odious and seditious Libel' because it 'seditiously, reproachfully, and outrageously tax[ed]' the king for his controversial actions in parliament.[120] Its 'nipping and checking' tone was deemed incompatible with the 'humble obedience of a good, quiet and peaceable subject'. In reply, Balmerino's lawyers argued that his petition was no libel, but rather a 'Remonstrance by supplication' in which the supplicants, as members of parliament, acted 'for the publick'.[121] The failure of this argument indicates both the unusually sharp tone of Haig's petition and the king's animosity towards collective criticism.[122]

Haig's petition represented an escalation in the assertiveness of petitioning practices, trying to reach a king who saw the expression of grievances as insubordination. Though Charles had been unable to establish a new judicial body to investigate seditious complaints, he and his officers restricted the expression of grievances in conventions and parliaments. With complaints not being aired in national assemblies, petitioners pointed to the unhappiness of subjects at large whose consciences were strained by religious reforms. Though Charles reprieved Balmerino from the death penalty after his conviction for sedition, the trial created disquiet. The king's expectation of silent obedience clashed with the customary idea

---

[118] Howell (ed.), *A Complete Collection of State Trials, Vol. III*, 604–8.

[119] The earl of Rothes was also questioned but the crown chose to make an example of Balmerino. 'Lesing-making', *DOST*; Rogers (ed.), *The Earl of Stirling's Register of Royal Letters*, ii, 838; Macinnes, *Charles I and the Making of the Covenanting Movement, 1625–1641*, 138.

[120] Rogers (ed.), *The Earl of Stirling's Register of Royal Letters*, ii, 808.

[121] An act of 1594 applied the penalties of leasing-making to anyone concealing slander against the crown. *RPS* 1594/4/26, 8 June 1594.

[122] Howell (ed.), *Complete Collection of State Trials, Vol. III*, 591–659.

70   Public Opinion in Early Modern Scotland, c.1560–1707

that monarchs should listen to the grievances of their people, stimulating criticism even from royalists like William Drummond of Hawthornden, better known for his poetry in praise of the Stewarts.[123] As the next section will show, the trial by no means discouraged adversarial petitioning; instead, it taught organisers to avoid direct criticism of the king and seek evidence of extra-institutional support in the form of signatures and crowds.

2.4   Petitions and Counter-Petitions under the Covenanters and Cromwell, 1637–1659

In 1637, the king's imposition of a new liturgy for the Scottish kirk stimulated an innovative petitioning campaign featuring repeated supplications made in the name of local and national communities, backed with male subscriptions. To avoid charges of sedition, these supplications to the privy council concentrated their criticism on the Scottish bishops instead of the king, while encouraging large crowds of men and women to gather to present the supplications and hear anticipated answers. In rejecting what he saw as a tumultuous and seditious attack, Charles created a face-off that ended in open rebellion. After the defeat of the king in the Bishops' Wars (1639–40), the Covenanter regime re-established personal petitioning to parliament as a bellwether of good government, but civil conflict stimulated collective petitions and counter-petitions in response to the English civil war and the 1647 Engagement. After the conquest of Scotland by English forces in 1651, the Cromwellian commonwealth took some of the sting out of assertive petitioning by hearing petitioned desires on the terms of a forced union, but the expression of petitioned opinions from Scotland tended to be restricted by an unwillingness to acknowledge the authority of a government imposed by force. In 1659 a new style of collective petition, offered by dissenters with male and female hands gathered from across Scotland, generated controversy over whether this represented national opinion.

The promulgation of controversial new canons in 1636 and a prayer book in 1637 by royal authority stimulated a persistent and increasingly participatory petitioning campaign from August 1637. This followed violent protests made at the first reading of the new prayer book in Edinburgh in July, orchestrated by 'matrons of the mercantile community'

---

[123] Spiller, 'Drummond, William, of Hawthornden (1585–1649)'.

Petitions 71

with the cooperation of female servants.[124] According to the earl of Rothes, when an unnamed 'good and religious woman' asked why 'no ordinare nor lawfull means were used' against the prayer book, resistance turned to petitioning.[125] On 23 August, three ministers from St Andrews presbytery asked the privy council to lift penalties imposed on them for failing to acquire two copies of the prayer book as demanded by a royal proclamation. Stating that 'in the matters of Gods worschip we are not bound to blind obedience', the ministers provided 'Reasons' for their stance which included popular preferences: the book was not approved by the general assembly or parliament, its imposition was contrary to the liberty of the kirk and the free judgment of its clerics, and 'the people' would not accept any change in their customary practices. This was accompanied by an 'information' elaborating the clerics' constitutional and theological points.[126] Several nobles and gentlemen seconded the petition with letters 'remonstrat[ing] both the evills of the book, and the illegal introductione therof'. They warned the council that if the prayer book continued to be imposed, 'all' would 'generallie refuse it, and numerouslie and confusedlie petition his Majestie'. After extensive debate, the council agreed to convey to the king 'the clamors and fears of many subjects from divers corners of the kingdom'.[127]

Before an answer could be received from London, a general supplication in name of the estates and commons gathered in Edinburgh was handed to the privy council on 20 September, joined by a tranche of supporting petitions including, on 26 September, a petition from the town council of Edinburgh.[128] To lend credence to the premise that the supplications spoke for the nation at large, these auxiliary petitions were presented as the consensual views of constituent units of the kirk and realm. An account by the earl of Rothes reported sixty-eight local petitions, while privy council records show forty-five from seven burghs, four presbyteries and thirty-four rural parishes. All came from south of the Tay, mostly from Fife, Lanarkshire and Ayrshire.[129] The general petition had been made 'very smoothe' by consultation with John Stewart, first earl of Traquair, the king's treasurer and leading officer in Scotland. The text opened with

---

[124] Macinnes, *Charles I and the Making of the Covenanting Movement*, 159–60.

[125] Leslie, *Relation*, 18.   [126] *Ibid.*, 45–7.

[127] *Ibid.*, 5–7. According to John Livingston, a second petition from the west was also submitted, 'the one not knowing of the other'. Tweedie (ed.), *Select Biographies: Edited for the Wodrow Society Chiefly from Manuscripts in the Library of the Faculty of Advocates*, i, 159.

[128] Leslie, *Relation*, 47–8; Row, *History*, 485.

[129] Leslie, *Relation*, 8, 47–8; *RPCS* ser. 2, vi, 699–716.

72   Public Opinion in Early Modern Scotland, c.1560–1707

assurances of loyalty and asked the privy council to submit the grievances of the estates and commons to the king.[130] The burgh of Glasgow's petition stated that though they had complied with recent religious changes, they found themselves mystified by the liturgy and compelled to beg the council for relief. The petitioners sought to enlist the sympathy of James Stewart, fourth duke of Lennox, a prominent courtier, by ranking themselves in the street by the tolbooth as he arrived in Edinburgh. The council agreed to send Lennox as an emissary to the king with the national petition and Edinburgh's petition.[131]

The affront given by agitated crowds in Edinburgh led Charles to withhold a direct answer to the petitions. Instead, when even greater numbers gathered for the next privy council meeting in October, they were ordered to leave the city.[132] The petitioners objected to this 'peremptorie unlawfull charge' in another collective supplication to the privy council on 18 October asking them again to represent their case to the king. This document added a formal complaint against the bishops, accusing them of betraying the king's good intentions by producing an unsuitable liturgy and canons imposed by unconstitutional means.[133] The text was written by David Dickson, a minister at Irvine in North Ayrshire who had been pursued for non-compliance with the Perth articles. Dickson also was involved in the July demonstrations and a September petition from the presbytery of Irvine.[134] The copy given to the privy council was not signed, but a separate parchment was signed by 482 nobles, shire gentlemen, burgesses and parish clergy in Edinburgh.[135] The collection of signatures was justified as necessary to identify the complainants, emphasising the formal legalism of the supplications.[136]

Copies of the October supplication were circulated to presbyteries and burghs for the collection of local subscriptions.[137] This process of grassroots engagement represented a significant development from the September petitions which had been subscribed by ministers, town officers or gentlemen on behalf of their communities. The presbytery of Kirkcudbright offered the signatures of 459 male adherents, including notarised signatures for those unable to write.[138] These began with five

---

[130] Leslie, *Relation*, 47.   [131] *Ibid.*, 9; Row, *History*, 485.
[132] *RPCS*, ser. 2, vi, 536–7; Leslie, *Relation*, 13–4. So many shire gentry were in town that they had to meet in a courtroom in the Tolbooth. Leslie, *Relation*, 20.
[133] Leslie, *Relation*, 16   [134] Holfelder, 'Dickson [Dick], David (c.1583–1662)'.
[135] Fleming, *Scotland's Supplication*, 370–8.
[136] Fleming and Ogilvie (eds.), 'National Petition', 243.   [137] Leslie, *Relation*, 21.
[138] *RPCS*, ser. 2, vi, 709–15.

Petitions 73

ministers and a group of leading laymen, followed by blocks of signatures from parishes including proprietors, tenant farmers, ordinary inhabitants and two more clergymen. Two baillies, several burgesses and a notary signed for the burgh of Minnigaff 'in name of the rest of the communitie' and the provost, two baillies, five town councillors and several merchant and trade burgesses and other indwellers signed for the burgh of Kirkcudbright.[139] The petition thus combined clerical signatories with lay hands from rural and urban parishes, reflecting the various communities within the presbytery.

Faced with the king's order to disperse, the petitioners expressed dismay that 'the Counsell wold not so much as take notice of the eminent and sensible grievances of the subjects'. Far from being unruly crowds, the gatherings were said to convey the 'lawfull concurrence of the rest of the subjects'.[140] The engagement of women in this fight as members of the kirk was signalled by a separate, and unusual, petition from the 'men, women, children and servants' of Edinburgh, though this was not signed by any women and its text indicated stereotypically negative views of female opinions by assuring the king that the people's protests were not the 'needlesse noyse of simple women'.[141] The earl of Rothes similarly emphasised the legitimacy of the protests by noting that the assembled people carried no weapons, displaying only 'cryes and tears' as true supplicants. But he also admitted that members of the privy council had to ask dissident nobles to escort them safely through a shouting 'thronge'. In September, angry crowds had intimidated the burgh council of Edinburgh into joining the petitioning campaign. Leaders sought to corral these energies in November by organising assemblies by the estate, known as the Tables, with commissioners to attend coordinating meetings. They considered submitting yet another petition to defend themselves from imputations of rebellion, but were informed that the king would not hear any further petition on church matters. Instead, they negotiated terms with the privy council to leave Edinburgh until an answer was received from the king.[142]

On 7 December, a proclamation conveyed the king's decision to postpone an answer again because of the affront given by 'disorderlie, tumultuous and barbarous insolencies', though he assured his subjects that he would maintain religion in Scotland as 'presently profest'.[143] Privately,

---

[139] *Ibid.*, 700–8.   [140] Leslie, *Relation*, 13–4.   [141] [Balquanhall], *Large Declaration*, 41.
[142] Leslie, *Relation*, 15, 19–20, 23–7, 32; *RPCS*, ser. 2, vi, 544–5.
[143] Leslie, *Relation*, 33–4; *RPCS*, ser. 2, vi, 546–7.

74   Public Opinion in Early Modern Scotland, c.1560–1707

leaders were warned that 'the king took their maner of supplicating togither to be a combining and mutinous forme' and that the submission of supplications by the estates together was an inappropriate replication of 'the representative body of the whole Estates'. Nevertheless, on 21 December, the commissioners submitted a 'bill' to the privy council adhering to their September and October supplications, defending themselves against aspersions of rebellion and asking the council to intercede with the king. In an oral statement, the cleric James Cunningham asked the council to emulate Esther, an Old Testament queen who begged her husband, King Ahasuerus, not to massacre the Jews, in petitioning the king on their behalf. They agreed, promising to resubmit the petitions to Charles.[144]

The king's answer, provided by proclamation on 19 February 1638, failed to defuse the conflict. Refusing to see petitions as an invitation to negotiate, Charles took personal responsibility for the prayer book, making it impossible to avoid sedition by blaming the bishops. He stated that the supplicants' unauthorised meetings and subscriptions had 'injured' his royal authority, but because they acted from a 'preposterous zeale', he would not bring charges against them, as long as they stopped their rebellious resistance.[145] As described in Chapter 1, the supplicants countered the king's proclamation with a protestation at Stirling, Linlithgow and Edinburgh. As the next chapter explains, they then reinforced their movement by renewing a 1581 anti-Catholic confessional oath with a new bond of mutual defence, creating what became known as the National Covenant. This collective oath was circulated by supporters to be sworn by all communicants in Scotland's towns and parishes and signed by males. The earl of Rothes argued that this oath allowed the subjects to affirm their loyalty to the king, being 'utherways barred from access'.[146]

After distributing the covenant for national subscription, the supplicants – now Covenanters – continued to use petitions to oppose the king in the name of the people. After refusing to accept a new petition in March, in June the king sent a commissioner to Scotland, James Hamilton, third marquis of Hamilton, who received a fresh supplication and a remonstrance from the Covenanters.[147] These asked for unrestricted meetings of the Scottish parliament and general assembly to review the prayer book and other innovations in religion. In July, the king stated privately that he would 'rather die than yield to those impertinent and

---

[144] Leslie, *Relation*, 35–40, 50–1; *RPCS*, ser. 2, vi, 554.   [145] *RPCS*, ser. 2, vii, 3–4
[146] Leslie, *Relation*, 125.   [147] *Ibid.*, 92–100, 121–3, 126–8; Row, *History*, 491–2.

Petitions 75

damnable demands'.[148] By September, he had conceded to meetings of the nation's assemblies, but his commissioner tried to dissolve the general assembly shortly after it opened in November 1638 when it became clear that he had no control over the meeting. The assembly continued to meet and sent a supplication to the king that not only 'humbly beg[ged]', but 'certainly expect[ed]' that Charles I would understand why they continued to meet, as the attempted dissolution was so 'contrarie to the desire and expectations of all your Majesty's good people'.[149]

In this period of resistance, traditional ideas about petitioned grievances underpinned unusually assertive and persistent arguments in the name of aggrieved people, launching a powerful movement that by 1639 was able to field men in arms against an absent king. Compared to the attempted *coup* of 1596, the breadth and depth of social support for the movement was a key factor in its success, realised in part by the gathering of local subscriptions on supplications followed by the swearing of the new covenant oath by congregations across Scotland.[150] The resulting Covenanter regime restored petitioning as a means of complaint and dialogue, loosening earlier restrictions. From 1640, petitions could be presented 'in open and plaine parliament' without prior scrutiny.[151] Various committees and sub-committees were created to consider petitions, starting with a 1641 'committie for the billis' containing representatives from each estate.[152] Across the 1640s, parliament handled numerous private petitions from men and women relating to wartime exactions and damages.[153] In 1649, complaints on oppressions in the levying and quartering of troops led parliament to order the formation of committees in every presbytery to hear and resolve complaints locally.[154]

As England descended into civil war in 1642–3, a contest for Scottish support triggered an exchange of petitions claiming to speak for the Scots. A petition was given on 31 May 1642 to the privy council from 'many noblemen, gentlemen, burgeses and ministers occasionallie meiting at Edinburgh' who supported the National Covenant and the English parliament, asking the council to maintain the terms of the 1641 Treaty of London. This claimed to speak in the name of themselves and others who

---

[148] Leslie, *Relation*, 83–4; Fleming, *Scotland's Supplication*, 70.   [149] *AGA*, 33–5.
[150] Steve Murdoch has suggested that the confidence of the Covenanters also rested on the knowledge that sympathetic Scottish officers in foreign service could bring home trained troops to fight the king. Murdoch, 'Preparation and propaganda'.
[151] *RPS* 1640/6/31, 6 June 1640.   [152] *RPS* 1641/7/52, 28 July 1641.
[153] Stewart, 'Petitioning in early seventeenth-century Scotland', 313–20.
[154] *RPS* 1649/5/203, 5 July 1649.

76   Public Opinion in Early Modern Scotland, c.1560–1707

would have signed, given the opportunity.[155] This was countered a few days later with a cross-petition presented by two nobles and two gentlemen urging the king's side on behalf of the 'Nobilitie, Gentrie, Burrows, Ministers and Commons' of Scotland. An unsympathetic privy council refused to record the second petition, having given a positive answer to the prior supplication. A print of the first petition claimed to represent the 'entire body' of Scotland more truly than the second.[156] The subsequent 1642 general assembly echoed this by claiming that no ministers had joined the second petition, making it unrepresentative of the clerical estate.[157] In January 1643, a new petition, again from nobles, lairds, burgesses and ministers (the last especially from Fife) gathered in Edinburgh and now with the explicit support of the kirk's executive body, the commission of the general assembly, was countered with a royalist cross-petition signed by forty-one individuals, including eight noble-men.[158] The petitions disputed whether a letter from the English parliament asking for Scottish support in their conflict with Charles I should be printed alongside a letter from the king urging the Scots not to be swayed by the arguments of his opponents. Both were printed, facilitating the eventual agreement of the 1643 Solemn League and Covenant. To support the first petition and undermine the cross-petition's claim to represent the nation, a declaration by the commission of the general assembly against the malignancy shown in the 1643 cross-petition was printed with a 'necessary warning' to be read from all pulpits.[159]

Petitions again expressed competing voices as the controversial Engagement, agreed in December 1647 with the king, broke the hege-mony of the covenants. On 1 March 1648, the commission of the general assembly made a declaration to parliament against the Engagement and printed copies to be read from the pulpit.[160] The commission then advanced eight 'desires' to the parliament, to which a committee gave answers.[161] A 'representation' from the commission gave their

---

[155] RPCS, ser. 2, vii, 260–3.
[156] Anon., The True Petition of the Entire Body of the Kingdome of Scotland. See also Anon., The Petition of the Kingdome of Scotland and Anon., The Petition of the Nobilitie, Gentrie, Burrows, Ministers and Commons of the Kingdom of Scotland.
[157] AGA, 64.
[158] RPCS, ser. 2, vii, 372–3, 597; Spalding, The History of the Troubles and Memorable Transactions in Scotland and England, 319.
[159] Commission of the General Assembly, A Declaration against a Crosse Petition and A Necessary Warning to the Ministerie of the Kirk of Scotland; Stevenson, The Scottish Revolution, 1637–1644: The Triumph of the Covenanters, 258–61. See chapter 4.
[160] RCGA, ii, 373–82, 388–90; RPS 1648/3/21, 9 March 1648.
[161] RCGA, ii, 403–5; RPS 1648/3/41, 22 March 1648, 1648/3/47, 27 March 1648.

Petitions 77

unsympathetic 'sense' of these answers and reaffirmed the original desires, to which parliament provided further answers.[162] Crowds played a role in this high-stakes petitionary dialogue when a meeting of the commission was disrupted by 'a multitude', said to be 'countenanced by some members of parliament'.[163] On 11 May, parliament attempted to counter the kirk's influence in the localities by writing to presbyteries asking them to endorse a 4 May order for a levy in favour of the king.[164] This letter cited an act of 1584 prohibiting the derogation of the authority of parliament, in effect accusing antagonistic clergy of seditious speech.[165] Nevertheless, in Fife, Lanarkshire and Peeblesshire, as Stewart has found, several kirk sessions, presbyteries and the University of St Andrews supplicated their committees of war asking them to petition parliament against the levy.[166] On 1 June, supplications against the levy from seventeen presbyteries, one synod, three kirks, nine shire committees of war and three burghs were presented to parliament.[167] Countering these anti-levy messages were pro-levy supplications from two shire committees of war, eight papers from the wards of Glasgow subscribed by 'ane great number of handis', and dissenting members' protestations against supplications from war committees in Fife and East Lothian.[168]

In this civil conflict, supporters of the Engagement recognised a need to satisfy the concerns of petitioners to secure wide support for the levy. In Haddingtonshire, the committee of war wrote to the parliament indicating their acquiescence with the levy, contrary to supplications from the presbyteries of Haddington and Dunbar, and asked the estates to address the supplicants' fear of a breach of covenant, so that 'thir mistakes and divisiones may be removit' and 'the ministerie and others may be satisfied in thair consciences'.[169] The estates provided formal answers to the petitioners, assuring them that they remained committed to the covenants and that the Engagement would provide 'saifety' against English sectaries.[170]

Opinion at large remained highly salient as tenant farmers rose in arms against the levy on 11–12 June 1648 at Mauchline Moor in Ayrshire, as discussed in Chapter 3, and the Whiggamore Raid in September produced

---

[162] *RCGA*, ii, 420–23; *RPS* 1648/3/52, 29 March 1648.
[163] *RPS* A1648/3/17, 31 March 1648; *RCGA*, ii, 427–8.   [164] *RPS* 1648/3/104, 4 May 1648.
[165] *RPS* 1648/3/166, 11 May 1648.   [166] Stewart, *Rethinking the Scottish Revolution*, 282.
[167] *RPS* 1648/3/178, 1 June 1648.
[168] *RPS* 1648/3/178, 1 June 1648, 1648/3/181, 2 June 1648, 1648/3/188, 3 June 1648, 1648/3/183, 2 June 1648, A1648/3/26, 7 June 1648. I thank Andrew Lind for bringing the Glasgow subscriptions to my attention.
[169] *RPS* A1648/3/25, 7 June 1648.   [170] *RPS* 1648/3/219–20, 10 June 1648.

78   Public Opinion in Early Modern Scotland, c.1560–1707

a hardline 'Kirk party' regime dependent on anti-Engagement opinion. A 16 January 1649 act of parliament castigated the 1648 parliament for ignoring 'the many earnest and humble petitions from severall shyres and the most pairt of provinciall synods and presbyteries and the just and necessary desyres, remonstrances and declarationes of the commissioners of the church' and, in forcing the levy, 'causing the people to sin after they had declared by thair petitions the same was against the light of thair consciences'.[171]

The execution of Charles I on 30 January 1649 created new conflicts as the Kirk Party regime recognised Charles II and allowed him to act as king after he swore the covenants in June 1650. Hardliners responded by expressing their fear of the new king's ungodliness. As Cromwell advanced on Scotland with an English army, a printed 'remonstrance and supplication' asked that malignants be purged from the army and the king's household and guard.[172] After the defeat of Scottish forces at Dunbar in September 1650, more remonstrances appeared from the synod of Perth, the synod of Glasgow and Ayr and an association of 'gentlemen, officers and ministers attending the Western forces'.[173] Known as the Western Remonstrance, this asserted that the nation's understanding of the terms agreed with Charles II, described as 'the sense of this Kingdom', had been betrayed. Like contemporaneous protestations, this paper was described as a 'testimony' for 'the discharge of our consciences' on the eve of battle with Cromwellian forces.[174] This unusual expression of the 'privat thoughts' of a group of individuals had a significant political impact. The commission of the general assembly acknowledged 'sadd trueths' in the paper while regretting its tendency to 'breid divisions in this Kirk and Kingdome'.[175] In a 'humble Remonstrance and Petition', the commission urged parliament to take the Western Remonstrance to heart.[176] Though parliament acknowledged some of the faults charged by the remonstrants, this did not satisfy hardliners.[177] In December 1650, as shown in Chapter 1, a party known as the Protesters split away from the institutional kirk, contributing to the conquest of Scotland by Cromwellian forces.

[171] *RPS* 1649/1/29, 16 June 1649.
[172] Officers of the Scottish Army, *To the Right Honourable Lords and the Others of the Committee of Estates, the Humble Remonstrance and Supplication of the Officers of the Army*; Spurlock, *Cromwell and Scotland*, 28.
[173] Stevenson, *Counter-Revolution*, 156; Haig (ed.), *The Historical Works of Sir James Balfour*, iv, 119.
[174] *RCGA*, iii, 95–106.   [175] *RCGA*, iii, 126–8, 130–2.
[176] *RCGA*, iii, 137–41; *RPS* A1650/11/3, 30 November 1650
[177] *RPS* A1650/11/3, 14 December 1650; *RCGA*, iii, 163.

Petitions 79

Under Cromwellian control, petitioning was allowed when it served the purposes of the conquerors, creating some space for the expression and invocation of opinion at large. From February 1652, deputies from Scotland's shires and burghs were required to assent to the creation of a united commonwealth and were invited to give their advice on how to achieve this to the 'best satisfaction' of 'the People of Scotland'. Many delegates added 'desires' to their assents requesting concessions on religion, forfeitures and judicatures. Wigtownshire was typical in asking that Scotland's religion not be altered, so that the union 'may with more Cherefullnesse bee accepted by the generallity of this Nation.'[178] In rejecting the tender of union, the burghs of Lanark and Glasgow and shires of Kirkcudbright and Moray detailed their 'sence' of the propositions, including the complaint that the proposed union was 'not presented to the full and frie deliberation of the people in their collected bodie'.[179] Later in 1659 when the Commonwealth parliament reconsidered its terms of union with Scotland, several Scottish members made a 'humble address' asking that the union be settled so that 'the pepill' of Scotland 'may be secured in their liberty'.[180]

Petitioning by the kirk during the Cromwellian period was constrained by an unwillingness to acknowledge the government in London with a formal address, leading Protesters and Resolutioners to favour collective letters and 'testimonies' over formal petitions. The Protesters sent a letter of grievances to Cromwell in January 1652 and produced a manuscript 'Declaration or Testimonie' in 1553 against the union and its 'vast toleration'. Both were signed in name of the clergy and laity attending Protester meetings.[181] When Cromwell invited delegates to discuss a new 'ordinance' for Scotland's clergy and universities, the Protesters sent a declaration and the Resolutioners sent 'Some Considerations' and 'Greevances concerning the affairs of the Kirk of Scotland with Remedies thereof'.[182] In 1656, proposals for the management of the kirk provided to Cromwell by a Protester delegation were blocked by Resolutioners and competing petitions were sent to the council in Scotland.[183] A Protesters'

---

[178] Terry, *Cromwellian Union*, 15, 38, 39–44, 53–5, 61–2, 70–1, 76–7, 77–8, 78–83, 91, 96–7, 100–1, 107–15, 117–8, 122–7, 148–9, 157–60, 162–3, 171–3.

[179] *Ibid.*, 34–5, 74–5, 112–5, 116–7, 118–20, 133–4, 139–40, 150–3, 161–2.   [180] *Ibid.*, lxxxix.

[181] McCrie, *Life of Mr. Robert Blair*, 292–4; Terry, *Cromwellian Union*, 7, 28; Stephen (ed.), *Register of Consultations*, i, 1–36. See chapter 1 on Protester testimonies.

[182] Stephen (ed.), *Register of Consultations*, i, 71–87; MacKenzie, *The Solemn League and Covenant of the Three Kingdoms and the Cromwellian Union, 1643–1663*, 130–2.

[183] Laing (ed.), *Robert Baillie*, iii, 573; Stephen (ed.), *Register of Consultations*, i, 191–3.

80 Public Opinion in Early Modern Scotland, c.1560–1707

plan in April 1659 to have synods petition the new Lord Protector Richard Cromwell against religious toleration was resisted by Resolutioners because the petition would have endorsed the forced union.[184]

When a collection of dissenting individuals petitioned in 1659 for freedom of worship, Protesters and Resolutioners both issued public statements rejecting these desires as unrepresentative. On 28 July 1659, a 'humble Petition and Address' from 'some well-affected Persons in Edenburgh, and other places near adjacent in Scotland in Name and Behalf of Themselves, and several others in that Nation' was presented to the Commonwealth parliament.[185] As Scott Spurlock has shown, this petition offered a 'humble Desire' for religious toleration with the signatures of one female and over 200 male members of Baptist, Quaker and other sects in Edinburgh, the west of Scotland and as far north as Orkney.[186] According to an antagonistic 'testimony' by the presbytery of Edinburgh, hands had been gathered 'to severall Copies' in 'severall parts of the Countrey', revealing a unique attempt to frame a national petition with local subscriptions (rather than being signed by adherents gathered in Edinburgh).[187] The presbytery rejected this by attributing the petition to the 'dross and scum' of the nation, no part of the 'truly godly, Ministers and people, throughout the land'. A group of nine Protester clergymen also printed a statement against the petition, reasserting the covenants, sworn by the body of the people and backed by the convictions of the godly, as a barrier to toleration.[188] Moreover, it was argued in a parliamentary committee that toleration would 'discontent the godly, the ministry, the incorporations, and body of Scotland' and would contravene the terms of union agreed by the nation's deputies in 1652.[189]

The innovative supplications campaign of 1637, sealed with the 1638 National Covenant, had placed public opinion at the centre of Covenanting political culture. The support of the people was courted in 1642–3, 1648 and 1650–1 as opinion split over the English civil war, the Engagement and the rule of Charles II. By 1649, the ruling regime relied on grassroots support mobilised in the Whiggamore Raid, but hardliners

---

[184] Laing (ed.), Robert Baillie, iii, 392–3.
[185] *Journals of the House of Commons, vol. VII*, 736; *Some Sober Animadversions* (London, 1659), 1–2.
[186] An earlier Quaker petition included seventeen women among forty-two signatories. Spurlock, *Cromwell and Scotland*, 189–194.
[187] Presbytery of Edinburgh, *A Testimony and Warning of the Presbytery of Edinburgh, against a Late Petition* (1659), 5.
[188] *Ibid.*, 3, 5; Anon., *A Testimony to the Truth of Jesus Christ*, [36].
[189] Terry, *Cromwellian Union*, lxxxix–xciii.

Petitions 81

began to split away with the Western Remonstrance. The significance of the views of the people and nation in political discourse and strategies is indicated by the invocation of 'the sense of this Kingdom' and the consciences of the people by the Covenanters and the Cromwellian consultation on union. But petitioning activity could be strongly resisted when unwelcome, as in 1659 when kirk parties attacked an innovative national petition for religious toleration. At the same time as the synod of Glasgow was considering whether to petition against religious toleration in 1659, one of its kirk sessions quashed 'misorderly' petitioning by 'almost all the householders' against an unwanted minister.[190] This synod could contemplate participative petitioning for its own ends but could not entertain uninvited petitions from the commons. With the restoration of Charles II in May 1660, disruptive petitioning practices would be blamed in part for the downfall of monarchical order, leading to new restrictions.

2.5 Constraints on Petitioning, 1660–1687

The restoration of Charles II stimulated a reaction against assertive petitioning. Though the conservative and royalist nature of the Restoration settlement created by the Scottish parliament in 1661 has long been recognised, this section will look more closely at the stance taken against petitioning by the reconstructed Stewart monarchy.[191] The Restoration parliament condemned tumultuous petitioning and executed a Protester clergyman on charges of sedition that included, as in Balmerino's case, an intent to petition. From 1660 to 1687, petitioning to parliament and king was constrained to prevent the public airing of grievances. By comparison, in England a 1661 act placed restrictions on adversarial petitioning on matters of church and state but the English parliament in 1679 reaffirmed the subject's right to petition parliament.[192] This allowed petitions in England's 1679–81 exclusion crisis to be countered by loyal addresses, maintaining a channel for the expression of grassroots opinions in English politics.[193] In Scotland, attempts to question or challenge monarchical policy by petition or letter were suppressed rigorously. Private petitions could be submitted to the monarch or parliament, but prior scrutiny of

---

[190] Laing (ed.), *Robert Baillie*, iii, 394.
[191] Buckroyd, *Church and State in Scotland, 1660–1681*, ch. 1; MacIntosh, *The Scottish Parliament Under Charles II, 1660–1685*, ch. 1.
[192] The English parliament also met more often in the Restoration period compared to the Scottish estates.
[193] Bowie, 'From customary to constitutional right'.

82   Public Opinion in Early Modern Scotland, c.1560–1707

parliamentary petitions was reintroduced, and dissidents had to resort to defiant public declarations (as seen in Chapter 1), illicit publications (as discussed in Chapter 4) or open rebellion to bring forward grievances.

In 1660, the Restoration regime quickly made it clear that adversarial petitioning would not be tolerated. Petitions aiding the Restoration were acceptable, including a petition from nobles, gentry and burgesses in London offering their 'humble opinion' that elections should be called for a parliament.[194] But when the Stirling minister James Guthrie met with other Protester clergymen in Edinburgh in August 1660 to concert a paper later described as a 'remonstrance', they were imprisoned and a proclamation was made against unauthorised meetings and seditious papers.[195] A subsequent proclamation on 20 September reasserted standing law against unauthorised convocations and leasing-making and barred any participation in state or church affairs outside of authorised assemblies.[196] Guthrie was charged with holding an unlawful meeting to prepare and disperse a 'slanderous and infamous pretendit petitione', 'thairby to sow sedition amongest his majesties subjects'. The criticisms of the king in his petition were said to be unwarrantable, despite the 'dress and garbe' of a 'humble petitione'. Guthrie also was accused of authoring the 1650 Western Remonstrance, containing 'seditious, treacherous and treasonable expressiones tending to the contempt and disdaine, slander and reproach of his majestie', and, as discussed in Chapter 4, an offensive 1653 tract, *The Causes of the Lord's Wrath against Scotland*.[197] In his defence, Guthrie claimed a clerical duty to point out sin, denied any intention to slander the king and insisted that he had convened a peaceful meeting 'for business in it selff lawful, to wit: humble petitioning of his majesty'.[198] The condemnation and execution of Guthrie made it clear that assertive petitioners would be subject to laws on sedition, as in Balmerino's case.[199] After the 1661 parliament revoked the Covenanters' parliamentary sanction for presbyterian church government, meetings of the synod of Fife and Galloway to prepare supplications against the return of bishops were dissolved and a proclamation banned any 'meddling' by clergy or laity with petitions on church government.[200]

---

[194] Airy (ed.), *The Lauderdale Papers*, i, 32; Airy (ed.), *Burnet's History*, i, 204.
[195] Airy (ed.), *Burnet's History*, i, 204–5; Charles II, *A Proclamation . . . against Unlawful Meetings and Seditious Papers*.
[196] Charles II, *A Proclamation against all Seditious Railers and Slanderers*.
[197] *RPS* A1661/1/67, 10 April 1661.   [198] *RPS* 1661/1/68, 10 April 1661.
[199] *RPS* 1661/1/90, 28 May 1661, 1661/1/362, 18 June 1661.
[200] Wodrow, *History*, i, 39–40 and appendix, 17–22; *RPS* 1661/1/158, 28 March 1661.

Petitions 83

Expressions of opinion in favour of an episcopalian settlement were welcomed as Charles II deliberated over Scotland's church settlement. A printed petition from the synod of Aberdeen in favour of episcopacy provided evidence of an appetite for the restoration of bishops, countering a letter from leading Resolutioner clerics in Edinburgh arguing that 'they were very considerable who were against Prelacy'. Contemporary histories highlight the prominence of national opinion in debates in the king's council over the church settlement, with arguments that 'the greater and honester part of the nation' preferred episcopacy being met with the view that Charles would 'lose the affections of the nation' if he brought back bishops.[201] The discussion included the suggestion that the temper of the nation should be measured. When the privy council was consulted on the 'inclinations of the nation', the council advised the king that episcopacy would 'give a general satisfaction to the main body of the nation'.[202] In a letter to the privy council dated 14 August 1661, Charles re-established episcopacy by his 'royall authority' and urged the privy council to cure the 'distempers' of recent times by preventing any seditious or unlawful meetings or discourse.[203]

With the church settled on episcopalian lines, uninvited petitions continued to be suppressed. In 1662, parliament declared against 'mutinous and tumultuary petitions' and required all office-holders to accept that collective petitioning was 'unlawful and seditious'.[204] Petitions were orchestrated when this suited the regime's purposes, as in 1669 when a petition from several moderate presbyterian ministers contributed to the granting of an indulgence.[205] Private petitions still could be handed to the parliament, privy council or monarch, but the presentation of petitions to parliament was constrained by the re-establishment of the Lords of the Articles. Written petitions and any oral complaints raised in open parliament were to be remitted to this committee for review.[206] Grievances conveyed to the king were rejected if they were deemed to question monarchical authority or betrayed any collective or public dissent.

The suppression of petitioning contributed to an armed presbyterian protest in November 1666, known as the Pentland Rising. This action was

---

[201] Airy (ed.), *Burnet's History*, i, 218, 234; Wodrow, *History*, i, 95.
[202] Airy (ed.), *Burnet's History*, i, 235–6. [203] *RPCS*, ser, 3, i, 28–9.
[204] *RPS* 1662/5/20, 24 June 1662, 1662/5/70, 5 September 1662.
[205] Cowan, *The Covenanters*, 76.
[206] *RPS* 1661/1/13, 8 January 1661; Mann, 'House rules', 128–9; Weiser, 'Access and petitioning during the reign of Charles II'; Airy (ed.), *Burnet's History*, ii, 39–41; *RPS* M1673/11/3, 17 November 1673.

84   Public Opinion in Early Modern Scotland, c.1560–1707

led by landowners and former army officers angered by the severe enforcement of laws against religious non-conformity in the southwest. The commander of these irregular forces later sought to justify armed action as a means to secure a channel for the expression of grievances: 'all ways of remonstrating and petitioning being taken from us, we were necessitated to draw together, that jointly we might the more securely petition his Majesty and council for redress'.[207] Though a petition was sent to the privy council, the crown responded with force, subduing the rising in the Pentland Hills outside Edinburgh.[208]

Other attempts to express grievances were deemed unacceptable if they questioned royal policy and authority. The archbishop of Glasgow, Alexander Burnet, was removed from his post after his synod issued a remonstrance against the 1669 indulgence.[209] In 1674, discontent with the Lauderdale regime led some burgesses to resist alterations to burgh election procedures ordered by the king. A letter from the Convention of Royal Burghs arguing that these changes betrayed long-standing custom was deemed 'most undutifull, impertinent and insolent'. The instigators were imprisoned and fined for unauthorised meetings and the dispersal of 'publick' copies of the letter.[210] Similarly, a group of advocates who objected to the king's rejection of any right of judicial appeal to parliament was forced to submit to Charles in 1675 after their 'humble address' was deemed a seditious combination.[211]

These restrictions led a group of presbyterian women to attempt to petition the privy council for freedom of worship in June 1674, to see whether their gender would make their supplication any more acceptable to the authorities. Dozens of women gathered at the steps of the council house as their leaders handed copies of a petition to councillors as they entered the building. Seeing this as a seditious petition and 'a disorderly rable', the council banished sixteen women from Edinburgh.[212] By contrast, in 1637, a similar group of presbyterian women had petitioned the

---

[207] Wallace, 'Narrative of the Rising at Pentland', 414.

[208] [Stewart of Goodtrees], *Jus Populi Vindicatum*, 9; *RPCS*, ser. 3, vi, 253.

[209] McIntyre, 'Saints and Subverters', 150, 153; McDougall, 'Covenants and Covenanters', 182; Cowan, *Scottish Covenanters*, 77.

[210] Marwick (ed.), *Extracts from the Records of the Convention of Royal Burghs*, iii, 639–42; *RPCS*, ser. 3, iv, 367–76, 396; Airy (ed.), *Burnet's History*, ii, 57.

[211] *RPCS*, ser. 3, iv, 337–8, 347–56, 379, 385–6, 393–5; Paton (ed.), *Report on the Laing Manuscripts Preserved in the University of Edinburgh*, i, 401; McCrie (ed.), *Life of Mr. Robert Blair*, 556; Ford, 'Protestations to parliament for remeid of law', 68–71; Jackson and Glennie, 'Restoration politics and the advocates' secession, 1674–1676'.

[212] *RPCS*, ser. 3, iv, 208, 241–2, 258–61, 295.

Petitions

privy council successfully, asking that presbyterian ministers expelled from Ulster be allowed to preach in Scotland. By 1674, however, the engagement of women in the presbyterian cause and their significance in maintaining presbyterian dissenting culture was well understood.[213] The wives of Scottish ministers typically were daughters of landowners, burgesses or clergy with relatively high literacy rates who actively helped their husbands in their clerical roles.[214] As well as ministers' wives, the 1674 indictment included two titled ladies, merchants' wives and other gentlewomen. With this case, the privy council made clear that its restrictions on petitioning would apply to women as well as men.

Though in 1675 discontent with the Lauderdale regime stimulated the leader of the parliamentary opposition, William Hamilton, third duke of Hamilton, to consider 'how the generality of the nation can be gott to send their complaints to the king', the threat of prosecution for sedition kept a lid on political petitioning.[215] In lieu of a petitioning campaign, James Stewart of Goodtrees published an unauthorised pamphlet addressed to the king describing the grievances of presbyterians in Scotland.[216] Only in 1678, when militia forces vigorously enforced bonds requiring heritors and masters to be responsible for the conventicling of tenants and servants, did several nobles travel to London to complain in person, defying a proclamation limiting access to the court in London.[217] Charles II agreed to hear them only because they were 'most humble' and apologised for breaking his ban on travel. Their complaints to the king, made in a private audience and to his council, managed to secure some relief, though the lawfulness of royal policy was defended.[218]

These complaints to the king on the stringency of the suppression of presbyterian conventicles did not prevent a revolt in 1679, triggered by the unpremeditated assassination of the archbishop of St Andrews by extremists. As noted in Chapter 1, a declaration made at Rutherglen on 29 May by a small group of militants was followed by a manifesto in more moderate terms at Hamilton on 13 June. As in 1666, armed action was justified as a 'last Remedie' to force the government to hear presbyterian

---

[213] McCrie (ed.), *Life of Mr. Robert Blair*, 153–4; Raffe, 'Female authority and lay activism in Scottish Presbyterianism, 1660–1740'. See chapter 3 on the engagement of women in the covenants and the pursuit of female Covenanters after the Restoration.

[214] Whyte and Whyte, 'Wed to the manse: The wives of Scottish ministers, c. 1100-c.1750', 223–4, 229.

[215] McMaster and Wood (eds.), *Supplementary Report*, 90; Airy (ed.), *Burnet's History*, ii, 57–8.

[216] [Stewart of Goodtrees], *An Accompt of Scotlands Grievances*.

[217] Charles II, *Proclamation Prohibiting the Nobility, and Others to Withdraw*. See chapter 3.

[218] Airy (ed.), *The Lauderdale Papers*, iii, 103–4.

86   Public Opinion in Early Modern Scotland, c.1560–1707

grievances. After the defeat of the rebellion by forces under the king's natural son James Scott, duke of Monmouth, petitions were handed to the duke asking the king for an indemnity and freedom of worship.[219] Charles' subsequent indemnity decried the 'pretext of representing Grievances'.[220] A loyal address from the 'noblemen, gentlemen and heritors of the sheriffdom of Ayrshire' asserted their 'detestatione' of presbyterian resistance, said to arise from 'the people' being misled by 'a few unsound, turbulent and hott headed preachers'.[221]

Attempts by James VII to secure toleration for Catholic worship from 1686 generated petitions revealing a split in opinion on the king's eventual toleration policy, described by Raffe as 'multi-confessional'.[222] Citing their consciences, ministers in the diocese of Aberdeen petitioned their bishop to urge him to resist any proposal in the 1686 parliament to lift penal limitations on Catholic worship.[223] During the ensuing parliamentary session, an unusual circular letter urged members of parliament to address James against toleration, as 'the only native and dutiful Way of redress for the Grievances that Subjects can have' (though no petition arose from this). James' subsequent establishment of freedom of worship for Catholics and other Christian dissenters by royal proclamation in 1687 was recognised by an address of thanks from a group of moderate presbyterian ministers, speaking on behalf of all of their brethren except 'disloyal' extremists who continued to reject the monarch's capacity to regulate the church.[224]

From 1660 onwards, unwanted petitioning in Scotland was suppressed by the application of laws against seditious speech and a return to prior review of petitions to parliament. Complaints on the restraint of presbyterian non-conformity were largely silenced, stimulating two armed uprisings justified as a means of expressing collective grievances. The supplication of the privy council by a group of presbyterian women in 1674 indicates an attempt to test the boundaries of these controls, but their gender did not make these petitioners any more acceptable. Complaints on royal policy through traditional channels, whether from bishops, burgesses or advocates, were also unwelcome; and leading nobles

---

[219] Wodrow, *History*, ii, 95 and appendix, 23–4, 31–2; McMaster and Wood (eds.), *Supplementary Report*, 100–1.

[220] Wodrow, *History*, ii, appendix, 28; Charles II, *A Proclamation. Containing His Majesties Gracious Pardon and Indemnity*.

[221] Paton (ed.), *Report on the Laing Manuscripts*, i, 416.

[222] Raffe, ''James VII's multiconfessional experiment and the Scottish revolution of 1688–1690'.

[223] Wodrow, *History*, ii, 590   [224] *Ibid.*, appendix, 173–7, 195.

became more cautious about expressing grievances to the king in person. By contrast, loyal addresses from recognised parts of the Scottish polity were received, though these were not as common as in England.

2.6 Conclusions

In 1590, Sir James Melville of Halhill recommended that James VI hold regular audiences to hear 'supplications and complantis' and 'get gud intelligence' of the 'greifis of your subiectis'.[225] This was standard advice for late medieval kings, who were expected to hold the hearts of their subjects by hearing their complaints. Yet in the context of the Scottish Reformation and the 1603 regal union, petitioning became much more than a simple process of personal pleading. The reformed kirk engaged in robust dialogue with James VI with assertive 'griefs', sparking violent protest in 1596 fronted by a petition. After this event, increasing episcopal and royal control of the kirk led clerical groups to petition unsuccessfully for meetings of the general assembly and against the controversial 1618 Perth articles. To reinforce their pleas, dissidents cited the opinions of like-minded brethren and laity and, when it was safe to do so, reinforced this with subscriptions. Charles I showed even more resistance to petitioned complaints, making his hostility clear with the pursuit of Lord Balmerino. In campaigning against Charles' new prayer book in 1637, supplicants took care to blame the bishops instead of the king and collected signatures from localities to boost their claim to speak for the nation. While the ensuing Covenanter regime re-established the hearing of petitions in parliament, from 1642 assertive petitions and counter-petitions purported to speak for an increasingly divided nation, contributing from 1650 to the conquest of Scotland by English forces. Public opinion remained visible in the ensuing British commonwealth with the orchestration of national consent for closer union and the expression of grievances in a handful of collective petitions, letters and declarations. When the Restoration regime sought to turn back the clock by outlawing 'mutinous and tumultuous' petitioning and restoring constraints on the submission of petitions to parliament and the king, the resulting constriction in petitioning meant that Scotland had no equivalent to the dialogic exchange of petitions and loyal addresses seen in contemporaneous England.

The Restoration regime's sensitivity to petitioning reveals its awareness of the affront presented to royal authority by clamorous petitions claiming

---

[225] Thomson, (ed.), *Memoirs of His Own Life*, 386.

to speak for the people or nation. Petitioners were meant to plead submissively for a remedy and submit passively to the recipient's judgement. But from the late sixteenth century, Scottish petitioning became more adversarial, with the repeated presentation of arguments on behalf of extra-institutional groups and the collection of grassroots subscriptions. Men and women joined crowds to present petitions, and, in a few instances, women petitioned in their own name. The difficulties of organising petitions meant that these tended to arise from shires near Edinburgh, though the 1659 petition for toleration was notable in encompassing Orkney. These campaigns, therefore, were not actually national, but they claimed to speak for clerics, laypeople or subjects at large. Though successive monarchs responded by quashing adversarial petitioning, Chapter 6 will show how the confirmation of a right to petition in the 1689 Claim of Right allowed collective petitioning to re-emerge and express the 'sense of the nation' at large.

CHAPTER 3

Oaths

Take heede therefore (my Sonne) to these Puritanes, verie pestes in the Church and common-weill of Scotland; whom (by long experience) I have found, no ... oathes nor promises binde, breathing nothing but sedition and calumnies.

James VI, *Basilikon Doron*, 1599[1]

Are yee not subjects of one Kingdome, members of one Kirk, professours of the same Reformed Religion, under one tye of solemne Covenants[?]

Commission of the General Assembly of the Church of Scotland, 22 March 1651[2]

[W]e for ourselves and all that will adhere to us, the representatives of the true Presbyterian Church and Covenanted Nation of Scotland ... do, by these presents, disown Charles Stewart ... by his perjury and breach of Covenant with God and his Church[.]

Sanquhar Declaration, 22 June 1680[3]

The ubiquity of sworn obligations in late medieval realms created what Andrew Spencer has characterised as societies 'built upon oaths'.[4] At the coronation of a Scottish monarch, proprietors, prelates and people swore, respectively, allegiance, fealty and obedience to the crown in return for promises of justice and security. Oaths established faithful duties for office-holders, clergy and guild members at their admission. Oaths of homage and fealty were supplemented by voluntary agreements known in late medieval Scotland as bands, establishing mutual obligations and alliances between lords and their followers and allies. In an era of limited governance and strong religious faith, these promises made before God were expected to bind the consciences of individuals. As Alasdair Raffe has

---

[1] James VI, *Basilikon Doron*, 49.   [2] *RCGA*, iii, 357.
[3] [Renwick and Shields], *Informatory Vindication*, 175–6.
[4] Spencer, 'The coronation oath in English politics, 1272–1399', 42.

89

90   Public Opinion in Early Modern Scotland, c.1560–1707

observed, 'oaths were a feature of a deeply religious society in which the threat of divine punishment for breaking one's word was thought to be more severe than any earthly sanction.'[5] As a result, oaths offered 'an opportunity to oblige, discipline and coerce the conscience'.[6] But the inculcation of conscientious opinions also facilitated demands for the satisfaction of sworn opinions.

The two preceding chapters have shown how political tensions arising from the Reformation and the 1603 Union of Crowns stimulated the remodelling of protestations and petitions into modes of collective protest, making extra-institutional opinions more visible in Scottish politics. Similarly, oaths and bands became a significant tool of indoctrination and engagement, reaching more frequently and deeply into society. Reformed beliefs were stipulated with confessional oaths, loyalty was enjoined with subscriptional bands and elements of both were combined in covenant oaths. Such oaths offered a means of controlling opinions among not just office-holders but entire communities, producing new levels of popular political engagement by obliging men and women to uphold certain political views. It also stimulated a rhetoric of national obligation inspired by the example of Old Testament covenants between God, king and people. It became possible to invoke a national sworn consensus to justify political action or resistance, even when actual opinion was divided, or to insist that policies align with covenanted consciences.

The rising prominence of oaths in this period has not escaped the notice of early modern historians. A large body of scholarship has explored the proliferation of demands for conformity and allegiance in post-Reformation England, including compulsory subscriptions, oaths of allegiance and test oaths, and the concurrent elaboration of casuistical justifications, equivocations and reservations.[7] Some of these oaths involved large-scale subscriptions, generating significant levels of political engagement. The 1584 Elizabethan Bond of Association has been described as a 'masterly piece of propaganda', designed to 'achieve a dramatic and public attestation of loyalty to Queen Elizabeth' that

---

[5] Raffe, 'Scottish state oaths and the revolution of 1688–1689', 174; Condren, *Argument and Authority in Early Modern England*, 236.

[6] Spurr, '"The strongest bond of conscience": oaths and the limits of tolerance in early modern England', 151.

[7] Jones, *Conscience and Allegiance in Seventeenth Century England: The Political Significance of Oaths and Engagements*; Hadfield, *Lying in Early Modern English Culture: From the Oath of Supremacy to the Oath of Allegiance*; Condren, *Argument and Authority*, part III; Vallance, 'Oaths, casuistry and equivocation: Anglican responses to the engagement controversy'; Donegan, 'Casuistry and allegiance in the English civil war'.

Oaths 91

involved ordinary male signatories as well as local elites.[8] In the civil war era, political oaths reached further into English society with the 1641 Protestation oath, the 1643 Solemn League and Covenant and 1649 Engagement.[9] As Ted Vallance has noted, these oaths made English politics more socially inclusive, with women in some cases being able to swear oaths aimed at parishioners or proprietors.[10]

In histories of Scotland, the 1638 National Covenant and 1643 Solemn League and Covenant have only recently been assessed as subscriptional oaths. Past generations of confessional historians have focused on the 'second Reformation' created by these covenants and celebrated the heroic resistance of dissenting Covenanters after the 1660 Restoration until the eventual reinstatement of presbyterian church government in the 1688–90 Revolution.[11] In works like the 1887 *Treasury of the Scottish Covenant*, the covenants of 1638 and 1643 anchored a tale of religious liberties won by 'the blood of the martyrs'.[12] In the twentieth century, conversely, fears of fascism and fundamentalism led some commentators to see the covenants as tools of indoctrination. In 1937, G. D. Henderson saw the 'compulsory signature' of the National Covenant as being 'very much in the spirit we associate with Nazi government', while more recently the Covenanters have been compared to Islamic extremists.[13] From the 1980s, however, revisionist interest in how Scottish events triggered the English civil wars, combined with a trend for studying Scottish and British national identity, has led historians to take a fresh look at the political thought and practices of the Covenanters.[14] Arthur Williamson has traced the idea of a covenanted Scottish nation from the 1581 Negative Confession to the 1638 National Covenant; John Ford has revealed the presence of the 1581 Negative Confession in printed debates over the 1618 Perth articles;

---

[8] Cressy, 'Binding the nation: The bonds of association, 1584 and 1596', 218.
[9] Walter, *Covenanting Citizens;* Walter, *Understanding Popular Violence;* Vallance, *Revolutionary England and the National Covenant: State Oaths, Protestantism, and the Political Nation, 1553–1682.* See also Morrill, 'An Irish Protestation? Oaths and the Confederation of Kilkenny'.
[10] Vallance, *Revolutionary England,* 222; Vallance, 'Women, politics and the 1723 oaths of allegiance to George I'.
[11] Cowan, 'The Covenanting tradition'; Langley, *Worship, Civil War and Community, 1638–1660,* 3.
[12] Johnston, *Treasury of the Scottish Covenant,* vi.
[13] Henderson, *Religious Life in Seventeenth-Century Scotland,* 170; Bambery, 'Terrorism and fanaticism'. I thank Neil McIntyre for bringing the Bambery article to my attention.
[14] Relevant works include Cowan, 'The making of the National Covenant'; Cowan, 'The political ideas of a Covenanting leader: Archibald Campbell, marquis of Argyll 1607–1661'; Steele, 'The "politick Christian": The theological background to the National Covenant'; Stevenson, 'The early covenanters and the federal union of Britain'; Cowan, 'The Solemn League and Covenant'; Macinnes, *The British Revolution, 1629–1660;* Coffey, *Politics, Religion and the British Revolutions;* Mullen, *Scottish Puritanism, 1590–1638.*

92   Public Opinion in Early Modern Scotland, c.1560–1707

Jane Dawson has extended Jenny Wormald's ground-breaking study of late medieval bands to assess Protestant practices of banding and covenanting; and Laura Stewart has compared the latter to contemporaneous English bonds and oaths.[15] A desire to see history from below has inspired analysis of the swearing and reception of the Scottish covenants, led by Ted Cowan's emphasis on the 'truly remarkable' requirement that these oaths be subscribed by all subjects.[16] Specialised studies have amended an overly schematic picture of a covenanted south and conservative north by showing conflict and struggle between covenanters and royalists in many parts of Scotland, including Scotland's universities.[17] In considering how Covenanter hegemony was established in the face of royal authority and royalist sympathy, Stewart has argued that the swearing of the 1638 National Covenant across Scottish parishes helped to make a 'covenanted public'. By reconstructing communal swearing events, Stewart and Jamie McDougall have highlighted the participation of women alongside men.[18] Michelle Brock's micro-study of Ayr has demonstrated how a persuasive minister could create profound popular engagement with the cooperation of local magistrates and guilds; conversely, Chris Langley has observed that some local figures were 'ill-positioned to cope' with the demands of the Covenanters.[19] The tenacity of covenanting commitments has been traced beyond the 1660 Restoration by McDougall and Neil McIntyre, building on Mark Jardine's analysis of the separatist United Societies, and Raffe has noted how presbyterian dissent required Restoration regimes to make greater use of oaths of allegiance.[20] Though

---

[15] Williamson, *Scottish National Consciousness in the Age of James VI: The Apocalypse, the Union and the Shaping of Scotland's Public Culture*, ch. 3; Ford, 'The lawful bonds of Scottish society: The Five Articles of Perth, the Negative Confession and the National Covenant'; Wormald, 'Bloodfeud, kindred and government in early modern Scotland'; Wormald, *Lords and Men in Scotland: Bonds of Manrent, 1442–1603*; Dawson, 'Bonding, religious alliance and covenanting, 1557–1638'; Stewart, *Rethinking the Scottish Revolution: Covenanted Scotland, 1637–1651*, 90–102.

[16] Cowan, 'The Covenanting tradition', 122–3; Cowan, 'The making of the National Covenant', 82.

[17] Adams, 'The making of the radical south-west: Charles I and his Scottish kingdom, 1625–1649'; Robertson, 'The Covenanting north of Scotland, 1638–1647'; Kennedy, 'The Covenanters of the northern Highlands: politics, war and ideology'; Barrett and Mitchell, 'Plunder in the north'; Cipriano, 'The Scottish universities and opposition to the National Covenant, 1638'; Lind, '"Bad and Evill Patriotts"? Royalism in Scotland during the British Civil Wars, c.1638–1651'.

[18] Stewart, *Rethinking the Scottish Revolution*, ch. 2; McDougall, 'Covenants and Covenanters'; see also McDougall, 'The reception of the 1643 Solemn League and Covenant'.

[19] Brock, 'Plague, covenants, and confession: The strange case of Ayr, 1647–8'; Langley, *Worship, Civil War and Community*, 8.

[20] McDougall, 'Covenants and Covenanters'; McIntyre, 'Saints and subverters: The later Covenanters in Scotland c.1648–1682'; McIntyre, 'Presbyterian conventicles in Restoration Scotland'; Jardine, 'The United Societies: Militancy, Martyrdom and the Presbyterian Movement in Late-Restoration

the re-established presbyterian kirk did not renew the covenants after the 1688–90 Revolution, Colin Kidd has indicated how opinions on the incorporating Union of 1707 continued to be shaped by the obligations of these oaths, thought by some to bind the nation in perpetuity.[21]

This scholarship has provided a better sense of who swore the Scottish covenants, how and with what consequences. This chapter will embed these insights into a comprehensive study of political oaths from early Protestant bands to the suspension of oaths of conformity by James VII in 1687. This will trace the increasing use of oaths to shape and corral opinions and the increasing reach of oaths across the social scale, involving women as well as men. Although oaths were designed to bind consciences, they also foregrounded the opinions of subjects, making it possible to claim the adherence of the sworn nation. Over time, the proliferation of oaths made it easier to imagine the political nation as a body of individuals holding opinions – and more difficult to ignore the political force of these committed individuals.

In this chapter, a range of oath types will be distinguished, including assertory confessions, bands of manrent, association, friendship, mainte-nance and obedience, and oaths of allegiance, obedience and abjuration. The first section will consider the use of collective oath-taking before 1638 by Protestants and the early reformed kirk. The creation of a national confessional oath in 1581 allowed supporters of presbyterian church government to invoke the freely covenanted consciences of the nation, while the crown made greater use of oaths of obedience and allegiance to force conformity to an increasingly episcopalian and erastian kirk. The second section will show how a programme of ostensibly national oppo-sition to the crown was embedded with the 1638 National Covenant, countered by the 1638 King's Covenant, extended with the 1643 Solemn League and Covenant and shored up with subsequent renewals and re-affirmations. The final section will show how the grassroots commitments inculcated by these covenant oaths required Restoration governments to deploy counter-oaths as political tests that eventually reached almost as deeply into Scottish society as the original covenants. Under James VII, however, the tenacity of covenanted opinion stimulated a radical shift away from confessional oaths with the short-lived adoption of an oath of civil allegiance.

Scotland, 1679–88'; Raffe, 'Scottish state oaths and the revolution of 1688–1690'. Raffe has also traced reaffirmations of the covenants in 'Confessions, covenants and continuous reformation'.

[21] Kidd, 'Religious realignment between the Restoration and the Union', 153–7.

3.1 Subscriptional Bands before the National Covenant

In sixteenth-century Scotland, a 'band' indicated a promissory compact, as in a band of matrimony, manrent or caution. In the 1580s, the St Andrews parish kirk recorded promises of marriage in a 'Band Buik'.[22] 'Bond' became a common variant of band by the late seventeenth century. Though historians tend to use 'bond', this chapter will reflect contemporary language.[23] From the mid-fifteenth century, Scotland's nobles routinely created bands of manrent and maintenance with their followers, described by Wormald as 'a mutual exchange of obligations, verbally sworn and set down in writing' before witnesses.[24] Because lands might be held from multiple lords, a band of manrent provided an exclusive promise of loyalty and aid in quarrels to one lord, excepting the superior allegiance due to the crown. In return, the lord swore a band of maintenance promising protection and support.[25] Similarly, bands of friendship agreed alliances between lords, creating regional or kin-based coalitions (again excluding any combination against the monarch).[26] Bands typically committed signatories for life and could impose obligations on heirs.[27] A sworn, signed and witnessed band was meant to bind the consciences of its parties, though a 1568 proclamation complained, 'what bands and subscriptions can perswade them to be true, that are facile with their hands to subscrive[?]'.[28] In the mid-sixteenth century, bands were an obvious choice for Protestant reformers seeking to knit themselves into a resistance movement and subsequently for leaders who wished to commit king and people to the defence and maintenance of the reformed kirk.

In the early stages of the Scottish Reformation, Protestant leaders used voluntary bands to commit signatories to shared aims in church reform, prioritising conscience over lawful obedience to the monarch. In December 1557, several Protestant noblemen signed a band later known as the 'First Band of the Lords of the Congregation', promising together to advance Protestant preaching and worship and defend themselves from adversaries.[29] As the Reformation rebellion began to unfold in May 1559,

---

[22] Fleming (ed.), *Register of the Minister Elders and Deacons of the Christian Congregation of St Andrews*, ii, 545.

[23] 'Band, n.', *DOST*.

[24] Wormald, *Lords and Men*, 26, 48. 'Manrent' referred to the condition of being a sworn man. 'Manrent, n.', *DOST*.

[25] Dawson, 'Bonding, religious alliance and covenanting, 1557–1638', 155–6.

[26] *RPS* 1425/3/6, 12 March 1425; *RPCS*, ser. 1, iii, 648–9; *RPS* 1585/12/15, 10 December 1585.

[27] Wormald, *Lords and Men*, ch. 2, appendix C.   [28] Calderwood, *History*, ii, 410.

[29] Laing (ed.), *Works of John Knox*, i, 273–4. Knox also described a 1556 band among Protestants in the Mearns, but as Mullen and Dawson note, it is not clear if this was a formal signed band. Mullen, *Scottish Puritanism*, 177; Dawson, 'Bonding, religious alliance and covenanting', 156–9.

Oaths 95

bands promising mutual aid were signed in Perth and Stirling by leaders of Lowland Protestant cells.[30] In July, a ground-breaking 'Generall Band' to form 'ane body' for 'mayntayning of the trew religioun' was signed in Edinburgh and St Andrews. A surviving copy from St Andrews shows 331 hands including the provost, two baillies and many ordinary inhabitants.[31] Later in April 1560, a band was signed at Leith by forty-nine nobles and gentry agreeing to 'joyne togidder' to advance reformation by working with the English to expel French troops.[32]

In the first decade after the 1560 Reformation, bands continued to tie signatories to the achievement of kirk reforms. In January 1561, a band promising to support the First Book of Discipline (a book of policy for the newly reformed kirk) was signed by 'a great parte' of the nobles attending a convention of estates.[33] In 1562, ninety-one Protestants from the south-west signed a band promising to support preaching and aid 'the hoill body of the Protestantis'.[34] In 1567, the earl of Bothwell banded with nobles and bishops to support his controversial marriage to Queen Mary and the ensuing civil war between supporters of the queen and the infant James VI featured banding on both sides.[35] On the king's side, sixty-two nobles and thirteen 'Comissioners for townes' signed a band shortly before the 1567 coronation of James VI vowing to defend the 1560 Reformation parliament, 'ruit out' idolatry and defend James. The coronation oath imposed on the infant king was described as a mutual band sworn by king and people, obliging James to defend the reformed kirk, while the people promised to maintain the king in these endeavours.[36] Further bands reinforced Jacobean regencies including a 1569 band of obedience with sixty-six signatures.[37]

The first Protestant band for subscription by all members of the Scottish church was created in 1581, stimulated by concerns for the security of the Reformation under the rising influence of Esmé Stewart, first duke of

---

[30] Calderwood, *History*, i, 327–8; *TSP*, ii, no. 78; Wormald, *Lords and Men*, 410–11; Dawson, 'Bonding, religious alliance and covenanting', 160–1; Mullen, *Scottish Puritanism*, 177–8.

[31] Fleming (ed.), *Register of St Andrews*, i, 6–10; Dawson, 'Bonding, religious alliance and covenanting', 161–2; Stewart, *Rethinking the Scottish Revolution*, 92.

[32] Hewison, *The Covenanters*, i, 28–9; Wormald, *Lords and Men*, 411; Dawson, 'Bonding, religious alliance and covenanting', 162–3.

[33] Calderwood, *History*, ii, 50; Spottiswood, *History*, ii, 62–7.

[34] Dawson, 'Bonding, religious alliance and covenanting', 164–5.

[35] Calderwood, *History*, ii, 352–4, 358, 419, 488; *RPCS*, ser. 1, i, 367–8; Goodare, 'The Ainslie bond'.

[36] *APGA* i, 106–10; Calderwood, *History*, ii, 378–83; Dawson, 'Bonding, religious alliance and covenanting', 168–9.

[37] Calderwood, *History*, ii, 412–3; *TSP* ii, no. 235.

96   Public Opinion in Early Modern Scotland, c.1560–1707

Lennox, a French Catholic cousin of the young James VI.[38] A public confession of faith for the king's household was mooted by the privy council in February 1580 along with a call for greater adherence to reformed worship and discipline in the king's household. This was followed by a proclamation in April requiring all persons to profess the reformed faith publicly, with male and female recusants to be reported.[39] A new anti-Catholic confession with a subscriptional band was sworn by 'othe' and endorsed by 'hand writ' by James, Lennox and thirty-seven other members of the king's household on 28 January 1581. This combined an assertory profession of beliefs with a promissory band, made by a collective 'we', to aid the king in his defence of the Protestant religion and the realm.[40] Known to contemporaries as the King's Confession, the text boldly stated that the reformed faith had been 'openly professed' by the 'whole body of this Realme' for 'a long tyme'.[41]

The oath was to be circulated by ministers and lay commissioners for subscription by all 'parochiners' in Scotland with refusers to be reported to the king's household. A fine was stated for negligent clergy and the confession and order for subscription were printed as a 'good example to all men'. The general assembly confirmed these orders in April 1581 and, noting uneven compliance, reiterated them in October 1581 with a threat of deprivation for noncompliant clergy.[42] Writing a generation later, the historian John Row emphasised the 'diligence' of the clergy in collecting subscriptions from all parishioners.[43] From 1587, college students routinely subscribed the confession and, according to a later account, 'many judges and burgesses' subscribed on entry to these offices.[44] These claims for widespread and continuing subscription, so useful to the later Covenanters, cannot be confirmed from extant evidence, but surviving documents from Fife do show deep social engagement in some parishes, including women and illiterate parishioners whose names were recorded by notaries. James Hewison noted a copy with 743 hands from the parishes of Anstruther, Pittenweem and Abercrombie in Fife and McDougall has tallied 830 signatures in the Kinghorn kirk session records, including at least sixty women's names.[45]

---

[38] Spottiswood, *History*, ii, 267–8.   [39] *RPCS* ser. 1, iii, 264–5, 277.
[40] Ford, 'Lawful bonds', 50.   [41] James VI, *Ane Short and General Confession.*
[42] *APGA*, ii, 512, 515–8, 526–7; Calderwood, *History*, iii, 501–6.   [43] Row, *History*, 73.
[44] [Calderwood], *An Answere to M. I. Forbes of Corse His Peaceable Warning*, sig. A2r; Leslie, *Relation*, 125.
[45] Hewison, *The Covenanters*, i, 103; NRS CH2/472/1, Kinghorn Kirk Session Records, ff. 249–58; McDougall, 'Covenants and Covenanters', 57. I am grateful to Jamie McDougall for showing me the Kinghorn subscriptions. See also Stewart, *Rethinking the Scottish Revolution*, 93 n.21.

Oaths

97

Though a renewed call for subscription specified that the oath be sworn by 'all men', the example of Kinghorn shows that women could be considered eligible for a confessional oath.[46]

After rapid shifts of regime in 1582–3, a controversial subscription was used in 1584 to impel clerical obedience to acts of parliament known to presbyterians as the 'Black Acts'.[47] These included an assertion of the monarch's jurisdiction over ecclesiastical causes and courts, a strengthening of the office of bishop and a condemnation of seditious speech from pulpits.[48] As noted in Chapter 1, when the acts were proclaimed on 25 May 1584, a public protestation for the liberties of the kirk was made at the mercat cross in Edinburgh, after which several clerics fled to England.[49] All benefice holders were required to subscribe a statement of 'submissioun and fidelitie' to the king and 'obedience' to their prelate, promising as a collective 'we' to obey the acts or lose their livings.[50] The subscription supplemented a requirement that new entrants accept the 1560 confession and swear an oath of allegiance to the king.[51] To implement the subscription, noblemen were commissioned to work with bishops. When some parish clergy refused to sign, James insisted that conscience could not override the law, though he proposed a clerical conference and a printed tract to help soothe troubled minds.[52] After negotiations, limited explanations were allowed: the addition 'according to God's word' was accepted, though a statement by the presbytery of Ayr on the 'devilish' nature of the acts was not. Under threat of deprivation, most clerics agreed to sign by March 1585.[53] The fugitive minister of Haddington parish in East Lothian, James Carmichael, attacked the forced

---

[46] *APGA*, ii, 724–5.

[47] On the 1582 Ruthven Raid and its unmaking, see Reid, 'Of bairns and bearded men: James VI and the Ruthven Raid'.

[48] *RPS* 1584/5/7–15, 22 May 1584; MacDonald, 'The Subscription Crisis and church-state relations, 1584–1586', 222–6.

[49] Calderwood, *History*, iv, 62–5, 72. Others had already fled after a failed coup in April. MacDonald, 'Subscription Crisis', 224–30.

[50] The 1584 compulsory subscription with its threat of deprivation can be compared to a slightly earlier 1583–4 subscription of obedience targeting Puritan clergy in England. Macdonald, 'Subscription Crisis', 227; Collinson, *Richard Bancroft and Elizabethan Anti-Puritanism*, 43–4.

[51] *RPS* 1584/5/75, 22 August 1584. An oath of allegiance for new entrants was required from 1571 (*APGA*, i, 212, 220, 231) and was required of penitent rebels after the Marian civil wars: *RPS* A1573/1/5, 26 January 1573. The 1560 confession was ratified in 1567 and remained the statutory standard for adherence to the true church. *RPS* A1560/8/3, 17 August 1560, A1567/12/3, December 1567, 1579/10/21, 10 November 1579, 1581/10/20, 29 November 1581.

[52] *RPCS*, ser. 1, iii, 702–3. See chapter 4 for the tract by Archbishop Patrick Adamson.

[53] Stuart (ed.), *The Miscellany of the Spalding Club*, iv, 69–70; Laing (ed.), *Miscellany of the Wodrow Society* 432–6; MacDonald, 'Subscription Crisis', 234–8.

98 Public Opinion in Early Modern Scotland, c.1560–1707

subscription as 'unlawful, unhonest, ungodlie, compellit, controvertit, misliket, urget and thristit out'.[54] As Williamson has shown, this unwanted oath stimulated Carmichael to reinterpret the 1581 confession and band as a compact made freely with God, king and people comparable to Old Testament covenants and in stark contrast to the forced subscription.[55]

Further defensive bands, including renewals of the 1581 confessional band, were stimulated by intensifying fears of counter-reformation between 1585 and 1590. Members of parliament subscribed a collective 'band anent the trew relligioun' in July 1585 affirming a Protestant league with England.[56] This followed the circulation of a Bond of Association in England from October 1584 promising to defend Elizabeth I from her enemies.[57] Anticipating a Spanish invasion, the 1588 general assembly asked all parish ministers to encourage a voluntary re-subscription of the 1581 confession and band.[58] The king re-subscribed with his household and leading clerics, and surviving documents from Edinburgh, Stirling and the Maxwells of Pollock near Glasgow indicate local subscription in universities, presbyteries and noble families.[59] After the Catholic earl of Huntly was found intriguing with the Spanish, the king marched to the northeast and, in Aberdeen on 30 April 1589, required subscriptions from lairds and burgesses to a band promising to rise in arms and defend the true religion at the king's call, supplemented with contractual bands of peace and financial sureties for the less trustworthy.[60] Recurring fears of Spanish interference and criticisms that James was being soft on Scottish Catholics led the king to march again to Aberdeen early in 1593 and extract another band. Signed by James and 161 noblemen and lairds, the band committed subscribers to support the king and each other against 'intestine and forraign enemies'.[61]

In March 1590, national re-subscription of the 1581 confession of faith was demanded with a new 'generall Band' to distinguish 'godlie and weil affected' subjects from Catholic enemies. All parishioners were to renew

---

[54] Laing (ed.), *Miscellany of the Wodrow Society*, 440–2.
[55] Williamson, *National Consciousness*, 68.
[56] *RPS* A1585/7/2, 31 July 1585; Spottiswood, *History*, ii, 327–9, 346–8.
[57] Cressy, 'Binding the nation', 218–20. [58] Calderwood, *History*, iv, 672.
[59] NRS RH1/2/427; Hewison, *The Covenanters*, i, 128 n3, 482–3.
[60] *RPCS*, ser. 1, iv, 375–80; Spottiswood, *History*, ii, 396; MacDonald, *The Jacobean Kirk, 1567–1625*, 41.
[61] Calderwood, *History*, v, 232–5, 774–5; Row, *History*, 155; *CSP Scot*, xi, 70–1. This was supplemented with individual bands of caution relating to the general band: *RPCS*, ser. 1, v, 45–9, 51–2.

Oaths 99

the confession while all male 'erles, lords, barons, freeholders, gentlemen, inhabitants of our burrowes, and other our leiges whatsomever, of what rank and degree that ever they be' were to subscribe a band promising to convene their men in arms when called by the king.[62] This new band had an elaborate scheme for implementation in which lay and clerical commissioners were to convene the lieges and gather subscriptions to the confession and band on printed copies in civil districts (sheriffdoms, stewartries and royal burghs). Progress reports were due to the presbytery of Edinburgh by 20 May and refusers were to be pursued in church courts. A printed tract with the confession, band, act of privy council and blank pages for separate signatures on the confession and band was produced for attendees to take home after the 1590 general assembly.[63] Biblical verses printed on the cover identified the renewed band with Old Testament covenants.[64] A surviving subscribed copy from Carmichael's parish of Haddington shows the signatures of male magistrates and proprietors on the band, while the confession included later signatures by three marrying couples, with the women signing in their own hands.[65]

The general assembly sought to corral clerical opinion with a new subscription in August 1590 requiring all presbyteries to endorse a copy of the Second Book of Discipline. This presbyterian book of policy had been produced in 1578 and registered by the general assembly in 1581 but had not received monarchical or parliamentary approval. The assembly's 1590 subscription sought to coerce clerical conformity to presbyterian principles, enforced with ecclesiastical penalties. Any 'negligent' presbytery was to 'receive publick rebuik of the haill Assemblie' and individual non-subscribers were to be excommunicated. The order was repeated in July 1591 with a fine of forty shillings for any non-compliant moderator.[66] The presbytery of Haddington, including Carmichael, signed in September 1591, citing the 1590 order.[67]

In 1596, with the king favouring Catholic advisers amidst fresh fears of a Spanish invasion, many clerics felt that 'all these faire shewes' of banding

---

[62] The 1590 renewal and band were authorised by the privy council and endorsed by the general assembly while James was away in Denmark. Because a 1585 act confirmed that only the monarch could make 'leaguis and bandis' with his subjects, the 1590 band emphasised the king's 'allouance' despite his absence. *RPS* 1585/12/15, 10 December 1585.

[63] *RPCS*, ser. 1, iv, 463–7; Calderwood, *History*, v, 45–52, 87, 89–91; *APGA*, ii, 756–61.

[64] James VI, *The Confession of Faith, Subscrived by the Kingis Maiestie and his Houshold Togither with the Copie of the Bande*. The verses were Joshua 24:25, 2 Kings 11:17 and Isaiah 44:5.

[65] NLS MS Grey 753. I am grateful to Jamie McDougall for bringing this source to my attention. See also Stewart, *Rethinking the Scottish Revolution*, 96–7.

[66] *APGA*, ii, 488, 773, 780.   [67] Laing (ed.), *The Miscellany of the Wodrow Society*, 403.

since 1581 had 'turned to no effect'.[68] Citing fears of 'Spainards', the general assembly in March 1596 proposed measures including the creation of a parish militia.[69] On 30 March, a reported 400 clerics gathered in an emotionally charged session to confess their sins and make a 'promise of amendment', raising their hands to 'testify' to a 'new league with God'. Termed a 'covenant', this oath was to be emulated at all synodical and presbyterial meetings.[70] The assembly records do not state whether the 1581 confession was part of the 1596 'covenant', though a later 1618 source suggests that the confession was renewed at this time.[71] This is also implied by the reprinting of the 1581 oath with a claim that it had been subscribed previously by the 'haill estatis'.[72] The synod of Fife renewed 'the covenant between God and his ministrie' with fasting and tears of repentance, while in the presbytery of St Andrews a 'verie frequent assemblie' of gentlemen and burgesses heard sermons on Old Testament covenants, vowed personal reformation and mutual defence and formulated local plans for a Protestant militia. Calderwood and Row claimed that the covenant was 'renewed likewise in the parishes', but royal disapproval prevented this in Edinburgh.[73]

In this heated atmosphere, divisions between the kirk and king led both sides to try to control clerical opinions with subscriptions. As discussed in Chapter 2, when the king brought charges against a leading cleric for seditious sermons, presbyteries were asked in October 1596 to subscribe a paper rejecting crown jurisdiction over clerical speech. In turn, James proposed that a 'band of duetifulnesse' should be signed by all clergy. Rejecting a band drafted by a clerical committee, James demanded a stricter 'prooffe of obedience', without which (as in 1584) the clergy would not receive their stipends.[74]

Violent resistance to the king erupted shortly after this on 17 December 1596, as shown in Chapter 2, when agitated clergy and laypeople raised their hands to 'vow and sweare to uphold the present state of religioun against all opponers whatsomever' and brought a petition to the king

---

[68] Calderwood, *History*, v, 233.

[69] *APGA*, iii, 859–60. This followed orders from the privy council in 1595 authorising proprietors and clergy in the presbyteries to call out 'the people' in case of invasion and to make proposals for the defence of the nation. MacDonald, *Jacobean Kirk*, 59.

[70] *APGA*, iii, 869–70.   [71] *APGA*, iii, 1164.

[72] Anon., *A Short and General Confessioun of the Trew Christian Faith according to Goddis Word, and Actis of our Parliamentis, Subscryuit be the Kingis Majestie, his Houshald, his Nobilitie and Haill Estaitis of this Realme.*

[73] Calderwood, *History*, v, 433–7; Row, *History*, 163–4.

[74] Calderwood *History*, v, 486, 490–6, 500–1.

against his Catholic counsellors.[75] James responded to the disorders by issuing a band of obedience for clergy on 21 December. This stated that the king was 'soverane judge' over public or private clerical speech and that the swearers' consciences required them to obey the king.[76] The king also reiterated the 1584 act against seditious words and required all magistrates and noblemen to silence any disloyal talk in their hearing. In reply, it was argued that the 1581 King's Confession and the oaths of allegiance sworn by new clerics made the band of obedience superfluous. Moreover, the 'woefull example' of the 1584–5 subscription provided a warning for 'weake brethrein' who signed ungodly bands.[77] Clerical resistance to the band eventually led James to agree on a compromise with the general assembly on the regulation of sermons.[78]

As James strengthened his control of the Scottish kirk after 1596, his opponents increasingly saw the 1581 confession and band as a presbyterian constitution endorsed by the nation.[79] In 1605, James Melville contended for regular meetings of the general assembly by citing the word of God, Scots law, the 'continuall custom' of the reformed kirk and, his final and most 'ungainstandable' argument, that 'the king's Majestie, the whole ministers, counsellers, nobilitie, estats, and subjects of the realm' had promised to maintain the kirk as established in 1581 under the Second Book of Discipline with regular meetings of the general assembly. The 1581 oath, he asserted, had been 'so reverenced' that it was 'sworn and subscribed' again with a 'generall band' in 1590.[80] Activist clergy insisted on renewing the confession in the synod of Lothian in 1604 and the presbytery of St Andrews in 1606.[81] Similar arguments relying on the 1581/1590 oaths appeared at the 1606 Hampton Court Conference and in a protestation against the rule of bishops, drawn up for submission to the 1606 parliament. The latter urged the estates to recognise that the oath they and 'the whole subjects' had sworn prevented them from 'setting up again the dominioun of bishops'.[82] In a manuscript paper, the minister Alexander Hume argued that the 1581 band bound swearers 'by a solemn othe' to uphold the kirk as established at that time 'to thair lyves end', making perjurers of those bishops who previously had 'exhorted the people

---

[75] *Ibid.*, v, 512.   [76] *RPCS*, ser. 1, v, 352.   [77] Calderwood *History*, v, 522–4, 531–4.
[78] *Ibid.*, 610–5, 622. *APGA*, iii, 895–6.
[79] On early modern constitutions, see Bowie, '"A legal limited monarchy": Scottish constitutionalism in the Union of Crowns, 1603–1707', 135.
[80] Calderwood *History*, vi, 317–9, see also 331.   [81] *Ibid.*, 268–9, 560.
[82] Row, *History*, 233; Calderwood *History*, vi, 487.

102   Public Opinion in Early Modern Scotland, c.1560–1707

and nobles of the land, to subscrywe'.[83] Similarly, articles given to the 1618 general assembly against innovations in worship concluded that 'subscrivers of the [1581] Confession of Faith, by their oath therin conteaned' promised 'to continue in the obedience of the doctrine and discipline of this church, and to defend the same according to their vocation and power, all the dayes of their lives'. It was noted that the oath had been printed as a witness to the world, making these backslidings all the more shameful.[84] An admonition to the 1621 parliament warned 'ye cannot cleanse yourselfs of despising the oath and covenant of God, solemnlie sworne and subscribed by all estates'.[85] When the 1621 parliament ratified the Perth articles, Row felt that the nation's oath with God had been 'publictlie broken'. God's judgement was indicated with 'the lowdest thunder-clap that ever Scotland heard', followed by a deluge that prevented the bishops from parading 'magnifickly mounted and apparelled' in the ceremonial riding that normally closed the parliamentary session.[86]

While presbyterians emphasised the nation's sworn commitments, James VI and his son Charles I built support for the episcopalian kirk by exacting oaths of obedience from clergy and office-holders.[87] Both Stewart and Vallance have highlighted a shift from the collective 1581/1590 King's Confession in Scotland and the 1584 Association in England to the imposition of new oaths of allegiance in both realms after 1603.[88] In 1607, James introduced a new 'Oath of Allegiance and Acknowledgement of Royal Supremacy' for all civil and ecclesiastical office-holders in Scotland. Ostensibly aimed at Catholics (like James' 1606 oath of allegiance in England), the terms of the oath also targeted presbyterians by requiring swearers to acknowledge and defend the superiority of royal courts in all causes.[89] The 1610 general assembly and 1612 parliament confirmed an oath of allegiance and obedience for new clergy and these were published in an official 1620 handbook for ordinations.[90] Speaking in 1622, Archbishop Spottiswood expressed the view that there was 'no lesse reason to requyr the

[83] Laing (ed.), *Miscellany of the Wodrow Society*, i, 570, 573–4.
[84] Calderwood *History*, vii, 330–1.   [85] *Ibid.*, 468, 484.
[86] Row, *History*, 330; Laing (ed.), *Miscellany of the Wodrow Society*, i, 572.
[87] Row, *History*, 324–5, 327–8, 331; Laing (ed.), *Original Letters*, ii, 662–4, 671. The 1571 general assembly had required new clergy to swear oaths of allegiance to the king and obedience to their prelate at their ordination. *APGA*, i, 212, 220, 231.
[88] Stewart, *Rethinking the Scottish Revolution*, 98; Vallance, *Revolutionary England*, 26–7.
[89] *RPCS*, ser. 1, vii, 374–5; Jones, *Conscience and Allegiance*, appendix, 272–3; Vallance, *Revolutionary England*, 26.
[90] *APGA*, iii, 1097; *RPS* 1612/10/8, 23 October 1612; Laing (ed.), *Miscellany of the Wodrow Society*, i, 599–607. A promise never to decline the king's jurisdiction was omitted from the 1620 handbook.

subscriptioun of Ministeris for obedience of Church Actis, than the subscription of laicks for thair professioun in Religion.'[91] In 1626, Charles I demanded a further 'band of conformitie' for new clergy.[92] This elaborated the required oath of obedience, adding promises to defend the monarch's prerogative over ecclesiastical causes, obey and respect the bishops and publicly defend episcopal church government.[93] Those who would not subscribe were refused parishes, including Robert Douglas, later minister of Kirkaldy and a leading Covenanter.[94] As noted in Chapter 2, grievances submitted to the 1630 convention of estates and reiterated in 1633 included a complaint that this new oath was unlawful and unworkable.[95]

James' use of more targeted bands and oaths extended to the Gaelic-speaking western isles where the 1609 Statutes of Iona demanded obedience to the king and the reformed kirk. Following negotiations led by Andrew Knox, bishop of the Isles, a band of obedience was signed by nine 'principall gentilmen' in August 1609 acknowledging the king's superiority in civil and ecclesiastical causes and promising to profess the reformed religion. Signatories undertook to obey an associated set of rules which required support for reformed worship and discipline in the parishes, among other reforms.[96] Martin MacGregor has emphasised the importance of the band in enforcing these statutes by 'the chiefs' solemn oath'.[97]

Bands and oaths had helped to make the Reformation in Scotland and hold together the reformed church against perceived enemies, so that when James and his son Charles enhanced the power of bishops and pressed for innovations in worship, especially the 1618 Perth articles, their presbyterian opponents could cite the sworn consciences of the nation as a barrier to these changes. A 1610 protestation by the presbytery of Haddington asked that church discipline not be altered, 'so that we and our flocks may be preserved from the infamous notes of inconstancie and perjurie'.[98] When the lawyer William Haig drafted a supplication to Charles I after the 1633 parliament, he begged the king to relieve 'your good people's consciences', 'the minds of most of your good people' being in 'perplexity' over the conflict between allegiance and conscience created by 'church

---

[91] Laing (ed.), *Original Letters*, ii, 682.
[92] Haig (ed.), *The Historical Works of Sir James Balfour*, ii, 142–4.   [93] Row, *History*, 359–61.
[94] Laing (ed.), *Original Letters*, ii, 682; Row, *History*, 349.   [95] Row, *History*, 350–1, 359–60.
[96] *RPCS*, ser. 1, ix, 24–27.
[97] After a 1614 rising on Islay, the band was renewed with fresh promises in favour of the kirk and in 1616, recalcitrant individuals swore obedience with cautioners to a new set of statutes emphasising economic and social compliance. *RPCS*, ser. 1, x, 773–90; MacGregor, 'The Statutes of Iona', 114, 122, 126–7, 129–31, 136–8.
[98] Calderwood, *History*, vii, 126.

104   Public Opinion in Early Modern Scotland, c.1560–1707

novations'.[99] Regardless of the actual reach of the 1581 band and its renewals, national commitment was presumed. In 1638, faced with the imposition of a controversial prayer book by royal authority, presbyterian dissidents again renewed the 1581 confession with a new general band. The oath resulting from this bold move would become known as the National Covenant.

3.2   The Covenanters and Cromwellian Conquest, 1637–1652

In 1638, presbyterian dissenters used the 1581 confessional oath to weaponise opinion at large. Locked in a face-off with Charles I over his new prayer book, as described in previous chapters, these adversaries achieved an extraordinary level of social engagement by disseminating the 1581 confession with a new band, later making it a required oath for all subjects and a test oath for office-holders. Emotionally intense subscription events for men and women in their congregations and communities created an apparent consensus. When Charles countered by renewing the 1590 confession and general band, this King's Covenant achieved only limited subscription. But open rebellion in 1639–40 and an Anglo–Scottish alliance against the king created with the 1643 Solemn League and Covenant encouraged royalist resistance. When the hegemonic hold of the Covenanter regime cracked with the 1647 Engagement, a hardline regime renewed the Solemn League in 1648 and required Charles II to swear the covenants in 1650 before taking up his crown after his father's execution. The young king's obvious reluctance created fatal divisions among Covenanted opinion, allowing Oliver Cromwell to conquer Scotland and impose a British union with a subscription of civil obedience.

The 1638 National Covenant emerged when supplications against the prayer book were met with an unsympathetic royal proclamation on 20 February 1638. Leaders realised that they needed a 'band of unione' to keep their movement together.[100] The lawyer Archibald Johnston of Wariston proposed a 'reneuing' of 'that same Covenant subscribed be our ancestours, with such additions as the corruptions of this tyme necessarilie required, and such Acts of Parliament as was against Poperie or in favours of the true religione.'[101] Drafted by Johnston of Wariston and the cleric Alexander Henderson, the text reaffirmed a presbyterian constitution, sealed with a new general band committing swearers to the

---

[99] Howell (ed.), *A Complete Collection of State Trials*, 604–8. See chapter 2.
[100] Leslie, *Relation*, 69.   [101] Leslie, *Relation*, 73; Paul et al. (eds.), *Diary*, i, 319.

Oaths 105

defence of the true religion. The opening lines reminded swearers that the original confession had been authorised and sworn by the king in 1581 and 1590, authorised by the privy council and general assembly and sworn by 'all ranks'. The closing band declared that 'present and succeiding generationes in this land are bound to keepe' their 1590 'nationell oath and subscriptione' to the church as constituted at that time. Scotland's 'noblemen, barrones, gentlemen, burgess, ministeris and commons', having failed to secure relief from 'manifold innovationes' with 'supplicationes, complaintes and protestationes', promised to 'labour by all meanes laufull to recover the puritie and libertie of the Gospell' and to 'resist all these contrary errouris and corruptiones according to our vocationes and to the wtermost of that power that God heath put in our handis all the dayes of our lyffe'.[102]

This renewal of the 1581 confession was highly controversial. It had no sanction from the monarch, privy council or general assembly. The new band treated ordinary subscribers as political agents, justifying their rejection of ecclesiastical innovations on the subscribers' 'knowledge and consciences of our duetie to God'. Loyalty to the king was made conditional with a promise to maintain the king's authority 'in the defence and preservatione of the foirsaid true religioun, liberties and lawes of the kingdome'.[103] Earlier bands had used similar language in promising to support the king in his actions against Catholic enemies; but if the king himself betrayed the kirk, where did loyalty lie? For John Campbell, first earl of Loudoun, Charles was forcing his people to make an impossible choice between their sworn loyalty to God and the king.[104] The new covenant implied that loyalty was due first to the kirk, yet the text also could support a royalist reading. Lastly, as in previous general bands, swearers in 1638 promised to bind together against all adversaries. This cohesiveness had been directed against Catholic enemies previously but had disturbing implications in 1638. Was this an unlawful combination against the king?

The renewed oath gained credibility by being presented not just as a confession and general band but as a covenant between God and the nation.[105] The association of the 1581 oath with the Biblical idea of a covenant has already been noted. In contemporary religious culture, the growing prominence of federal or covenant theology and the idea and practice of personal covenanting allowed the oath to be understood as a

---

[102] *RPS* 1640/6/36, 6 June 1640.   [103] *RPS* 1640/6/36, 6 June 1640.   [104] Leslie, *Relation*, 39.
[105] Dawson, 'Bonding, religious alliance and covenanting', 171.

106   Public Opinion in Early Modern Scotland, c.1560–1707

covenant that made each swearer, as Louise Yeoman has put it, 'God's man in the world, a partaker of his cause'.[106] More than just a witness to an oath, God became a party in a national compact. The importance of the covenant for every swearer individually and collectively was reinforced by a sense of international Protestant mission against imperial Catholicism, giving Scotland a special millenarian role in the re-establishment of God's kingdom on earth.[107]

National adherence, or at least the appearance of it, quickly emerged as a key aim and theme. Forceful preaching on a fast day in Edinburgh prepared the ground for 'many thousands' of greater and lesser nobles to swear and sign the covenant on 28 February, followed by hundreds of ministers and burgesses on 1 March and burgh inhabitants on 2 March. For the minister John Livingston, the subscribing estates and commons were equivalent to 'the whole body of the land'.[108] Copies of the covenant, with a justification of its lawfulness written by Johnston of Wariston, were carried by leading subscribers back to their localities.[109] The justification asserted that this was not an illegal private band against the king, but a 'publict covenant of the collectiue bodie of the kingdom with God for God and the king', previously accepted by 'subjects of all degrees, from the hiest to the lowest, in the whole kingdome' and now signed in Edinburgh by 'the greater part of the lieges'. Indeed, the oath's renewal was an 'innocent', 'readie' and 'powerfull' way to remind the nation of its covenanted obligations. For those clergy who feared the covenant would conflict with prior oaths of obedience, they were asked only to forbear the practice of the Perth articles. Sympathetic clergy were urged to 'exhort' their colleagues to sign and 'discountenance them' if they proved obstinate.[110]

Clergy, landowners and urban magistrates cooperated to implement the covenant oath in civil and ecclesiastical jurisdictions: noblemen and gentry led in shires and stewartries while clergy worked with ruling elders in rural parishes and magistrates in burghs.[111] In some localities, uncooperative clergymen were side-stepped. In the parish of Burntisland, for example, the burgh council and presbytery brought in another minister when the local

---

[106] Yeoman, 'James Melville and the Covenant of Grace', 575; Mullen, *Scottish Puritanism*, ch. 6; Steele, 'The "politick Christian"'.
[107] Burrell, 'The apocalyptic vision of the early Covenanters', 3–6; Gribben, *The Puritan Millennium*, 103–5; Williamson, "Scotland and the rise of civic culture, 1550–1650', 91–100.
[108] Tweedie (ed.), *Select Biographies*, i, 159.
[109] Paul et al. (eds.), *Diary*, i, 323; Leslie, *Relation*, 79–80, 82. Livingston rode to London with copies and letters to 'friends at court of both nations': Tweedie (ed.), *Select Biographies*, i, 159.
[110] Leslie, *Relation*, 79, 90–1.   [111] Stevenson, 'The National Covenant', 259, 264–98.

clergyman refused the covenant.[112] The contemporary historian Row claimed that 'in a few dayes' the covenant was 'sworne and subscryved almost by all, Aberdeen onlie excepted.' Though an exaggeration, the reach of the covenant was greater than might have been expected for an unauthorised oath. Success relied on vigorous persuasion as delegations were sent to Glasgow, St Andrews and Aberdeen and north to Moray and Inverness.[113] In Glasgow, Johnston of Wariston would not allow academics to sign with an explanation reserving royal authority, insisting on unconditional subscription.[114] In the royal burgh of Inverness, representatives of the Covenanters worked to 'to cleir all doubtis and scruples', securing a commitment from regional nobles to liaise in turn with 'the whole gentrie, ministers and borrowis [burghs]' in their territories.[115] In the royal burgh of Elgin, the local minister would not sign the covenant, but the 'haill people' were convened to hear a 'little speech' by a visiting minister and the magistrates led the subscription of the 'community altogether', with 'very few refusing'.[116] The Covenanter delegation was least successful in Aberdeen, where resistance was shown among college staff, magistrates and local nobles. The king's commissioner, the marquis of Hamilton, wrote to the town in August urging them to continue to 'hinder the subscription' of the covenant.[117]

The implementation of the covenant in sympathetic parishes aimed to engender wholehearted acceptance through what Brock has described as 'a fundamentally local, communal process'.[118] According to diaries and kirk session records, typically the covenant was presented to congregations after a fast with an explanation of the text, making reference to Biblical covenants. After hearing the text read out, the congregation stood, raised their right hands and together swore orally.[119] This included male and female communicants, with the youngest in their early teens.[120] With a charismatic preacher, the swearing ceremony could be a fervent emotional

---

[112] Stewart, *Rethinking the Scottish Revolution*, 104.

[113] Row, *History*, 489, 493–6; Leslie, *Relation*, 82, 98, 104–10; Stevenson, 'The National Covenant', 288–9.

[114] Cipriano, 'Scottish universities', 27.   [115] Kennedy, 'Covenanting government', 106–7.

[116] Spalding, *History of the Troubles*, 48.   [117] *Ibid.*, 55.

[118] Brock, 'Plague, covenants and confession', 131.

[119] Paul et al. (eds.), *Diary*, i, 327–9, 331, 334–6, 338; Hay Fleming, *Subscribing of the National Covenant*; Stewart, *Rethinking the Scottish Revolution*, 109–14; Stewart, 'Authority, agency', 95–7; McDougall, 'Covenants and Covenanters', 57–8.

[120] The 1616 general assembly required religious instruction to age 14 after which a communion token could be earned by demonstrating knowledge and understanding (*APGA*, iii, 1123). Johnston of Wariston mentions lasses and lads when describing the swearing of the covenant in his parish of Currie, probably meaning young communicants (Paul et al. [eds.], *Diary*, i, 328).

108   Public Opinion in Early Modern Scotland, c.1560–1707

experience.[121] In Lanark and other southwest parishes, Livingston described 'all the people generally and most willingly concurring' with 'tears dropping from their eyes'.[122]

After swearing, men signed the document, with notaries providing endorsements for those unable to write. The wording of the band ('for our selves, our falloweris and all other wnder ws') defined subscribers as male lieges, signing for liegemen, tenants, servants and dependent women (as in the 1590 general band).[123] In practice, many dependent men and, more rarely, women also signed.[124] Extant covenants include signatures by male tenants and craftsmen and undesignated names suggesting subordinate men and servants. In a surviving covenant from the Maybole parish in Ayrshire, a small number of women's names appear, including Jean Hamilton, countess of Cassillis.[125] Signatures were placed carefully in hierarchical order, reproducing local political communities in what was intended as a display of unanimity. On some parchments prepared in Edinburgh, leading lords appended their signatures as an encouragement for others to follow. When accused of intimidation, John Leslie, sixth earl of Rothes insisted that 'they wold not admit ane unwilling, let be a forced hand.'[126] Not all covenants reflected the signatures of a single parish. In Edinburgh, trade incorporations signed separate covenants and in the Carrick district in Ayrshire, a covenant circulated over several parishes for signature by local elites including landowners, a few merchants and four clergymen.[127]

The process of swearing the covenant in local communities stimulated and acknowledged the opinions of individuals not normally considered part of the political nation, including women. Widespread support for the covenanted cause can be seen in the phalanx of supporters that gathered for the arrival of the king's commissioner, the marquis of Hamilton, in

---

When the commission of the general assembly renewed the Solemn League in 1648, one of its aims was to capture those too young to swear the oath in 1643: *RCGA* 1648–49, 78. Children old enough to sit quietly were expected to attend church, so probably younger children would have been present for the ceremony but would not have sworn the oath (Todd, *Culture of Protestantism*, 31, 37–8, 90). I am grateful to Scott Spurlock for his advice on this point.

[121] Schmidt, *Holy Fairs: Scotland and the Making of American Revivalism*, ch. 1.
[122] Tweedie (ed.), *Select Biographies*, i, 160.   [123] *RPS* 1640/6/36, 6 June 1640.
[124] The Book of Nehemiah provided a model for the taking of covenants by all men and women of sufficient knowledge and understanding with the adherence of social elites being recorded (Nehemiah 10: 1–28). Stevenson, 'The National Covenant', 263–98.
[125] Stevenson, 'The National Covenant', 259, 269; Hewison, *The Covenanters*, i, 484; Imrie, 'The Carrick covenant of 1638', 108.
[126] Leslie, *Relation*, 122.
[127] Stevenson, 'The National Covenant', 259; Imrie, 'The Carrick covenant of 1638'.

early June 1638. It was reported that gentry lined the road for a mile and a half from Musselburgh, 600 ministers stood at Leith and 20,000 men and women gathered along the thoroughfare from Leith to Edinburgh.[128] As shown in Chapter 2, female opposition to the 1637 prayer book in Edinburgh indicated the engagement of godly women in religious politics. Early in 1637, the cleric Robert Baillie wrote that 'almost all our nobilitie and gentrie of both sexes' considered the prayer book 'little better than the Masse'.[129] Having sworn the covenant, ordinary women could feel empowered to continue to defend the kirk. In Kinghorn parish in Fife (where some women had subscribed the 1581 confession), a group of women led an attack on a suspected episcopal agent in July 1638 after the community had sworn the covenant.[130]

When proclamations against the covenant failed to halt its spread, in September 1638 Charles offered his own renewal of the King's Confession and 1590 general band in what became known as the King's Covenant. Though Charles was reluctant to embrace a general band, this tactic offered a means to rebuild a lawful consensus alongside concessions offered in a proclamation on 22 September 1638. After months of negotiations, Charles agreed not to enforce the prayer book, the 1636 canons, the 1618 Perth articles and the oath of conformity for new clergy and to call meetings of the general assembly and parliament.[131] The king acknowledged widespread discontent among his subjects, expressing a wish to 'satisfie not onlie thair desires, but even thair doubts' so that 'all our good people may be fullie and cleerelie satisfied' about his intentions towards the kirk.[132] The privy council subscribed the king's renewed band with its promise to support the king against his enemies and ordered 'all his Majesties lieges of whatsoever estat, degree or quality' to follow suit, naming lay commissioners in each sheriffdom to work with parish clergy to collect subscriptions on printed copies over the next two months.[133] Stevenson has estimated that the King's Covenant gained perhaps 28,000 signatures in a minority of parishes and burghs. About half of these came from the northeast where nobles and clergy were more active in implementing the oath.[134] Row reported that George Gordon, second marquis of Huntly acquired the most signatures, from the shires of Aberdeen and Banff.[135] An extant copy from Angus contains over 1000 signatures of

---

[128] Leslie, *Relation*, 115.   [129] Laing (ed.), *Letters and Journals of Robert Baillie*, i, 4.
[130] McDougall, 'Covenants and Covenanters', 59.   [131] *RPCS*, ser. 2, vii, 64–74.
[132] *RPCS*, ser. 2, vii, 64–5.   [133] *RPCS*, ser. 2, vii, 71, 75–7.
[134] Stevenson, *Scottish Revolution*, 110–1; Stevenson, 'National Covenant', 299.
[135] Row, *History*, 500.

male proprietors, magistrates, craftsmen and tenants from several parishes and the royal burgh of Arbroath.[136] A copy from the parish of Glenisla in Blairgowrie shows the signatures of one landowner and two tenants in their own hands, followed by forty-four notarised tenant subscriptions.[137] In Glasgow's college, academics signed the King's Covenant more willingly than the previous covenant.[138] In Ayr, however, 'a great part of the gentry and burghers' prepared a protestation against the King's Covenant, and others in southeastern shires were similarly reluctant, preferring to wait for a meeting of the general assembly.[139]

Though the King's Covenant was not a complete flop, it failed to create a national consensus behind the king's concessions. Unwilling to trust Charles, leading Covenanters felt that his band targeted them as internal enemies. Conversely, some royalists hesitated to sign because (as the Covenanters had argued previously) the 1581 confession predated the disputed innovations and could be seen to endorse obsolete kirk practices. Some subscribers got around this by signing with explanations indicating their acceptance of prelacy and the Perth articles.[140] This problem was compounded in December 1638 when, after rejecting the office of bishop and the Perth articles as inconsistent with the 1581 confessional constitution of the church, the general assembly condemned explanations on the King's Covenant in favour of episcopacy as 'repugnant to the genuine and true meaning' of the original oath.[141] The assembly barred all members of the kirk from swearing the King's Covenant, referring them instead to the National Covenant with a new statement against bishops and the Perth articles.[142] The 1638 assembly deposed at least eleven clerics for refusing the National Covenant and established special commissions to pursue nonconformity, leading to the deposition of fifty-two ministers in 1639.[143]

Historians have tended to accept that the National Covenant was as national as its architects intended. For Allan Macinnes, the Covenanters expressed a 'national consensus' against Charles' 'authoritarian' rule, while John Morrill stated that 'we must conclude that the Covenant was, in

---

[136] McDougall, 'Covenants and Covenanters', 52. I am grateful to Jamie McDougall for sharing his transcription of the covenant subscriptions (NLS MS 34.5.15).

[137] NRS GD16/57/31. [138] Cipriano, 'Scottish universities', 27.

[139] McMaster and Wood (eds.), *Supplementary Report*, 100.

[140] Row, *History*, 500–1; Stevenson, *Scottish Revolution*, 111.

[141] *AGA*, 13–21 and reiterated in 1639: *AGA*, 36–7. [142] *Ibid.*, 31–2.

[143] Stevenson, 'Deposition of ministers in the Church of Scotland under the Covenanters, 1638-1651', 324–5.

Oaths

aspiration and effect, a document of the Scottish nation. Most men took it and few resisted it.'[144] Yet contemporaries recognised that the face-off between the National Covenant and the King's Covenant created two camps. For Row, these were the 'Covenanters' and the 'Malignants, or Anti-covenanters'.[145] Supporters of the king saw the Covenanters as an unlawful and seditious 'confederacy'.[146] Though royalist resistance usually is associated with Aberdeen and the north-east, anti-covenanters appeared elsewhere. Recent studies have highlighted Burntisland on the Firth of Forth, where the local cleric refused the oath and was deposed, and the parish of Douglas in Lanarkshire, where the minister chose to sign the King's Covenant.[147] In St Andrews, the burgh's commissioner, minister and university academics refused to sign, though many inhabitants welcomed the covenant.[148] Andrew Lind's study of Glasgow suggests that as early as 1638, 'a strong Royalist faction was active in the city, drawing on the support of individuals from all ranks of society'. Though dozens of women rioted against the reading of the 1637 prayer book and Glasgow supplicated against the book, leading figures in the burgh embraced the King's Covenant instead of the National Covenant.[149] Faced with the general assembly's order to subscribe the covenant, some royalist clerics in Scotland fled to Charles' court, hoping that his forces would overcome the Covenanter regime.[150]

Faced with these divisions, the Covenanter regime strove to embed a hegemonic understanding of the National Covenant, turning it into a compulsory oath required for access to offices and assemblies. Parish-level re-subscription of the revised oath after December 1638 was urged, though this was patchy. On the Carrick covenant, for example, there were just seven signatures under an addendum on bishops.[151] Clergy were pursued for non-compliance, leading to the deposition of over ninety ministers by 1643.[152] The threat of deposition brought some clerics around, including the recalcitrant minister in Douglas who agreed to swear the National

---

[144] Macinnes, *The British Revolution*, 105, 107; Morrill, *The Nature of the English Revolution,* 109.
[145] Row, *History,* 500.   [146] Spalding, *History of the Troubles,* 49.
[147] Stewart, *Rethinking the Scottish Revolution,* 103–5; McDougall, 'Covenants and Covenanters', 53–4.
[148] Laing (ed.), *Letters and Journals of Robert Baillie,* i, 62, 64; Cipriano, 'Scottish universities', 12–3, 18–24.
[149] Lind, 'Battle in the burgh'.   [150] Stevenson, 'Deposition of ministers', 326.
[151] McDougall, 'Covenants and Covenanters', 50–1; Imrie, 'Carrick covenant', 118.
[152] Stevenson, 'Deposition of ministers', 326. Whereas in 1585, clergy were deprived by civil authority through the withholding of stipends, in 1638–43 presbyteries, the general assembly and special commissions deposed ministers from their spiritual offices.

112   Public Opinion in Early Modern Scotland, c.1560–1707

Covenant in 1639.[153] After nullifying in 1638 the disputed oath for clerical entrants, the general assembly in 1640 required the covenant to be sworn by new clergy and schoolmasters.[154] Speaking 'in name of all of the subjects and congregations whome wee represent', the 1639 general assembly secured civil authorisation of the covenant. A 30 August directive from the privy council ordered that the oath should be 'subscryved be all his Majesties subjects of what rank and qualitie soever, in tyme coming', including members of parliament.[155] The king's commissioner, the earl of Traquair, subscribed in 1639 with a declaration indicating that he signed unreservedly as the earl of Traquair but with limitations as royal commissioner to parliament.[156] Meeting in June 1640 without royal permission, parliament ratified the privy council's order for subscription of the National Covenant.[157] The regime secured retrospective royal approval for the covenant in the 1641 Treaty of London.[158] In 1643, the general assembly ordered printed copies to be prepared for a re-swearing in all parishes, universities, presbyteries and synods, with careful archiving of signed copies.[159] Some localities recorded covenant signatures to help track compliance while others hung signed covenants on public display.[160] The Assembly in 1644 tightened the net by calling on ministers to take note of any disaffected individuals who escaped subscription by 'unconstant abode'.[161] However, as Macinnes has noted, more remote areas evaded these 'unprecedented pressures on the Scottish localities', including the Gaelic-speaking areas of Badenoch, Skye and the Outer Hebrides.[162]

To reinforce the consensual authority created by the enforced swearing of the National Covenant, the Covenanter state also employed supplementary bands and subscriptions. During the Bishops' Wars (1639–40), recruits entering the Covenanter army had to confirm their covenanted commitments.[163] Early in 1640, subscriptional bands were circulated in presbyteries and burghs to encourage voluntary donations to the war against the king.[164] Livingston describes a gift of £45 from his 'little and poor' parish of Stranraer, with one woman donating a dowry intended for

---

[153] McDougall, 'Covenants and Covenanters', 54.   [154] AGA, 6–9, 45.
[155] Ibid., 40–1; RPCS, ser. 2, vii, 131–2.
[156] RPS C1639/8/3, 6 September 1639; Stevenson, 'National Covenant', 265.
[157] RPS 1640/6/34–36, 6 June 1640.   [158] Stevenson, Scottish Revolution, 216.   [159] AGA, 75.
[160] Stevenson, 'The National Covenant', 262; Stewart, Rethinking the Scottish Revolution, 116.
[161] AGA, 99–100.   [162] Macinnes, 'Scottish Gaeldom, 1638–51', 70.
[163] Stewart, Rethinking the Scottish Revolution, 258.
[164] RPS 1640/6/41, 8 June 1640; Stevenson, 'Financing of the cause', 90–1; Stewart, Rethinking the Scottish Revolution, 101. The 1640 parliament converted this into a compulsory new tax known as the Tenth Penny.

Oaths 113

a recently deceased daughter.[165] More controversially, the 1640 parliament set a new collective band to be taken by all members of the kirk and kingdom.[166] The band required all subjects ('noblemen, barrones, burgess and otheris') to 'wnanimouslie with heart and hand testifie by there subscriptione' to the legitimacy of the 1640 parliament as 'frie, lawful and necessary' and promise to uphold its decisions in 'ther severall stations and callings'.[167] This band, with its echo of the 1584 subscription of obedience, was condemned by the 1641 general assembly and it was later reported that 'it was not thought expedient by the State that that band should be pressed through the kingdom'.[168] After the Treaty of London, however, a new oath for members of parliament required them to defend the 'puritie of religione as it is now established in this kingdome'.[169] Key individuals were targeted with personal oaths: on being defeated by Covenanter forces in 1639, the marquis of Huntly secured his submission with an oath to maintain the established religion according to the 1581 confession; and the 1641 parliament extracted a promise from Charles I to uphold the Treaty of London 'for now and evir'.[170]

By 1640, however, royalist dissidents were using collective bands to undermine the Covenanters' consensus. The Cumbernauld band was signed by a splinter group of twenty nobles in August, led by James Graham, fifth earl and later first marquis of Montrose. Asserting that the aims of the National Covenant had been undermined by the 'particular and indirect practicking of a few', the subscribers promised to collaborate for the 'safety' of the 'Religion, Laws and Liberties' of Scotland as defined by the 1638 covenant.[171] Recognising this as a substantial challenge to their necessary fiction of national conformity, the regime imprisoned Montrose and burned the band.[172] When royalist cross-petitions in June 1642 and January 1643 tried to co-opt the covenant's stated obligation to the king (as noted in Chapter 2), an incensed commission of the general assembly asked clerics to preach against 'false interpretations' of the covenant.[173]

---

[165] Tweedie (ed.), *Select Biographies*, i, 164.   [166] *RPS* 1640/6/34–36, 6 June 1640.
[167] *RPS* 1640/6/61, 10 June 1640.
[168] *AGA*, 48, 171; *RPS* 1641/7/75, 9 August 1641. Parliamentary peers in 1641 were required to sign the 1640 band. *RPS* 1641/7/96, 13 August 1641.
[169] *RPS* 1641/7/96, 13 August 1641, A1641/8/1a, 17 August 1641.
[170] Gordon, 'Oath to the Covenanters (c.1639)', *MPESE*; Robertson, 'House of Huntly', 7; *RPS* 1641/8/21, 26 August 1641.
[171] Hewison, *The Covenanters*, i, 357; Macinnes, *British Revolution*, 137. The influence of the earl of Argyll was a particular concern.
[172] Hewison, *The Covenanters*, i, 359.
[173] Commission of the General Assembly, *A Necessary Warning to the Ministerie;* Stevenson, *Scottish Revolution*, 258–61.

114   Public Opinion in Early Modern Scotland, c.1560–1707

The making of an alliance between covenanted Scotland and parliamentarian England produced a new national subscriptional oath in 1643, the Solemn League and Covenant. Approved by the Scottish parliament and the general assembly, the 1643 oath was to be taken by all subjects: 'noblemen, barrones, knichts, gentlemen, citizenes, burgesses, ministeres of the Gospell and comones of all sortes'.[174] Swearers entered a 'mutuall and solemne league and covenant', promising in their stations to preserve the reformed kirk in Scotland and advance further reformation in England and Ireland; suppress 'poperie, prelacie, superstitione, heresie, shisme and profainnes'; preserve the Scottish parliament and kingdom; bring malignants to justice; pursue moral reformation; and uphold the Treaty of London, tying themselves to these terms and each other for the rest of their lives. Echoing the conditional terms of the National Covenant, they undertook to defend the king 'in the preservatione and defence of the true religione and liberties of the kingdome'.[175]

Though the Solemn League achieved only patchy subscription in England, wider engagement was secured in Scotland with the continuing cooperation of ecclesiastical and civil authorities. The commission of the general assembly ordered that the oath be 'received, sworn and subscribed by all Ministers and Professours in this Kirk'. Printed copies were produced with blank pages for subscriptions. Over two Sundays, ministers were to read the oath, explain its terms and present it for swearing and subscription, reporting any refusers to their presbytery. Kirk session clerks were authorised to sign for those unable to write, though urban parishes tended to use local notaries. Sheriffs, burgh magistrates and shire committees of war were to aid parish clergy in enforcing the oath, armed with civil penalties extending to the confiscation of 'rents and goods'. Alongside the 1638 covenant, the Solemn League was to be a test oath for any civil or ecclesiastical office.[176] McDougall's review of presbytery and kirk session records has shown widespread compliance with surviving evidence of female subscription in three parishes (Newbattle in Midlothian, Elgin in Moray and Aberlady in Haddingtonshire).[177] Because the 1643 general assembly previously had ordered the re-subscription of the National Covenant (as noted above), in some cases both oaths were administered at the same time. General subscription of the Solemn League encouraged

---

[174] *AGA*, 86.   [175] *RPS* 1643/6/75, 17 August 1643, 1644/6/147, 14 July 1644.
[176] Commission of the General Assembly, *A Solemn League and Covenant*; Stevenson, 'Solemn League', 157–8, 161–2.
[177] McDougall, 'Covenants and Covenanters', 66–9.

Oaths 115

cooperation with a new levy to wage war against the king, a 1645 directory of worship and a 1647 confession of faith arising from the Westminster Assembly. In approving the directory, the general assembly stated that Anglo–Scottish uniformity in religion had been 'long and earnestly wished for by the godly and well-affected'.[178]

Compliance with the Solemn League was not complete; some nobles refused the oath (including Montrose), and in the north, royalist landowners evaded the efforts of their presbyteries.[179] The kirk continued to remove uncooperative ministers, deposing seven in 1644.[180] In January 1645, Montrose and fifty-two nobles and gentlemen signed a 'Band of Unione' for 'mutuall assistance and defence', known as the Kilcumin Band. Designed to consolidate a royalist uprising, the oath emphasised the consciences and 'just sense' of the swearers in declaring their duty to God and the king.[181] Mackay gentry in Caithness also banded against the Covenanting regime.[182] In a proclamation outlawing Montrose, the Covenanter regime cited his apparent repudiation of his 'Oath in the Covenant'.[183]

With the collapse of royalist resistance in 1646, the Covenanters sought to exclude 'malignants' from kirk and state. While leading nobles faced treason trials, middling and lower status men were fined and barred from public office by a 1646 'act of classes' and required to profess repentance before church courts.[184] At least thirty-one clergy were deposed by the kirk between 1645 and 1647, many for cooperating with royalist rebels.[185] The kirk also took steps to quash an attempt by George Mackenzie, second earl of Seaforth in 1646 to promulgate a subscriptional band calling for national unity for king and kirk according to the terms of the National Covenant – but not the Solemn League. Copies of Seaforth's 'humble remonstrance' were circulated in the north and sent to the committee of estates but, as Stevenson has observed, this solo move by the earl had little means of amassing support.[186]

An agreement known as the Engagement, made late in 1647 by moderate Scottish nobles to support Charles I against English forces, stimulated

---

[178] *AGA*, 115–6, 158–9; *RPS* 1645/1/65, 6 February 1645, 1645/7/24/18, 2 August 1645.
[179] Kennedy, 'Covenanting government', 107; McDougall, 'Covenants and Covenanters', 67–8.
[180] Stevenson, 'Deposition of ministers', 328.
[181] Napier, *Memorials of Montrose and His Times*, ii, 172–4. I thank Andrew Lind for this reference.
[182] Kennedy, 'Covenanting government', 96.   [183] Napier, *Memorials of Montrose*, ii, 163.
[184] *RPS* 1645/11/110, 8 January 1646; Stewart, *Rethinking the Scottish Revolution*, 249–52.
[185] Stevenson, 'Deposition of ministers', 328.
[186] Commission of the General Assembly, *A Declaration against a Late Dangerous and Seditious Band*; Stevenson, *Revolution and Counter-Revolution*, 41.

a clash of opinions over its compatibility with the Solemn League and Covenant. Determining that the Engagement was 'destructive' to the covenants, the commission of the general assembly denounced the 'Prelaticall and malignant party' and 'discovenanters'. In negotiations with the committee of estates, the commission asked that Charles I commit himself to the covenants before being allowed to resume his powers as a king and that the Engagement be imposed with a new national oath administered by the kirk. When the Hamilton regime disregarded these demands and proceeded to order a levy for the king, the commission advised presbyteries to 'make conscience of their solemn vowes' and reject this 'unlawfull' Engagement.[187]

The 1648 levy was undermined by an ensuing split in grassroots opinions which parliament attempted to patch with a national subscription of obedience. When some shire committees of war raised objections, they were assured that parliament was acting 'according to the covenant' and that they would 'imploy nane in our armie bot such as have signed the Solemn League and Covenant'.[188] Nevertheless, many, especially in the Lothians, Fife, Lanarkshire, Ayrshire and Galloway, felt that the levy was inconsistent with their sworn obligations. There were crowd protests in Edinburgh and resistance in Glasgow, leading parliament on 10 June 1648 to make evasion of conscription a capital crime and to order all 'members of parliament, noblemen, barons, burgesses and all other subjects and inhabitants of the kingdom' to endorse the legitimacy of the 1648 diet and its legislation.[189] The general assembly rejected the subscription, declaring it inconsistent with the covenants, the publicly expressed views of the church and the oath of parliament sworn by members, and urged parish clergy not to support the levy.[190] When about 2000 armed men gathered on 11 June at a communion service on Mauchline Moor in Ayrshire led by seven clergymen, a rising against the levy seemed imminent.[191] But as Stevenson has pointed out, because nobles like Argyll could wait on events, no senior leadership emerged for a march on Edinburgh. The gathering was broken up by government forces and Mauchline Moor dissidents were required to sign the new subscription.[192]

---

[187] *RCGA*, i, 363–4, 373–82, 404–5, 528–30.
[188] *RPS* 1648/3/219–220, 10 June 1648. See chapter 3.
[189] Stevenson, *Revolution and Counter-Revolution*, 89–90; *RPS* 1648/3/217–8, 10 June 1648. Subscriptions were to be collected by 1 August.
[190] *AGA*, 170–1.   [191] *RPS* 1649/1/30, 16 January 1649.
[192] Stevenson, *Revolution and Counter-Revolution*, 91; Anon., *Ane Information of the Publick Proceedings*, 3. On the importance of noble leadership for risings, see Robertson, 'House of Huntly', 8–9 and Bowie, 'Popular resistance and the ratification', 12–3.

Oaths

The subsequent defeat of Engager forces in England led to a regime change and a return to a hardline endorsement of both covenants. Taking losses in England as evidence of God's disapproval, anti-Engagement nobles, gentry and ordinary men from Ayrshire and Lanarkshire made an armed march to Edinburgh known as the 'Whiggamore Raid' that allowed Argyll and the 'Kirk party' to establish a new government in September 1648.[193] To restore a correct understanding of the Solemn League, the commission of the general assembly on 6 October 1648 ordered its national renewal. Precise instructions were given for the reading of the Solemn League with a new paper, *A Solemn Acknowledgement of Publick Sins and Breaches of the Covenant, and a Solemn Engagement to all the Duties Contained Therein*, to congregations in December on a day of public humiliation and fasting. Literate laypeople were to study printed copies of these texts. After hearing the documents read again on the following Sunday, all were to swear the covenant followed by subscription on freshly printed copies. The *Solemn Acknowledgement* reinterpreted the Solemn League in its new circumstances, condemning both malignancy and 'detestable indifferency and neutrality'. The *Solemn Acknowledgement* also rejected the estates' endorsement of the Engagement as unrepresentative of national views expressed in protestations, petitions and the commission's own declaration. As McIntyre has noted, a 'Solemn Engagement' within this text acted as a supplementary oath as part of the commission's re-framing of the Solemn League.[194]

This renewal aimed to reinvigorate covenanted opinion and exclude unrepentant Engagers from kirk and state. Anyone who had taken part in the Engagement levy or sworn an oath or subscription acknowledging the Engagement, even if they had believed it would achieve the ends of the covenants, were suspended from communion. Leeway was provided for marginal cases: proprietors who had been coerced into supporting the levy could make repentance to their presbytery and any 'common people' who had gone into the levy were to stand for a public rebuke by the minister.[195] All individuals, from elites to commoners, were required to be responsible for their own opinions and actions, including, in Dumfries presbytery,

---

[193] Stevenson, *Revolution and Counter-Revolution*, 95–9.

[194] *RCGA*, ii, 78–88; *A Solemn League and Covenant for Reformation* (Edinburgh: Evan Tyler, 1648); McIntyre, 'Re-framing the Covenant: The Reception and Legacy of *A Solemn Acknowledgement* (1648) in Scotland and Beyond'.

[195] *RCGA, ii*, 163–9; Commission of the General Assembly, *The Explanation of a Former Act* (Edinburgh: Evan Tyler, 1648).

'women malignantly disposed'.[196] McDougall's survey has found a high level of compliance with the renewal of the Solemn League and the disciplining of Engagers in the localities, though not all Engagers cooperated.[197] In July 1649, the general assembly published yet another subscription, a 'Declaration and Acknowledgement' requiring Engagers to admit the unlawfulness of the Engagement and promise to uphold the covenants before they could be returned to communion.[198] Ministers who had supported or failed to resist the Engagement were pursued, with twenty deposed in 1648 and at least fifty-two more in 1649.[199] A call in the *Solemn Acknowledgement* for a civil purge was answered with the Act of Classes in January 1649.[200] This act removed Engagers from all central and local public offices in favour of those who 'have continowed constant in the covenant'.[201] Parliament also praised those who had appeared in arms at Mauchline Moor, overturning their forced subscription to the Engagement levy by declaring that this gathering was 'not onlie laufull bot a zealous and loyall testimony to the truth and covenant'.[202]

Despite the purging of Engagers, events caused a further split in opinions over the covenants. After the execution of Charles I on 30 January 1649 in London, his son was proclaimed as Charles II but the Kirk party regime insisted that he swear the covenants. Agreeing only after the failure of a final attempt by Montrose to retake Scotland by arms, Charles made it obvious that he accepted the covenants grudgingly. The cleric John Livingston, a member of the delegation sent to Charles in the Netherlands, decried the king's 'bare subscriving or swearing some words without any evidence it was done from the heart'.[203] The defeat of Scottish forces by Cromwell on 3 September 1650 at Dunbar only reinforced fears among hardliners that God's cause had been betrayed. A spectrum of opinions was expressed publicly: hardline remonstrances came to the committee of estates from several synods and the 'western association', a group of lairds and ministers with levied forces in the west of Scotland; moderate views came from the synod of Fife, urging the rehabilitation of repentant Engagers; and royalism was seen in another attempted rising for the king early in October, after which a group of royalist nobles signed the 'northern band and oath of engagement' indicating their wish to assist in the defence of the covenanted nation.[204]

---

[196] McDougall, 'Covenants and Covenanters', 95.   [197] *Ibid.*, 87–96.   [198] *AGA*, 201–3.
[199] Stevenson, 'Deposition of ministers', 330.   [200] *RCGA*, ii, 86.
[201] *RPS* 1649/1/43, 23 January 1649.   [202] *RPS* 1649/1/30, 16 January 1649.
[203] Tweedie (ed.), *Select Biographies*, i, 171.
[204] Haig (ed.), *The Historical Works of Sir James Balfour*, iv, 108, 129–30.

Under the pressure of an English invasion, the kirk split into factions known as Resolutioners and Protesters (as seen in Chapter 1).[205] Invoking an image of covenanted unity found in the book of Zechariah, the minister James Kirkton later referred to these divisions as the breaking of Scotland's 'staff of bands'.[206] Though the coronation of Charles I on 1 January 1651 emphasised mutual obligations formed between king and people by their reciprocal oaths, by May parliament had dropped the covenants as a test for civil office in order to employ former Engagers in the defence of the realm.[207] The Engagers had to promise to maintain recent laws in favour of the kirk, while conversely the leaders of the western remonstrance were required to repudiate their stringent opinions and 'obleidge themselfes never to medle with the lyke heirefter'.[208]

The National Covenant had been designed to set the opinions of the laity at large against the judgement of the monarch by asking individuals to suspend their practice of church innovations until these could be considered by authorised assemblies. When the Covenanters succeeded in taking control of these assemblies, they re-imposed the National Covenant with a declaration against bishops in hopes of creating a national commitment to presbyterian church government. This grand experiment in the mass coercion of consent aimed to harness public opinion with the help of exhortations and the threat of exclusion from civil and ecclesiastical office. But the National Covenant created a paradox: it enjoined obedience to a set of truths defined by law and custom while also stimulating individuals to reflect on current affairs and act according to their consciences. Opinions became more relevant to political outcomes as men and women chose to adopt or refuse the National Covenant and responded to events according to their sworn commitments. As the covenanted consensus weakened from 1643 with the imposition of the Solemn League and the ensuing civil wars, a proliferation of supplementary bands, subscriptions and renewals could not force the resulting range of opinions back into uniformity. The potential leverage of public opinion was realised when the Covenanters came to power on the shoulders of their subscribers and secured a constitutional revolution on the back of the Bishops' Wars and when half-hearted levies doomed the Engager and Kirk party regimes.

---

[205] Stevenson, *Revolution and Counter-Revolution*, 150–63.
[206] Kirkton, *Secret and True History*, 52–3.
[207] Bowie, '"A legal limited monarchy": Scottish constitutionalism in the Union of Crowns, 1603–1707', 142–4; *RPS* A1651/5/5, 30 May 1651, A1651/5/7, 2 June 1651.
[208] *RCGA*, iii, 352–3; *RPS* A1651/5/10, 4 June 1651; Haig (ed.), *The Historical Works of Sir James Balfour*, i, 309.

120   Public Opinion in Early Modern Scotland, c.1560–1707

After 1651, governments sought to reassert control over opinion at large not by disseminating new national oaths but by applying oaths of allegiance, obedience and abjuration to selected groups and individuals.

3.3   After the Covenants: Oaths from Cromwell to the Revolution

Building on an initial study of oaths by Raffe, this chapter will assess the use of oaths in the Cromwellian and Restoration periods to show how these regimes attempted to control opinion at large.[209] It will argue that the Cromwellian regime sought quiescence through oaths of civil obedience combined with toleration for forms of Protestant worship, allowing individuals to maintain their covenanted opinions as long as they did not threaten the stability of the regime. When the Stewart monarchy was restored in 1660, however, the government of Charles II imposed new oaths antithetical to covenanted consciences. These stringent oaths forced individuals to decide how far to comply with the civil and ecclesiastical establishment. When substantial numbers chose partial or complete separation and some offered violent resistance, promises of lawful behaviour were demanded from individuals, with failure leading to their removal from Scottish society by imprisonment, banishment or execution. The radicalisation of dissenting opinions from 1679 stimulated new oaths in 1681 and 1684 to stamp out militancy, targeting all men and women in certain districts in 1684 and all males in 1685. In 1687, James VII's desire to secure freedom for Catholic worship led to a substantial shift in the management of opinion with the lifting of confessional oaths, leaving public speech constrained only by the law of sedition.

Apparent consent for the making of a British commonwealth in 1652 was created by requiring two of Scotland's three estates to subscribe to a tender of union, followed by individual oaths for office-holders. In a state of military occupation, the parliamentary burghs and shires of Scotland were ordered to send deputies to Dalkeith in February 1652 to sign a declaration accepting a union of Scotland and England.[210] As in England, however, where a national oath of engagement for the kingless Cromwellian commonwealth was resisted by presbyterians because it contradicted the Solemn League, many covenanters in Scotland objected to the subscription because it contradicted both the National Covenant and Solemn League.[211] Kirsteen MacKenzie has emphasised the extent of

---

[209] Raffe, 'Scottish state oaths'.   [210] Terry (ed.), *Cromwellian Union*, 11–5.
[211] Vallance, *Revolutionary England*, 161–2. See chapter 2 on petitions against union.

Oaths

resistance to the union on covenanted grounds, encouraged by Protester and Resolutioner clergy.[212] Glasgow could not provide its subscription, 'beinge unsatisfied in our conscience'. The 'burgess[es] and neighboures' of Lanark would have been ready to enter into a covenanted union but could not accept England's tender without 'farder satisfaction in our conschiences thairanent', being 'bound by the Law of God and oath of Covenant agreeable thereto to endeavour the preservation of the Liberties of this Nation and Just fundamentall Lawes thereof.' Similarly, representatives of Morayshire in the north stated 'we dare not in our Consciences yeild our Consent'. A key issue was the religious toleration required by the English commonwealth, which promised 'sadd effects'.[213]

When the commonwealth was formed nonetheless, the regime focused on quieting Scottish public opinion with civil oaths, capitalising on Scotland's internal divisions. All electors and office-holders were required to sign a declaration confirming their consent to the union and promising 'that wee will Live peaceably vnder and yeald obedience unto the Authoritye of the Parliament of the Comon-Wealth of England Exercised in Scotland'.[214] As the Protesters complained, 'engagements in things civill are pressed whilst covenants in things religious are casten loose'.[215] After the formation of the 1653 Protectorate, new oaths of allegiance were provided for office-holders.[216] A 1653 royalist rising led by William Cunningham, eighth earl of Glencairn, did not endorse the Solemn League and failed to attract significant support outside of royalist circles in the north and central Highlands and northeast.[217] Resolutioner ministers urged 'the conscientious keeping' of the covenants and reasserted their allegiance to the Stewart composite monarchy as defined by the Solemn League.[218] In September 1655, Protester clergy, urged by Samuel Rutherford and led by Archibald Johnston of Wariston, drafted a new covenant to rally the godly, but in November this was dropped for fear that the English regime would see it as a dangerous 'combination' even though it made no mention of the 'Kings interest'.[219]

From 1660, the restored government of Charles II sought to neutralise the Scottish covenants by declaring them unlawful and requiring selected subjects to accept this by oath. This focus on personal, rather than national, oaths echoed the practice of Charles I who, after the failure of

---

[212] MacKenzie, *Solemn League*, 104–6.   [213] Terry (ed.), *Cromwellian Union*, 34–5, 74–5, 112.
[214] *Ibid.*, 64–5.   [215] Stephen (ed.), *Register of Consultations*, i, 21.
[216] Vallance, *Revolutionary England*, 177.   [217] McDougall, 'Covenants and Covenanters', 121–8.
[218] Laing (ed.), *Robert Baillie*, iii, 295.   [219] Paul et al. (eds.), *Diary*, iii, 6–12.

his 1638 King's Covenant, in 1639 required Scotsmen in his London court to swear not to covenant, band, protest or rebel against him.[220] With a sweeping Rescissory Act, the 1661 parliament negated previous authorisations of the covenants.[221] It then approved a new oath for 'places of publict trust' with a sworn acknowledgement of Charles II as 'supream governour of this kingdome over all persones and in all causes' and a subscription indicating acceptance of the 1661 legislation.[222] A further restriction on public offices was added in 1662 with an act condemning 'treasonable and sedicious positions infused into the people' by 'unlawfull oaths' during the 'late troubles' and banning from public office any person convicted of seditious speech or actions.[223] Finally, on 5 September 1662 parliament replaced the 1661 acknowledgement with a succinct 'declaration' that all office-holders were to subscribe after taking the oath of allegiance. This affirmed that the making of 'leagues and covenants', taking up arms against the king and 'all these gatherings, convocations, petitions, protestations and erecting and keeping of councill tables, that wer vsed in the begining and for carieing on of the late troubles' were 'unlawfull and seditious' and that 'ther lyeth no obligation upon me or any of the subjects' from the covenants.[224]

These assertory subscriptions were used to purge civic posts. Orders were sent to the president of the court of session, sheriffs and the royal burghs requiring them to have the declaration signed by all lawyers, judges and shire and burgh officers, including commissioners of excise, justices of the peace and burgh councillors. Printed copies of the declaration were provided for the subscription. No explanations or reservations were allowed, and refusers were to be reported.[225] Enforcement in the burghs was backed with a threat to revoke trading privileges from the non-compliant.[226] It was announced in February 1664 that any office-holder would be turned out if a signed declaration was not returned by April.[227] Orders for burgh magistrates and councillors to take the declaration were renewed in 1679 and extended to burghs of barony and regality in 1680.[228]

---

[220] 'Oath Offered to the Scots in London' (1639), *MPESE*.

[221] *RPS* 1661/1/67, 9 February 1661, 1661/1/158, 28 March 1661.

[222] This parliament swore a new oath of allegiance to the king. *RPS* 1661/1/7, 1 January 1661, 1661/1/88, 27 February 1661; Raffe, 'Scottish state oaths', 180.

[223] *RPS* 1662/5/20, 24 June 1662.   [224] *RPS* 1662/5/70, 5 September 1662.

[225] *RPCS*, ser. 3, i, 455–6, 473.   [226] *RPS* 1663/6/33, 7 August 1663.   [227] *RPCS*, ser. 3, ii, 2.

[228] Charles II, *A Proclamation, Appointing the Magistrates of Burghs of Regality and Barony, and their Clerks, to Take the Oath of Alleadgeance, and Signe the Declaration*; Charles II, *A Proclamation Anent*

Oaths 123

Resistance to the 1662 declaration indicates a crisis of conscience in strongly covenanted communities, especially in Galloway, Ayrshire, Renfrewshire, Lanarkshire, Fife and the Lothians. In the Galloway burgh of Stranraer, the council withdrew from service to avoid the declaration and in Ayrshire, a newly elected slate in the burgh of Irvine found that they were 'not cleare to subscryve'.[229] By January 1664, the magistrates of Edinburgh had not yet all signed. Resistance appeared among shire officers too; in Orkney, three new justices of the peace refused the declaration.[230] In 1665, Ayr struggled to form a council because so many burgesses refused the declaration. In September 1666, the council demanded again that sheriffs and royal burghs implement the declaration after Michaelmas elections and report refusers.[231] Yet implementation continued to be problematic for years in some districts. More than a decade later, in March 1676, the privy council had to order the removal of elected councillors in Ayr who had not taken the declaration and in 1680, officers were elected to Newtown of Ayr, a baronial burgh, without taking the declaration.[232]

Alongside the declaration, the restoration of episcopacy in 1661–2 required every subject, clerical and lay, to consider how far they would honour their covenant oaths. In a return to prior practice, clergy were required to swear an oath of obedience to their bishop alongside an oath of allegiance.[233] Individuals had to choose whether to conform to an uncovenanted church, accepting that the monarch and his parliament could void the covenants, or remove themselves partially or wholly from the church, upholding their covenant oath as a perpetually binding tie. As McDougall has shown, men and women made personal decisions on how best to reconcile their beliefs with their circumstances. A substantial number occupied a middle ground, seeking to avoid civil penalties without rejecting the covenants. Some bishops and presbyteries allowed ministers and schoolmasters to take an oath indicating their satisfaction with the church settlement but not repudiating the covenants. Some parishioners attended church but avoided contentious elements like thanksgiving services on 29 May celebrating the Restoration.[234] In some parishes, conforming clerics struggled to form a kirk session as elders refused to serve.[235]

---

the Murtherers of the Late Archbishop of St Andrews, and Appointing Magistrates and Councils of Burghs Royal to Sign the Declaration at Michaelmas Next.

[229] *RPCS*, ser. 3, i, 549, 617–8.   [230] *RPCS*, ser. 3, ii, 134–5.

[231] *RPCS*, ser. 3, ii, 95, 110–1, 191–2.   [232] *RPCS*, ser. 3, iv, 551; *RPCS*, ser. 3, vi, 590–2.

[233] McDougall, 'Covenants and Covenanters', 152–4, 170.   [234] *Ibid.*, ch. 4.

[235] *RPCS*, ser. 3, ii, 111–2.

124   Public Opinion in Early Modern Scotland, c.1560–1707

About 300 clergymen felt compelled to leave the kirk and many parishioners followed them to house and field conventicles or sought them out for marriages and baptisms. Though most apparent in the southwest, conventicling appeared across southern Scotland and in some northern parts.[236]

The Restoration regime responded by criminalising nonconformity with stiff penalties designed to force dissenters back into the established church. From 1663, all subjects were required to attend their parish church, with tiered fines for landowners, burgesses and tenants.[237] Both civil and ecclesiastical penalties were applied to nonconformist clergy with deprivation of stipends and deposition from the ministry. When some heritors continued to pay stipends to deposed clergy, this was considered seditious.[238] Heritors were made responsible for protecting their parish clergy from violence offered by 'disaffected and disloyall persons'.[239] Royal troops were used to police restive districts, extracting fines with intimidation, violence and quartering.[240]

Oaths and bands continued to be an important tool in the government's suppression of resistance as part of an expansion in the state's capacity for coercive control. An armed protest in November 1666, known as the Pentland rising, triggered a more aggressive application of the 1662 declaration. Stimulated by a clash between troops and dissenters in Dumfriesshire, several thousand men in arms on foot and horseback gathered from across the southwest and moved towards Edinburgh. Believing that the coronation of Charles II represented a 'most solemn Indenture betwixt him and his People', the rebels renewed the Solemn League at Lanark and sent a petition to the privy council asking for relief from penalties for nonconformity.[241] To secure the capital city, the privy council imposed a new oath of loyalty on the Edinburgh town guard.[242] Weakened by a lack of noble leadership and miserable winter weather, a band of about 800 armed protesters were defeated by royal forces in the Pentland Hills near Edinburgh.[243] After the rising, the king was advised

---

[236] *RPCS*, ser. 2, i, 30–2, 269–70; *RPS* 1662/5/9, 27 May 1662; Cowan, *Scottish Covenanters*, 50–7; Hyman, 'Church militant', 54–7.

[237] *RPS* 1663/6/19, 10 July 1663.   [238] *RPCS*, ser. 3, i, 403–4.

[239] *RPS* 1669/10/19, 30 November 1669.

[240] *RPCS*, ser. 3, i, 350. Additional forces were offered by the 1663 parliament: *RPS* 1663/6/64, 23 September 1663.

[241] Wallace, 'Narrative of the Rising at Pentland', 405; [Stewart of Goodtrees and Stirling], *Napthali*, 128; [Stewart of Goodtrees], *Jus Populi Vindicatum*, 9; Wodrow, *History*, i, 245–6; McDougall, 'Covenants and Covenanters', 179; Raffe, 'Confessions, covenants', para. 18.

[242] *RPCS*, ser. 3, ii, 213; Wallace, 'Narrative', 426–7.   [243] Wallace, 'Narrative'. See chapter 2.

Oaths

that 'those principles which are pretendit for the ground of this rebellion are so rooted in many severall places throw the kingdome' that 'more vigorous application of your Majesties authority' was needed. The oath of allegiance and the 1662 declaration were required of anyone suspected of being 'active and leading persons in the disaffected party'. Imprisoned rebels had to accept the declaration to be released, with refusers being sent to Barbados as indentured servants.[244] Men who had refused public office or left the kirk were not to keep high-value horses unless they signed the declaration. In addition to the disarming of heritors in southwest shires, a new militia was created in 1669 led by 'loyall and weill principled' officers and extra regiments were added to the regular forces in 1674.[245] Troops continued to be quartered on conventiclers to extract fines and provide surveillance.[246]

For those who refused the declaration, personal bands promising compliance could be substituted. In October 1667, an indemnity offered a pardon for anyone 'seduced and misled' into the rebellion in return for the swearing of a band 'for keeping the publict peace' with a promise not to rise in arms. A reported 218 rebels signed the band, with several hundred mostly 'very mean persons' remaining fugitives early in 1668.[247] Commissioners also extracted this band from most of the 'considerable heritors' in disaffected shires. They, in turn, were to require their tenants and servants to sign bands under threat of disarming and eviction.[248] Individual bands also were used by kirk sessions to enforce church attendance. In Morayshire, reluctant parishioners at Alves parish agreed with their 'hand at the pen' to come to church or incur physical punishment.[249] Alongside stiff fines for attendance and the death penalty for clergymen leading field conventicles, a 1670 act required a bond of 5,000 merks (3,333 Scots pounds) for any clergyman caught leading a house conventicle. Men were fined for conventicles hosted by their wives, with the fine being doubled if the mistress was present at the meeting.[250] As scholars

---

[244] *RPCS*, ser. 3, ii, 228, 307.

[245] All arms except gentlemen's swords were to be taken from heritors in Lanarkshire, Renfrewshire, Ayrshire, Wigtownshire and the Stewartry of Kirkcudbright. *RPCS*, ser. 3, ii, 267–8, 272–5; *RPS* 1669/10/14, 19 November 1669.

[246] Cowan, *Scottish Covenanters*, 87.   [247] Airy (ed.), *The Lauderdale Papers*, ii, 96.

[248] *RPCS*, ser. 3, ii, 348–50, 365–6; Airy (ed.), *The Lauderdale Papers*, ii, 52.

[249] McDougall, 'Covenants and Covenanters,' 164.

[250] *RPS* 1670/7/11, 13 August 1670. This act was renewed in 1672 with fines for uncooperative magistrates and in 1681 the fines on field conventicles were doubled: *RPS* 1672/6/51, 4 September 1672, 1681/7/26, 29 August 1681. Fines were also set for irregular baptisms: *RPS* 1670/7/12, 17 August 1670.

126   Public Opinion in Early Modern Scotland, c.1560–1707

have emphasised, this points to the essential role played by wives and mothers in the maintenance of covenanting beliefs and dissenting behaviours in households across the social scale.[251] As records of non-attendance reveal, some wives chose to dissent with or without their husbands.[252]

Increasing attempts were made to impose bands in the late 1670s as conventicling reached what was called 'an unsufferable pitch' in some areas.[253] In 1674, heritors and burgh magistrates in targeted regions again were required to extract bands of obedience from tenants and burgesses for themselves and their households.[254] Non-compliance increasingly could lead to expulsion through transportation to the colonies as an indentured servant.[255] Performance of banding, however, was patchy after the 1674 order, with renewed orders in 1677 and 1678.[256] In the spring of 1678, bands were enforced in the southwest with the quartering of about 8,000 troops, including militia forces known as the Highland Host.[257] The extreme nature of this pressure on landlords is indicated by a complaint made to the king in London that 'it was an unheard-of stretch to oblige men to be bound for others in matters of religion and conscience'.[258] The pressure led some dissenters to consider removing themselves from Scottish society, as seen in a 1679 petition to England's Massachusetts Colony asking to settle one hundred godly families with a minister and schoolmaster.[259]

Alongside these attempts to control public behaviour, the government sought to gauge clerical and lay opinions to see if indulgences or an accommodation scheme might reduce unlawful conventicling. As McIntyre has outlined, this showed a desire to achieve civil peace by creating a space for covenanted consciences within the national church. An indulgence would allow a dissenting cleric to practice his spiritual office in a designated parish without taking the declaration or oath of allegiance. The success of this, however, rested on whether dissenting clerics were

---

[251] Raffe, 'Female authority and lay activism in Scottish Presbyterianism, 1660–1714'; McSeveney, 'Non-Conforming Presbyterian Women in Scotland, 1660–1679'; McDougall, 'Covenants and Covenanters', 172, 176, 187–9, 193–4.

[252] *RPCS*, ser. 3, x, 549–50.   [253] Airy (ed.), *Burnet's History*, ii, 143.

[254] *RPCS*, ser. 3, iv, 197–200; Charles II, *A Proclamation, Oblidging Heritors and Masters*; Raffe, 'State oaths', 182.

[255] Cowan, *Scottish Covenanters*, 92.

[256] Charles II, *A Proclamation, Oblidging Heritors and Masters* (1677 version); Charles II, *A Proclamation, for Offering the Band Obliging Heretors and Masters*.

[257] *RPCS* ser. 3, v, 206–9; Airy (ed.), *Burnet's History*, ii, 144–5; Cowan, *Covenanters*, 91; Hyman, 'Church militant', 65.

[258] Airy (ed.), *Burnet's History*, ii, 148; Airy (ed.), *Lauderdale Papers*, iii, 103–4. See chapter 2.

[259] Paul, 'Scottish emigrants'. I thank Georgina Hodges for this reference.

willing to acknowledge the authority of an uncovenanted monarch in order to take the indulgence. The government consulted several ministers and identified three opinion groups: moderate Resolutioners who were likely to accept an indulgence, more hardline Protesters and a radicalised fringe most active in conventicling.[260] These groupings were confirmed when indulgences were implemented in 1669 and 1672. A little less than half of the deposed clergy, mostly Resolutioners, were settled in vacant parishes in Ayrshire, Lanarkshire, Renfrewshire and Galloway with some in the Lothians, Argyllshire and elsewhere.[261] Dissenting gentry proved more willing to hear indulged services, while their tenants tended to refuse.[262] A parallel proposal to accommodate clergy under a reformed episcopate foundered in part on grassroots opposition to prelacy despite a promotional 'preaching tour'. As Ian Cowan has noted, the touring clerics found that 'the peasantry were more than their equals in debates on the nature of ecclesiastical government'.[263]

Alongside indulgences, the government applied charges of sedition and treason against dissenters who felt compelled to resist uncovenanted royal authority. An armed uprising was defeated at Bothwell Bridge near Hamilton in Lanarkshire on 22 June 1679, with several hundred killed and over 1,000 taken prisoner. Deploying the militia to hunt fugitives, the privy council prosecuted rebels for treason, executing two preachers. Prisoners of lesser social status, including tenants, weavers and artisans, were released if they swore not to take up arms against the king, while propertied prisoners were required to give bands of caution with penalties ranging from 500 to 5000 merks. Hardline prisoners who refused a band were shipped out as indentured servants. About fifteen clerics were allowed to give a band of caution to the privy council to lead house conventicles in certain areas, though this indulgence was not extended to any Bothwell rebels.[264]

After the Bothwell rising, a militant minority revived the outlawed practice of collective banding to repudiate their loyalty to an uncovenanted monarchy, triggering an intensification of government efforts to extinguish these opinions in a period known in presbyterian histories as 'the Killing

---

[260] McIntyre, 'Saints and Subverters', 146, 149–50.
[261] If indulged ministers refused collation from the bishop or to attend church courts, they forfeited their stipends and were confined to their parish but could still lead worship. *RPCS*, ser. 3, iii, 38–40, 586–91.
[262] McIntyre, 'Saints and Subverters', 151, 167, 169–70.
[263] Cowan, *Scottish Covenanters*, 76–9; McIntyre, 'Saints and Subverters', 156.
[264] *RPCS*, ser. 3, vi, 253–4, 257–61, 63–6; Cowan, *Scottish Covenanters*, 96–102.

128 Public Opinion in Early Modern Scotland, c.1560–1707

Times'. In the southwest, a loose network of praying societies had formed, known variously as the United Societies, the 'Society people' or the Cameronians, after the preacher Richard Cameron, ordained in the Netherlands in 1679 and killed by government troops in July 1680.[265] Shortly before his death, one year after Bothwell, Cameron and twenty-five other men signed a collective band promising to defend each other in disowning Charles' uncovenanted government and his erastian indulgences.[266] This was followed by a public repudiation of Charles II for his breach of covenant made at the Nithsdale royal burgh of Sanquhar on 22 June in the name of 'the covenanted Nation of Scotland'.[267] A new covenant was written by outlawed minister Donald Cargill to bind swearers in opposition to the uncovenanted king and his 'Oppression' of 'Consciences, civil Rights and Liberties'. Cargill's covenant confirmed the obligations of prior covenants and asserted that Charles II was an 'unlawful' ruler because he had broken his 'Coronation Compact'. Repudiating hereditary monarchy, the signatories promised to establish and defend a self-governing body ruled by God's laws that would deliver 'righteous Justice' on the ungodly.[268] Imprisoned extremists later stated that they were compelled to own this document.[269] In September 1680, Cargill performed a public excommunication of Charles II and other leading figures at a field conventicle at Torwood in Stirlingshire, the text of which was posted in public places in Edinburgh.[270]

The view of the privy council was that these extremists had moved beyond 'the sentiments of tender consciences' to 'fanatical principles' dangerous to monarchy and society.[271] They began to pursue ordinary men and women not just for illegal behaviour but for their opinions alone, as refusal to disavow militant declarations became an act of treason subject to the death penalty. The confirmed executions of thirty-one men and women between 1679 and 1681 included two unmarried women who were active in extremist networks: Marion Harvie, a young servant girl from the harbour town of Bo'ness on the Firth of Forth and Isobel Alison, an older woman from Perth. The two were executed in Edinburgh on 26 January 1681 after refusing to disown the Sanquhar declaration and Cargill's covenant (though Lord Lauder of Fountainhall, a court of session judge, felt that as women they should not have been given 'the credit of a

---

[265] Jardine, 'United Societies', ch. 1; Pearce, 'Cameron, Richard'.
[266] Jardine, 'Declarations –1680 Sanquhar'; *RPCS* ser 3, vi, 584.
[267] *RPCS*, ser. 3, vi, 481–3; Wodrow, *History*, ii, appendix, 47. See chapter 1.
[268] Wodrow, *History*, ii, appendix, 43–7.   [269] *Cloud of Witnesses*, 87.
[270] Callow, 'Cargill, Donald [Daniel]'; RPCS ser 3, vi, 584.   [271] *RPCS*, ser. 3, vi, 582.

Oaths

public suffering').[272] In addition, women and men in a cult-like group led by John Gibb, a ship's captain in Bo'ness, were apprehended and imprisoned in Edinburgh in May 1681. From February, this breakaway group had been living rough, fasting, praying, singing psalms and preaching according to their consciences. With no ordained minister, the Gibbites were said to have allowed knowledgeable women to preach. From their Edinburgh prison, some of the women threw rubbish at the king's brother James, duke of York and Albany, when his coach passed their window. Concluding that the Gibbites were more deluded than dangerous, the privy council whipped those who refused to abjure their views.[273]

At the same time as the government faced intransigent presbyterian opinions, they also had to manage concerns about the Catholicism of the duke of York, the king's brother and heir. A band of association was signed by a group of students in December 1680 during a visit by James to Scotland, committing themselves to stage an illegal pope-burning on Edinburgh's High Street on Christmas day.[274] Hearing of these plans, the authorities asked the students to sign a bond promising not to burn the pope, but 'very few or none of the Boys would subscribe'.[275] Because the students managed to evade the authorities and perform their protest, from February 1681 all new university students were required to swear the oath of allegiance, promise to attend church and give a bond for peaceable behaviour.[276]

A new confessional oath was authorised by the Scottish parliament on 31 August 1681, aimed equally at 'popery and phanaticisme'.[277] This oath returned to Scotland's original 1560 confession instead of the Covenanters' 1581 oath, combining this with elements from the oath of allegiance and declaration confirming the royal supremacy and rejecting the covenants. Swearers promised to teach the confession to their children and agreed not to covenant, convene without authority or rise in arms against the king. To prevent equivocation, swearers asserted that they took the oath according to its 'plain, genuine sense' without any mental reservations or evasions.[278] This new oath, known as the Test, was not to be taken by all subjects, but by 'all persons in offices and places of publict trust civill, ecclesiastical and

---

[272] Jardine, 'Table: Judicial Executions of Militant Presbyterians'; *Cloud of Witnesses*, 77–94; Doak, 'Militant women: the execution of Isabel Alison and Marion Harvie, 1681'; Lauder of Fountainhall, *Historical Observes of Memorable Occurrents in Church and State*, 26.

[273] Wodrow, *History*, ii, appendix, 79–84; Somerset, 'Walter Ker', 86–96.

[274] Anon., *A Modest Apology for the Students of Edenburgh Burning a Pope*, 9.

[275] Anon., *The Scots Demonstration of their Abhorrence of Popery*.   [276] *RPCS*, ser. 3, vii, 28–30.

[277] *RPS* 1681/7/29, 31 August 1681.   [278] Condren, *Argument and Authority*, 248–50.

130   Public Opinion in Early Modern Scotland, c.1560–1707

military'.[279] The Test was to be sworn orally in front of superior officers or commissioners and recorded in court registers.[280] The inclusion of schoolmasters, regents and chaplains indicates the importance of these figures in conveying covenanted opinions to a new generation. As McDougall has shown, in the 1670s authorities singled out chaplains and nonconformist schoolmasters for their sinister influence on the young.[281]

The Test was refused not just by hardline presbyterians, but by episcopalians who felt that the 1560 confession was incompatible with prelacy. Despite the publishing of an explanation offering a very general reading of the confession, some clerics signed with reservations and others rejected the test altogether, leading to the deposition of up to eighty episcopalian ministers.[282] As shown in Chapter 1, presbyterian militants burned the Test act on 12 January 1682 in the royal burgh of Lanark with a declaration highlighting the consciences of the people. This was followed on 8 November 1684 by another statement of 'our firm Resolution of constant Engagement to our Covenant and Obligations' and warned that they would defend themselves from anyone inhibiting 'the Ends of our Covenants'. This statement was posted on market crosses and kirk doors in a handful of burghs and printed as an *Apologetical Declaration*.[283]

Armed with the 1681 Test, the government pursued those holding militant opinions.[284] Military officers were commissioned to hold crown courts in disturbed areas and circuit courts were added in 1683 and 1684.[285] At a court in Kirkcudbright on 10–11 October 1684, a group of men including tenants, a miller, a gardener and a 'violer' took the Test 'upon their kneys with uplifted hands', while a court at Glasgow imposed the Test on all freeholders in Renfrewshire and all heritors and masters of families in the barony burghs of Renfrew and Paisley. Lord Fountainhall

---

[279] *RPS* 1681/7/29, 31 August 1681, 1681/7/49, 17 September 1681. The king's Catholic brother and heir, James, duke of Albany and York, was exempted from the Test.

[280] *RPCS*, ser. 3, vii, 246.

[281] McDougall, 'Covenants and Covenanters', 190. Both Richard Cameron and Donald Cargill worked as chaplains to dissenting lairds early in their careers and some chaplains led house conventicles, including John King, chaplain to Lord Cardross in Perthshire. Wodrow, *History*, ii, appendix, 91; Cowan, *Covenanters*, 84. A further proclamation in 1683 reiterated the requirement that teachers working in private households take the test: *RPCS*, ser. 3, viii, 178–9.

[282] Wodrow, *History*, ii, appendix, 61–2; Raffe, 'State oaths', 183; Cowan, *Scottish Covenanters*, 109; *RPCS*, ser. 3, vii, 239, 242.

[283] Renwick and Shields, *Informatory Vindication*, 176–91; Wodrow, *History*, ii, appendix, 137–8.

[284] The government also applied a new act making it treason to defend the lawfulness of assassination. *RPS* 1681/7/39, 13 September 1681.

[285] Privy councillors convened circuit courts in 1684. *RPCS*, ser. 3, viii, 135, 143, 180–1, x, xv–xvi; Charles II, *A Proclamation, Allowing a Further Diet to the Commons For Taking the Test*; Cowan, *Scottish Covenanters*, 111, 114, 116, 120.

observed, 'All courses were set on foot to spread the Test, to make it as universall as the Covenant was, which it [was] to root out'. Unlike the covenants, however, the Test was not applied to women. Instead, female suspects were required to enact bands of obedience or give monetary bonds of caution.[286]

Both men and women were subject to a new oath of abjuration enacted on 30 December 1684 in response to the *Apologetical Declaration*.[287] Heritors and burgh magistrates in southern shires and the north between the Spey and Ness rivers were ordered to convene all individuals over the age of 16 and require them to reject the treasonous principles found in the *Apologetical Declaration*. In an echo of the covenants, an oral oath was to be followed by subscription (by all who could write) on a large paper for each parish. But anyone refusing the oath was to be taken to the nearest authorised magistrate for trial and immediate execution.[288]

The threat of summary execution turned the mass swearing and subscription practices of the Covenanters into a much more sinister attempt to extirpate disruptive opinions. Instructions issued on 13 January 1685 ordered the drowning of women who were 'active in these courses in a signall manner'.[289] Alongside forty-five men known to have been executed for treason between 1682 and 1685, Margaret McLachlan, a widow aged about 60, and Margaret Wilson, an unmarried woman aged about 18, were condemned and reportedly drowned at Wigtown on 11 May 1685 for refusing the abjuration.[290] Both were nonconformists from the parish of Penninghame north of Wigtown. Though their executions have been disputed, records confirm their trial and sentence and Jardine has argued convincingly for the likely performance of their execution. Jardine also has shown that another Galloway woman was prosecuted by a court in Kirkcudbright for refusing the abjuration. Named as a fugitive in 1684 for aiding rebels, Grizel Fullarton appears to have escaped a sentence of drowning by finally agreeing to take the abjuration oath.[291]

Oaths were extended further under James VII in response to a presbyterian uprising against the new king and a declaration by the United

---

[286] Lauder of Fountainhall, *Historical Notices*, i, 445, 448.   [287] *RPCS*, ser. 3, x, 236–7, 239–42.
[288] Charles II, *A Proclamation for Discovering such as Own, or Will Not Disown a Late Treasonable Declaration of War*; Wodrow, *History*, ii, appendix, 138–40; *RPCS*, ser. 3, x, 102; Cowan, *Covenanters*, 119, 121.
[289] *RPCS*, ser. 3, x, 107.   [290] Jardine, 'Table: Judicial executions of militant Presbyterians'.
[291] In May 1684, 1,819 individuals were named as outlaws, including twelve women. Wodrow, *History*, ii, appendix, 104–20; Jardine, 'United Societies', 48, 247–50; Jardine, 'The "Petitione for Margaret Lachlisone" of 18 April 1685', 'The first post-martyrdom sources of 1687', 'The "Galloway" memorandum of the Killing Times', 'The woman who never was'.

132   Public Opinion in Early Modern Scotland, c.1560–1707

Societies in favour of the covenants, both made in May 1685. Having fled to Dutch exile after being convicted of treason for taking the Test with an explanation, the earl of Argyll landed on Scotland's west coast on 20 May hoping to stimulate a rising of Campbells and covenanters against James as an uncovenanted Catholic monarch. Recent studies of this attempt have confirmed that militants mistrusted Argyll, despite his covenanting rhetoric, while swift military action by the government discouraged moderates from rising.[292] Separately, the United Societies made a protestation against the accession of an uncovenanted and unlawful Catholic king on 28 May with an armed force at Sanquhar, reiterating previous renunciations of allegiance.[293]

Meeting during these acts of defiance, James' first parliament condemned the covenants and extended the Test and bands to control dissent. New acts made it treason to swear the 1638 or 1643 covenants or defend them in writing or speech. After debate over whether the Test should be extended to 'ignorant People' and women, parliament required the Test of all Protestant proprietors, masters of ships and all adult male inhabitants in the burghs.[294] A new law required all proprietors to compel their tenants to 'live peaceably and regularly, free of all fanaticall disorders', by a clause in their tack (lease) or a signed bond, forfeiting half of their movables on failure. Parliament also confirmed the fining of husbands for their wives' conventicling.[295] It was further ordered that all subjects were liable to take the oath of allegiance on demand. The death penalty for refusing the 1684 abjuration oath was confirmed and extended to anyone attending a field conventicle.[296] At the same time, an indemnity allowed lesser fugitives to be readmitted to society by taking the oath of allegiance.[297] These oaths and bands aimed to establish control of Scottish opinions through male householders, but, as in previous instances, this approach met with resistance from landlords and tenants.[298] The oath of allegiance was refused by a group of twenty-eight men and women who were banished to the colonies in August 1685.[299]

By 1686, James had initiated a radical shift in his approach to the management of public opinion, towards what Raffe has called a 'multi-

---

[292] Doak, 'The "vanishing of a fantosme"? The 1685 Argyll Rising and the 'Covenanting' opposition'; Kennedy, 'Rebellion, government and the Scottish response to Argyll's rising of 1685'.
[293] Renwick and Shields, *Informatory Vindication*, 101–8. See chapter 1.
[294] Wodrow, *History*, ii, 523; *RPS* 1685/4/34, 13 May 1685.
[295] *RPS* 1685/4/23, 6 May 1685, 1685/4/57, 2 June 1685; Wodrow, *History*, ii, 521.
[296] *RPS* 1685/4/44, 22 May 1685; 1685/4/28, 8 May 1685, 1685/4/52, 2 June 1685.
[297] Cowan, *Covenanters*, 125.   [298] Wodrow, *History*, ii, 589.
[299] 'Banishment from Scotland, 1685'.

confessional experiment'.[300] After failing to convince the 1686 Scottish parliament to allow freedom of worship for Catholics, James exercised his royal prerogative on 12 February 1687 to suspend penal laws against dissent, allowing worship in private buildings for Catholics, 'moderate Presbyterians' and Quakers. This abandoned the principle of universal Protestantism established by Scottish law since the 1560 Reformation and enjoined since then by successive confessional and civil oaths. Even the religious toleration offered by the Cromwellian regime had only extended to forms of Protestantism. James' indulgence aimed to provide 'Ease' to 'tender Consciences' and 'unite the Hearts and Affections of our Subjects'. Though James never held a Scottish coronation, being unable to swear to uphold the reformed kirk, he stated that his subjects' 'Obedience and Service' were due to him 'by their Allegiance' and that no 'Difference in Religion' could alter this. A new oath of allegiance acknowledged him as 'rightful King' and 'supreme Governor' with a promise of non-resistance.[301] Within a month of the indulgence, presbyterian ministers were not required to take this oath, 'or any other Oath whatsoever', subject to their good behaviour.[302] From the end of June, presbyterians were allowed to worship in any building as long as they provided advance notification of the meeting to a crown officer and 'nothing be preached or taught among them, which may any ways tend to alienate the Hearts of Our People from Us or Our Government'.[303]

James' indulgences allowed freedom to covenanted consciences within traditional limitations on seditious speech and unauthorised meetings, if James was recognised as a rightful king. This policy had some precedent in the oaths of obedience implemented by the Cromwellian regime and Restoration bands for public peace, which, unlike a confessional oath, declaration or test, merely demanded civil non-resistance. But James' indulgence went further in requiring no oath or band from 'those whose Principles we can with any Safety trust'.[304] This was followed with a general pardon for those previously convicted of rebellion or leasing-making.[305] But not all were willing to accept the king's new terms. The United Societies made a testimony against the toleration in January 1688, asserting their intention to continue with field conventicles rather than

---

[300] Raffe, 'James VII's multi-confessional experiment'.
[301] Wodrow, *History*, ii, appendix, 187–9; *RPCS*, ser. 3, xiii, 123–4.
[302] Wodrow, *History*, ii, appendix, 192; *RPCS*, ser. 3, xiii, 138.
[303] Wodrow, *History*, ii, appendix, 194; *RPCS*, ser. 3, xiii, 156–8.
[304] Wodrow, *History*, ii, appendix, 187.
[305] James VII, *A Proclamation Containing His Majesties Gracious and Ample Indemnity*.

134   Public Opinion in Early Modern Scotland, c.1560–1707

acknowledge the royal supremacy or toleration for Catholics. Conversely, many dissenting ministers accepted James' toleration, joining a collective address in July 1687 thanking the king for his concessions.[306] In dissenting districts, meeting houses were set up and kirk sessions re-established. Yet laws against seditious speech did not stop indulged and established ministers from making fervent sermons against Catholicism.[307] As will be seen in the next chapter, James' inability to counter anti-Catholic opinions allowed William of Orange to launch an invasion in November 1688 with widespread support in Scotland.

3.4 Conclusions

From the Reformation to the Revolution, oaths offered the potential to create extra-institutional support for a regime or its opponents by engaging and directing the consciences and behaviour of swearers. Traditional bands, by which men and lords bound themselves to mutual promises of alliance and service, were repurposed by early reformers to build an associational movement. During the reign of James VI, both kirk and state created compulsory subscriptional bands and oaths for clerics and the laity at large. The 1581 King's Confession came to be seen by presbyterian activists as a voluntary national endorsement of presbyterian church government, allowing them to argue that subsequent shifts towards episcopacy and the royal supremacy broke the nation's covenant with God and offended the consciences of swearers. In response, the crown made greater use of individual oaths to create a more compliant church and nation, including a 1584 subscription and oaths of allegiance and obedience. From 1638, national adherence to a presbyterian constitution was re-asserted when men and women of all social levels were invited and then required to swear the National Covenant. Presented in compelling community settings, this remarkable oath sustained a successful armed rebellion and an ecclesiastical and constitutional revolution by 1641 in the name of the covenanted nation. As events unfolded with the swearing of the 1643 Solemn League, however, this hegemony was strained by civil conflict. Public adherence became essential to the stability of regimes as levies were weakened by arguments over the obligations of the covenants, while royalists used bands of association to facilitate resistance. A striking number of auxiliary bands, subscriptions and renewals sought to maintain

---

[306] Renwick, *The Testimony of Some Persecuted Presbyterian Ministers*. See chapter 2.
[307] Raffe, 'James VII's multi-confessional experiment', 366–8.

appropriate covenanted opinions, enforced with threats of deposition, exclusion from office or excommunication. After taking Scotland into a commonwealth with a forced subscription, the Cromwellian regime made no attempt to control opinion with confessional oaths; instead, individual oaths of civil allegiance were required from office-holders. But divisions in Scottish opinion ensured that a 1653 rising failed because it could not appeal to covenanters and royalists. When the Restoration government demanded that office-holders subscribe to the royal supremacy, episcopalian church government and the unlawfulness of the covenants, covenanted individuals navigated this new environment with difficulty, choosing to conform wholly, partially or not at all as their consciences allowed. Where minds could not be changed, the government sought to control behaviour with bands of obedience for male householders, removing the obstinate through imprisonment, banishment and execution. Extreme judicial rigour was applied to men and women in disturbed districts, especially between 1681 and 1684, until James VII removed confessional oaths in order to secure Catholic toleration.

Like previous chapters, this chapter has confirmed the significance of conscientious commitments in forming early modern public opinion. Understood as a mental faculty separate from reason and emotion, the conscience was believed to regulate an individual's beliefs and actions according to God's laws and sworn obligations.[308] By promising to uphold constitutional and ecclesiastical principles, oath-takers could express and act on their opinions as a testimony to the truth. As George Gillespie stated in 1648, 'I cannot but discharge my conscience in giving a Testimony.'[309] This chapter also has shown how, from the Reformation to the Revolution, oaths provided an essential means of shaping and controlling opinions in a context of constitutional instability. Disputes over royal powers and forms of church government were fought out through competing oaths with deep social reach. The innovative swearing of confessional oaths in a parish context stimulated men and women to act according to their views, creating a problem of control addressed by supplementary bands and counter-oaths enjoining allegiance, obedience and abjuration. As a result of this dynamic, this era saw substantial expansion in the power of the state to police the behaviour and even the thoughts of men and women at large.

---

[308] Spurr, '"The strongest bond of conscience"', 152.
[309] Gillespie, *An Usefull Case of Conscience*, 29. I thank Neil McIntyre for bringing this source to my attention.

While the first two chapters showed how extra-institutional opinions could be presented publicly through protestations and petitions for political ends, with some consideration of how these devices could stimulate and engage opinion, this chapter has focused on how opinions were shaped and controlled by the swearing of oaths and how this influenced political outcomes. The next chapter will consider how oral, written and printed communications contributed to the management of extra-institutional opinions, highlighting the language in which collective opinions were represented in public discourse.

CHAPTER 4

Public Communications

But becaus the malicious hearts of our conspired enemies ... seduce the true and simple people ... we have thought good to notifie and make knowne the certaintie of the whole mater, for satisfactioun of those whose judgement yitt remaineth in suspense.

Proclamation, 14 May 1568[1]

[I]t is hard to compell a conscience even to that which is just, before it be perswaded.

David Hume of Godscroft to Bishop James Law of Orkney, 1608[2]

[N]one can justly blame any, who is a Subject to the Monarch of Great Britain, modestly to endeavour the satisfaction of his Reason, Judgement and Conscience.

A Brief Account of His Sacred Majestie's Descent (1681)

In the early modern era, print technology and expanding literacy enabled a substantial expansion in the circulation of persuasive messages. Accounts of England's post-Reformation print culture and public sphere have traced the burgeoning of public debate through printed pamphlets, petitions and newsbooks produced, with varying levels of censorship, in London's unusually large and concentrated print market.[3] But, as Peter Lake has emphasised, this scholarship describes England and should not be taken as a model for early modern Europe.[4] Moreover, as Andrew Pettegree has observed in relation to Reformation studies, 'by elevating the book in this way as a primary instrument of change, we are promoting a view of reading that is essentially modern.'[5] An understanding of how public communications shaped and expressed public opinion requires the study of formats relevant to particular historical contexts. For early modern Scotland, that

---

[1] *TSP* no. 197; Calderwood, *History*, ii, 405–12.   [2] Calderwood, *History*, vi, 730.
[3] See historiographical discussion in Introduction.
[4] Lake, 'Publics and participation: England, Britain and Europe in the "post-Reformation"', 849.
[5] Pettegree, *Reformation and the Culture of Persuasion*, 8.

138   Public Opinion in Early Modern Scotland, c.1560–1707

means studying oral and manuscript formats alongside print, recognising that the printing press provided an increasingly important but not yet transformative technology in this northern realm. The inclusion of formal oral communications, including proclamations, sermons and Gaelic political poetry, will help to explain the engagement of those who were less likely to have had the opportunity to learn to read, especially women and vernacular Gaelic speakers. The inclusion of circular letters and manuscript tracts will reveal the circulation of political polemic despite active censorship. These robust oral and manuscript patterns of communication combined with a rising flow of English and Scottish prints to produce a distinctive communications culture in early modern Scotland.

Compared to its southern neighbour, Scotland's smaller print market was constrained to a greater degree by relative costs, was less centralised and had a more devolved regulatory system. Though the nature of the Scottish print market has been construed as providing 'shallower foundations' for a public sphere, nevertheless this differing context produced appeals to Scottish opinion at large and concepts of national opinion.[6] This book has started to explain this phenomenon by examining protestations, petitions and oaths, with some mention of print, manuscript and oral communications relating to these devices. This chapter will provide a broader assessment of public communications and their influence on opinion politics. It will ask how monarchs and their opponents used persuasive messages and censorship to stimulate, express and contain the opinions of men and women across Scotland. In considering how collective opinions were presented in public, especially in proclamations and political pamphlets, it will identify the language used to describe and imagine opinion at large.

Differences in vernacular language will complicate this assessment. Because Scots was the primary language of the kirk and crown, this chapter will focus on communications in this language. Sometimes called 'Inglis' in contemporary sources, Scots was a dialect of English predominantly spoken in the south and north-east of Scotland.[7] The Scots language remained distinct from English in the early modern period, though some Anglicisation occurred with the diffusion of English books and tracts to Scotland, the migration of English printers to Scotland and increased travel by Scots to England after the 1603 regal union. Because Latin was required

---

[6] Harris, 'The Anglo–Scottish treaty of union, 1707 in 2007: Defending the Revolution, defeating the Jacobites', 44.
[7] 'Inglis, n.', *DOST*.

Public Communications

to study law, medicine and theology at continental universities, Scotland's cultural elite continued to value this language, with Scottish humanists producing fine neo-classical poetry and prose in manuscript and print.[8] This meant that the framing of public communications in Scots instead of Latin signalled a desire to address broader audiences. By the late sixteenth century, parliamentary laws were being printed in Scots for 'the knawlege of all the subjectis'.[9] When former archbishop Patrick Adamson submitted a Latin document to the synod of St Andrews in April 1581 abjuring erastian episcopalianism, his brethren insisted that he resubmit it in the vernacular 'that all might understand'.[10] The resulting paper was printed as anti-episcopalian propaganda in 1598 'for the great benefite of many'.[11]

The Scots language, however, had limited social reach in the north and west, roughly contiguous with the geographical Highland region, where vernacular Gaelic (often called 'Irish' in Scottish sources) was spoken. Literacy for educated clan elites and learned orders included Scots, Latin and Classical Common Gaelic, a written form used across Scotland and Ireland.[12] To improve the cultural integration of his realm, James VI aimed to expand Scots fluency and literacy among clan chiefs and gentry in the western isles, approving in 1609 orders that 'everie gentilmen and yeamen' in this area should send their heir to a Lowland school to 'speik, reid and wryte Inglische'.[13] By 1639, Glasgow hosted four 'Inglische scoolls' and in 1654, there were ten masters of 'Scotis scooles'.[14] In the northern and eastern Highlands, clan elites sent their sons to burgh schools, with some attending grammar school in Edinburgh.[15]

Beyond the educated clan chiefs, gentry (*fine*), bards (*filidh*) and clergy, official communications in the *Gàidhealtachd* relied on oral translation. Protestantism was embedded in much of the Highlands by multi-lingual clergy who worked from Latin and Scots texts and a handful of Gaelic prints, including a translation of a Genevan liturgy (1567), an Irish New Testament (1602) and a few editions of catechisms (1631, 1651, 1688)

---

[8] Reid, *Bridging the Continental Divide*; Reid and McOmish (eds.), *NeoLatin Literature and Literary Culture in Early Modern Scotland*; Verweij, *The Literary Culture of Early Modern Scotland: Manuscript Production and Transmission, 1560–1625*, ch. 1.

[9] *RPS* 1592/4/67, 5 June 1592.   [10] Quoted in Mullen, *Episcopacy*, 71.

[11] Adamson, *The Recantation of Maister Patrik Adamsone*, sig. A1r.

[12] Dawson, 'The *Gàidhealtachd* and the emergence of the Scottish Highlands', 282–4.

[13] *RPCS* ser. 1, ix, 29. In 1616, mastery of 'Inglische' was required for the inheritance of property. *RPCS* ser. 1, x, 775.

[14] *ERBG*, i, 397 and ii, 284–5.

[15] Macinnes, 'Crowns, clans and *fine*: the 'civilising' of Scottish Gaeldom, 1568–1637', 47.

140   Public Opinion in Early Modern Scotland, c.1560–1707

and psalms (1659, 1684, 1702, 1705).[16] From 1648, the kirk sought to improve the availability of bilingual clergy by providing bursaries to train Gaelic speakers for the ministry. Yet this region also had a strong cultural tradition of spoken and sung verse and poetry. Composed by learned bards and men and women of gentry status, poetry could communicate political ideas through gatherings in landed households. Allan I. Macinnes has emphasised the historical value of hundreds of vernacular Gaelic poems and songs composed in response to the turbulent events of the Covenanting revolution. Increasingly devised by local elites, including women, these provided 'political propaganda and social comment' designed to 'disseminate topical information and to formulate public opinion'.[17]

Among Scots speakers, political communication was aided by rising literacy. As elsewhere in Europe, this change was enabled by three over-lapping factors: basic schooling slowly became more available through the provision of parish schools; socio-economic development made education a more worthwhile attainment, especially in burghs; and reading became a desirable skill for the godly. Also typical was the pattern of more men being educated than women and more women being able to read than write, making female signature literacy a useful benchmark for minimum literacy rates. In a review of sixteenth-century legal papers, Margaret Sanderson found signature literacy rates of about 70 per cent for noblewomen and 30 per cent for female relatives of lairds and burgesses, while female relatives of tenant farmers or small proprietors were very unlikely to write.[18] By the mid-seventeenth century, literacy had improved, especially in urban areas. In Glasgow, the burgh council stipulated that poor children should be educated at no charge alongside fee-paying scholars (though the opportunity cost of lost wages and labour probably prevented some parents from taking up this offer).[19] Rab Houston's analysis of covenants signed in 1638 and 1643 showed male signature literacy of 47 to 68 per cent in Lowland urban parishes (with the highest literacy in Edinburgh) and much lower rates of 10 to 30 per cent in rural parishes. Houston has posited a 'very approximate estimate' of 25 per cent male signature literacy as a national average for the 1640s, from which a modestly higher rate of reading literacy could be supposed. By c.1700, most middling tenant

---

[16] MacLean, *Typographia Scoto-Gadelica, Or, Books Printed in the Gaelic of Scotland from the Year 1567 to the Year 1914*, 49, 65, 69–70, 83, 317–21; Dawson, 'Calvinism and the Gàidhealtacht in Scotland'; Meek, 'The Reformation and Gaelic culture: perspectives on patronage, language and literature in John Carswell's translation of "The Book of Common Order"', 37–41.

[17] Macinnes, 'Scottish Gaeldom, 1638–1651', 59, 63, 76.

[18] Sanderson, *A Kindly Place? Living in Sixteenth-Century Scotland*, 137.   [19] *ERBG*, ii, 284–5.

Public Communications

farmers, craftsmen and merchants were likely to be literate (c.70–80 per cent) and literacy among male servants and labourers had risen to perhaps 50 per cent, with rates remaining lower in rural areas, especially to the north.[20] Personal testimonies suggest higher reading rates in godly households, encompassing servants and females. Across this period, literacy accelerated as attainment was passed to the next generation. In schools and the home, the core learning texts were the Bible, the catechism and the psalm book, emphasising the fundamental connection between reading and religion in this era.[21] Though Scottish presses produced far less of the cheap printed storybooks and ballads that fed popular literacy in England, these texts circulated north via pedlars.[22]

As reading slowly expanded, so too did Scotland's domestic print market. Printing was established in Edinburgh by royal licence from 1507, with ballads, breviaries and bibles featuring in early print runs. Scottish printers published liturgies, psalm books, scriptural commentary, practical piety, medieval and contemporary poetry, pamphlets, catechisms, schoolbooks and songs for local markets.[23] As Adam Fox has noted, early modern Edinburgh remained 'overwhelmingly the biggest hub of Scottish printing', fed by monopolies granted to printers for the church and crown.[24] However, presses were established in Aberdeen from 1622 and Glasgow from 1638, each supporting a small regional print economy sustained by university theses and, in Aberdeen, a long-running almanack.[25] Alastair Mann's analysis of the total annual book and single-sheet outputs shows slow growth before 1630, spikes in the 1640s and around the 1660 Restoration and more substantial growth from the 1680s and especially the 1690s.[26] As will be seen, growth reflected an increasing recourse to print by crown and kirk for administrative purposes, including the printing of proclamations, acts and oaths.[27] Chapbook and broadside ballad printing increased from the 1680s, confirming the downward spread of literacy as demand increased for ephemeral print.[28] After a few short-

[20] Houston, 'The literacy myth?: Illiteracy in Scotland 1630–1760', 86, 88, 90–9.
[21] Smout, 'Born again at Cambuslang', 122–6.
[22] Stevenson, 'Reading, writing and gender in early modern Scotland', 340–1; Hill, 'The lamentable tale of lost ballads in England, 1557–1640'.
[23] Stevenson, 'Reading, writing and gender', 338–43.
[24] Fox, 'The emergence of the Scottish broadside ballad in the late seventeenth and early eighteenth centuries', 173.
[25] Bevan, 'Scotland', 698; Walsby, 'Cheap print and the academic market: the printing of dissertations in sixteenth-century Louvain'.
[26] Mann, *Scottish Book Trade*, 215. [27] *RPCS*, ser. 3, i, 635.
[28] Fox, '"Little story books" and "small pamphlets" in Edinburgh, 1680-1760: The making of the Scottish chapbook'; Fox, 'Emergence of the Scottish broadside ballad', 172.

142   Public Opinion in Early Modern Scotland, c.1560–1707

lived editions, regular domestic newspapers were established by licence from 1699, providing news more cheaply than imported papers with the added benefit of local advertisements.[29]

In this era, the scale of Scottish printing was limited by high investment and running costs, with presses, type, skilled workers and high-quality paper all needing to be imported.[30] Books purchased by educated elites in Scotland continued to be imported from larger print centres, including Antwerp, Amsterdam, London and Paris, aided by exemption from import duties before 1676.[31] The paucity of illustrations in Scottish prints signals a key limitation in the market not rectified until the 1730s.[32] While German broadsides featured engravings of individual witches and their grisly executions, it is only on a London print of a Scottish manuscript tract, the 1591 *Newes from Scotland*, that a similar image can be found.[33] As a consequence, visual images will not be a significant factor in this chapter (though Chapter 6 will consider a notable exception from 1701).

Censorship also restricted the supply of domestic print for political purposes. While in England the Stationers' Company managed the large and concentrated London print market, no guild or company oversaw Scotland's dispersed presses. Authorised printers to the crown and church were named with monopoly powers over certain genres. Pre-publication censorship was imposed through a licensing system by which a specified agent of the crown (privy council, bishop, general assembly, university or burgh council) reviewed individual works and gave permission to print. An act of 1552 ordered that no printer 'prent ony bukis, ballattis, sangis, blasphematiounis, rymes or tragedeis, outher in Latine or Inglis toung' without review and licencing on pain of confiscation of goods and banishment.[34] In 1568, the general assembly ordered Edinburgh printer Thomas Bassandyne to recall a psalm book found to contain a profane ballad and reminded him to secure a license for any future publications.[35] In practice, many uncontroversial texts were published without prior review, especially as print volumes expanded, but licenses for individual

---

[29] Bowie, 'Newspapers, the early modern public sphere and the 1704–05 *Worcester* affair', 12–3.
[30] Mann notes that French paper was imported from Amsterdam, Rotterdam and Middelburg with English paper being imported from the 1680s. Mann, *Scottish Book Trade*, 67, 80, 135.
[31] Mann, *Scottish Book Trade*, 73, 137–8.
[32] Rock, 'Richard Cooper Sr and Scottish book illustration', 82–3.
[33] Warfield, 'Witchcraft illustrated: the crime of witchcraft in early modern German news broadsheets'.
[34] *RPS* A1552/2/26, 1 February 1552.   [35] *APGA*, I, 125–6.

Public Communications

works were sought when printers anticipated difficulties or wished to secure monopoly protection (for example for lucrative almanac titles). When offensive titles slipped through the net, requirements for review were renewed.[36] Provocative tracts might be printed without identifying the publisher, author or date of publication. Yet the relative smallness of Edinburgh and other printing towns made it difficult to hide underground printers like London's 1588–9 Marprelate press, seen by historians as an important catalyst for public debate in Elizabethan England.[37]

Offensive public communications could attract capital charges of sedition for the printer or author. From 1425, a series of laws against leasing-making sought to prevent discord between monarch and people caused by false or disrespectful news or talk. The making and spreading of seditious slander was outlawed on pain of death and loss of goods. From the late sixteenth century, these laws were reiterated and expanded as successive regimes responded to the increasing circulation of political arguments.[38] Initially expressed in terms of speech, by the 1580s the laws mentioned written or printed works and authors. Under these laws, indigenous and imported texts could be pursued for post-production censorship. In 1584, parliament ordered all copies of George Buchanan's *Rerum Scoticarum Historia* (1682) and his *De Jure Regni apud Scotos* (1679) to be handed in for the removal of 'syndrie offensive materis worthie to be delete', with a fine of £200 for refusers.[39]

These limitations on domestic printing ensured that manuscript texts remained significant. Though poor survival rates impede study, Sebastiaan Verweij has traced the circulation of manuscript poetry and prose through courtly, urban and landed networks in the Jacobean period.[40] Manuscript offered an efficient means of circulation in like-minded circles, such as the epistolary community of godly gentry in Fife whose exchanges in the early seventeenth century have been uncovered by Jamie Reid-Baxter.[41] In a more public mode, handwritten placards and pasquils (pasquinades or libels) were posted on doors or left on church seats to make anonymous

---

[36] Mann, *Scottish Book Trade*, 139–41.
[37] Black, 'The Martin Marprelate Tracts'; Bevan, 'Scotland', 689.
[38] *RPS* 1425/3/23, 12 March 1425; 1458/3/38, 6 March 1458; 1540/12/25, 10 December 1540; A1555/6/40, 20 June 1555; 1567/4/12, 19 April 1567; 1584/5/14, 22 May 1584; 1585/12/9, 10 December 1585; 1594/4/26, 8 June 1594; 1640/6/51, 9 June 1640; A1700/10/57, 31 January 1701; 1703/5/191, 16 September 1703; Mann, *Scottish Book Trade*, 164.
[39] *RPS* 1584/5/14, 22 May 1584.   [40] Verweij, *Literary Culture*.
[41] Baxter, 'Elizabeth Melville, Lady Culross: new light from Fife'.

144   Public Opinion in Early Modern Scotland, c.1560–1707

attacks on civic figures.[42] In January 1558, urban support for religious reformation was signalled by the posting of notices threatening unproductive friars with eviction in the name of the poor and disabled of Scotland.[43]

Public modes of oral communication included proclamations and sermons. Promulgation by open proclamation was required to activate ordinances and prevent subjects from arguing that they were unaware of new rules. After being read aloud at the mercat (market) cross or tolbooth (council house) in designated burghs, a proclamation text was posted for further consultation.[44] Manuscript copies were sent to the relevant officers and increasingly copies were printed.[45] As elsewhere in Europe, sermons were central to the formation of reformed Protestant culture and attendant political commitments.[46] Macinnes has noted that 'the pulpit was the main medium of propagating Covenanting ideology' in Gaelic-speaking regions.[47] Powerful speaking skills were encouraged in Scottish clergy by university instruction in rhetoric followed by practical training for expectants in the presbyteries.[48] Parish clergy stayed abreast of current affairs through the Scottish reformed kirk's hierarchical network of church courts, reaching from the kirk session to district presbyteries, regional synods and the general assembly. As previous chapters have indicated, these authorised channels could be appropriated, whether by the staging of collective protestations at the mercat cross or making open attacks on crown policy from the pulpit.

This chapter will assess practices of public persuasion and the rhetoric of public opinion in a context of slowly expanding communications. The first

[42] 'Pasquil(l), Pasquile, *n.*', *DOST*. The term derives from anti-papal poems attributed to a fictional 'Pasquillus' posted on statues on New Year's Day in sixteenth-century Rome. MacDonald, *George Lauder (1603-1670): Life and Writings*, 22.

[43] Knox, *Works*, i, 320–1.

[44] MacCannell, 'Cultures of Proclamation: The Decline and Fall of the Anglophone News Process, 1460–1642'; Der Weduwen, '"Everyone has hereby been warned": the structure and typography of broadsheet ordinances and the communication of governance in the early seventeenth-century Dutch Republic', 251–2.

[45] *TSP* no. 240; *APGA* i, 177–8. It is likely that printed proclamations were sold in Scotland. MacCannell has found evidence of this in England. In Dutch cities, prints could be distributed free of charge. During the Cromwellian occupation of Scotland (1650–9), proclamations were printed and sold. MacCannell, 'Cultures of Proclamation', 133–7; Der Weduwen, '"Everyone has hereby been warned"', 252; Spurlock, 'Cromwell's Edinburgh press and the development of print culture in Scotland', 194.

[46] Todd, *The Culture of Protestantism*, ch. 1; Pettegree, *Reformation and the Culture of Persuasion*, ch. 2.

[47] Macinnes, 'Scottish Gaeldom, 1638–1651', 64.

[48] By 1600, most Scottish clerics had at least attended college and by 1638 nearly all held a Master of Arts degree, with some clerics completing postgraduate study on the continent. Whytock, *"An Educated Clergy": Scottish Theological Education and Training in the Kirk and Secession, 1560–1850*, 1–55.

Public Communications 145

section will show how post-Reformation concerns about misleading 'bruits', or rumours, stimulated increasingly elaborate efforts to inculcate correct opinions in the subjects at large.[49] While metaphorical figures could be employed to speak for the realm, the estates and the people, after the 1581 confessional band, more direct claims could be made about the laity's sworn commitments. The second section will consider what Mann has called a 'flood of propaganda' appearing from 1638.[50] Going beyond the protestations, petitions and covenant oaths already discussed, this will evaluate efforts to manage grassroots opinions and the difficulties faced by the king and his royalist supporters in this. The third section highlights a range of efforts by the Restoration government to build a royalist consensus, aided by selective reprinting of English pamphlets, and concurrent attempts by presbyterian dissenters to sustain and express the nation's 'true' opinion. Though print will feature in this chapter, attention will be paid to oral and manuscript communications to capture the unique and changing communicative context of early modern Scotland.

4.1 Bruits, Broadsides and Books, 1560–1636

In her account of medieval Stewart kings, Katie Stevenson has emphasised the promotion of their stature as imperial monarchs through written and visual propaganda.[51] For the sixteenth century, there is no assessment of public communications in Scotland comparable to Lake's study of Elizabethan 'politics of publicity', though exchanges during the Marian civil war have been described by Jane Dawson as 'the first major Scottish propaganda war aimed at swaying a wide spectrum of the political nation'.[52] Led by literary and intellectual scholars, research for this period has tended to focus on key texts and authors, including Buchanan, Andrew Melville and James VI.[53] This section, therefore, will provide a new angle on this period by considering how public communications sought to

---

[49] 'Brute, Bruit, n.', *DOST*.

[50] Mann, 'Embroidery to enterprise: the role of women in the book trade of early modern Scotland', 142.

[51] Stevenson, *Power and Propaganda: Scotland 1306–1488*.

[52] Lake, *Bad Queen Bess?: Libels, Secret Histories, and the Politics of Publicity in the Reign of Queen Elizabeth I*; Dawson, *Scotland Re-Formed, 1488–1587*, 270–1. For the Reformation period, see Tapscott, 'Propaganda and persuasion in the early Scottish Reformation, c.1527–1557'.

[53] Mason and Smith (trans and eds.), *A Dialogue on the Law of Kingship among the Scots*; Burns, *The True Law of Kingship: Concepts of Monarchy in Early-Modern Scotland*; Reid and Mason (eds.), *Andrew Melville (1545–1622): Writings, Reception, and Reputation*; McGinnis and Williamson (trans and eds.), *The British Union: A Critical Edition and Translation of David Hume of Godscroft's De Unione Insulae Britannicae*; Verweij, *Literary Culture of Early Modern Scotland*.

146   Public Opinion in Early Modern Scotland, c.1560–1707

influence opinions at large from the personal reign of Mary I to the early rule of Charles I. This will show that though secrecy in government affairs remained the norm, a desire to manage opinions in a context of religious and political conflict led the crown to use proclamations, pamphlets and books to spread authorised information, including books written by James VI himself. At the same time, censorship blocked challenging communications, forcing dissidents to rely on oral and manuscript circulation and overseas presses. In this era, a distrust of plebeian capacities encouraged an emphasis on correcting the people's misunderstanding of events. Representations of public opinion tended to be metaphorical, as writers employed allegorical figures to express national grievances. By the 1620s, however, change can be discerned as presbyterian authors contrasted the sworn commitments of the people with the decisions of the 1618 general assembly.

As David Coast has emphasised, because commoners were thought to be susceptible to false arguments, disrespectful murmurs were feared as a seditious precursor to rebellion.[54] To shape opinions, Scottish governments published authorised information and persuasive arguments through proclamations that assumed a capacity in listeners to hear and understand. When Mary's reputation came under attack in her short personal reign, the queen sought to correct her people's mistaken attitudes. A proclamation on 15 September 1565 excoriated written and spoken 'untrew reportis' designed to 'fyle [pollute] the eyis of the blind peopill'.[55] It offered instead a justification for royal policies and promised to pass desired legislation at a future parliament.[56] Again in 1567, the queen attacked damaging rumours that had 'perswadit' the people to think badly of her. Asserting that her reign could be compared to the 'maist happie tyme . . . in mannis memorie', she made 'plane declaratioun of hir mynd and part to all hir gude subjectis' so they could resolve their doubts.[57]

Mary's opponents also played for public support, calling on audiences to take action as right-thinking members of the church and nation. During this period of civil conflict, rumours, drawings, placards, broadsides and proclamations all sought to undermine Mary's moral authority.[58] In 1567, after the murder of Mary's husband Henry, 'placardes and billis and

---

[54] Coast, *News and Rumour in Jacobean England: Information, Court Politics and Diplomacy, 1618–25*, 82–3.
[55] 'Fyle, v.', *DOST*.   [56] *RPCS*, ser. i, i, 372; 'Fyle, v.', *DOST*.
[57] *RPCS*, ser. i, i, 514–5; *TSP* no. 170.
[58] McElroy, 'Imagining the "Scottis natioun": populism and propaganda in Scottish satirical broadsides', 323–4; Cranstoun (ed.), *Satirical Poems of the Time of the Reformation*, ii, 82.

ticquettis of defamatioun' were 'sett up under silence of nycht in diverse publict places'.[59] In September 1565, a muster for the queen was countered with a call urging all Scotsmen to defend the reformed kirk and nation 'as they would be compted right worshippers, and faithfull members of this common wealth'.[60] Similarly, a printed proclamation of 11 June 1567 asked listeners to recognise 'the most miserabill stait of this Common Weill' and help secure the realm.[61] An elaborate rhetorical foray from May 1568 spoke as if in the voice of the infant James, explaining the actions of the King's party and refuting narratives provided by the Queen's party that threatened to mislead 'the true and simple people'.[62]

Alongside proclamations, anti-Marian satirical ballads were circulated on broadsides printed in Edinburgh by Robert Lekpreuik, later named printer to the King.[63] Distribution of these poems outside of Edinburgh is suggested by the printing of multiple editions and evidence of circulation to provincial towns like Montrose.[64] As Tricia McElroy has observed, these verses were 'expertly sculpted out of literary tradition', using sophisticated rhetorical forms to convey political messages to educated elites in Scotland and England.[65] These constructions indicated a role for the people as distressed commoners who expressed national grievances and pursued personal moral reformation, guided by right-thinking Scottish nobles. A 1567 dialogue between two gentlemen, *Ane Declaratioun of the Lordis Just Quarrel*, referred to the election of kings by a popular majority in ancient times, though, as in Buchanan's political works, the responsibility for contemporary political action was given to aristocrats, not the people at large.[66] The 'common breist' might 'burst' with 'sorrow' at the queen's immoral conduct, but it was the nobles who would 'couragiouslie Hazard thame self to saf vs all fra shame'.[67] Similarly, though the 1572 *Lamentation of the Comounis of Scotland* spoke in the voice of traders, craftsmen and farmers whose livelihoods were lost to civil war, their only role was to express their complaints and call on God for vengeance.[68]

Other texts adopted female figures to express the grievances of the people and the nation, including the kail-selling Maddie, a plebeian truth-telling character, and 'Lady Scotland', wife to 'Sir John the

---

[59] *RPS* 1567/4/12, 19 April 1567.   [60] Calderwood, *History*, ii, app, 575.
[61] *TSP* no 172; *RPCS*, ser. 1, i, 519–20.   [62] *TSP* no. 197; Calderwood. *History*, ii, 405–12.
[63] Cranstoun (ed.), *Satirical Poems*, i; McElroy, 'Imagining the "Scottis natioun"', 324–5.
[64] Cranstoun (ed.), *Satirical Poems*, ii, 76; Verweij, *Literary Culture*, 33.
[65] McElroy, 'Imagining the "Scottis natioun"', 326–7.
[66] Mason, 'People power? George Buchanan on resistance and the common man'.
[67] Cranstoun (ed.), *Satirical Poems*, i, 57–64.   [68] *Ibid.*, i, 221–5.

148   Public Opinion in Early Modern Scotland, c.1560–1707

Commonweil', a personification of Scotland's common good. Evoking the soundscape of the marketplace, *Maddies Proclamation* conflated the voices of women hawking their wares with official voices heard at the mercat cross. Addressing her audience as 'my Lords', Maddie expressed sadness for the assassination of the regent Moray and charged her listeners to stay true to the 'contractit band' sworn at the coronation of the young James VI in 1567.[69] Another tract, *Maddeis Lamentatioun*, called on the 'commonis' to mourn Moray while urging his noble allies to be true to his memory.[70] A more elite female voice spoke for the realm in *The Complaint of Scotland*. This ballad conveyed grief and anger for Scotland's 'deir', the murdered Moray, and called on both the 'nobill Lordis' and 'commouns' to avenge the nation.[71] The *Lamentatioun of Lady Scotland* presented an elaborate allegory in which civil war among the people of Scotland (the offspring of Lady Scotland and Sir John the Commonweil) had caused Sir John to flee, leaving Lady Scotland bereft. In her lamentation, Lady Scotland castigated each sector of Scottish society – lords, lairds, lawyers, merchants, crafts and yeoman commoners – for their moral failings and called for individual reformation, giving each man a personal role in the nation's cause.[72]

Continuing instability in the minority of James VI stimulated further proclamations to combat rumours, asking reasonable men not to be hoodwinked like the silly multitude. In 1578, these countered 'untrew reportis and malicious inventis' with the 'simple trewth'. When the trial of former regent James Douglas, fourth earl of Morton in 1581 stimulated 'seditious and sclanderous bruittis', a proclamation explained the purpose of the trial.[73] The young king's favour for his French Catholic cousin, Esmé Stewart, first duke of Lennox, stimulated another proclamation in 1581 confirming Lennox's conversion to Protestantism against seditious rumours believed by 'the symple people'.[74] A further proclamation identified these 'maist false and untrew bruites and informationis' as seditious attempts to use religion as a pretext for rebellion, ordering all lieges, including nobles and kirk ministers, to stop repeating such rumours lest they influence 'the simple multitude' who were 'maist subject to change and mutabilitie'.[75] After Lennox's death in 1583, a proclamation sought to suppress 'libellis, in write and prent, in prois and ryme' about the duke.

---

[69] *Ibid.*, i, 149–55. Dated by Cranstoun to c. April 1570 (vol. ii, 100). See chapter 3 on this band.
[70] *Ibid.*, i, 144–8.   [71] *Ibid.*, i, 95–99.
[72] *Ibid.*, i, 226–39. See conclusion for discussion of a similar John the Commonweal character in Sir David Lindsay's earlier 1552 play, *Ane Satyre of the Thrie Estaitis*.
[73] *TSP* no. 377, 383, 448; *RPCS*, ser. 1, iii, 3–4, 15, 388.
[74] *TSP* no. 457; *RPCS*, ser 1, iii, 431–2.   [75] *TSP* no. 465; *RPCS*, ser. 1, iii, 492.

Public Communications 149

This proclamation expressed confidence in 'the judgement and censure of all godlie, honnorable and reasonable personis' by expecting them to recognise the falsity of these texts.[76]

At the same time, greater control was exerted over public communications by imprisoning printers, offering rewards for the identification of authors, reiterating licensing regulations and applying sedition laws to all, including ministers in the pulpit. Reacting to the 1574 printing of an objectionable dialogue pamphlet on church affairs, the privy council imprisoned the printer and insisted on pre-publication review to ensure texts were 'godlie and tollerable'.[77] A £500 reward was offered in February 1583 for the identification of the author of a seditious 'pasquil' posted in St Giles' Kirk.[78] In the same year, a new privy council ordinance required the licensing of books, ballads, songs, rhymes or tragedies and in 1584 a controversial slate of parliamentary acts included an elaboration of the law against seditious speech holding all subjects responsible for slanderous talk, regardless of social rank.[79] The act also claimed civil jurisdiction over clerical speech, indicating unhappiness with oppositional sermons.[80]

With more attention being paid to the political capacity of subjects at large, the king and his agents provided more extensive persuasive arguments for crown policies. To justify the controversial 'Black Acts' of 1584, archbishop Adamson published in Edinburgh and London an explanatory tract, *A Declaratioun of the Kingis Maiestes Intentioun and Meaning Toward the Last Actis of Parliament*. This presented a corrective to false 'brutis' and the 'seditious interprises' of 'rebellious subiects' who acted 'under Pretext of Religion'.[81] As is well known, James himself wrote and printed a series of vernacular books with didactic purposes. Using an accessible dialogue format, his 1597 *Daemonologie* explained the threat posed by witches and urged magistrates to pursue them; the *Trew Law of Free Monarchies* (1598) argued that the Stewart monarchy was not limited by law and defended James' claim to the English throne; and *Basilikon Doron* (1599) outlined his practical view of the monarchy in the form of an advice book for his son Henry.[82] Having first printed *Basilikon Doron* in an exclusive edition,

---

[76] *RPCS*, ser. 1, iii, 583–4.
[77] Calderwood, iii, 301; *TSP* no. 316; *RPCS*, ser. 1, ii, 387; Bardgett, 'Foure parische kirkes'. The printer, Robert Lekpreuik, had been pursued for unlicensed printing in 1570, 1571 and 1572. Henderson, 'Lekpreuik [Lekprevick], Robert'.
[78] *TSP* no. 483; *RPCS*, ser. 1, iii, 549–50.   [79] *RPCS*, ser. 1, iii, 587.
[80] *RPS* 1584/5/14, 22 May 1584. See chapters 1 and 3 for more on clerical speech and the 1584 act.
[81] *RPCS*, ser. 1, iii, 702–3; Adamson, *A Declaratioun of the Kingis Maiestes Intentioun*, sig. Aiir.
[82] James VI and I, *Political Writings*; Normand and Roberts (eds.), *Witchcraft in Early Modern Scotland*, ch. 10; Burns, *The True Law of Kingship*; Rickard, *Authorship and Authority: The*

150   Public Opinion in Early Modern Scotland, c.1560–1707

James authorised a larger print run to refute 'calumnies' raised by pirated manuscript copies, ensuring that 'the honest godly sort' would not be misled.[83] After the 1603 union, James published an anonymous defence of the English oath of allegiance in 1607, followed by an acknowledged edition in 1609. As Jane Rickard has commented in relation to *Daemonologie*, these books sought to establish James as 'a source of knowledge to be appreciated and revered'.[84] In 1616, James provided a national textbook on royalism with *God and the King*.[85] A dialogue text explaining the oath of allegiance and asserting the royal supremacy, the book was ordered to be acquired by all Scottish school teachers (male or female, teaching in Latin or Scots), all universities and 'everie familie within this kingdom quhair thair is ony that can reid'. All ministers were to be given an abridged version to rehearse with their flocks. These extensive requirements reflected the king's understanding that 'the terrour of lawes withoute instructioun and edificatioun is bot ane imperfyte remeid [remedy]'.[86] The burgh of Perth ordered 500 copies and the master of the grammar school at Ayr took seventy in English and thirty-four in Latin at eight shillings per book, though in 1620, the king's agent, James Primrose, complained that some customers were slow to pay and others had expressed violent resentment towards the book.[87]

Other authors produced written and printed books in favour of James' policies and oral and printed poems flattering him as king. James' accession to the English throne in 1603 stimulated poetry celebrating his greatness and mourning his departure from Scotland, while his pursuit of a closer British union stimulated the production of more poetry and several pro-union pamphlets.[88] His sole return visit to Scotland in 1617 led to the public presentation and printing of over 130 poems and speeches.[89] Though most of these were presented in Latin, James' progress included elaborate visual pageantry as he moved through the Borders, Fife and central and western Lowlands, going as far north as Perth and including Stirling, Glasgow and Dumfries.[90]

Writings of James VI and I; Lake, 'The king (the queen) and the Jesuit: James Stuart's *True Law of Free Monarchies* in context/s'.
[83] James VI and I, *Political Writings*, 4–5.   [84] Rickard, *Authorship and Authority*, 105.
[85] [Mocket], *God and the King*; Porter, 'Mocket, Richard'.   [86] *RPCS*, ser. 1, x, 530–1, 534–8.
[87] *RPCS*, ser. 1, xi, 392, xii, 42–3, 118–9, 229, 601.
[88] Galloway, *The Union of England and Scotland, 1603–1608*, 30–57.
[89] Green, 'The king returns'; King, 'Ἐπιβατήριον ad Regem in Scotiam redeuntem' (1617); Anderson, 'Ecloga I' and 'Ecloga II' (1617).
[90] MacNeill, 'The Scottish progress of James VI'. For James' 1591 wedding, see Stevenson, *Scotland's Last Royal Wedding*.

Public Communications 151

Alongside these promotional efforts, James asserted greater control over oppositional speech and writing after the arrest of two presbyterian booksellers stimulated a violent disturbance against the king in December 1596, as discussed in Chapter 2.[91] In February 1597, the king's printer, Robert Waldegrave, was found guilty in the Court of Justiciary of 'tressonabill Imprenting' for having printed an annotated copy of a 1592 parliamentary act in favour of the presbyterian kirk given to him by John Howison, minister in Cambuslang parish. Intended as presbyterian propaganda, copies had been purchased by Howieson and other clerics.[92] Though Waldegrave was not executed for treason, his trial made clear the riskiness of presbyterian printing after December 1596. This was enhanced by James' re-establishment of an episcopal court with jurisdiction over clerical communications.

These print controls restricted the king's presbyterian opponents to manuscript publication and the occasional use of overseas printers. The Calvinist Schilders press in Middelburg was employed to publish accounts of controversial general assemblies held in 1606 and 1610.[93] Activist clerics used circular letters to speak to the laity and their fellow brethren, sometimes stimulating public exchanges with Scottish bishops. In 1584, two exiled clergymen circulated a letter to their Edinburgh congregation. When archbishop Adamson printed a reply, the clerics' wives, Jonet Guthrie and Margaret Marjoribanks, responded to Adamson with a manuscript paper. Though claiming to speak in the 'simple stile' of 'simple weomen', they provided close arguments showing a deep knowledge of classics, Latin, contemporary theology and international religious politics.[94] In 1608, the presbyterian laird David Hume of Godscroft began to exchange letters with James Law, bishop of Orkney. Outlining his views on parity in church government, Hume asked Law for 'a verie simple searche of the truth'.[95] Hume promised to keep their exchange private, so that his letters are known only through copies obtained by the minister and presbyterian historian David Calderwood.[96] A subsequent exchange with William Cowper, bishop of Galloway, however, became more public. In 1613, Cowper was attacked by an unknown 'lying Libeller' and responded with a printed *Apologie* in which he provided his 'honest

---

[91] Calderwood, *History*, v, 511.

[92] Pitcairn (ed.), *Ancient Criminal Trials in Scotland*, ii, 2–3, 14–7; Mann, *Scottish Book Trade*, 142–3.

[93] Anon., *A Faithfull Report of Proceedings*; Anon., *A Briefe and Plaine Narration*; Mann, *Scottish Book Trade*, 78–9.

[94] Calderwood, *History*, iv, 126–41. I am grateful to Jamie Reid-Baxter for this reference.

[95] *Ibid.*, vi, 728.   [96] Reid, 'Hume of Godscroft', 191–2.

152 Public Opinion in Early Modern Scotland, c.1560–1707

testimonie' for episcopacy and castigated his opponents as 'barking Dogges'. Hume and others 'answered him in writt', 'because the presse was not patent to them', with Hume sharing 'sundry Copies' of his answer before Cowper had seen it.[97] Offended by this 'publicke writing', Cowper printed his *Dikaiology* (justification) in London with a response to Hume's letter.[98] A third example is provided by Alexander Hume, a civil lawyer turned parish minister, who in 1608 or 1609 addressed himself to the clergy at large with an admonitory letter arguing against an erastian episcopate.[99]

Printed presbyterian works became more visible after 1618, when controversial changes to Scottish worship practices were pushed through a general assembly in Perth. Despite a 1615 privy council order requiring the licensing of Scottish tracts printed abroad, opponents of the Perth articles printed a series of unauthorised tracts on Dutch presses.[100] Though Calderwood noted in the foreword to his *Perth Assembly* that the 'meanes of printing and publishing are to us very difficill', he managed to have his tract printed in Leiden and smuggled into Scotland by June 1619 when the king ordered universal obedience to the Perth articles and forbade writing, reading or distributing any 'libells, pamphlets, or books' against the articles.[101] Bookshops and homes in Edinburgh were searched and the bookseller James Cathkin was arrested and questioned before the king in London.[102] In July, *Perth Assembly* was condemned as seditious for encouraging a 'sinister oppinioun' of the king 'in the hairtis of the simple and ignorant multitude'. All copies were to be handed in and burned at the Edinburgh mercat cross.[103] Three clerics were questioned by the bishops' court of high commission on the collection of money for the publication of *Perth Assembly*.[104] A further order in 1625 ordered ships to be searched for seditious tracts printed in the Low Countries.[105]

When conformist clergy used presses in London and Scotland to defend the Perth articles, Calderwood, who had fled to the Netherlands, arranged the publication of responses. Defences included two tracts by David Lindsay, bishop of Brechin; a justification of the articles by Bishop Cowper, printed in London in 1619; and a tract on kneeling for

---

[97] Calderwood, *History*, vii, 180.   [98] Cowper, *The Bishop of Galloway*.
[99] Wodrow, *Miscellany*, i, 569–90.
[100] Mann, *Scottish Book Trade*, 79, 167; Stewart, '"Brothers in Treuth"', 154.
[101] [Calderwood], *Perth Assembly*, A3r; Calderwood, *History*, vii, 380–1; *RPCS*, ser. 1, xi, 579–81.
[102] Calderwood, *History*, vii, 382–3; Mann, 'Embroidery to enterprise', 142–3.
[103] *RPCS*, ser. 1, xii, 15–6.   [104] Row, *History*, 324–5.   [105] Mann, *Scottish Book Trade*, 78.

Public Communications

communion published at St Andrews in 1620 by John Michaelson, minister of Burntisland.[106] Responses included an allegorical text, *The Speach of the Kirk of Scotland to Her Beloved Children* (1620), addressed to the clergy and parliamentary estates of Scotland, and *A Dialogue betwixt Cosmophilus and Theophilus anent the Urging of New Ceremonies upon the Kirke of Scotland* (1621), written for a general audience.[107] In *The Speach,* Calderwood urged his readers to recognise an imbalance in the public debate on the Perth articles: 'To the one, the presses are open and free: to the other, it is not safe or possible to print even a few words of this sort'.[108]

Pamphlets against the Perth articles credited godly readers with the capacity to form and express conscientious opinions, though writers were still worried about the multitude. In *Perth Assembly,* Calderwood placed his trust in the 'sincerer sort', referring the truth of his arguments to 'the tryall of every iudicious Reader, making conscience of his oath, promise, subscription and puritie of his profession'.[109] *The Speach* raised the fear that 'public contradictions' in worship would confuse the commons and lead them to error and irreligion, especially those who had only a super-ficial understanding of their faith based on 'external shewes'.[110] To help the ordinary layman, the *Dialogue* was written in a 'short', 'plaine' and 'generall' style for 'the information of the simple and unlearned'.[111] Theophilus (lover of God) argued that while the Perth articles might be legal, they went against the consciences of those who had sworn confes-sional bands in 1581 and 1590. Swearers had adopted their views after careful reflection and inspiration: they 'swore their resolution and perswa-sion of the truth', a persuasion 'wrought in their hearts by God's spirit' and their understanding of 'his word'.[112] Taking confessional oaths as a man-ifestation of national consent, the *Dialogue* provocatively suggested that these collective, extra-institutional commitments overrode the capacity of the 1618 general assembly to represent 'the whole body' of the kirk.[113] With the voting of the Perth articles, 'the good people perceive[d]' the iniquity of the 1618 assembly.[114] These challenging views excited a 1620 proclamation against 'turbulent' clergy and laity who 'preferr[ed] thair

---

[106] Ford, 'Conformity in conscience: the structure of the Perth Articles debate in Scotland, 1618–1638', 258–9.

[107] [Calderwood], *The Speach of the Kirk of Scotland to Her Beloved Children*; [Murray], *A Dialogue betwixt Cosmophilus and Theophilus*. See also [Calderwood], *A Solution of Doctor Resolutus, His Resolutions for Kneeling*; [Calderwood], *A Defence of Our Arguments.*

[108] [Calderwood], *The Speach of the Kirk*, 90.   [109] [Calderwood], *Perth Assembly*, 'To the Reader'.

[110] [Calderwood], *The Speach of the Kirk*, 24–25, 74–75.

[111] [Murray], *A Dialogue betwixt Cosmophilus and Theophilus*, A2r.   [112] *Ibid.*, 8, 5.

[113] *Ibid.*, 11.   [114] *Ibid.*, 27.

154   Public Opinion in Early Modern Scotland, c.1560–1707

awin conceittis and opinionis to the ordinanceis of the generall Churche'.[115]

As questions of church government divided late Jacobean Scotland, both sides appropriated a stock plebeian character, Jock Upaland, to express what each saw as common-sense views. After the appointment of a commission to provide James VI with greater executive control of the kirk, a 'rusticall letter' in the name of Jock Upaland was written to the commissioners in 1597. While noting that the commons had some 'weaknesse' in understanding, Jock Upaland asserted that regular doctrinal instruction 'these manie yeeres bygone' had allowed them to see that the king and kirk were taking an 'evill course', misled by 'wicked counsellers'. Threatening violent resistance if this course were not corrected, Jock Upaland turned away accusations of sedition by blaming the king's advisers for alienating the people's affections.[116] Around 1618, however, a royalist writer turned this straight-talking character to the king's cause with a manuscript dialogue, 'Jok up Landis Newes and Dreame'. This told the story of a visit by Jock to the home of a 'Guid man' (a substantial tenant or small proprietor). Asked for news, Jock lampooned the presbyterians by recounting a dream in which James VI handed control of the kirk to them and then watched as the headless kirk fell into chaos. In the closing, Jock wished that precise 'puritanes' and 'sighing sisters' would learn from his dream.[117]

After his accession in 1625, Charles I continued his father's practice of using proclamations and print publications to instruct opinion at large. However, his rapid implementation of controversial policies outstripped the persuasive power of his communications. Just four months after his accession, Charles proclaimed, orally and in print, that he intended to enforce the Perth articles. Noting that he would have preferred to ignore 'foolish rumours', Charles spelt out his intentions so that 'the vnstable mynds of the vulgare sort' would not be misled.[118] According to the presbyterian historian John Row, this 'made many honest people to have harder thoughts of the King than they had before'.[119] Charles also struggled to win over landowners to an ambitious plan to reform the payment of teinds (tithes), despite the publication in 1627 of an authorised pamphlet supporting this policy. Voiced by a Scottish 'Respublica', this unique

---

[115] RPCS, ser. 1, xii, 280–1.   [116] Calderwood, History, v, 655–68.
[117] Baxter (ed.), 'Jok up Landis Newes and Dreame'. I am grateful to Jamie Reid-Baxter for sharing his unpublished transcription and commentary.
[118] RPCS, ser. 2, i, 91–2; Charles I, A Declaration of his M. Pleasure Anent Religion; TSP no. 1428.
[119] Row, History, 340.

Public Communications

pamphlet combined an expression of the king's intention ('The mind of the king my head') with favourable accounts of the views of the kirk and noble estate ('The minde of the chvrch my heart' and 'The minde of the barrons my body'). In contrast to the previous use of allegorical figures to express oppositional grievances, this tract conveyed royalist sentiments with an updated representation of the realm.[120] Yet in targeting the landowners alienated by royal policy, this tract portrayed a polity comprised of the king, church and barons, with no place for ordinary people. Charles also authorised a 1627 pamphlet addressing the subjects at large, *An Aduertisement to the Subjects of Scotland*, with a warning against Spanish ambitions and internal discord. After a dedication to Charles, a foreword to readers called on 'vpright Subjects' to 'carrie publicke, and not private Mynds'.[121] Though the readership of this tract would have been narrow, its rhetorical appeal to all 'subjects' rather than the nobles or estates was more inclusive than the image of Respublica.

Charles' 1633 Scottish coronation should have provided an opportunity for the king to win over hearts and minds, but Chapter 2 has shown how Charles fueled resentment by suppressing petitions and debate in the accompanying parliament. Nor was he always aided by royalist poetry or poets. Alongside two books of Latinate encomia and an account of his reception in Edinburgh, a handful of poems in Scots were printed.[122] While the fawning *King Charles His Birthright* named Charles 'father to the Common-well' with mental powers that 'farre surpasse[d] vulgar heads', the more ambiguous *Scotland's Welcome to her Native Sonne* included a long list of 'just complaints' articulated by a maternal figure of Scotland.[123] These economic grievances indicated resentment of the 1603 union, which had left Scotland as a 'mourning Widow' awaiting the return of her husband, the king.[124] Instead of assuaging these concerns, the king pushed through parliamentary acts for a land tax and a new tax on annualrents (investment income). The proclamations announcing these new taxes insisted that 'the wisest eye can finde no blemish in the temper of all our

---

[120] Cockburn of Langtoun, *Respublica De Decimis*.

[121] Hay of Naughton, *An Aduertisement to the Subjects of Scotland*, sig. B2r. Hay held a Fife barony and served as a Justice of the Peace. In July 1626, Charles ordered the archbishop of St Andrews to review and license Hay's book, promising to reward Hay when convenient. *RPCS*, ser. 2, i, 345n.

[122] Green, 'The king returns', 161; Anon., *The Entertainment of the High and Mighty Monarch*. The latter included poems by William Drummond of Hawthornden, who also wrote poetry marking the deaths of Prince Henry and James VI and James' 1617 visit.

[123] Anon., *King Charles His Birthright*, sig. A2v.

[124] Lithgow, *Scotland's Welcome to Her Native Sonne and Soveraigne Lord, King Charles*.

156   Public Opinion in Early Modern Scotland, c.1560–1707

royall actions', 'each Estate' being 'most sensible' of the king's goodness.[125] But as Chapter 2 has explained, the king's aggressive management of the 1633 parliament led to capital charges being brought against John Elphinstone, second Lord Balmerino, for possessing a draft of a petition from dissatisfied members of parliament. The alienation created by this prosecution can be seen in the penning of a letter against the trial by the royalist poet William Drummond of Hawthornden.[126]

From the reign of Mary to Charles, political and religious divisions stimulated the presentation of persuasive arguments in a range of formats. Because the uneducated multitude was thought to be easily misled, efforts were made on all sides to instruct them in correct opinions. The crown offered information by proclamation and printed books while censoring seditious speech, sermons and print, forcing presbyterians to rely more on manuscript publication and overseas printing. Across these communications, typical representations of the nation included Maddie and Jock Upaland as common-sense voices and Lady Scotland as the motherland. Before the accession of Charles, however, the imagery of public opinion was becoming less abstract as presbyterian writers placed their trust in sincere consciences and treated the swearing of confessional oaths as a form of national consent. Even royalist writers made more direct appeals to the nation, with tracts invoking the mind of the estates and speaking to subjects at large.

4.2   The Satisfaction of the Subjects, 1637–1659

Though generations of historians have studied canonical printed texts from the Covenanting era, such as Samuel Rutherford's 1644 *Lex Rex*, more recently historians have considered the wider deployment of public arguments for political ends in Scotland and England. Joad Raymond and Sarah Waurechen have highlighted the printing of Scottish pamphlets for English audiences from 1638.[127] John Ford has traced lines of printed argument in Scotland from the Perth articles to the 1638 National Covenant, while David Stevenson and Alistair Mann have shown how the Covenanter regime capitalised on its control of Scottish presses by

---

[125] Charles I, *Charles by the Grace of God ... One Taxation;* Charles I, *Charles by the Grace of God, King ... One Yearly Extraordinary Taxation.*
[126] Spiller, 'Drummond, William of Hawthornden'.
[127] Raymond, *Pamphlets and Pamphleteering*, ch. 5; Waurechen, 'Covenanter propaganda and conceptualisations of the public during the Bishops' Wars, 1638–40'.

Public Communications

blocking royalist printing in Scotland after 1638.[128] Sal Cipriano's examination of anti-covenant writings by university intellectuals confirms the difficulties that royalists faced in disseminating their views.[129] Laura Stewart has described the creation of a Covenanted public, highlighting 1637–39 and 1648 as key moments of public debate.[130] Scott Spurlock's study of printing in the later years of the Covenanter regime shows how important printing was to the kirk's control and how its leaders turned to presses in Aberdeen when English forces appropriated Edinburgh's presses for Cromwellian and Protester publications.[131]

Having already evaluated the protestations, petitions and oaths so important to the stimulation and expression of opinions in this period, this section will add an assessment of printed, written and oral publications, including proclamations, texts circulated for dissemination from the pulpit and Gaelic poetry. This will reveal a divergence in attitudes towards the opinions of the people at large. While Charles and his royalist allies focused on providing information to bring confused subjects back to obedience, the Covenanters demanded the satisfaction of thoughtful consciences, emphasising the sworn commitments of the laity at large. This theme also emerged in the radical claim that the National Covenant could not be unmade without the consent of every swearer. As published communications proliferated across two decades of conflict, this question of satisfaction – whether extra-institutional opinion should be respected or simply made the target of persuasive communications – became increasingly pertinent. Still, the tactical nature of the Covenanters' approach to public opinion was revealed when the kirk split in late 1650 and the resulting Resolutioner faction started to criticise the populism of their Protester opponents.

The early success of the Covenanters relied in part on the weakening of normal licencing controls in 1637 and the securing of press capacity for Covenanter works from 1638. A censorship order was issued in October 1637 against George Gillespie's *Dispute against the English–Popish Ceremonies*, printed in the Netherlands, but, according to a contemporary report, the book was protected by powerful figures and the proclamation

---

[128] Ford, 'Conformity in conscience'; Stevenson, 'A revolutionary regime and the press'; Mann, *Scottish Book Trade*. See also Coffey, *Politics, Religion and the British Revolutions*.
[129] Cipriano, 'The Scottish universities and opposition to the National Covenant'.
[130] Waurechen, 'Covenanter propaganda'; Stewart, *Rethinking the Revolution*.
[131] Spurlock, 'Cromwell's Edinburgh press'; Spurlock, *Cromwell and Scotland*, chs. 1–3.

158   Public Opinion in Early Modern Scotland, c.1560–1707

only encouraged greater sales.[132] By 1638, George Anderson's Edinburgh press was working for the Covenanters. The December 1638 general assembly was served in Glasgow by an Anderson press brought from Edinburgh, with the press of Robert and James Bryson being added to Covenanter service in 1639–41. Expressing a desire to avoid 'infecting and disquyeting the mindes of God's people', the 1638 assembly ordered its clerk to take over the licensing role previously performed by bishops for religious texts.[133] The Raban press in Aberdeen came under severe pressure after publishing anti-covenant works by Aberdeen academics in 1638 and with the outbreak of war in 1639, the king's printer, Robert Young, fled Edinburgh. From London, Young published proclamations for the king and a *Large Declaration Concerning the Late Tumults in Scotland*, discussed below. After the resolution of the conflict in 1641, Young and the English printer Evan Tyler both acted as printers to the king in Edinburgh, printing for the Covenanter-controlled kirk and state. As Stevenson has shown, three presses (Tyler, Bryson and Raban) were marshalled to print 1,000 copies of the 1643 Solemn League for parish subscription.[134] Printing became a more regular part of the practices of both the general assembly and the parliament, with matters of immediate interest being printed for easier dissemination.[135]

Like the National Covenant itself, Covenanter tracts stressed the responsibility of every subject to take an appropriate view on religious controversies and act accordingly. In the contestation of the Perth articles, Calderwood had encouraged civil disobedience by arguing that the laity incurred personal guilt when they accepted communion in the kneeling position required by law.[136] In 1637, Gillespie's *Dispute* urged his readers to 'make diligent search and enquiry for the Treuth'. The laity should resist lawful but evil innovations in worship, for only this would 'exoner your owne consciences'.[137] He further argued that the offending of 'tender

---

[132] Gordon, *History of Scots Affairs*, 120; *RPCS*, ser. 2, vi, 537. Mann describes Gillespie's book as 'a remarkable co-production' by Willem Christiaenez van der Boxe in Leiden and John Canne of Amsterdam. Both printers were fined by Dutch authorities. Mann, *Scottish Book Trade*, 69, 83.

[133] *AGA*, 30. The clerk was Archibald Johnston of Wariston, the author of the National Covenant and several public protestations.

[134] Stevenson, 'A revolutionary regime and the press', 315–30.

[135] E.g., Church of Scotland, *In the National Assemblie at Edinburgh the Fourth Day of August 1641*; Parliament of Scotland, *Questions Exhibited by the Parliament now in Scotland Assembled*; *RPS* 1643/6/29, 13 July 1643, 1644/1/65, 31 January 1644, 1644/1/119, 16 April 1644.

[136] [Calderwood]. *A Dispute vpon Communicating*, 29–31. The logical conclusion of this position was at least partial separation from the kirk, contributing to a rise in conventicling from 1619. Stevenson, 'Conventicles in the kirk, 1619–37'.

[137] [Gillespie], *A Dispute against the English-Popish Ceremonies*, sig. Cr, C2r.

Public Communications 159

consciences' constituted a sinful scandal which the church was obliged to avoid.[138]

Covenanter tracts replaced allegorical national figures with portraits of the people united in covenant, speaking through pamphlets, petitions and protestations. Early in 1639, a printed *Information* aimed at England presented a rationale for the Scottish rebellion from the 'nobility, barrons, borrows, ministers, and commons' of Scotland, 'the bodie of a Church and Kingdome'. This insisted on their loyalty to the king as 'professed in our Supplications', 'sworn in our solemne Covenant' and 'publickly declared before God and men in all our Protestations'.[139] A subsequent tract published in Edinburgh and Amsterdam provided a vindication of Scottish resistance in the form of a 'remonstrance' from the estates and commons of Scotland.[140] Refuting a 27 February proclamation made in England condemning the Covenanters as rebels, this tract offered a 'true and full information', based on published protestations and petitions, to 'convince the consciences' of English readers.[141] A 1639 tract urged Scottish clerics to build lay support in Scotland by reading the *Information* for England to their congregations alongside the acts of the 1638 general assembly and the assembly's supplication to the king.[142]

As Richard Cust has demonstrated, Charles believed that the opposition to his new prayer book had been whipped up by clerical firebrands who wished to constrain crown powers and enhance their own. This idea had been expressed in his father's condemnation of 'Democraticke' presbyterians in *Basilikon Doron* and, according to Row, was urged by his advisors.[143] The notion that Scottish religious resistance was a cloak for an anti-monarchical rebellion became a standard theme in royalist communications. Convinced that the commons were easily misled, Charles seems to have believed that '[i]f he could communicate with the loyalist majority', 'they would return to the fold'.[144] Persuasive arguments would restore his people to obedience, for they, as an April 1639 proclamation stated, had been 'cunningly seduced by vthers' to 'blindly run themselffes in to undutiful and seditious courses'.[145] However, Charles' inability to accept the substance of presbyterian grievances limited the effectiveness of his efforts. As a Covenanter tract from 1638 warned, anything the king might

---

[138] *Ibid.*, sig. Dd4v-Ee2v.   [139] [General Assembly], *An Information to All Good Christians*, 4–5.
[140] Mann, *Scottish Book Trade*, 83–4.   [141] Anon., *Remonstrance of the Nobility*, 4, 5.
[142] Row, *History*, 510.   [143] Row, History, 508.   [144] Cust, 'Charles I and popularity', 241–51.
[145] Charles I, *Charles by the Grace of God King of Scotland ... Whairas We Have by Many Fair and Calm Waies.*

gain from imposing his new prayer book would be cancelled by 'the losse hee may make of his good Subjects affections'.[146]

Royalist responses to the National Covenant echoed the idea that the people had been misled.[147] Between July and November 1638, the Raban press in Aberdeen printed lengthy disputations between a group of local academics and clergy, known as the Aberdeen Doctors, and Covenanter envoys, attracting the praise of the king.[148] John Forbes of Corse, the professor of divinity at King's College in Aberdeen and son of Bishop Patrick Forbes of Aberdeen, also published in manuscript and then in print a short and simple tract aimed at a wide readership, *A Peaceable Warning to the Subjects of Scotland*.[149] Rejecting the National Covenant as unauthorised, Forbes and other Aberdeen divines insisted that the laity did not have sufficient understanding to follow their consciences and were being deluded by the Covenanters into disobedience. In the earlier Perth articles debates, Forbes had dismissed presbyterian arguments on Jacobean confessional bands as an attempt to 'terrify weaker consciences.'[150] In his *Peaceable Warning*, he downplayed the 1581 confessional oath as a short-lived anti-Catholic device designed to instruct 'the simple people' in the tenets of their faith.[151] William Strang, principal of Glasgow's college, sought to redirect attention to the King's Covenant, Charles' renewal of the 1590 confessional band, with a manuscript tract in favour of subscription.[152]

In reply, Covenanter publications demonstrated an escalating emphasis on opinion at large as established by the National Covenant.[153] A set of printed 'Reasons' explaining why the National Covenant could not be superseded, penned by Archibald Johnston of Wariston, included the extraordinary suggestion that the 'expresse consent of the meanest of all the subscribers' would be required, because legal compacts could not be unmade without the approval of all parties.[154] A similarly expansive view was expressed by Calderwood in an answer to Forbes' *Peaceable Warning*. Calderwood developed his previous emphasis on the authority of

---

[146] [Gillespie], *Reasons for which the Service Booke, Urged upon Scotland Ought to Bee Refused*, sig. A2v. This was a short, accessible version of Gillespie's 1637 *Dispute*.

[147] Cipriano, 'Scottish universities', 18–9, 25; Ford, 'Lawful bonds', 55–60. For parish-level opposition see chapter 3.

[148] Stewart, 'The "Aberdeen Doctors" and the Covenanters', 35–36; Spalding, *Troubles*, 55.

[149] Forbes of Corse, *Peaceable Warning*, 5.   [150] Quoted in Ford, 'Lawful bonds', 52.

[151] Forbes of Corse, *Peaceable Warning*, 18.   [152] Cipriano, 'Scottish universities', 27–9.

[153] See Chapter 3 on the King's Covenant.

[154] [Johnston of Wariston], *Reasons Against the Rendering of our Sworne and Subscribed Confession of Faith*, sig. Cv.

Public Communications

161

confession oaths through 'collective' rather than 'representative' approval, superseding the ratification of the Perth articles by the general assembly in 1618 and parliament in 1621.[155]

In February 1639, after the abjuration of episcopacy by a rebellious general assembly in December 1638, Charles published a book in his own name to supplement his proclamations and royalist tracts. The *Large Declaration* was composed by Walter Balcanquhall, the Scottish dean of Rochester, with input from Charles. The book opened by asserting that the king's 'manie Proclamations' should have made his good intentions clear to any unbiased man, but the king's subjects were being misled by seditious enemies 'impatient of all laws and government'. Therefore, the king was determined to ensure his 'true hearted and loyall subjects' understood matters correctly.[156] The book reproduced the supplications, proclamations and protestations issued from September 1637 to December 1638 with marginal comments refuting Covenanter arguments. Totalling 430 pages, the book sought to prove that 'wicked contrivers' were using religion as a 'cloak' to 'muffle the face of the multitude', staging a revolution with the people's unwitting compliance.[157] The text shows that in 1637 Charles had been aware that a new service book might offend 'the mindes and dispositions' of his northern subjects.[158] But he could not understand the depth of feeling in Scotland against the liturgy he had imposed, attributing resistance to the book to the 'madd Multitude' and the succumbing of the 'better sort' to 'madnesse'.[159]

When the king moved in arms against Scotland in the Bishops' Wars (1639–40), even royalists found themselves hard pressed to speak well of him. In his 1639 *Tweeds Teares of Joy, to Charles great Brittains King*, the soldier–poet George Lauder blamed '[s]editious sycophants' for stirring Charles to wrongful anger against 'his mother', the realm of Scotland. Lauder showed deep antipathy to Charles' prayer book and sympathy for the resistance to it: 'the name did wound/The people's hearts and ears, who begg'd with tears/No puppet play might interrupt their prayers'.[160] Lauder's commitment to the Scottish presbyterian kirk was expressed more strongly in his 1641 *Caledonias Covenant, or Ane Panegyrick to the World*. Addressing an international audience, Lauder used a female figure of

---

[155] [Calderwood], *An Answere to M. I. Forbes of Corse*, sig. Cr.
[156] Cust, 'Charles I and popularity', 248; [Balcanquhall], *Large Declaration*, 1–2.
[157] [Balcanquhall], *Large Declaration*, 2–6, 15.   [158] *Ibid.*, 16–17.   [159] *Ibid.*, 30–1, 34.
[160] MacDonald, *George Lauder*, 257–63, quotes at lines 10–11, 108–10.

162   Public Opinion in Early Modern Scotland, c.1560–1707

Caledonia to express the nation's 'heauy Grieffe' against Charles, implying national unity behind the Covenanting cause.[161] A royal visit to Scotland in August 1641 stimulated strikingly few published encomia in contrast to 1617 and 1633.[162]

After the Bishops' Wars, Charles sought to turn the Covenant to his own purposes by pointing out that the oath bound Scottish swearers to support the crown. In a speech to the 1641 parliament, later printed, Charles promised satisfaction to his subjects while reminding them that by their 'nationall oath' they had to maintain his royal authority.[163] In January 1643, to prevent his English parliamentary opponents from securing Scottish aid, Charles ordered his Scottish privy council to publish to all parishes a letter from the English parliament and his response, so that his subjects could 'perceave the subtle wayes which is used to corrupt their fideliteis and alledgeance'.[164] This was followed by a printed proclamation early in June urging loyalty on the king's 'loving subjects' according to 'their owne solemn Nationall Covenant'. Charles condemned misleading propaganda directed at Scotland by English parliamentarians, attributed England's civil conflict to a few discontented people and asserted his good intentions.[165]

To sustain public support for their fight with the king, the Covenanter-controlled kirk and parliament applied sedition laws to royalist speech while printing propaganda for wide audiences. In 1640, the estates classed proclamations made during the Bishops' Wars as seditious speech and threatened to apply leasing-making laws to anyone still advising the king against the Covenanters.[166] In January 1643, the committee of estates responded to the king's propaganda by printing a directive from the general assembly calling on all clergy to 'warn the People' against royalist malignants. Those found to be acting or speaking against the Covenanter regime were to be disciplined before their presbytery as 'dis-covenanters'. This was published with 1,000 copies of a declaration against a royalist cross-petition (discussed in Chapter 2) and directions for a national fast

---

[161] *Ibid.*, 54–56. G[eorge] L[auder], *Caledonias Covenant*, sig. Av.
[162] Sillitoe, 'Rediscovering the progresses of Charles I', 101; [G.], *The Speech Which Was to Have Been Delivered to the Kings Majestie.*
[163] Charles I, *The Kings Majesties Speech in the Parliament at Edinburgh the Seventeenth Day of August, 1641.*
[164] *RPCS*, ser. 2, vii, 359–63, 372–4; *TSP* no. 1770. See chapter 2 on petitions preceding this request.
[165] *RPCS*, ser. 2, vii, 429–34; *TSP* no. 1788.
[166] *RPS* 1640/6/59, 9 June 1640, 1640/6/51, 9 June 1640.

'to all the people, that they be not deceived and drawn away from their stedfastnesse.'[167] Later in 1643, two remonstrances from the commission of the general assembly to the estates were printed with answers designed to satisfy concerns.[168] In January 1644, Scottish action against their king was justified by reference to the 'informations, declarations and remonstrances' published to 'all the world'.[169]

By 1645, military setbacks forced kirk leaders to address fresh persuasions to the subjects at large while taking further steps to suppress discordant talk. After securing a royalist victory at Kilsyth in August, the marquis of Montrose indicated his desire, for 'the Contentment of all his Majesty's good Subjects', to print explanatory tracts by William Drummond of Hawthornden.[170] This was prevented by the subsequent defeat of his royalist insurrection, but a few royalist pamphlets, probably printed at Aberdeen, recounted victories won by the marquis and urged 'people of all sorts' to recognise this as a sign of God's wrath against a 'seditious faction'.[171] These were answered by the general assembly with a *Solemn and Seasonable Warning* to be read to the Scottish people and army from all pulpits under threat of ecclesiastical censure for refusers.[172] To ensure that no one's conscience misinterpreted events, the *Warning* explained that recent military defeats indicated God's wrath for slackness and not, as royalist 'Sons of Belial' argued, sinful rebellion. '[E]very Person in every Family' was asked to reflect and repent, while 'all sorts both of high and low degree' were reminded of the 'bond on their consciences' requiring them to support the war effort.[173] This was followed in 1646 by another print to be read from all pulpits to 'all Estates and Degrees of Person throughout the Land'. This warned against 'false glosses of the Covenant' advanced by subtle enemies and urged constancy in the Solemn League's Anglo–Scottish alliance.[174] The commission of the general assembly also published a condemnation of a 'humble remonstrance' produced by George Mackenzie, second earl of Seaforth, a leader in the royalist

---

[167] General Assembly, *A Necessary Warning to the Ministerie of the Kirk of Scotland*, 6–7, 10; *TSP* no. 1778. Some clerics complained that the Committee of Estates should not speak for the kirk, with a reported fourteen presbyteries refusing to read these missives from the pulpit. Spalding, *History of the Troubles*, 321–2.

[168] *RPS* 1643/6/11, 27 June, 1643/6/18, 4 July, 1643/6/21, 6 July, 1643/6/29, 13 July 1643.

[169] *RPS* 1644/1/66, 31 January 1644.

[170] The desired tracts included Drummond's 1638 *Irene: A Remonstrance for Concord, Amity and Love Amongst his Majesty's Subjects*. Drummond of Hawthornden, *Works*, 157, 163. I thank Andrew Lind for this reference.

[171] Anon., *The Copie of a Letter*, 8; Anon., *The True Relation of the Late and Happie Victorie*.

[172] *AGA*, 122–8.   [173] General Assembly, *A Solemne and Seasonable Warning*, 6–7, 16.

[174] Commission of the General Assembly, *A Solemne and Seasonable Warning to All Estates*, 3.

164   Public Opinion in Early Modern Scotland, c.1560–1707

uprising, interpreting this call for national unity as a 'dangerous and seditious band' designed to 'deceive the simple'.[175] In the same year, the general assembly recommended that persons making 'disaffected speeches' be subject to kirk discipline.[176] From February 1646, an executive committee of parliament established new requirements for any books, especially histories, to be reviewed by a crown official before publication, and for any books coming from outside Scotland to be checked before sale.[177]

These efforts were directed at print and oral communications circulating in support of Montrose's 1644–6 royalist uprising. A history of these events was published in Latin and English in the Hague and Paris in 1647–8. The author, a former Scottish bishop and chaplain to Montrose in his campaign, described his adulatory account as a 'short and plaine discourse' designed to combat 'venimous tongues & pens' that targeted 'the ignorant, and unwarie world' (though his criticism of other royalist leaders led Charles I to disown the book).[178] Praise for Montrose also circulated in vernacular Gaelic poetry, such as *Soraidh Do'n Ghramach* (A Song of Greeting to Montrose) by Iain Lom of the MacDonalds of Keppoch. This political poem urged the royalist clans to rise again if Montrose returned.[179]

In 1647, kirk leaders stoked opposition to an accommodation with Charles I by printing 'humble remonstrances' to parliament and the committee of estates.[180] These were joined by an unusual tract, the *Humble Remonstrance of the Citizens of Edenburgh to the Convention of the Estates*. Though this made no explicit claim to speak for the people of Edinburgh beyond the title, the text drew on civil law, Biblical examples and theories of original sovereignty to argue for the people's capacity to make covenants with God and the king and the responsibility of magistrates and assemblies to correct tyrant kings on behalf of the people. However, the text rejected any role for an unbridled multitude by narrowing its definition of 'the people' to those with delegated or representative authority. Citing conciliar theory, the author placed political agency in the

---

[175] Commission of the General Assembly, *A Declaration against a Late Dangerous and Seditious Band*; Stevenson, *Revolution and Counter-Revolution*, 41.

[176] *AGA*, 139.   [177] Spurlock, 'Cromwell's Edinburgh press', 183.

[178] Stevenson, 'Wishart, George (1599–1671)'; Wishart, *The History of the Kings Majesties Affairs in Scotland*, preface.

[179] MacKenzie (ed.), *Orain Iain Luim: Songs of John MacDonald, Bard of Keppoch*, 28–33.

[180] Commission of the General Assembly, *The Humble Remonstrance of the Commission of the General Assembly*; General Assembly, *To the Right Honourable Committee of Estates, the Humble Remonstrance of the Commissioners of the General Assembly*; RPS 1646/11/231, 11 February 1647.

Public Communications

hands of the 'Officers and Deputies of the Kingdom', who acted on behalf of the nation.[181]

The eventual Engagement with Charles agreed late in 1647 stimulated an outburst of print, featuring publications against the Engagement by the kirk, ineffective efforts to censor these and an innovative but short-lived attempt to provide persuasive counter-arguments in an authorised newspaper. Early in March 1648, the commission of the general assembly sent 2,000 copies of a disapproving *Declaration* against the Engagement to the presbyteries for 'timeous and dew warning' to the 'whole kirk and kingdom'. The commission ignored a request from parliament that they should not print this statement until the estates could provide a public answer to it.[182] John Twyne, printer for the Tyler press, was called to parliament for questioning, but the kirk's licensing powers meant that Twyne was released when he showed his orders from the commission. In April, the parliament responded with its own declaration in favour of the Engagement, followed by the printing of a 4 May act for a levy.[183] The commission replied on 5 May with a *Short Information* attacking parliament's declaration and demanding 'satisfaction to our consciences'.[184] This was again sent to the presbyteries with orders that ministers read it in pulpits and 'disperse copies'. The clergy also were ordered not to read any parliamentary papers in favour of the levy.[185] Despite this injunction, the parliament's need to raise the 'haill fensible persones' for the king led it on 11 May to take the unusual step of communicating directly to the presbyteries. An 'extraordinary addresse' urged the clergy to 'stirr up the people by your preaching and prayeris and all utherwayes in your calling to a cheerefull obedience to our orders'.[186] A month later, the estates responded to petitions against the levy submitted by synods and presbyteries. Arguing that the levy was 'much misconstrued', a printed letter sought to provide information 'for the satisfactioune of all suche as are satisfieable'.[187]

---

[181] Anon., *Humble Remonstrance of the Citizens of Edenburgh*, 22–4, 28–9.

[182] Commission of the General Assembly, *A Declaration*; *RCGA*, ii, 385, 388–90; *RPS* 1648/3/21, 9 March 1648. Previously, the kirk's remonstrances had been printed with answers from the estates.

[183] *RPS* 1648/3/83, 20 April 1648, 1648/3/104, 4 May 1648; *TSP* no. 1954.

[184] Though this item was printed, the Commission's order allowed that it be published in 'writt or print', as convenient. *RCGA*, i, 531.

[185] Commission of the General Assembly, *A Short Information from the Commission of the General Assembly*; *RCGA*, i, 528–31.

[186] *RPS* 1648/3/104, 4 May 1648, 1648/3/166, 11 May 1648; *TSP* no. 1957.

[187] *RPS* 1648/3/220, 10 June. See chapter 2.

166   Public Opinion in Early Modern Scotland, c.1560–1707

This paper war led the committee of estates to restrict the kirk's printing while increasing its own propaganda output. It curtailed the kirk's licensing capacity on 16 June 1648 with a proclamation requiring prior review by the committee of any books and pamphlets published on any press in the kingdom 'under pain of death'.[188] By August the commission of the general assembly was complaining that 'the Presse is not patent to our papers', to the detriment of 'the people of God in this land who expect information from us'.[189] In the same month, the committee of estates published Scotland's first domestic newspaper. Headlined 'God Save King Charles' and decorated with the royal arms, this was titled *Ane Information of the Publick Proceedings of the Kingdom of Scotland*. Countering what Stevenson has called 'the unrivalled power of the Kirk's propaganda machine', the paper aimed at 'the un-deceiving of such as are apt to be mis-led' and, showing more sensitivity to public opinion than Charles had previously, 'the satisfaction of the Kingdom'.[190]

Plans to publish further issues were curtailed by the defeat of the Engager army at Preston. Gaelic royalist poetry expressed frustration when the nation's divisions over the Engagement led to this defeat in August 1648.[191] After the execution of Charles I in London in January 1649, the taking of Inverness by Mackenzie royalists stimulated the execution of George Gordon, second marquis of Huntly in Edinburgh.[192] Lom's *Cumha Morair Hunndaidh* (A Lament for the Marquis of Huntly) celebrated the young Charles Stewart as the rightful king, noted that all of Europe was talking of his father's unjust execution and urged Charles to take back his kingdom with the help of his loyal subjects. Lom condemned the kirk for treating royalists 'as if they were unbaptised outcasts, for having stood up for [Charles] as heir to the crown'.[193]

As the Engagers fell from power in 1649, the ensuing 'Kirk party' regime sought to re-establish a hegemonic understanding of the covenants. Having proclaimed Charles II as king, the regime demanded that he swear the covenants before returning to rule Scotland in person. The general assembly printed in July 1649 a *Seasonable and Necessary Warning and Declaration* calling on the nation to hold firm against English sectaries and

---

[188] *TSP* no. 1962; Spurlock, 'Cromwell's Edinburgh press', 183.
[189] Commission of the General Assembly, *Answer of the Commissioners of the General Assembly*, 4. A 31 July declaration was not printed. *AGA*, 171–81.
[190] Stevenson, 'Scotland's first newspaper', 124; *Ane Information of the Publick Proceedings*, 2.
[191] Macinnes, 'Scottish Gaeldom 1638–51', 86–7.
[192] Huntly had been captured in late 1647 after a previous uprising.
[193] MacKenzie (ed.), *Orain Iain Luim*, 49–55.

Scottish malignants. This urged the laity to 'labour for more knowledge', 'without which they may easily be deceived' and to accept Charles as the king only when 'satisfaction' had been given for their consciences.[194] The commission of the general assembly published a series of national exhortations culminating in October with, as discussed in Chapter 3, a *Solemn Acknowledgement of Public Sins and Breaches of the Covenant* to accompany a renewal of the Solemn League.[195]

Competing public appeals again were made when the marquis of Montrose launched another royalist uprising. A *Declaration* by Montrose was printed at Gothenburg late in 1649, followed by editions in London and Scotland. Montrose urged all Scotsmen to return to 'dutyfull Obedience' as subjects, husbands and fathers, promising that Charles would pardon them, 'the People (in Generall) Having been but Ignorantly misled'.[196] One edition used large type, possibly to facilitate reading aloud to crowds or congregations. This was answered in January 1650, well ahead of Montrose's landing on mainland Scotland in April 1650, with prints urging the covenanted nation to oppose Montrose and his malignant followers. These included a printed *Declaration* from the committee of estates and another national warning 'to Kirk and Kingdom' from the commission of the general assembly.[197]

When Cromwellian forces marched into Scotland and occupied Edinburgh later in 1650, contending messages continued to address the people of Scotland. After the English parliament made a public declaration justifying the invasion, a broadside written in the name of 'the people of Scotland' argued that the English incursion was 'sinfull and unlawfull'. This asserted that Scotland should not be held responsible for their 1648 invasion of England because the Engagement had been opposed by 'the Body of the Ministrie' and 'the Body of the people'.[198] With Edinburgh under Cromwellian control, a printed response in the name of the English army aimed to 'perswade the Hearts and Consciences of those that are godly in Scotland' that the execution of Charles I, the establishment of a republican commonwealth and the English invasion

---

[194] General Assembly, *Remonstrance and Declaration*, 7, 8, 11; *AGA*, 203–11. No Scottish print of this text has been found but the London print cited here mentions an Edinburgh edition.

[195] Commission of the General Assembly, *A Short Declaration to the Whole Kirk and Kingdom;* Commission of the General Assembly, *An Information of the Present Condition of Affairs.*

[196] Graham, *Declaration of His Excellency James Marqves of Montrose*, 1, 6. See Bibliography for editions.

[197] Committee of Estates and the Commission of the General Assembly, *A Declaration of the Committee of Estates ... Together with a Declaration and Warning.*

[198] Anon., *For the Under-Officers and Souldiers of the English Army, from the People of Scotland.*

168   Public Opinion in Early Modern Scotland, c.1560–1707

all served God's purposes and 'the good of the people'.[199] A printed retort by the general assembly denied that the godly of Scotland could be 'satisfiable' or 'inclinable' to these arguments.[200] Three further English tracts demonstrated, as Spurlock has emphasised, a desire to loosen the hold of the Scottish kirk on the people's consciences, though they found that these were countered by 'Slanders' spread by Scottish ministers.[201] Other republican propaganda included a tract purporting to describe a meeting of Scottish republicans in Perth and two tracts accusing Charles II of Catholicism.[202]

Turning to an Aberdeen press to print an account of the January 1651 coronation of Charles II, the commission of the general assembly appealed to the covenanted nation even as the kirk was splitting into Protesters and Resolutioners over a new levy.[203] While moderates supported the employment of repentant malignants in the army to prevent English conquest, hardliners insisted that this would betray the covenanted cause. The commission managed to print in January and March texts for parish clergy to read from the pulpit, though conditions of war and noncompliance by Protester ministers lessened their circulation.[204] In a January *Solemn Warning*, the commission castigated those who were 'speaking disrespectfullie' of the covenanted cause. Lest the people be misled by 'fayr and enticing words', the commission showed how the English invasion had broken the Solemn League. Moreover, they argued, any who supported the 'Sectarian Armie of England' was committing 'unnatural Treacherie' to 'their Native Countrey', risking 'the enthralling us and this ancient Kingdom in bondage and slaverie'. The commission called on 'all ingenuous, honest and godlie hearts' to consider the consequences of ignoring a lawful call to arms. Holding the people's consciences in 'tender respect', the commission expected that their arguments would address any 'scruple in the myndes of honest people', except for those 'willfullie resolved unto

---

[199] Army of England, *A Declaration of the Army*, 4–5.

[200] General Assembly, *A Short Reply to a Declaration Intituled, the Declaration of the Army of England*, 1.

[201] Spurlock, *Cromwell and Scotland*, 12, 14, 20–31; Stevenson, 'Reactions to ruin, 1648–51: "A Declaration and Vindication of the Poore Opprest Commons of Scotland," and other pamphlets', 257–60.

[202] Stevenson, 'Reactions to ruin', 1648–51', 258–9; Spurlock, 'Cromwell's Edinburgh press', 188–90.

[203] Douglas, *The Form and Order of the Coronation*. The coronation is discussed in chapter 3 and the Protester–Resolutioner split in chapter 1.

[204] Commission of the General Assembly, *A Solemn Warning to All the Members of this Kirk*; Commission of the General Assembly, *A Short Exhortation and Warning to the Ministers and Professours of this Kirk*; RCGA, iii, 216–226, 346–52.

the contrarie'. For incorrigibles, the commission appended an act threatening excommunication.[205] A second tract, *A Short Exhortation and Warning*, cautioned against the people being 'seduced' by the 'the wynde of Strange Doctrine' and called on all Scots to resist the 'impious monster of Toleration' and contribute to the defence of the realm according to their station. Citing past church acts against malignancy and the censoring of speech and books, the commission banned any speaking, writing or publishing of papers against a new levy, under pain of ecclesiastical censure.[206]

To undermine support for the Scottish levy, Cromwell authorised the printing of a letter to the commission from Stirling presbytery showing Protester concerns.[207] This presented lay opinion as a reason to disobey the levy, arguing that the recruitment of malignants would cause 'great scandal and grief of heart to many of the poor people of God throughout the Land'.[208] The commission, in turn, printed a response, again using the Aberdeen press. Noting that the Stirling letter was 'abroad in the hands of many', the commission argued for the lawfulness of the levy to defend the country from foreign invasion, reassuring readers that former malignants would only be accepted if they expressed repentance for their errors.[209]

This split between Protesters and Resolutioners, discussed in more detail in previous chapters, stimulated demonstrations of public adherence in contending publications. Subscribed protestations presented to the 1651 general assembly were printed in 1652 by the Protester minister Samuel Guthrie with a refutation of a text by the Resolutioner minister James Wood. Wood's anti-Protester *Vindication* had circulated in manuscript before being reproduced by Guthrie (and printed by Resolutioner hands in London).[210] Guthrie also reproduced the 1648 *Solemn Acknowledgment*, establishing this publication alongside the 1638 and 1643 covenants as a benchmark for right-thinking consciences.[211] Guthrie appealed for public support from those seeking

---

[205] Commission of the General Assembly, *A Solemn Warning*, 4–5, 8, 11. 18–9.
[206] Commission of the General Assembly, *A Short Exhortation and Warning*.
[207] Spurlock, 'Cromwell's Edinburgh press', 181, 187.
[208] Presbytery of Stirling, *Remonstrance of the Presbyterie of Sterling*, 9, 11–2.
[209] Commission of the General Assembly, *The Answer of the Commission of the Generall Assemblie*, 5.
[210] Anon., *An Answer to the Declaration of the Pretended Assembly at Dundee*, sig. a2r.
[211] [Guthrie], *The Nullity of the Pretended Assembly at St Andrews & Dundee*. Guthrie's refutation of Wood's *Vindication of the Freedom & Lawfulnes of the Late Generall Assembly* also was printed separately as [Guthrie], *A Vindication of the Freedome and Lawfullnesse, and so of the Authority of the Late General Assembly*. [Wood], *Vindication of the Freedom & Lawfulnes of the Late Generall Assembly*.

170   Public Opinion in Early Modern Scotland, c.1560–1707

'to know, debate and for thy edification decern on what side Truth and Justice is'.[212] In response to Wood's claim that four out of five presbyteries accepted the kirk's public resolutions for a levy, Guthrie asserted that at least half contained some objectors, listing names as evidence. He also drew a parallel between what he saw as the people's unanimous rejection of the Engagement and the disapproval of the 'generality' of the godly for the public resolutions.[213] The Tyler press continued to stimulate this debate by printing a Resolutioner attack on a second protestation delivered to the 1652 general assembly at Dundee.[214] A Protester answer to this tract appeared in 1653 decrying the 'Public provocations in Print' issued by Resolutioners, complaining that 'in this corrupt age calumnies passe for truth among the generality of people'.[215] As negotiations attempted to close the Protester–Resolutioner schism in 1652, the Protester point of view was advertised in two more tracts claiming to speak for like-minded ministers, kirk elders and laymen.[216] Guthrie published in 1653 the *Causes of the Lord's Wrath Against Scotland*, blaming English conquest of covenanted Scotland on the moral failings and backsliding of the king and the Resolutioners.[217]

When the Cromwellian regime in 1652 pursued a tender of union to create a British commonwealth, Scottish responses were restricted to manuscript formats. Chapters 2 and 3 have shown how some localities cited their covenanted consciences in expressing resistance to the tender. At about this time, however, a manuscript tract spoke in favour of English hegemony, asking only that the invaders not force Scottish consciences into perjury nor retain in power any Covenanter leaders. Speaking on behalf of the 'poore opprest Commons of Scotland', this excoriated the ruling classes for their repeated levies and complained bitterly against the Protesters for tearing apart the kirk. Though in the style of Jock Upaland, the words were presented in name of the actual oppressed commons rather than a stock character.[218] Divisions between ministers meant that the kirk made no formal response to the tender of union. A handwritten remonstrance was addressed to Cromwell by Protesters in January 1652,

---

[212] [Guthrie], *A Vindication of the Freedome and Lawfullnesse, and so of the Authority of the Late General Assembly*, 5.
[213] [Guthrie], *The Nullity of the Pretended Assembly*, 78–80, 112–4.
[214] Anon., *The Protestation Given in by the Dissenting Brethren*.
[215] Anon., *An Answer to the Declaration of the Pretended Assembly at Dundee*, sig. a2r.
[216] Anon., *The Representation, Proposition and Protestation of Divers Ministers, Elders and Professors*; Anon., *Reasons Why the Ministers, Elders, and Professors, who Protested*.
[217] [Guthrie], *The Causes of the Lord's Wrath*.
[218] Stevenson, 'Reactions to ruin, 1648–51', 260–5.

Public Communications

followed by further testimonies in 1653 and 1654.[219] The Protesters also issued in 1653 a manuscript declaration against the rise of independent sects, while Resolutioner James Wood warned against congregationalism in a tract printed in Edinburgh.[220]

Between 1657 and 1659, greater access to the press allowed Resolutioners and Protesters to reinvigorate their public exchanges. The Resolutioners launched a fresh effort to discredit the Protesters, publishing in London a *True Representation* for the 'undeceiving' of those deluded by 'mis-representations'. Attributed to the future archbishop James Sharp, this text condemned the separation created by the Protesters and the 'reproaches and calumnies' that they had 'published to the world in print.' According to Sharp, the Resolutioners were 'perswaded in [their] consciences' to maintain the established church government.[221] This was followed by an Edinburgh print of a *Declaration* by Wood describing Resolutioner attempts to find peace 'consistent with the simple freedom of our own judgements'.[222] A response from the Protesters, also printed in Edinburgh, claimed that although the *True Representation* was 'diligently spread both at home and abroad' and handed to 'publick persons' in Scotland and England, the Protesters continued to claim 'the hearts of most of the Godly in the Land'.[223] The publishing of a petition for toleration in 1659 from independent sects in Scotland triggered the printing of a Protester testimony asserting the nation's covenanted commitments, backed with clerical subscriptions.[224]

This section has shown how public opinion came to the fore after 1637 as oral, written and printed political communications rose rapidly. For the presbyterian historian Row, so many tracts were printed in 1638 that he could not list them all.[225] The Covenanters seized control of Edinburgh's presses to justify their rebellion in the name of the nation's sworn commitments, while royalists circulated manuscript tracts and managed to print a few in London and Aberdeen. Charles and his royalists aimed to rectify the misinformation of the people, while the Covenanters sought to maintain a hegemonic hold on the consciences of the nation. Montrose's risings and the Engagement allowed more royalist communications to emerge, including Gaelic political poetry and an Edinburgh newsbook, countered by multiple warnings to the covenanted nation.

---

[219] See Chapter 3.   [220] Spurlock, *Cromwell and Scotland*, 142–4.
[221] [Sharp], *A True Representation*, 2, 31, 40, 48.   [222] [Wood], *A Declaration of the Brethren*, 3.
[223] Anon., *Protesters No Subverters*, 3.
[224] Anon., *A Testimony to the Truth of Jesus Christ*. See chapter 2.   [225] Row, *History*, 446.

172   Public Opinion in Early Modern Scotland, c.1560–1707

From 1651, English appeals joined Resolutioner and Protester publications, creating a cacophony as each interest group sought to influence and speak for the people, or at least the godly, of Scotland with printed and written papers.

4.3   Persuasive Publications after the Restoration, 1660–1687

Tim Harris has emphasised the extent to which the crown after 1660 recognised the importance of wooing popular support across the three British kingdoms. Convinced that his father had lost the hearts of his people, Charles II paid more attention to the management of public opinion.[226] In Scotland, this meant strict censorship combined with proclamations, pageantry and pamphleteering, including the reprinting of English texts for Scottish readers. Harris' emphasis on the crown's communication strategy fits with recent studies of Restoration print, censorship and political culture in Scotland. Clare Jackson has shown how royalist writers sought to rebuild the public image of the crown by transforming Scotland's ancient line of kings into an absolute monarchy with a remodelling of the Fergusian origin myth and the rejection of a Buchananite elective monarchy.[227] Laura Doak has pointed to royalist campaigns staged during visits by the king's brother and heir and shown how, in turn, militant presbyterians appropriated public platforms for rebellious declarations and unrepentant scaffold speeches.[228] In offering the 'culture of controversy' as a framework for understanding public religious debate in this era, Raffe has acknowledged the significant participation of ordinary people in debate and protest while emphasising the extent to which God's truth remained the ultimate authority in these controversies.[229] As Raffe and Jackson both have shown, Restoration presbyterians continued to claim divine authority for their church government, while writers for episcopacy emphasised the indifferency of church government, sidelining the people's consciences.[230]

Drawing on these insights, this section will show how oral, manuscript and print publications contributed to an ongoing contest for allegiance to

---

[226] Harris, 'Publics and participation', 750–1.
[227] Mann, *Scottish Book Trade*, ch. 3; Gardner, *The Scottish Exile Community in the Netherlands, 1660-1690*; Jackson, *Restoration Scotland*, ch. 6.
[228] Doak, 'On Street and Scaffold: the People and Political Culture in Restoration Scotland, c.1678–1685'; Mann, *James VII*, ch. 4.
[229] Raffe, *Culture of Controversy*, 5–21.
[230] Raffe, 'Presbyerians and Episcopalians'; Jackson, *Restoration Scotland*, ch. 5.

Public Communications

the restored monarchy and episcopalian kirk and how this affected the vocabulary of public opinion. The re-establishment of an episcopalian church in 1662 by royal authority turned committed Covenanters into a minority dissenting movement that no longer could speak for the laity at large. Presbyterian writers in the 1660s responded by emphasising, and even exaggerating, the extent of national enrolment in the covenants before 1660 in order to contrast this with a subsequent collapse in covenanting zeal. Unable to claim majority adherence, they urged the truly godly to stay the course. By 1679, hardliners defined themselves as a righteous remnant of the true national kirk, rejecting a degenerate majority. Bold declarations of presbyterian opinion were countered by royalist claims for the loyalty of the nation to the Stewart monarchy. Episcopalian writers urged rational readers to reject presbyterian cant, while reprinted English Exclusion tracts portrayed the opinions of reasonable gentlemen.

In the early stages of the Restoration, calls for the adherence of the godly gave way to royalist appeals to the loyalty and obedience of the subject. Moving south in 1659, the Protectorate army called for the 'unprejudiced faithfull' to concur with them and, early in 1660, the covenants and Robert Douglas' 1651 coronation sermon were reprinted.[231] By the summer of 1660, however, royal proclamations expressed the king's expectation that his 'loving subjects' would demonstrate their loyalty to his re-established government.[232] Female representations of the realm re-appeared in Edinburgh-printed encomia like *Laetitia Caledonicae or Scotland's Raptures,* a poem expressing a female Caledon's 'unuterable happinesse' and calling on each 'Loyall Heart' to reject the covenants and be true to the king above all else.[233] Printed sermons by moderate clergy in Edinburgh, Aberdeen, Linlithgow and Stirling all emphasised the duties of a loyal subject.[234] In *Crunadh an Dara Rìgh Tearlach* (The Crowning of King Charles II), Lom described the return of the king to 'a hundred thousand welcomes' and proposed to travel south from his

---

[231] Monck, *A Declaration of the Commander in Chief of the Forces in Scotland*; Officers of the Army in Scotland, *A Declaration of the Officers of the Army in Scotland to the Churches of Christ in the Three Nations*; *The National Covenant of the Kirk of Scotland and the Solemn League and Covenant; A Solemn League and Covenant.*

[232] Charles II, *His Majesties Gracious Proclamation Concerning the Government of his Ancient Kingdom of Scotland.*

[233] Anon., *Laetitiae Caledonicae or Scotland's Raptures.*

[234] L[aurie], *God Save the King;* R[amsay], *Moses Returned from Midian;* Symson, *Mephibosheth;* Scrougie, *Mirabilia Dei.*

174   Public Opinion in Early Modern Scotland, c.1560–1707

'high mountain glen' for the coronation, or at least the execution of the earl of Argyll in Edinburgh.[235]

The revolution made by the Restoration parliament from January 1661, including an Act Rescissory wiping out the legislative basis for a covenanted Presbyterian kirk, was recounted by Thomas Sydserf, the son of a former bishop, in a short-lived royalist newsbook, *Mercurius Caledonius,* and five news separates. Sydserf's reportage included the state burial of Montrose in January 1661, celebrations in Edinburgh marking the English coronation of Charles II in April (with the comment that the coronation sermon by the future Archbishop Sharp was 'quite of another strain' to Robert Douglas' 1651 sermon), the burning of the Solemn League in London on 22 May and an elaborate feast and festivities in Edinburgh marking the king's birthday on 29 May.[236] Across his publications, Sydserf blamed seditious clergymen for whipping up popular presbyterianism and only mentioned opinion at large when it supported his story, typically in noting the appearance of jubilant crowds.[237] Sydserf asserted that his papers were useful in alerting 'all Fanaticks whatsoever' to the government's changed tune.[238] When leading Resolutioner clerics complained to the king about his impertinence, however, his newsbook was silenced. As Julia Buckroyd has suggested, in the early months of 1661 Charles II could not afford to alienate moderate presbyterian clergy.[239] Still, the value of a royalist paper was recognised by the privy council, with some perhaps recalling the Engagers' newsbook of 1648. In December 1661 a license was provided to Edinburgh postmaster Robert Mein to print a weekly 'diurnall' for 'preventing false news which may be invented by evil and disaffected persons'.[240] As postmaster, Mein circulated London papers to Scottish burghs, though he does not appear to have taken up the opportunity to produce a domestic news digest.[241]

The king's re-established government pursued the regulation of seditious speech and print with vigour.[242] In August 1660, eleven Protester

---

[235] MacKenzie (ed.), *Orain Iain Luim,* 77–81.
[236] [Sydserf], *Mercurius Caledonius* (8 January 1661); *Edinburghs Joy; The Work Goes Bonnely On.*
[237] [Sydserf], *Edinburghs Joy,* 6; Buckroyd, '*Mercurius Caledonius* and its immediate successors, 1661', 15, 19.
[238] [Sydserf], *Edinburghs Joy,* 2.
[239] Buckroyd, '*Mercurius Caledonius*', 21; Laing (ed.), *Letters of Robert Baillie,* iii, 454.
[240] *RPCS,* ser. 3, i, 115.
[241] The judge Lord Fountainhall referred to a short-lived *Edinburgh Gazette* as the 'Edenborough Weeklie Gazet' in 1680. Lauder of Fountainhall, *Historical Observes of Memorable Occurents in Church and State from October 1680 to April 1686,* 33.
[242] The privy council licensed a religious book by David Dickson, translated from Latin 'to Inglish, for more publique use' soon after restarting in July 1661: *RPCS,* ser. 3, i, 12.

ministers, including James Guthrie, were arrested for meeting to frame a remonstrance to the king. This was followed by the burning of two totemic Covenanter books, Rutherford's 1644 *Lex Rex* and Guthrie's 1653 *The Causes of the Lord's Wrath Against Scotland*, in Edinburgh and St Andrews. Guthrie was executed for sedition and Robert McWard, a Protester minister in Glasgow, was banished for a seditious sermon.[243] When unlicensed prints of Guthrie's dying speech appeared in Edinburgh, the privy council reasserted the requirement that all books be licensed.[244] Teeth were added to the policing of seditious words with a parliamentary act passed on 24 June 1662. Stating that the troubles of the past two decades had been caused by certain 'treasonable and sedicious positions' which had been 'infused into the people' by a 'multitude of sedicious sermons, lybells and discourses preached, printed and published', the act confirmed the death penalty for the expression of rebellious doctrines by 'writeing, printing, preacheing or other malicious and advised speakeing'. In addition, any person defending the covenants or undermining the authority of the king or bishop by 'writeing, printing, praying, preacheing, libelling, remonstrating or by any malicious and advised speiking' would be excluded from office in state and kirk and prosecuted for sedition.[245] This made clear that clerical and lay speech alike would be prosecuted by civil authorities. As Mann has shown, strict clauses were added to contracts with Scottish staple ports requiring these Dutch burghs to prevent the export of seditious books to Scotland.[246]

Despite these restrictions, Covenanter exiles managed to publish texts in the Netherlands to justify and support their minority dissenting movement.[247] Though Jamie McDougall has shown that many individuals in Scotland sought ways to conform partially to protect their consciences and their safety, exiled pamphleteers urged an uncompromising separation from the episcopalian church.[248] Because these authors could no longer claim the adherence of the nation, they praised the universality of covenanted commitments before 1660 and urged the godly to maintain their opinions in the face of external pressure. When the exiled minister John

---

[243] Charles I, *His Majesties Gracious Letter Directed to the Presbytery of Edinburgh; RPS* A1661/1/90, 28 May 1661; Buckroyd, 'Bridging the gap: Scotland, 1659–60', 22; Gardner, 'McWard [Macward], Robert'. See chapter 2 on Guthrie.

[244] The council later explained that the licensing order applied only to new books, not routinely printed textbooks. *RPCS*, ser. 3, i, 73, 90, 119. In 1662 they confirmed that the bishop of Glasgow was to review works printed by Robert Sanders in Glasgow: *RPCS*, ser. 3, i, 272.

[245] *RPS* 1662/5/20, 24 June 1662.   [246] Mann, *Scottish Book Trade*, 78.   [247] *Ibid.*, 84–5.

[248] McDougall, 'Covenants and Covenanters', ch. 4.

176   Public Opinion in Early Modern Scotland, c.1560–1707

Brown published in Rotterdam his 1665 *An Apologeticall Relation of the Particular Sufferings of the Faithfull Ministers and Professors of the Church of Scotland since August 1660*, he explained that he wrote in English rather than Latin to ensure that the godly in Scotland would have their 'doubts cleared, scruples removed and their judgements convinced', allowing them to resist a 'popish prelaticall malignant party' and a 'sinful and backslyding Generation'.[249] Also published in Rotterdam, *Naphtali, or the Wrestlings of the Church of Scotland* (1667) underlined the breadth of the 'public Profession of the Truth' in Scotland before 1660, asserting that the kirk had been 'of equal extent with the Nation'; conversely, the 'present Defection' encompassed 'the greatest part of all Ranks'.[250] To encourage conscientious dissenters, *Napthali* reprinted the covenants and the 1648 Solemn Acknowledgement alongside final testimonies by Guthrie and other dying Covenanters. The latter contributed to an emerging martyrology seen also in the circulation of Archibald Johnston of Wariston's 1663 dying speech and later scaffold messages.[251]

The abandonment of the covenants by the Scottish parliament encouraged dissidents to highlight extra-parliamentary opinion. The presbyterian lawyer James Stewart of Goodtrees, one of the authors of *Napthali*, provocatively argued in his 1669 *Jus Populi Vindicatum* that national opinion could be represented by the people at large. Neil McIntyre has shown how, in the absence of noble leadership for presbyterian dissent, Stewart developed the populist implications of the covenants by combining a theory of original sovereignty with the bonds of the covenants to argue that conscientious commoners could revolt against a backsliding monarch. While Buchanan, Rutherford and the author of the *Humble Remonstrance of the Citizens of Edenburgh* assumed that nobles, magistrates or parliament would act on behalf of the nation, Stewart's aim was to justify the ordinary individuals who marched in arms from the southwest in the 1666 Pentland rising. In contending that the 1661 Restoration parliament had been unrepresentative, Stewart employed the phrase 'the true sense of the nation' to suggest that the nation's opinions – not just their grievances – could be identified outside of an authorised assembly of the estates.[252]

---

[249] [Brown], *Apologetical Relation*, 'Epistle to the Christian Reader'.
[250] [Stewart and Stirling], *Naphtali*, sig. A2v, A3v.
[251] *RPCS*, ser. 3, i, 584; King and Kid, *The Last Speeches of the Two Ministers*.
[252] McIntyre, 'Representation and resistance in Restoration Scotland: the political thought of James Stewart of Goodtrees (1635–1713)'.

Public Communications

The privy council responded to presbyterian publishing with post-production censorship. *An Apologeticall Relation* was denounced in February 1666 for endeavouring to 'seduce the lieges' and 'strengthen the disaffected in their rebellious principalls'. This was followed by condemnations of *Naphtali* in December 1667 and *Jus Populi* early in 1671 in similar terms.[253] All three books were burned in Edinburgh near the mercat cross and a large fine of £2,000 was set for owning any of these titles.[254] Women, as well as men, were pursued for dangerous books: Jane Ramsay of Shielhill, the widow of James Guthrie, and her daughter Sophia were exiled to Shetland in 1666 when they refused to reveal how they had obtained a copy of a banned book.[255]

Alongside these restrictions, episcopalian writers sought to persuade subjects to obedience. Stewart of Goodtrees had argued that covenant-swearers needed good reasons 'to renunce what they have been fully perswaded was truth'.[256] The bishop of Orkney, Andrew Honyman, took up this challenge by writing responses to *Naphtali* and *Jus Populi*, having previously published a case for conformity in 1662.[257] In a 1669 tract, Honyman expressed doubt that his book would have any impact on the 'prejudices of the multitude' or zealots whose 'wrathful humours' overtook their reason but hoped that the judicious would hear his arguments.[258] Also in 1669, the episcopalian minister Gilbert Burnet provided a set of six dialogues pitched for 'meaner capacities'. Like Forbes of Corse, he accused the Covenanters of seeking to 'terrifie simple people', especially women. He argued that rational men should recognise covenanting 'cant' and value unity and order over superstitious precision.[259] As Raffe has shown, by painting the presbyterians as irrational enthusiasts, episcopalian writers transformed their sworn commitments into mad fanaticism.[260] To this, Burnet added feminisation by identifying rational conformity with masculinity.

In response, presbyterian communications sought to bolster godly resistance, especially after the contested indulgences of 1669 and 1672. Relatively short, readable tracts from Dutch presses joined manuscript letters circulating from exiled ministers to dissenters in Scotland and

---

[253] *Jus Populi* was condemned again in 1673 and 1680. McIntyre, 'Representation and resistance', 174.

[254] *RPCS*, ser. 3, ii, 138–9, 375–6, iii, 265, 296–7; Charles II, *A Proclamation Anent* Jus Populi.

[255] *RPCS*, ser. 3, ii, 139. [256] McIntyre, 'Representation and resistance', 173.

[257] McDougall, 'Covenants and Covenanters', 149–50.

[258] Honyman, *Survey of Naphtali Part II*, 'To the Reader'.

[259] [Burnet], *A Modest and Free Conference*, sig. A4r, 41. [260] Raffe, *Culture of Controversy*, ch. 5.

178   Public Opinion in Early Modern Scotland, c.1560–1707

locally composed tracts, such as a 1672 'testimony against the embracing of the liberty granted to some ministers in Scotland' written by 'some privat christians'.[261] These texts moved along dissenting networks, revealed by the arrest of a chapman in July 1680 who carried letters between dissenters.[262] In 1671, McWard answered Burnet's dialogue with *The True Non-Conformist*, hoping to sustain 'the Lord's faithful remnant in this hour of great & manifold temptations'.[263] By 1678, the stringent pursuit of conventiclers led him to publish *The Poor Man's Cup of Cold Water, Ministered to the Saints and Sufferers for Christ in Scotland*. Making a virtue of the smallness of the movement, this developed the trope of a 'little flock' of faithful, persecuted Christians, the 'poor remnant' of the covenanted nation.[264]

While hardliners directed underground literature at the godly, the privy council used public proclamations to instruct Scottish subjects in loyal obedience.[265] These were published by the erastian state in 'all places needful', including parish kirks.[266] In September 1683, an announcement of the discovery of a plot to kill the king was made at all kirks in conjunction with a national fast.[267] Some proclamations gave subjects responsibility for combatting non-conformity, forcing individuals to choose to dissent or collaborate. In 1669, for example, a proclamation alerted all subjects to the king's determination to enforce laws against conventicles and required heritors to report separatist preachers.[268] In 1680, Fife heritors arrested for failing to attend a muster against a 1679 presbyterian rising tried to argue that they had not been bound to attend because the proclamation had not been made as required at 'the severall mercat croces', but the state rejected this argument.[269]

As Doak has emphasised, the continuing importance of proclamation as a mode of engagement made the usurpation of this platform by

---

[261] Gardner, *Scottish Exile Community*, 52; NLS Wodrow Quarto XCIX, item 24, A testimony against the embracing of the liberty granted to some ministers in Scotland, 3 September 1672, ff. 179–90.

[262] Lauder of Fountainhall, *Historical Notices of Scotish Affairs*, i, 269.

[263] [McWard], *The True Non-Conformist*.

[264] [McWard], *Poor Man's Cup of Cold Water*, 2. Other writings by McWard and Brown against an accommodation scheme and the 1679 band required of indulged ministers provided intellectual rationales for hardline resistance for more educated readers. [McWard], *The Case of the Accommodation*; [McWard], *Banders Disbanded*; [Brown], *History of the Indulgence*. Gardner, *Scottish Exile Community*, 53.

[265] For more on royal proclamations, see Doak, 'On Street and Scaffold', ch. 3.

[266] *RPCS*, ser. 3, i, 95–6, 510.   [267] Lauder of Fountainhall, *Historical Notices*, i, 450–1.

[268] *RPCS*, ser. 3, iii, 62.   [269] Lauder of Fountainhall, *Historical Notices*, i, 254.

presbyterian hardliners even more significant.[270] Public testimonies against royal authority made between 1679 and 1685, discussed in Chapter 1, stimulated the government to emphasise the dangers of presbyterian fanaticism through proclamations and printed papers. A proclamation issued after the June 1680 discovery of Cargill's new covenant described it as a deeply disturbing combination in which swearers promised to abjure Charles II as a usurper and set up a new government for the true covenanted people under Mosaic law.[271] In November 1680, a proclamation called for the arrest of 'turbulent and fanaticall persons' in a 'schismaticall and ungovernable party' responsible for 'insolencies, murthers and treasons'.[272] The privy council agreed to an order by the king to publish militant papers 'to the end that our dutifull and loyall subjects, being informed, may have a just abhorrence of the principles and practices of these villaines'.[273] Subsequently printed papers included a Gibbite paper and a testimony by James Russell.[274] The latter, a 'prodigious and traiterous libel', was said to have been printed 'for the satisfaction and information of all of His Majesties Loyal and dutiful Subjects'.[275] This was followed by the burning of the 1643 Solemn League and other seditious papers by the hangman in January 1682 (though the judge Lord Fountainhall wondered why the privy council would encourage people to buy and read the Solemn League, a document that he felt was 'old and buried').[276]

While militants sought to speak for 'the true presbyterian and covenanted people of Scotland', royalist propaganda encouraged the people's love for their restored monarch and the ancient Stewart line of kings.[277] Enthusiastic communications celebrated the presence of Charles' brother James in Scotland from November 1679 to February 1680 and October 1680 to March 1682, displaying Scottish loyalty to English as well as domestic readers during the English Exclusion crisis.[278] A printed letter to the king from the Scottish privy council effusively reported that James' first visit had stimulated a 'just abhorrence of these seditious Persons and pernicious Principles' responsible for past troubles. This sentiment was

---

[270] Doak, 'On Street and Scaffold', ch. 3, 5.
[271] Charles II, *A Proclamation Declaring Mr. Richard Cameron, and Others, Rebels and Traitors.*
[272] *RPCS*, ser. 3, vi, 583.   [273] *Ibid.*, 495.
[274] *TSP* ii, no. 2519; Privy Council, *A True and Exact Copy of a Treasonable and Bloody Paper;* Raffe, *Culture of Controversy*, 124.
[275] Russell, *A True and Exact Copy of a Prodigious and Traiterous Libel.*
[276] Lauder of Fountainhall, *Historical Notices*, i, 346.   [277] *RPCS*, ser. 3, vi, 584.
[278] Doak, 'On Street and Scaffold', ch. 2.

180   Public Opinion in Early Modern Scotland, c.1560–1707

apparent in 'all degrees of Person' and the 'Nobility and Gentry of both Sexes', with 'no Libel, no Pasquil' appearing during James' residence.[279] Authorised accounts chronicled James' arrivals in Scotland in November 1679 and October 1680 and a progress in February 1681, showing how loyal officers, nobles, magistrates and crowds turned out to welcome the duke and his family.[280] Appended to the October 1680 account was another letter from the privy council to the king, expressing the 'profound respect, and sincere Kindness' shown by Scottish subjects to James and thanking Charles for allowing them to let 'the world see' their loyalty to the Stewart line, their 'chief Glory, and only security'.[281] Lord Fountainhall described this as 'a boast to hector the House of Commons and the generality of the English nation' on the question of exclusion.[282] Positive reports of Scotland's welcome to the king's Catholic successor flowed back into the northern realm through the *London Gazette*, while vernacular praise poetry was printed in Edinburgh.[283] One poet mourned the departure of James by asserting that 'our Hearts must frieze' without the warming rays of 'Caledon's Sun' and that 'all Scotland' loved James, 'except some clownish Boors'.[284]

This publicity was enhanced by the reprinting in Edinburgh of anti-Exclusion tracts alongside Scottish pamphlets in favour of James' succession. The greater availability of English tracts in Scotland by 1680 can be seen in Lord Fountainhall's frequent references to such titles in his *Historical Observes* for 1680–6.[285] English tracts tended to feature gentleman narrators advancing arguments for rational readers. *A Civil Correction of a Sawcy Impudent Pamphlet,* for example, responded to Exclusionist pamphlets in the voice of a thoughtful reader, while *The True Protestants Appeal to the City and Country* concluded that 'you shall never see this Nation secured in a happy Peace, till Sober, Wise, Judicious and moderate men, by Moderate, Cool and healing Councils, rescue both the Church and State' from 'Schismaticks'.[286] These joined Scottish tracts like *A Brief Account of his Sacred Majestie's Descent,* which asserted that 'none can justly blame any, who is a Subject to the Monarch

---

[279] Privy Council, *A Letter to His Majesty from his Privy Council in Scotland.*
[280] Mann, *James VII,* 140.
[281] Privy Council, *A True Narrative of the Reception of their Royal Highnesses.* See also *A Letter Directed from the Council of Scotland to the King.*
[282] Lauder of Fountainhall, *Historical Notices,* i, 275.   [283] *London Gazette* 1623 (6–9 June 1681).
[284] L., *Albion's Elegie, or a Poem upon the High and Mighty Prince James,* 5, 7, 13.
[285] Lauder of Fountainhall, *Historical Observes.*
[286] [Nalson], *The True Protestants Appeal to the City and Country,* 4.

of Great Britain, modestly to endeavour the satisfaction of his Reason, Judgement and Conscience'.[287]

Despite censorship efforts, including a January 1680 order for all 'gazetts and news letters red in coffie-houses' to be reviewed prior to sale, counter-messages attacking James' Catholicism appeared.[288] During James' visit in 1680, a group of Edinburgh college students managed to stage an embarrassing pope-burning in the capital on Christmas day.[289] A short tract, possibly printed in Edinburgh, emphasised the authorities' efforts to quash this event, insinuating their favour for Catholicism. The king's horse guard was said to have been deployed at a gallop under 'his Majesties Standard Royal' to prevent any violence to Catholics.[290] This account was supplemented by a London print describing the event as a 'Publick Testimony' against Catholicism. Though insisting that the students did not mean to insult anyone other than the pope, the tract closed with a stinging reference to James' Catholic faith.[291] After this event, some Edinburgh elites signalled their political sympathies by wearing either blue hat ribbons with anti-Catholic slogans or royalist red ribbons.[292]

A greater challenge was made in May 1685 with the printing of a manifesto by Archibald Campbell, ninth earl of Argyll on a press brought from Amsterdam to Kintyre to rally presbyterians to rise against the accession of a Catholic monarch.[293] Yet this declaration in name of 'the Noblemen, Barrons, Burgesses & Commons of all sorts now in armes in the Kingdom of Scotland, with the concurrence of their true and faithfull Pastors' failed to convince Lowland presbyterians to join an uncovenanted rebellion.[294] In reply, Lom marked the defeat of Argyll with *Oran Do Mharcus Atholl* (A Song to the Marquis of Atholl), celebrating the bravery of the marquis as 'Lieutenant appointed by the King' against those 'who wear head-dress of religion'.[295]

While continuing to combine messages in favour of royal policy with controls on seditious speech, James VII ramped up the crown's publicity

---

[287] Anon., *A Brief Account of his Sacred Majestie's Descent*, 1.
[288] Lauder of Fountainhall, *Historical Notices*, i, 248.   [289] Doak, 'On Street and Scaffold', ch. 4.
[290] Anon., *The Scots Demonstration of their Abhorrence of Popery*.
[291] Anon., *A Modest Apology for the Students*, 7, 10, 18.
[292] Lauder of Fountainhall, *Historical Observes*, 19.
[293] Argyll brought a printer from the Amsterdam printing house of Jacob van der Velde to operate the press. Mann, *Scottish Book Trade*, 152.
[294] Campbell, *Declaration and Apology of the Protestant People*; Doak, 'The "vanishing of a fantosme"?'.
[295] Mackenzie (ed.), *Orain Iain Luim*, 166–77, 301.

182   Public Opinion in Early Modern Scotland, c.1560–1707

efforts by installing a printer to the king's household in Holyrood to publish pro-Catholic materials. At his accession, English accounts of his Westminster coronation and celebratory poems were reprinted in Edinburgh alongside a loyalist sermon by James Canaries, minister at Selkirk.[296] Controls on seditious speech were reasserted with proclamations in June and September 1686, the latter being ordered for quarterly promulgation.[297] When proposals for the toleration of Catholic worship were put to the parliament in 1686, printed tracts supported this measure while opponents were restricted to manuscript publication and authors were investigated.[298] As Mann has shown, the printer James Glen was pursued late in 1687 for publishing an unlicensed anti-Catholic tract, while the Holyrood printers James Watson (from 1685) and Peter Bruce (from 1687) answered anti-Catholic tracts and defended James' 1687 indulgence for Catholic and dissenting worship.[299] As Chapter 3 has shown, with this indulgence Catholic and non-conforming clerics could preach freely, constrained only by regulations on seditious speech; yet this did not stop clerics, conformist as well as dissenting, from speaking against the king's Catholicism.

With the restoration of the monarch and the bishops in 1660–2, episcopalian royalists strove to win back the subjects to quiet obedience while presbyterian dissenters sought to sustain what Stewart of Goodtrees called the 'true sense of the nation'. Censorship restricted unwanted printing in Edinburgh, forcing dissenters to rely on manuscript and Dutch-printed tracts. On the royalist side, episcopalian pamphlets, crown proclamations, royal pageantry and propagandistic reprints of seditious texts were supplemented by the republication in Edinburgh of moderate English tracts. While presbyterian dissenters urged adherence to the nation's sworn commitments, episcopalian and royalist discourse condemned disorderly schism and sedition under the cloak of religion. The importation of a press by the earl of Argyll did not ensure the success of his 1685 rising but indicated his desire to facilitate public communications. The Catholic James VII also sponsored a press, contributing to the formation of fears for the church that the censorship of seditious talk could not wholly suppress.

---

[296] James VII, *This Day Being the Festival of St George;* Settle, *An Heroic Poem;* Canaries, *A Sermon Preacht at Selkirk.*
[297] James VII, *A Proclamation against Slanderers and Leasing-Makers;* TSP no. 2671, 2678.
[298] Wodrow, *History,* ii, 594–5.   [299] Mann, *Scottish Book Trade,* 152; Mann, *James VII,* 188.

4.4 Conclusions

This chapter has not asked whether a public sphere was created through the consumption of printed tracts in early modern Scotland. Instead, it has considered how far persuasive arguments, in oral, handwritten and printed forms, were addressed to men and women at large for political purposes by the crown and its opponents, and what rhetorical forms were used to represent and express extra-institutional opinions in these communications. This has shown how religious reformation and regal union made public opinion something that monarchs needed to manage and that dissidents could exploit, using a range of formats. In Scotland's distinctive communicative context, the continuing importance of oral communications helped to engage women and Gaelic-speakers. As extra-institutional opinion came into greater focus, its representation in tracts shifted from abstract figures and stock characters expressing general grievances to more direct and bold claims about the allegiances and opinions of the laity and the nation.

Under Mary and James VI, the crown and its supporters supplied propagandistic arguments in proclamations, tracts, poems, pageantry and books while censoring political and religious printing. These restrictions forced opponents to rely more on oral sermons, circular letters and tracts published by overseas presses. At this stage, the rhetoric of public opinion focused on a fear of false reports and emphasised the susceptibility of ordinary subjects to misleading information. Elites ventriloquised their opinions through stock characters or female figures of Scotland. However, books by the adult James VI demonstrate the crown's increased commitment to proactive persuasion, going beyond mere correction of false rumours to influence audiences with readable dialogues and the cachet of a royal author. Charles I also directed proclamations and tracts at his Scottish people, but his unwillingness to acknowledge complaints meant that his messages often missed their mark. Royalist tracts by writers like Forbes of Corse were overtaken by the volume and range of Covenanter communications and the stringency of Covenanter censorship, though Gaelic poetry and prints from London or the continent were less easy to suppress. As internal divisions worsened, Engager, Kirk party and Cromwellian regimes competed for the allegiance of the godly. From 1661, strict censorship pushed presbyterian exiles to use Dutch presses, manuscript messages and oral declarations to urge followers to stay the course. Hardliners presented themselves as the true covenanted kirk and nation, however small. Reprinted covenant texts remained the touchstone

184   Public Opinion in Early Modern Scotland, c.1560–1707

for presbyterian consciences, while royalist and episcopalian discourse, including imported or reprinted English tracts, emphasised the satisfaction of moderate, masculine minds.

In this period from the 1560 Reformation to the eve of the Williamite Revolution, a wide range of attitudes towards public opinion was on display, from revulsion to respect. Many elites still feared that the silly multitude could be misled – Lord Advocate Sir George Mackenzie of Rosehaugh in 1680 reportedly said that 'permitting the common peeple to read the Scriptures did more evill than good' – but over time counter-arguments became as important as censorship.[300] With rising literacy, written and printed publications could reach middling to lower ranks, including female readers and especially in urban areas, while oral sermons, proclamations and political poetry continued to engage Scots and Gaelic speakers across the social scale. The next two chapters will show how public communications, combined with protestations, petitions and oaths, allowed concepts like 'the inclinations of the people' and 'the sense of the nation' to become prominent in Scottish political discourse after 1688.

[300] Lauder of Fountainhall, *Historical Notices*, i, 311.

CHAPTER 5

The Inclinations of the People

[T]here is nocht ane mayr ignorant & ane mayr blynd thyng in this varld as is til adhere to the iudgement of the comont pepil quhilk hes nothir consideratione nor rason.

Dame Scotia, The Complaynt of Scotland (1550)[1]

[P]relacy and the superiority of any office in the church above presbyters, is and hath been a great and insupportable grievance and trouble to this nation, and contrary to the inclinationes of the generality of the people ever since the reformatione (they haveing reformed from popery by presbyters) and therfor ought to be abolished.

1689 Claim of Right[2]

The Revolution of 1688–90 reinforced the greater prominence of extra-institutional opinion in Scottish political culture as public support for William of Orange lent plausibility to a constitutional claim for the people's preferences in church government. When the invasion of England by Dutch forces in November 1688 led to the flight of James VII and II, presbyterians in Scotland mobilised grassroots agitations for a revolution in the church as well as the state. National assemblies in each kingdom offered the Scottish and English crowns to William and his wife Mary Stewart, led in Scotland by a cadre of returned exiles and sympathetic nobles and backed by squads of armed presbyterians on the streets of Edinburgh. A set of limitations on royal power, known as the Claim of Right, and an accompanying list of complaints (the Articles of Grievances) were attached to the offer of the Scottish crown.[3] The Claim of Right included the assertion, quoted above, that most people in Scotland preferred presbyterian church government.

---

[1] [Wedderburn], *The Complaynt of Scotland*, 99. [2] *RPS* 1689/3/108, 11 April 1689.
[3] Bowie, "'A legal limited monarchy'", 146–8.

185

186   Public Opinion in Early Modern Scotland, c.1560–1707

This clause has only recently attracted historiographical attention, having been accepted as simple fact by generations of presbyterian historians. For C.S. Terry, writing in 1920, 'the inclinations of the majority rejected a prelatical establishment'.[4] In 1959, however, the Rev. Thomas Maxwell sought 'a fair review', setting aside 'personal predilections', and concluded that 'there was a division in Scotland with strong support for both sides'.[5] This was consolidated by Andrew Drummond and James Bulloch's 1973 study of the post-Revolution church which made clear that the veracity of the claim for a presbyterian consensus was 'highly doubtful'.[6] Although research stimulated by the 1989 tercentenary tended to emphasise the conservative nature of the Revolution in Scotland, Tim Harris has shown that the Scottish constitutional settlement was more radical than in England and David Onnekink has proposed that the Williamite period should be seen as 'a transformative period of political experimentation'.[7] While noting the unusual nature of the inclinations clause, Alasdair Raffe has warned that it should not be seen as evidence of the legitimacy of public opinion in a Habermasian sense; instead, this assertion of popular preferences was 'accidental', designed to renew the presbyterian church without acknowledging the covenants.[8] Harris, too, has stressed the tactical nature of the inclinations clause, arguing that the placing of a statement about popular feelings in the Claim of Right, instead of the Articles of Grievances, was a 'deliberate strategy' designed to 'ensure that the new monarchs would be required to abolish the institution of episcopacy'.[9] This successful gambit had a major impact not just in Scotland, Harris observed, but in England, because it led Anglicans to harden their stance against English presbyterians, making comprehension impossible in 1689.[10]

The analysis of early modern public opinion in the preceding chapters suggests that the inclinations clause arose from a deeper context and had a greater significance than has been recognised. By the time of the Revolution, extra-institutional opinion had become a force in Scottish politics. This chapter will show how reliance on public opinion was

[4] Terry, *A History of Scotland*, 481.   [5] Maxwell, 'Presbyterian and Episcopalian in 1688', 25, 37.
[6] Drummond and Bulloch, *The Scottish Church 1688–1843*, 4.
[7] Harris, 'The people, the law and the constitution in Scotland and England: A comparative approach to the glorious revolution'; Onnekink, 'The earl of Portland (1689–1699): a re-evaluation of Williamite policy', 231.
[8] Raffe, *Culture of Controversy*, 10.
[9] Harris, 'The people, the law and the constitution', 46–53; Harris, *Revolution: The Great Crisis of the British Monarchy, 1685–1720*, 403.
[10] Harris, 'Publics and participation', 753.

The Inclinations of the People 187

signalled from the earliest stages of the Revolution, allowing leaders to capitalise on an explosion of publicly expressed enthusiasm for presbyterian church government that overwhelmed a much smaller number of Williamite voices speaking for prelacy. Moreover, the inclinations clause reinforced the stature of public opinion by presenting 'the generality of the people' not as a dangerous and easily misled multitude, but a body with meaningful opinions on questions of church governance. Though expressed in the traditional language of complaint and grievance, the placing of this clause in a ratified instrument of government gave it a degree of constitutional authority. That authority was contested by episcopalians, partly by deriding vulgar opinion, but also by challenging the accuracy of the clause with demands for the direct measurement of popular preferences. Until the 1707 Act of Union superseded the Claim of Right with a new constitutional guarantee for the Scottish presbyterian church, the inclinations clause stimulated a running debate on the actual preferences of the people for church government. Episcopalian writers proposed polls and politicians offered collective petitions to prove their claims for the people's inclinations, leading some presbyterians to express ambivalence about their church's reliance on popular opinion. By the time of the Union, the rhetoric of the people's inclinations had become well-established within political parlance, allowing James Hamilton, fourth duke of Hamilton to express the fear that a treaty of union with England would be passed by the Scottish parliament 'inspyt of the inclinatione of the people'.[11]

5.1 The Making of the Inclinations Clause

William's instructions to George Melville, Lord Melville, a returned presbyterian exile acting as his agent in Scotland's 1689 convention of estates, show that the prince wanted to secure a moderate settlement in Scotland on lines already established by the English parliament's Declaration of Rights.[12] But the overturning of the covenants and re-establishment of episcopacy by law in 1661–2 meant that presbyterian government could not be claimed by legal right. The inclinations clause, with its expression of longstanding popular grievance, had to be placed in the Claim of Right to force the abolition of prelacy. This controversial move, later condemned by the episcopalian historian Gilbert Burnet as

---

[11] NRS GD406/1/5294, James duke of Hamilton to Anne duchess of Hamilton, 22 October 1706.
[12] Melville (ed.), *Letters and State Papers Chiefly Addressed to George, Earl of Melville, Secretary of State for Scotland, 1689-1691*, 2.

188   Public Opinion in Early Modern Scotland, c.1560–1707

'absurd', was foreshadowed with references to public opinion in Williamite communications and reinforced by a surge of extra-institutional support for presbyterian church government expressed by crowds, pamphlets and petitions.[13]

News of William's pending invasion and his eventual landing on the south coast of England on 5 November 1688 stimulated public communications for and against his venture, with Williamite voices quickly growing in volume. Separate declarations for Scotland and England from the prince of Orange were printed, with the Scottish version being pitched for a presbyterian audience through the influence of exiles.[14] The text emphasised William's desire to come to 'the Relief of so Distressed a Kingdom', listing complaints that included not just James' 'Absolute Monarchy' and the encouragement of Catholicism but also alleged Caroline abuses including 'Hanging, Shooting and Drowning' of presbyterian dissenters without trial or mercy.[15] For Colin Lindsay, the Jacobite third earl of Balcarres, 'it was evident that [William] intended to sacrifice all to satisfy the Presbyterians'.[16] Copies of the declaration were spread on presbyterian networks and read publicly in towns including Edinburgh, Glasgow, Irvine and Ayr.[17] Too late, the privy council on 10 November 1688 issued a proclamation against the spreading of 'treasonable Papers' and 'false News', though counter-propaganda was provided with the printing of loyal addresses. Two weeks after the landing, the *London Gazette* printed an address by the Convention of Royal Burghs expressing a desire to 'let all Your other Subjects see' their steadfastness for James VII.[18] A similar message of adherence signed by twelve Scottish bishops was printed in the *Gazette* in November and reprinted in a London pamphlet alongside a loyal address from the University of St Andrews, while the king's printer in Holyrood reprinted a tract attacking William's declaration for England.[19] In December, however, the privy council indicated a change of heart (and personnel) with two proclamations ordering arms to be taken from Catholics and calling out the shire militia

---

[13]   Routh (ed.), *Bishop Burnet's History of His Own Time,* iv, 40.
[14]   Wodrow, *History,* ii, 647–9; Gardner, *Scottish Exile Community,* 187.
[15]   William of Orange, *The Declaration of His Highness William . . . for Restoring the Laws and Liberties of the Ancient Kingdom of Scotland*; Raffe, 'Propaganda, religious controversy and the Williamite Revolution in Scotland', 23–5.
[16]   Lindsay, *Memoirs Touching the Revolution in Scotland,* 13.
[17]   *London Gazette* 2398 (8–12 November 1688); Wodrow, *History,* ii, 649; Harris, *Revolution,* 375.
[18]   *London Gazette* 2401 (17–19 November 1688); Harris, *Revolution,* 370.
[19]   Wodrow, *History,* ii, appendix, 205; University of St Andrews, *The Address of the University of St Andrews*; Anon., *Some Reflections.*

The Inclinations of the People

to defend the Protestant religion.[20] After a gathering in London of over a hundred Scottish nobles and gentlemen early in January 1689, a Jacobite speech by James Hamilton, earl of Arran was printed in Edinburgh and London.[21] This was countered by a broadside describing how the assembled lords refused to 'give their Sense of the Earls Proposal' before signing an address inviting William to assume the administration of Scotland.[22]

A subsequent address to William from dissenting presbyterian clergy emphasised the religious views of the presbyterian people. As Elizabeth Hyman and Raffe have shown, James' 1687 toleration created a web of indulged presbyterian ministers who were ready to act when William's invasion gave them the opportunity.[23] These clergy recognised the favour shown by William's declaration, characterising it 'as Rain on the mown Grass'. Citing the opinions of dissenting presbyterians, bound 'by Light and Conviction of the Word of God, and the Conscience of many solemn Engagements', their address begged William to lift the 'Yoke of Prelacy' imposed not only 'against the Consent of the Church' but 'contrary to the Genius of the Nation'.[24] Noble endorsements were added to the address before its presentation to William in late February.[25] Reports hint at the drafting of an address offering the 'Grievances of many Thousands' in name of 'the People of Scotland, of all Sorts, especially of the Presbyterians there' and the preparation of a petition in favour of presbytery with 40,000 signatures.[26] Confirmed petitions include an address from the nobility, gentry, magistrates and inhabitants of Glasgow 'with others now in armes in the west of Scottland' and an address from the city of Edinburgh.[27] The address from the west celebrated the prince's 'Glorious undertaking' with a 'publick Testimony', informing him that they had 'taken up armes under your victorious bener for the ends exprest' in his declaration.[28]

Similarly encouraged by William's declaration, between November and March other presbyterians expressed their desire for a church revolution. While pope-burnings appeared in Edinburgh, Aberdeen, Dumfries and

---

[20] Wodrow, *History*, ii, 651 and appendix, 205–6; Harris, *Revolution*, 371–2.
[21] Hamilton, *A Speech Made by the Right Honourable the Earl of Arran*.
[22] William of Orange, *His Highness the Prince of Orange His Speech;* Wodrow, *History*, ii, 651; *RPS* 1689/3/36, 19 March 1689.
[23] Hyman, 'A church militant: Scotland 1661–1690', 70; Raffe, *Scotland in Revolution, 1685–1690*, ch. 2.
[24] Wodrow, *History*, ii, appendix, 211–12.   [25] Harris, *Revolution*, 382.
[26] Wodrow, *History*, ii, appendix, 207–11; Harris, *Revolution*, 382.
[27] McCormick (ed.), *State Papers and Letters Addressed to William Carstares*, 37; Whatley and Patrick, 'Persistence, principle and patriotism in the making of the Union of 1707: The Revolution, Scottish parliament and *squadrone volante*', 174.
[28] NRS GD3/10/3/10, Copy of an address from Glasgow to the Prince, 1688.

190   Public Opinion in Early Modern Scotland, c.1560–1707

Glasgow, Glasgow's fires also consumed episcopal effigies.[29] In central and southwestern shires, bands of presbyterians forcibly ousted an estimated 200 episcopalian ministers from pulpits and manses before and during the 1689 convention.[30] When clerics from the established church in the west petitioned William for his protection, a 6 February proclamation against the disruption of worship was disregarded in many localities.[31] A crowd of presbyterian women in Glasgow justified an attempt to exclude an episcopalian minister from the cathedral in February as a fulfilment of William's desire to stop the persecution of presbyterians.[32] Prominent in the removal of clergy were the Cameronians or United Societies, who had continued to meet regularly after rejecting the 1687 indulgence.[33] Returning to their practice of public testimony, the Societies published a statement early in January justifying the expulsion of prelatical clergy according to the Solemn League.[34] They also prepared a petition for the Scottish convention asking for the reinstatement of presbyterian church government, though they did not succeed in having this presented.[35] Just prior to the start of the Scottish convention in March 1689, they also renewed the National Covenant and Solemn League at Lesmahagow in Lanarkshire with an updated version of the 1648 Solemn Acknowledgement.[36]

Manifestations of opinion at large continued to reinforce the presbyterian cause during the convention of estates that opened on 11 March 1689 in Edinburgh. According to the earl of Balcarres, William Hamilton, third duke of Hamilton and other lords associated with the presbyterian cause brought armed retinues and encouraged 'a great number of rabble' to come to Edinburgh.[37] Armed men formed a phalanx around Parliament House carrying banners with the motto 'For Reformation According to the Word of God'.[38] The convention later voted an act of thanks to the 'persones well affected to the Protestant religion' who had come to Edinburgh and 'put themselves to armes' in order to 'secure the peace and quiet of this meeting'.[39] When 'six or seven of the western rabble' reportedly threatened

---

[29] Wodrow, *History*, ii, 649–51; Anon., *A True Account of the Trial, Condemnation and Burning*; Harris, *Revolution*, 372–6; Raffe, *Scotland in Revolution*, 110–15.

[30] Raffe, *Scotland in Revolution*, 115–7.

[31] [Morer, Sage and Munro], *An Account of the Present Persecution of the Church of Scotland in Several Letters*, 20–1; Raffe, *Scotland in Revolution*, 117.

[32] Raffe, 'Propaganda', 32.   [33] Jardine, 'The United Societies', ch. 5.

[34] Harris, *Revolution*, 376–8; Raffe, *Scotland in Revolution*, 116.   [35] Harris, *Revolution*, 382.

[36] Raffe, 'Confessions, covenants', para 21–3.   [37] Lindsay, *Memoirs Touching the Revolution*, 24.

[38] Balfour-Melville (ed.), *An Account of the Proceedings of the Estates*, i, 21, 33.

[39] *RPS* 1689/3/72, 28 March 1689.

The Inclinations of the People

to assassinate James Graham, viscount Dundee and former Lord Advocate Sir George Mackenzie of Rosehaugh, the convention showed little sympathy for what it termed 'private affairs'.[40] The convention required all Protestant subjects to be ready with 'their best horse and armes' to suppress any action in favour of James VII.[41]

As Raffe has emphasised, there was not an organised presbyterian 'party' in the convention and some members may have been undecided, but the election of Williamites had been encouraged by the opening of the burgh electorate to all burgesses and the lifting of the 1681 test oath from electors and commissioners.[42] Early in the convention, the election of the duke of Hamilton as president and the reading of an intransigent letter from James VII consolidated the Williamite camp and encouraged viscount Dundee and other committed Jacobites to abandon the meeting. Their departure allowed Melville to pursue William's private instructions for the restoration of 'the Government of the Church in the Presbiterian way', if 'that interest is strongest' in the convention.[43]

An attempt was made by episcopalian Williamites to counter the apparent strength of the presbyterian interest by publishing a memorial to William. George Mackenzie, viscount Tarbat and Sir George Mackenzie of Rosehaugh urged the prince to see that presbyterian numbers were 'not near so great' as it seemed, for 'though now [the presbyterians] appear numerous here, yet that proceeds from their being all here, upon design to make themselves appear considerable.' The activity of armed presbyterians in southwestern parishes and Edinburgh was designed, they argued, to 'persuade the Nation that they onely must give Measures, and that none can live peaceably there without complying with all their Inclinations'.[44]

As Tarbat and Rosehaugh feared, in the convention William's advisors played up the political force of presbyterian inclinations. The opinion of the people had not been mentioned in a 24 December letter from the Scottish privy council to William nor in the January address to William from Scottish nobles in London.[45] An early draft of the presbyterian clergy's address made no mention of the people's preference; instead, its reference to the 'genius of the nation' appears to have been added through

---

[40] Lindsay, *Memoirs Touching the Revolution*, 29, 33; *RPS* M1689/3/8, 22 March 1689.
[41] *RPS* M1689/3/5, 19 March 1689.
[42] Raffe, *Scotland in Revolution*, 132–3; Patrick, 'Unconventional procedure', 211–2.
[43] Melville (ed.), *Letters and State Papers*, 2.
[44] [Mackenzie and Mackenzie], *A Memorial to His Highness the Prince of Orange*, 6–7.
[45] Fraser, *The Melvilles Earls of Melville*, iii, 193; William of Orange, *His Highness the Prince of Orange His Speech*, 2.

192   Public Opinion in Early Modern Scotland, c.1560–1707

the influence of William Carstares, a former exile and personal chaplain to William.[46] William's formal letter to the convention, most likely written by Melville and Carstares, introduced the term 'inclinations' in urging regard for 'the generall interest and inclinationes of the people that, after so much trouble and great suffering, they may live happily and in peace.'[47] The convention echoed this language in its response, promising to secure Scotland's religion, laws and liberties 'upon solid fundations most agreeable to the generall good and inclinatione of the people'.[48] This language is striking in the way it added popular preferences to the more traditional concept of the common good. A 'committee for setleing the government', including Melville, proceeded to develop 'ane instrument of government to be offered with the croune for secureing the people from the greivances which doe affect them'.[49] The inclinations clause in the resulting Claim of Right was accepted by a majority vote, though more dissented from this measure than a clause declaring that James had 'forefaulted' the Scottish crown.[50]

The convention took care to ensure that William and Mary accepted the Claim of Right with the Scottish crown, though William resisted the imposition of conditions on his rule. The convention's emissaries were instructed to read the Claim of Right with the Articles of Grievances before the administration of the coronation oath.[51] An accompanying letter to William and Mary stated that the swearing of the coronation oath would be taken as 'testimony of your majestie and the queen's acceptance' of what the letter called the 'petitione or Claime of Right of the subjects of this kingdome'.[52] In England, William had given a speech on 15 February in which he promised to 'endeavour to support' the English Declaration of Rights and to 'concur in anything that shall be for the Good of the Kingdome'.[53] In his Scottish coronation, William gave no answer to the

---

[46] McCormick (ed.), *State Papers and Letters*, 37; [Mackenzie and Mackenzie], *A Memorial*, 10–23, 25. Wodrow called the Mackenzies' copy 'maimed and false' (*History*, ii, 652) but it appears to be a draft superseded by advice from London.
[47] *RPS* 1689/3/16, 16 March 1689. David Onnekink has emphasised the control of affairs by Melville and Carstares working under William's aide Bentinck in this period. Onnekink, 'The earl of Portland', 234–40.
[48] *RPS* 1689/3/58, 23 March 1689.
[49] *RPS* 1689/3/67, 27 March 1689 and 1689/3/95, 4 April 1689.
[50] Father Thomas Hay reported eighty-six votes for abolishing prelacy and thirty-two against, while the marquis of Tweeddale recorded 106 or 107 in favour and thirty-two against. Hay, *Genealogie of the Hayes of Tweeedale*, 76; Riley, *King William and the Scottish Politicians*, 9. Twelve votes were cast against the 'forefaulting' of James VII. Balfour-Melville (ed.), *An Account of the Proceedings*, i, 25–6.
[51] *RPS* 1689/3/168, 25 April 1689.   [52] *RPS* 1689/3/159, 24 April 1689.
[53] Schwoerer, *The Declaration of Rights, 1689*, 298.

The Inclinations of the People

Claim of Right, though he did pause during the coronation ceremony to express concern about a requirement in the Scottish coronation oath to pursue heretics.[54] A subsequent letter from William to the convention noted that the Claim of Right and Articles of Grievances had been read before the coronation oath and promised that 'yow shall alwayes find us ready to protect yow and assist yow in makeing such laws as may secure your religion, liberties and properties and prevent or redress whatever may be justly greivous'. Twice insisting that the interest of the crown could not clash with the 'true interest' of the people, William returned to the traditional idea that as king he would judge what was good for the nation.[55]

When the estates reconvened in June 1689, continuing pressure for the abolition of prelacy was countered by a campaign in favour of the comprehension of conformist episcopalian clergy. In response, presbyterian rhetoric defined the 'true' church as presbyterian and began to invoke divine right as well as popular preferences. The king's letter to parliament stated that the government of the kirk would be settled 'according to your desires and inclinations' and in keeping with this, a general address in name of (but not signed individually by) 'the Presbiterian ministers and professors of the Church of Scotland' was presented in this session and again in 1690.[56] Speaking on behalf of 'all that love the true reformed Protestant religion in this Land', the address left no space for comprehension. It blamed prelacy on self-serving clerics, equated episcopalianism with Jacobitism and asked parliament to settle the church according to 'the Word of God' and the ratification of presbyterian government by James VI in 1592. The address proposed the restoration of presbyterian clergy removed after 1661 and the abolition of patronage (as in 1649) so that congregations could call presbyterian ministers according to their preferences. The covenants were not mentioned, though the reinstatement of the Westminster catechisms and directory of worship 'formerly Received by the general Consent of this Nation' was requested.[57] However, the synod of Aberdeen submitted a competing address for 'ane union with all our Protestant brethren'. This asked that 'ministers of different persuasions in matters of church government' be allowed to make

---

[54] Cowan, 'Church and state', 176.

[55] *RPS* 1689/3/236, 24 May 1689. Melville, now secretary for Scotland, signed the letter on behalf of William and would have been responsible for its language.

[56] *RPS* 1689/6/5, 5 June 1689; Raffe, *Scotland in Revolution*, 140.

[57] Anon., *To His Grace ... The Address of the Presbyterian Ministers and Professors*; Stephen, 'Defending the Revolution: The Church of Scotland and the Scottish parliament, 1689–95', 32–3.

194   Public Opinion in Early Modern Scotland, c.1560–1707

proposals to a general assembly that would discuss the church settlement.[58] This episcopalian call was backed by *A Letter from the West*, which challenged the apparent dominance of presbyterian opinion in the south-west by arguing, in the persona of a reasonable gentleman, that both the covenants and the 1681 test should be eschewed in favour of a 'moderate Episcopacie' led by 'Learned Divines, gathered out of both Perswasions'.[59]

After the estates voted for an act abolishing the office of the bishop according to 'the inclinationes of the generalitie of the people', presbyterian and episcopalian interests continued to present competing communications until the church settlement was completed by parliament in its 1690 session.[60] In September 1689, as more doubts were raised about the actual inclinations of the people, a delegation appointed by a general meeting of presbyterian clergy travelled to London to reassure William and Mary.[61] In October, a printed address to William claiming to speak for 'the greatest part' of parliament complained that delays in the confirmation of presbytery had caused the 'visible Consternation and Discouragement of thousands of your good Subjects' and indicated parliament's desire to settle matters 'for the satisfaction of the Country'.[62] To support this address, the former presbyterian exile Robert Ferguson published a justification stressing the expectation of 'the Lieges' to have their 'Grievances Redressed' by the estates. Ferguson implied that the Scottish secretary Sir John Dalrymple of Stair had been seditious when he suggested in parliament that the king's interest in church governance might differ from the people's, causing the people to be 'allarm'd'.[63] Ferguson's tract reveals an intensification in the exchange of publications between Scotland and England as he argued against episcopalian lobbying and publishing designed to recruit Anglican support.[64] In response, a tract decried the 'peremptoriness' of this address and accused the king's opponents of trying to 'Amuse the unwarry multitude.'[65] An address to the reconvened parliament on 27 May 1690 from 'severall Ministers, in name of themselves, and others of the Episcopal Perswasion' asked again for a

---

[58] *RPS* A1689/6/8, 2 July 1689; Clarke, 'The Williamite episcopalians', 43.
[59] Anon., *Letter from the West*; Raffe, *Scotland in Revolution*, 141.
[60] *RPS* 1689/6/36, 22 July 1689; Clarke, 'Williamite episcopalians', 38–9; Halliday, 'The Club and the Revolution in Scotland 1689–90'.
[61] Stephen, 'Defending the Revolution', 35; Onnekink, 'The earl of Portland', 240.
[62] Anon., *An Address Sign'd by the Greatest Part of the Members of the Parliament*.
[63] [Ferguson], *The Late Proceedings and Votes*, 3, 6–7, 9.
[64] Clarke, 'Williamite episcopalians', 45; Raffe, 'Episcopalian polemic, the London printing press and Anglo-Scottish divergence in the 1690s', 24–7.
[65] Anon., *An Account of the Affairs of Scotland*, 4–5.

The Inclinations of the People

'Conference' to find grounds for a 'happy Union' in the kirk, but this was laid aside.[66] The tussle over church government finally was resolved with a 1690 act restoring the 'true' Protestant church according to 'the Word of God' and the 1592 act, by which presbyterian church government had been 'received by the generall consent of this nation to be the only government of Christ's church within this kingdome'. As had been requested by petition, pulpits were to be re-populated from a narrow base of clergy appointed before 1661, patronage in the selection of ministers was abolished and the 1647 Westminster Confession of Faith was ratified. The 1690 act reiterated the terms of the inclinations clause, asserting that a presbyterian settlement was best suited for 'the establishing of peace and tranquillity within this realme'.[67]

The 1690 act allowed church commissions to purge 'erroneous' clergy who disagreed with the presbyterian settlement. Already about 200 clergies had been removed by the privy council for refusing to pray for the new king and queen as ordered by the 1689 convention. More would be removed when a 1689 oath of allegiance and 1690 oath of assurance were extended from civil and military officers to all clerics in 1693. These post-Revolution oaths sought to confirm the civil allegiance of subjects by requiring swearers to accept William and Mary as monarchs, with the 1690 oath of assurance insisting that they held their crowns by right.[68] Unlike former covenant and test oaths, these oaths did not tie consciences to a confession of faith or form of church government, yet many clerics felt unable to swear them, having previously sworn allegiance to James VII. Some sympathetic officers allowed clerics to take the oath of assurance with an explanation, but general rigour produced a large body of deposed non-juring clergy despite pressure from William and the English bishops for accommodation.[69] Many sought to retain their pulpits as 'intruders' or preached in meeting houses.[70] This schism fuelled an ongoing battle over the terms of the inclinations clause and the 1690 presbyterian settlement. The next section will consider the contemporary meaning of the inclination clause before showing how the contestation of this clause reinforced

---

[66] Balfour-Melville (ed.), *An Account of the Proceedings*, ii, 180–1; Stephen, 'Defending the revolution', 39.

[67] *RPS* 1690/4/43, 7 June 1690.

[68] *RPS* 1689/6/11, 17 June 1689; 1690/4/161, 22 July 1690; 1693/4/50, 19 May 1693. The 1689 oath allowed those who accepted William and Mary as *de facto* monarchs to swear loyalty. Weil, *A Plague of Informers: Conspiracy and Political Trust in William III's England*, 37.

[69] Raffe, 'State oaths', 185–6. Clergymen and schoolmasters were required to subscribe the confession of faith: *AGA*, 285.

[70] Clarke, '"Nurseries of sedition?": The episcopal congregations after the Revolution of 1689'.

196   Public Opinion in Early Modern Scotland, c.1560–1707

the salience of 'the inclinations of the generality of the people' in political discourse.

5.2   The Meaning of the Inclinations Clause

Carefully crafted to facilitate a revolution, the inclinations clause, like the adversarial petitioning discussed in Chapter 2, reworked the traditional language of petitioned grievances into something that was more assertive but not too radical. By explaining the people's unhappiness with prelacy in terms of their historical 'inclinations', the wording suggested inbred tendencies and emotional responses over rational opinions or covenanted commitments. 'The people' elided the laity with the subjects, implicitly defining the people of Scotland as presbyterian while hinting at the disruptive power of a multitude of presbyterian men and women. By referring to the 'generality', the clause acknowledged, and just as quickly dismissed, episcopalian viewpoints. Despite the emphasis in this carefully engineered clause on history and the conventional language of grievance, its innovations did not escape criticism.

According to the Oxford English Dictionary, 'inclination' suggested a 'tendency or bent of the mind', a 'disposition' or a 'propensity'.[71] In leaning one way or another, a person did not necessarily express a worked-out position or rational stance; instead, an inclination suggested something more instinctual. When the cleric Robert Baillie wrote in 1637 that God needed to restrain men's 'humorous inclinations', he meant temperamental impulses influenced by bodily humours rather than the mind.[72] In similar terms, William Seton of Pitmedden commented in 1700 on the difficulties that arose when soldiers followed 'the itch of their own Inclination'.[73] Associating inclinations with emotions and the body, the Covenanter earl of Rothes described the 'secret motiones and inclinationes' of hearts in 1637.[74] These connotations complemented the traditional language of grievance, in which petitioners emphasised their distress and kings sought to retain their hearts. Prior to the Williamite invasion, presbyterian exiles in the Netherlands sent a spy to Scotland to assess 'the inclination and affection of the people of Scotland to the interests of the Prince of Orange'.[75] Natural inclinations also were known as one's 'genius' or 'genie'. As has been seen, the presbyterian clerics' address to William

---

[71] 'Inclination, n.' OED Online.   [72] Laing (ed.), Letters and Journals of Robert Baillie, i, 15.
[73] Seton of Pitmedden, The Interest of Scotland, 4.   [74] Leslie, Relation, 42.
[75] Lindsay, Memoirs Touching the Revolution, 7.

The Inclinations of the People

claimed that episcopacy was 'contrary to the Genius of the Nation'. The Scots 'genie' can be defined as an 'inherent ability' or 'natural aptitude', with etymological links to the French 'génie' and Latin 'genius', meaning disposition or inclination.[76] A 1689 pamphlet noted that it was the 'Genius' of the Scots 'to have a Monarchy', a 'natural bent' that had led them to rush to restore Charles II in 1660 without placing limitations on his prerogative.[77]

The contentious question of the people's intellectual capacity could be evaded by using the terms 'inclinations' and 'genius', suggesting an involuntary leaning that William had no choice but to accommodate. As this chapter's opening quote shows, in the 1550 *Complaynt of Scotland*, Dame Scotia, an abstract figure representing the realm and its interest, stated that 'there is nocht ane mayr ignorant and ane mayr blynd thyng in this varld as til adhere to the iudgement of the comont pepil quhilk hes nothir consideratione nor rason'. If given freedom, the labouring order inevitably would follow its inclinations and indulge its vices, being without 'education, eruditione nor ciuilitie' and therefore unable to regulate itself.[78] Instruction in reformed religion, however, could improve the people's capabilities. As discussed in Chapter 4, post-Reformation writers used stock figures like Maddie and Jock Upaland to represent an increasingly virtuous commoner voice. In a 1597 letter, Jock Upaland criticised the commission of the general assembly for allowing the king to be designated as the head of the Scottish church, 'which, as yee have instructed us, appertains not to him'.[79] The special capacity of the godly for moral probity led the Protesters to claim 'the concurrence of the generality of the Godly in the Land'.[80] Yet this could be countered by the spectre of the mindless multitude, as in 1638 when John Forbes of Corse rejected the idea that ordinary people should be asked to form their own religious opinions by swearing an unauthorised covenant. The inclinations clause sought to avoid this problem by suggesting that the acculturation of the people since the Reformation, 'haveing reformed from popery by presbyters', produced a less cerebral form of opinion.

'Inclinations' also avoided any reference to the consciences of the people and their sworn commitments. As has been noted, a national renewal of the covenants was not acceptable to William, even though many of the individuals backing his revolution would have welcomed this. Presbyterian

---

[76] 'Genie, n.', *SND*.   [77] Anon., *Allegiance and Prerogative Considered*, 7.
[78] [Wedderburn], *Complaynt of Scotland*, 99, 101.   [79] Calderwood, *History*, v, 655–68.
[80] Anon., *The Representation, Propositions, and Protestation*, 10.

198   Public Opinion in Early Modern Scotland, c.1560–1707

non-conformists split over this issue, with a militant wing continuing to dissent from the Revolution kirk and refuse allegiance to the Revolution monarchy because it was uncovenanted.[81] For others, the resettlement of the church on the 1592 act and Westminster confession was sufficient because it re-established the kirk on essential terms demanded by the covenants (no bishops and an Anglo–Scottish confession). Any explicit requirement in the inclinations clause for the satisfaction of covenanted consciences through the renewal of the covenants would have sunk this pragmatic settlement.

'The people' carried multiple connotations, indicating the subjects of the realm, male and female laypersons in the church of Scotland or a theoretical body that in the distant past had remitted its sovereignty to the Scottish monarchy. The covenants had equated membership of the church with subjecthood in the Scottish realm, so even though the inclinations clause seemed to refer to all Scots and did not mention covenanted consciences, it implicitly pointed to presbyterian people. As recalled by the presbytery of Hamilton in 1700, the covenants defined God's true people in Scotland, for by 'frequent repeated vowes national and solemn covenants this Church and Nation had with uplifted hands to the most high God avouched the Lord to be their God and themselves to be his people, and had sworn against popery, prelacy, schism and prophaneness, and that in a most distinguished manner, beyond all other protestant churches'.[82] In arguing in 1668 that 'the people of God in Scotland' should refuse to sign bands for peaceful behaviour, the dissident cleric John Brown indicated that the presbyterians were the true Scots.[83] Stewart of Goodtrees' 1669 *Jus Populi* portrayed the people as a presbyterian body that made contracts with their kings through coronations and covenants and could reclaim their original sovereignty from tyrants and covenant-breakers.[84] Similarly, by defining the true church of Scotland as presbyterian and rejecting episcopalians as seditious subjects in their 1689 address,

---

[81] NLS, Wodrow Quarto 16, Alexander Shields, 'To Sir R[obert] H[amilton] the answer of his protestation', c.1690. The three United Societies ministers, including Shields, joined the restored kirk. Raffe, 'Presbyterians and Episcopalians: the formation of confessional cultures in Scotland, 1660–1715', 587; Kidd, 'Conditional', 1156, 1159, 1161.

[82] NLS, Wodrow Folio 28, vol. 2, 'Act of the Presbyterie of Hamilton appointing a day of solemn humiliation and prayer, 30 July 1700', f.186.

[83] NLS, Wodrow Quarto 98, Brown, 'Whether or not it be lawfull for the people of God in Scotland to subscribe a bond wherein they oblige themselves to live peaceablie and not to lift armes etc under a pecuniall penalty, 1668', ff.169–72.

[84] See Chapter 4.

The Inclinations of the People

a group of presbyterian clerics and professors defined themselves as the people of Scotland. 'The people' also carried an unspoken but unsubtle threat of what might happen if presbyterian inclinations were not indulged. Presbyterians had risen in arms in 1666 and 1679, massed in arms in Edinburgh for the 1689 convention and, for several months before this, evicted hundreds of episcopalian clergy from parishes by force. To the Jacobite James Graham, first viscount Dundee, these were 'wild Hill-men', who reportedly threatened to assassinate him.[85]

Despite the apparent vigour of presbyterian activism, the inclinations clause cited the 'generality'. This useful phrase suggested a substantial majority, allowing episcopalian opposition to be recognised, but down-played as a minority view. Still, the evidence for a generality could be questioned. In 1652, Protester claims for the support of a 'generality' of the godly were met with Resolutioner accusations that they had collected signatures selectively 'amongst such as were conceived more inclinable to follow that Way'.[86] Similarly, as noted above, viscount Tarbat and Sir George Mackenzie tried to warn William early in 1689 that enthusiasm for a presbyterian kirk was illusory, created by an over-active faction. Shortly after the 1689 convention, Tarbat reminded Melville that only part of the kingdom preferred a presbyterian kirk, warning that 'if the other part of the nation be prest, they will kick, and in my apprehension overturn what will be now established'.[87] Episcopalians, as well as presbyterians, could act as a multitude. 'The inclinations of the generality of the people' was a carefully constructed statement of public opinion that avoided giving too much intellectual credit to the commons while eliding the people with presbyterians and hinting at the threat of unrest. Ratified by the Scottish convention and read to William and Mary before their coronation, the clause achieved constitutional credibility, but its weak points were targeted by episcopalians seeking to undermine the 1688–90 presbyterian settlement.

5.3 The Contestation of the Inclinations Clause

In his study of representations of public opinion in late Stuart England, Mark Knights has observed that the making of majoritarian claims in

---

[85] Balfour-Melville (ed.), *An Account of the Proceedings*, i, 33; Lindsay, *Memoirs Touching the Revolution*, 29.

[86] [Wood], *A Vindication of the Freedom & Laufulnes of the Late Generall Assembly*, title page.

[87] Melville (ed.), *Letters and State Papers*, 108.

200   Public Opinion in Early Modern Scotland, c.1560–1707

petitions posed the problem of 'how the majority was to be discerned', for 'the majority was itself often a representational construct'.[88] Like a petition, the inclinations clause advanced a majority view that could be attacked as inaccurate. Building on previous studies of pamphlet debates on episcopalian comprehension and toleration, this section will trace episcopalian responses to the inclinations clause, largely printed in London because of censorship in Scotland, and presbyterian defences produced in Edinburgh and London. This will focus on printed pamphlets, but will also include petitions, addresses, protestations and published acts of parliament. This will show that while opponents tried to dismiss and denigrate public opinion, they also queried the verity of the inclinations clause, called for the measurement of popular preferences and generated petitions as evidence for their position. In reply, some presbyterians stepped back from the inclinations clause, indicating its instrumentality by preferring the higher authority of God's word as cited in the 1690 act. Stretching from 1689 to toleration proposals in 1703 and beyond, these exchanges helped to embed the language of popular inclinations in Scottish political culture.[89]

Initially, episcopalian commentators tried to discredit the 'inclinations of the generality of the people' by equating 'inclinations' with bodily humours and 'the generality' with an over-zealous faction. A Jacobite memoirist, Father Thomas Hay, attributed the abolition of bishops to the 'humors of the generality of the people'.[90] In a 1690 pamphlet, Alexander Munro, the former principal of Edinburgh college, raised the spectre of unbridled sects and unfettered enthusiasm when he described religion as having degenerated into 'no more than every man's fantastic humour'.[91] The former Glasgow cleric John Sage referred to the presbyterian cadre running the re-established church as the 'Zealous Gang' and 'Phanaticks', reinforcing a rhetorical association between presbyterianism and fanaticism previously advanced, as Raffe has shown, by Restoration writers.[92] Munro argued that a 'Faction' had managed to convince William that both 'the Flower and Multitude of the Nation is for Presbytery'. With tongue in cheek, he suggested that if the western rabble

---

[88] Knights, *Representation and Misrepresentation*, 353.

[89] Bowie, *Scottish Public Opinion*, 36–7, 76–7; Raffe, 'Episcopalian polemic'; Raffe, *Culture of Controversy*, chs 4–6; Jackson, *Restoration Scotland*, 208–14; Maxwell, 'Presbyterian and episcopalian in 1688'; Lenman, 'Scottish episcopal clergy and the ideology of Jacobitism'; Leighton, 'Scottish Jacobitism, episcopacy and counter-Enlightenment'.

[90] Hay, *Genealogie of the Hayes of Tweeedale*, 76.   [91] [Monro], 'The fourth letter', 64.

[92] [Sage], 'The third letter', 57; Raffe, *Culture of Controversy*, 121–8.

The Inclinations of the People

were let loose on the Jacobites, the Jacobites would win, proving that the presbyterians were 'a clamorous and Inconsiderable Faction'.[93] Likewise, for Thomas Morer, an Anglican clergyman attached to a regiment in Scotland in 1689, the revolution had been made by a 'Faction' aided by mad Cameronians whipped up by calculating politicians.[94]

These authors also warned against the democratic implications of the inclinations clause, portraying the Claim of Right as a manifestation of radical theories of contractual monarchy and the people's right to resist already associated with presbyterians.[95] As has been seen, previous presbyterian pamphlets provided grounds for this attack, including Robert Douglas' 1651 account of a covenanted coronation compact and James Stewart of Goodtrees' 1669 assertion that the people could resist a monarch that broke his covenanted compact. A historical claim for the replacement of kings that broke their compacts was suggested by a 1689 reprint of the 1320 Declaration of Arbroath stating that 'the Nobility, Barons & Commons' would 'disown' any king who 'subvert[ed]' their Civil Liberties', and 'choose another'.[96] Yet, as Jackson has shown, few Williamite pamphleteers directly asserted popular sovereignty or a right of resistance, arguing instead that James had disqualified himself by ruling outside the law or that William's invasion was an act of providence.[97] One author argued that self-preservation, according to the 'the most binding Law, to wit, *Salus Populi Suprema Lex esto*', had impelled the Scots to accept the aid offered by God through William during the state of 'Anarchy' created by James' precipitous flight from the realm.[98] By contrast, Sage saw the convention as having made 'an Original Contract betwixt King and People', while the earl of Balcarres condemned the idea that the liberties in the Claim of Right were 'naturally and legally the rights of the people, inherent to them'.[99]

Despite this anti-populism, also expressed in attacks on the 'homely, course and ridiculous Expressions' used by some presbyterian ministers, episcopalian writers also, with some ambivalence, argued about the actual preferences of the people.[100] In 1690, Sage ridiculed the idea that 'the Scotch Laicks' should be made the 'infallible Judg of Controversies', but asserted that if this were to be the new rule, then it should be known that

---

[93] [Monro], 'The fourth letter', 65.   [94] [Morer], 'The first letter', 1–2.
[95] Leighton, 'Scottish Jacobitism', 8–9.
[96] Anon., *A Letter from the Nobility, Barons & Commons*, 1.
[97] Jackson, *Restoration Scotland*, 198–200.   [98] Anon., *Salus Populi Suprema Lex*.
[99] [Sage], 'The third letter', 57; Lindsay, *Memoirs Touching the Revolution*, 36.
[100] [Crokatt and Monro], *The Scotch Presbyterian Eloquence*, 22.

202   Public Opinion in Early Modern Scotland, c.1560–1707

the people preferred the episcopalian church. Countering 'English Pamphleteers' who accepted the inclinations clause as a statement of truth, Sage asserted that there was 'not a falser Proposition in the World'. Probing the questions of who were the people and whose opinion mattered, Sage stated, 'if by the People you mean the Commonalty, the rude, illiterate Vulgus, the third Man through the whole Kingdom is not Presbyterian; and if by the People you mean those who are Persons of better Quality and Education (whose sense in my opinion, ought in all reason to go for the sense of the Nation), I dare boldly aver, not the 13th'. Sage also provided a geographical assessment, portraying the presbyterians as a minority outside of a few western shires. Even in Glasgow, 'which has been so famous for its phanatick Zeal', 'the greater number of Citizens of the best quality are of Episcopal principles.' Outside of these areas, he noted the establishment of dissenting Episcopalian meeting houses and poor attendance at presbyterian services as evidence of lay support for the overturned church. Moreover, the balance was shifting towards episcopacy, for 'eyes are now beginning to open' and some who had accepted the revolution were 'beginning to have enough of [presbyterian] cant, and to be weary of their Sermons'. To indicate his confidence in his claims, Sage called for the measurement of the people's inclinations: 'let us have a Poll for it when they will, and you shall quickly see the Demonstration'.[101] Similarly, Morer argued that the episcopalians had both quality and quantity on their side, with strength among nobles and gentlemen nationally and among ordinary people in the north of Scotland. Morer felt that the presbyterians had taken unfair control of the elections to the 1689 Convention and he called for new elections to produce a more representative parliament.[102] By 1691, Munro too was arguing that the inclinations of the generality had changed, for the 'New and Pedantick Tyranny' of the Presbyterian regime had 'lost the greatest part of even of such of them, as they had formerly deluded'. While noting that 'the perverse Inclinations of the People, be no good Argument', he, like Sage, proposed a 'Poll of the whole Nation' to test its loyalties.[103] John Cockburn, a former doctor of divinity at Aberdeen, applied the principle of popular preference to the parish level by accusing presbyterians of betraying their own principles when they installed presbyterian clergy

---

[101] [Sage], 'The third letter', 57–60.
[102] [Morer], 'The first letter', 3–4. After 1689, no parliamentary elections were called until 1702.
[103] [Monro], *Presbyterian Inquisition*, 14–7.

The Inclinations of the People

'against the Will and Inclinations of the people' in the parishes.[104] These arguments for local preferences were reinforced by a collective petition to parliament in 1693 for episcopalian comprehension and a 1694 protestation against the authority of a committee of the general assembly made 'in the Name of the whole Ministers benorth the Tay'.[105]

Presbyterian authors quickly defended the inclinations clause and the church settlement with works published in London and Edinburgh. Writing for an English audience in *Plain Dealing* (1689), the medic John Gordon sought to prove the anti-prelatical opinions of 'the generality of the Scotch Nation' to 'any impartial unbyassed person indued with common Sense and Reason'. In response to Sage's call for a poll, Gordon offered quantitative estimates of popular presbyterian opinion. First considering population, he claimed that half of Scotland's shires were Presbyterian by 150 to 1 while the other half were presbyterian by two to one, yielding a national majority. Turning to social structures, he asserted that presbyterian heritors controlled two-thirds of the nation's land by rental value and, in addition, the 'Burgesses' and 'Commonalty' were 'all generally inclined to the Presbyterian Government'. Gordon capitalised on contemporary prejudices by excluding Catholics and what he called 'barbarous Highlanders' from his calculations, side-stepping the relative strength of episcopalianism in this region.[106] In a June 1690 sermon to the parliament, David Williamson measured his church's strength among the weightier part, 'the sober, judicious and Ingenuous', among whom only 'hundreds' might object to the presbyterian interest. He also reinforced a historical sense of this strength by praising the staunchness of presbyterians who 'did stand their ground, and owned their Principles since the Reformation from Poperie, by Presbiters'.[107] George Ridpath likewise asserted the historical and continuing appeal of the presbyterian kirk across Scottish society. A presbyterian expatriate writer based in London, Ridpath, wrote three pamphlets between 1693 and 1694 in the name of the Presbyterian laity using the *nom de plume* 'Will. Laick', an intriguing designation that updated Jock Upaland with a nod to the will of the laity.[108] In his first tract, Ridpath referred to his episcopalian adversaries as 'the Faction' and those who rose in arms with Dundee as

---

[104] [Cockburn], *A Continuation of the Historical Relation*, 15–6.
[105] Anon., *A Letter from a Presbyterian Minister*, 3–4; [Ridpath], *The Queries and Protestation*, 21, 30.
[106] [Gordon], *Plain Dealing*, 14–5, 27–8.
[107] Williamson, *A Sermon Preached Before His Grace, the King's Commissioner*, 19, 28.
[108] [Ridpath], *An Answer to the Scotch Presbyterian Eloquence*; [Ridpath], *A Continuation of the Answer*; [Ridpath], *The Scots Episcopal Innocence*.

204   Public Opinion in Early Modern Scotland, c.1560–1707

'Prelatists'. To the charge that presbyterians relied on plebeian backing, Ridpath pointed to the support of nobles and gentlemen in the 1689 convention. Wondering at 'the small appearance of the Prelatical Party by Protestation, Petition or Arms' while thousands of presbyterians came to Edinburgh for the convention, Ridpath dismissed Highland support for Dundee's uprising, attributing this to their 'Love to prey and not Zeal to prelacy'. Rejecting the reconstruction of an erastian episcopate under James VI as a political tactic to secure the English crown, he pointed to historical demands for presbyterian church government under James VI and Charles I and emphasised the 'sanguinary Laws and Tyranny' required to enforce episcopacy under Charles II. By portraying the Scottish bishops as deracinated creatures of the English church, Ridpath maintained a rhetorical identification of the Scottish people with the presbyterian church.[109]

In 1695, Sage reiterated his call for a national poll in a tract examining the evidence for popular preference for presbyterian church government. Sage emphasised the novelty of the inclinations clause: 'if I mistake not, there was never publick deed, before, founded, mainly, and in exprest terms, upon the Inclinations of the Generality of the People.'[110] To argue that no such inclination existed, Sage pointed to the absence of any instructions to members or petitions to the 1689 convention against prelacy. This disingenuous argument played to an English audience by mentioning instructions, which were not typical in Scotland, and skipping over the presbyterian petitions sent to William and later parliaments. He further noted that '[t]hey never so much as once offered at Polling the People about it' and 'durst never yet adventure to require from the Generality of the People, their Approbation of it.' The only evidence of popular support, therefore, was the 'Rabbling' of clergy by 'Rascally scum' in 'a corner' of 'the whole Nation'.

Because Gilbert Rule, the new principal of Edinburgh's college, had tried to evade the issue by characterising a poll as impractical, Sage pointed to recent poll and hearth taxes and the widespread swearing of the 1638 National Covenant as models for the direct measurement of opinion.[111] As Keith Brown has shown, early modern Scotland contained a range of voting and polling practices relating to the governance of guilds,

[109] [Ridpath], *An Answer to the Scotch Presbyterian Eloquence*, 35–41.
[110] [Sage], *Fundamental Charter of Presbytery*, 296.
[111] [Sage], *Fundamental Charter of Presbytery*, 298–311; *RPS* 1690/4/58, 14 June 1690.

The Inclinations of the People 205

burghs, parishes and shires.[112] The idea of a poll was not beyond contemporary imaginations. In 1661, discussions in the Scottish privy council on the church settlement had considered the possibility that opinion should be measured, since both sides claimed the support of the majority.[113] In 1688 in England, James VII and II launched 'the most extensive survey of political opinion ever conducted up to that point in British history' by asking over 2,000 royal office-holders in each county whether they would accept the repeal of penal laws against Catholic worship.[114] In Scotland in 1689, all burgesses had participated in elections for burgh commissioners to the Revolution convention and new burgh councils.[115] With these precedents, it was not unreasonable for Sage to suggest that opinion could be assessed by local commissioners like those appointed for collecting the 1693 poll tax.[116] Though Sage's call for a poll may have been a rhetorical gambit to imply confidence in his position, his repetition of the proposal and presbyterian attempts to dismiss it suggest some tenacity in the idea of measuring public opinion.

The accession of Queen Anne in 1702 encouraged episcopalian leaders in Scotland to try again to demonstrate popular sympathy, this time to secure toleration for dissenting worship. Asserting again congregational and national preferences, these claims were backed up with subscriptional petitioning. The campaign began with an address organised by the former archbishop of Glasgow, John Paterson, and presented to Anne in March 1703 in the name of the 'Suffering Episcopal clergy'.[117] Though the address did not mention popular opinion, its carrier was instructed to ask Anne 'to allow every parish to call such ministers as shall be most agreeable to their own inclinations' so that 'where the parish is intirely episcopal a presbyterian minister may not be thrust in upon them'.[118] Local addresses signed by episcopalians were organised to support this appeal. Though no extant addresses have been identified, these documents were cited by Anne's secretary of state, George Mackenzie, earl of Cromarty, to reinforce the argument for toleration of episcopalian worship. Formerly viscount Tarbat, co-author of the 1689 anti-presbyterian

---

[112] Brown, 'Towards political participation and capacity: elections, voting, and representation in early modern Scotland'.
[113] Airy (ed.), *Burnet's History*, i, 235–6.
[114] Sowerby, *Making Toleration: The Repealers and the Glorious Revolution*, 97–8.
[115] *RPS* 1689/3/134, 18 April 1689.   [116] *RPS* 1693/4/56, 29 May 1693.
[117] Clarke, 'The Scottish Episcopalians, 1688–1720', 136.
[118] Anon., *To the Queen's Most Excellent Majestie, the Humble Address and Supplication of the Suffering Episcopal Clergy*; NRS CH8/184, Copy instructions given to commissioner of noblemen, 1703.

206   Public Opinion in Early Modern Scotland, c.1560–1707

memorial to William, Cromarty wrote two tracts in favour of toleration in 1703. In the first, he did not attempt to deny popular support for presbytery but asserted strong backing for a toleration of episcopalian worship, declaring that it was 'Impudence to deny this truth, that at least the half of Scotland, do desire a Toleration'. Like Sage, he used the presence of episcopalians in apparently presbyterian places like Glasgow to imply their general ubiquity, stressing the support of the better sort: 'there is full proof ready to be shown by above 400 subscriptions of the prime Inhabitants of Glasgow'. Moreover, other signed petitions showed 'by two to one in Dundee; By 4 to one in Aberdeen, Especially of the Chief Merchants, and Burgers; By 3 to One in Elgin; And by 5000 Subscriptions in Fife; That a Toleration to Episcopal Ministers in these Places is earnestly desired.' Cromarty called on shire commissioners in the 1703 parliament, where proposals were being made for an act of toleration, to confirm that 'a Toleration is desireable by the greatest part of the Nation'.[119] In a follow-up tract, he stated that episcopalian dissenters numbered two for every three presbyterians, 'if not three to two'. Cromarty urged a toleration as 'a prudent Medium for Peace to the Nation' by resolving the ongoing conflict over the church settlement.[120]

Additional tracts by clerical writers urged a toleration, with most continuing to assert an episcopalian majority. George Garden, a nonjurant Aberdeenshire clergyman, condemned the imposition of presbyterian ministers on unwilling congregations and urged toleration of the 'peaceful' episcopalian people of Scotland. Garden played on the association of presbyterians with disorder by arguing that episcopalian ministers did not 'stir up the People against the Magistrate, nor Animate them to Rables'.[121] Garden countered the idea that the people had been 'reformed from popery by presbyters' by noting that the Scottish reformed church had maintained prelacy with the appointment of superintendents after 1560. Robert Calder, a nonjurant minister who led a meeting house in Aberdeen, stated that 'the Generality of the People in Scotland, in most places, have an Aversion to Presbyterie, and are inclin'd to Episcopacie'.[122] Another tract (as reported by James Hadow of St Mary's College in St Andrews in his pamphlet against toleration) proposed that the inclinations clause should be 'Rectifyed' by parliament.[123]

---

[119] [Mackenzie], *A Few Brief and Modest Reflexions*, 4–5.
[120] [Mackenzie], *A Continuation of a Few Brief and Modest Reflexions*, 4–5.
[121] [Garden], *The Case of the Episcopal Clergy*.
[122] [Calder], *Reasons for a Toleration to the Episcopal Clergy*, 124.
[123] [Hadow], *A Survey of the Case of the Episcopal Clergy*, 5.

The Inclinations of the People

This episcopalian campaign sparked a vigorous defence of the Claim of Right and its inclinations clause, heightened by Anne's promotion of closer union between presbyterian Scotland and episcopalian England. When the 1702 Scottish parliament ratified a request from the queen for union negotiations, it reminded Anne that the Scottish church was 'founded in the Claime of Right' and that presbytery represented 'the true interest and solid foundation of the peace and quiet of this kingdom'.[124] Though Anglo–Scottish union talks collapsed over the winter of 1702–3, Anne continued to stimulate presbyterian fears by issuing a letter to her privy council in February 1703 recommending a *de facto* toleration of peaceful dissenting ministers.[125] After elections in 1702, Anne's commissioner to parliament, James Douglas, second duke of Queensberry, sought to build a majority in the ensuing 1703 session by promising a toleration act to newly elected episcopalian 'Cavaliers' in exchange for their votes on a supply bill.[126]

The presbyterian response was vigorous. On 1 June 1703, the commission of the general assembly addressed parliament against the proposed toleration act, warning that toleration 'must unavoidably shake the foundation of our present happy constitution'. Toleration would 'disquiet the minds of Her Majesties best subjects' and 'increase Animosities, Confusions, Discords and Tumults'.[127] James Hadow insisted that toleration was unnecessary, because the episcopalians shared the same confession and did not suffer from penal laws; instead, toleration would be the thin edge of a wedge driving at the 'Restauration of Prelacy in this Church in spite of the Claim of Right'.[128] Led by Archibald Campbell, second duke of Argyll, a majority in parliament approved a parliamentary act asserting the authority of the Claim of Right and making it high treason to 'quarrel, impugne or endeavour by writing, malicious and advised speaking, or other open act or deed, to alter or innovate the Claim of Right or any article thereof'.[129] Aimed at episcopalian pamphleteers and addressers, the proposed act raised 'a long and hot debate'. The Aberdeenshire commissioner James More of Stoneywood asked if it would be treason for his constituents, which 'every body knew was generally of the episcopal

---

[124] *RPS* 1702/6/55, 25 June 1702.
[125] Anne, *Her Majesties Most Gracious Letter to the Privy Council of Scotland*.
[126] Szechi (ed.), *'Scotland's Ruine'*, 27–8.
[127] Commission of the General Assembly, *Unto His Grace ... The Humble Representation of the Commission of the Late General Assembly*.
[128] [Hadow], *A Survey of the Case of the Episcopal Clergy*, 3–4.
[129] *RPS* 1703/5/190, 16 September 1703.

208   Public Opinion in Early Modern Scotland, c.1560–1707

perswasion', to petition for 'a rectification of the present settlement of the presbyterian church government'. Sir William Hamilton of Whitelaw offered his view that addressing for a toleration would be allowed, but any attack on the legitimacy of presbyterian government would be considered a crime against the Revolution monarchy.[130]

Other writers joined Hadow in defending the authority of the Claim of Right, with some threatening popular mayhem should the inclinations clause be overturned. Robert Wylie, minister in Hamilton parish, asserted that 'Presbytery is now Incorporated in the Claim of Right, which is become a fundamental Charter of the Civil Government'. He warned of mass resistance should episcopacy return: 'Bishops in Scotland can never be maintain'd' without 'a standing Army to save them from the People'.[131] In commenting on a draft toleration act, another author cited a recent attack by a presbyterian crowd on a meeting house in Glasgow to prove that toleration 'can never be attempted without Blood, and the most fatal Discontents and Disorders'.[132] James Webster, a prominent Edinburgh clergyman, also referred to the disturbance in Glasgow, arguing that the 'Generality of the Nation have such an Aversion to Prelacy, that the Toleration will be fair to create great Tumults'.[133] John Bannatyne of Lanark parish warned that 'the Presbyterian Ministers will not be blown out of their Pulpits with the breath of an Proclamation, but will maintain their possession (their people adhereing to them) till they be dragged by Forces from their pulpits'.[134]

While these writers embraced the people's enthusiasm for presbytery, others could be ambivalent about the reliance of the kirk on the people's inclinations. In 1680, Cargill's covenant had asserted the 'word of God' as the sole source of authority in church government, explicitly rejecting 'plurality of votes'.[135] The 1703 parliament passed a statute affirming that presbytery was 'agreeable to the word of God', indicating a desire to reinforce this justification from the 1690 church act.[136] In a second pamphlet against toleration, Robert Wylie advised that it was a 'great Mistake' to see the Claim of Right as founding presbytery on 'the Inclinations of the People'. More precisely, he argued, the 'Foundation given in Law is our Reformation from Popery, and *That* is laid down as the

---

[130] Szechi (ed.), 'Scotland's Ruine', 35–6.   [131] [Wylie], *Letter from a Gentleman in the City*, 17.

[132] Anon., *Draught of an Act for Toleration with a Few Short Remarks*, 3. On events in Glasgow, see Bowie, *Scottish Public Opinion*, 37–9.

[133] [Webster], *An Essay upon Toleration*, 22.

[134] [Bannatyne], *A Letter from a Presbyterian Minister in the Countrey*, 5–6.

[135] Wodrow, *History*, ii, appendix, 44.   [136] *RPS* 1703/5/189, 16 September 1703.

The Inclinations of the People 209

Ground of the Peoples Inclinations'. It was the presbyterian church's historical 'Gospel Institution', founded in the word of God and confirmed by law, that provided the church's security, not the people. At the same time, however, Wylie took care to undermine episcopalian counter-claims by suggesting that the signatures on their addresses had been 'procured upon insinuated Encouragements'.[137]

As these exchanges demonstrate, the innovative inclinations clause opened a public debate on the preferences of the people on church government. The Claim of Right asserted that the people had been acculturated to presbytery since the Reformation, forming 'inclinations' that would be dangerous to disturb. When challenged on the veracity of this claim, presbyterians sought to reinforce the authority of this clause by associating episcopalians with Jacobitism, excluding the Highlands from calculations of national opinion, advancing divine sanction and historical law as the ultimate foundation for presbyterian church government or threatening violent disorder in defence of the kirk. Though initially, episcopalians ridiculed the idea that the vulgar people should determine questions of church government, the constitutional status of the Claim of Right led them to counter-assert a national desire for prelacy, or at least toleration of episcopalian meeting houses. Writers estimated the balance of opinion in terms of landed wealth and population and used contemporary models of taxation and oath-taking to imagine forms of direct polling.

5.4 Conclusions

The inclinations clause shows that by 1689 an assertion of the people's preferences on a question of church government had become plausible, though not incontestable. This unusual clause adapted the traditional language of complaint to argue that the people's post-Reformation acculturation, elsewhere described as their 'genius', justified the removal of bishops from the kirk. This premise had been enabled by the prince of Orange's published promise to provide a parliament to relieve the grievances of the Scottish people. Thereafter, the people's preferences were written into a presbyterian address, William's letter to the convention and the ensuing Claim of Right. Backed by grassroots activism stimulated by William's declaration, the convention's claim identified 'the generality of the people' with the laity of the formerly presbyterian kirk, neatly minimising episcopalian sympathies and hinting at the disruptive power

---

[137] [Wylie], *A Speech Without Doors, Concerning Toleration*, 3–4.

of this body. This clause excited controversy as episcopalians questioned the wisdom of letting plebeians determine church government; but the constitutional status of the Claim of Right, passed by the convention and read to the monarchs at their coronation, required its opponents to engage with the question of popular preferences. The ensuing debate appeared across pamphlets printed in London and Scotland, petitions, addresses and protestations, indicating the extent to which these methods for presenting collective opinions had become part of Scottish political culture, despite their repression during the Restoration period. Episcopalians proposed polls and provided estimates of the scale of their support with an emphasis on social weight, while presbyterians rejected polls as impractical or left the Highlands out of their own counter-guesses. This activity helped to make the 'inclinations of the people' a common phrase in post-Revolution discourse. In an address to parliament in 1706, the parish of Logie by Stirling employed well-established tropes in arguing that incorporating union threatened the presbyterian settlement 'established amongst us by the happy revolution which is not only most agreeable to the Generall inclinations of the people but also founded on the word of God'.[138] Also prominent in the union debates was another recently invented phrase, 'the sense of the nation'. The next chapter will consider what was meant by this phrase, how it gained prominence in Scotland's post-Revolution context and how it was deployed in hopes of defeating the 1706 treaty of union by undermining the legitimacy of its parliamentary ratification.

[138] Bowie (ed.), *Addresses Against Incorporating Union*, 210–1.

CHAPTER 6

The Sense of the Nation

And since it evidently appears ... that ther is a generall dislike and aversion to the incorporating union ... I do therfor further protest against concluding this and the following articles of this treaty untill her majestie shall be fully informed of the inclinations of her people, that, if her majestie think fitt, she may call a new parliament to have the immediat sentiments of the nation.

John Murray, duke of Atholl, 7 January 1707[1]

The previous chapter has shown how dissenting presbyterians grasped an opportunity to make a revolution in the Scottish church as well as the monarchy in 1688–90 by claiming that the Scottish people were inclined towards presbyterian church government, stimulating debate about what the people truly preferred and how these preferences should be measured. Alongside the 'inclinations of the generality of the people', phrases like 'the sense', 'the sentiments' or 'the mind' of 'the nation' also appeared in contemporary discourse by the time of the Williamite Revolution. If the inclinations of the people indicated the instinctive tendencies of the laity or commons, the sense of the nation suggested the thoughtful conclusions of a national political community. 'Sense' pointed to the workings of the mind, encompassing the 'mental faculties or faculty of reason or rationality, the power of reasoning, esp. as apparent in a sane person; wits; judgment; commonsense'. In a political context, this translated into a 'view, judgment or opinion held by a number of persons' or, crucially, 'a consensus'.[2] Similarly, 'sentiments', from the older Scots sensement and French sensément, indicated a judgement, verdict or opinion, including the conclusions of a parliament.[3] Sentiment also might indicate an emotional belief or inclination, a meaning that came to predominate in modern usage. In the early modern era, therefore, 'sense' or 'sentiments

---

[1] *RPS* 1706/10/212, 7 January 1707.   [2] 'Sens(e), n.', *DOST*.
[3] 'Sen(s)ement, n.', *DOST*; 'Sentiment, n.', *OED*.

211

of the nation' indicated rational, consensual opinions equivalent to the judgement of a meeting of the estates in parliament, though 'sentiments' could carry a more affective overtone.

'The nation' indicated a usefully amorphous political *communitas*. The nation could be interpreted as a synonym for the estates, the monarch's feudal charter-holders, consisting of nobles, prelates and royal burghs who met in parliament and together acted as the *sanior pars* of the nation at large. The estates embodied the community of the realm and, when gathered in parliament, they spoke for the commoners under their jurisdiction. At its most expansive, however, the nation could indicate the Scots as a national body, encompassing every subject in the kingdom. By eliding the parliamentary estates with the subjects at large, 'the nation' could indicate an inclusive political community that carried more weight than 'the people'.

The identification of the nation with all subjects was strengthened by the increasing engagement of ordinary men and women in public affairs through, as has been seen, the expansion of literacy and the widespread swearing of oaths and covenants. In addition, war brought national exactions to communities and households across Scotland. The Covenanter regime repeatedly recruited men aged from 16 to 60, known as the fencible men, for obligatory military service and a national militia was created after the Restoration.[4] With the raising of royalist revolts against the Covenanters and the Cromwellian regime, the deployment of Highland troops against the southwest in 1678, Covenanter uprisings in 1666 and 1679, and the Highland War of 1689–91, military action brought many ordinary men and women into direct contact with national affairs.[5] The Gaelic verses of Iain Lom on the 1645 battle of Inverlochy evoked both the triumph of the royalist victors and the 'wailing of the women of Argyll'.[6] The demands of war also drew more subjects into the payment of taxation. With the introduction of excise taxes in the 1640s and hearth and poll taxes from the 1690s, by the post-Revolution period only the poorest households were excluded from crown taxation.[7] The stringency of wartime demands can be seen in a 1649 parliamentary act seeking to resolve the 'manifold grievances and complaints within the kingdom against

---

[4] Furgol, 'Scotland turned Sweden: The Scottish Covenanters and the military revolution, 1638–51'; Lenman, 'Militia, fencible men and the home defence, 1660–97', 172–80.

[5] Roberts, *Clan, King and Covenant: History of the Highland Clans from the Civil War to the Glencoe Massacre*, chs 8–12.

[6] Mackenzie (ed.), *Orain Iain Luim*, 21–5.

[7] Goodare, 'Parliamentary taxation'; Stewart, *Rethinking the Scottish Revolution*, ch. 4; *RPS* 1690/9/14, 10 September 1690, 1693/4/56, 29 May 1693.

The Sense of the Nation

masters for oppressing their tenants'; and in a manuscript 1651 'Declaration and vindication of the poore opprest Commons of Scotland', which bemoaned 'new tyranicall inventions' that 'squized the verie livelyhood from us and our children'.[8] This extended, as Macinnes has noted, to Gaelic-speaking areas, where 'the rates of exaction were no less than elsewhere in Scotland, though geographic inaccessibility and family solidarity did afford a measure of immunity', and to women.[9] It was confirmed in 1646 that widows with liferent property were liable for land taxes because 'all persones and subjectis of this kingdome sould be lyable to ther proportionall pairt of all publict burdens'.[10] Likewise, the 1690 hearth tax encompassed female-headed households and the 1693 poll tax required payment from 'all persons of whatsoever age, sex or quality' above the age of 16. Developed in the Restoration as a means of spreading tax obligations downwards from proprietors, the poll represented a significant extension of the fiscal nation to nearly all subjects. Though women's political status remained marginal in legal and cultural terms, this chapter will show how overlaps between the covenanted, fiscal and political nation made it possible to imagine women participating in national polls.

Though parliamentary decisions could be challenged by pointing to 'the sense of the nation', parliament remained an authoritative counter to unwanted crown policies. Historians have emphasised the extent to which a cluster of reforms agreed in the 1689–90 Revolution settlement, including a right to frequent meetings of parliament, a right to petition the king and the abolition of the Lords of the Articles, revived the power and significance of the Scottish parliament.[11] Under William, the parliament flexed its muscles by conducting inquiries and addressing the monarch. Moreover, by 1698, as Riley has shown, a more substantial opposition had emerged, known as the Country party.[12] Its leaders adopted aggressive tactics and patriotic rhetoric to challenge the crown's management of parliament, in 1700 threatening to convene members independently and in 1702 walking out of parliament in protest.[13] Adversarial petitioning tactics from the Covenanting era were rediscovered as extra-institutional

---

[8] *RPS* 1649/5/203, 5 July 1649; Stevenson, 'Reactions to ruin', 260–4.

[9] Macinnes, 'Scottish Gaeldom, 1638–1651', 71.   [10] *RPS* 1646/11/66, 10 December 1646.

[11] Bowie, 'From customary to constitutional right'; Raffe, *Scotland in Revolution*, 144–7; Goodare, 'Parliament and politics', 248.

[12] Riley, *King William and the Scottish Politicians*, ch. 7.

[13] McCormick (ed.), *State Papers and Letters*, 544; Brown, 'Party politics and parliament: Scotland's last election and its aftermath, 1702–3', 249–50.

214   Public Opinion in Early Modern Scotland, c.1560–1707

petitions were presented to the king in 1700 and parliament in 1700, 1701 and 1706–7.[14]

The Country opposition accused crown ministers of betraying the nation's interests to serve an uncaring monarch and inconsiderate English neighbours. As Mark Goldie has observed, despite a century of regal union, Scotland and England were growing apart rather than together, riven by religious and economic differences.[15] Public opinion played a major role in this trend as, with more powers and weak oversight from London, the Scottish parliament passed legislation designed to satisfy opinion groups in Scotland. The result was a battle for control of the Scottish parliament from 1698 to 1707: could ministerial management keep the estates aligned with crown policy or would an oppositional majority break away, acting in the name of the nation?

Though there has been some study of lobbying in the post-Revolution period, the interplay between parliament and extra-parliamentary opinion remains under-explored outside of the Union debates.[16] This chapter will examine the expression of national concern and grievance, in and out of parliament, from the Revolution to the Union. It will show how, in the aftermath of the Revolution, William left his officers to manage Scotland with limited resources, relying heavily on presbyterian loyalty to the Revolution as he ran a major war effort and governed two composite polities. Missteps by the king's ministers were publicised internationally as printed news and commentary expanded in this period, eroding William's reputation in Scotland and creating conflicting interpretations of events in Edinburgh and London. Most notably, William's lack of support for a well-publicised patriotic joint-stock venture, the Company of Scotland, fuelled extra-parliamentary petitioning and pamphleteering from 1699. By 1702, Anne found herself pushing for closer union to resolve a succession crisis as reformers called for the transfer of prerogative powers to the Scottish parliament to allow the estates to better serve the nation. With the negotiation of a treaty of incorporating union in 1706, Anne's ministers sought to secure the consent of the nation through parliament in the face of extensive extra-parliamentary opposition involving men and women from across the social scale, though largely from Lowland areas. Radical calls were made for a referendum, extending even

---

[14] Bowie, *Scottish Public Opinion*, chs. 2, 6.
[15] Goldie, 'Divergence and Union: Scotland and England, 1660–1707'.
[16] Stephen, 'Defending the revolution'; Young, 'The Scottish parliament and the politics of empire: Parliament and the Darien project, 1695–1707'; Bowie, *Scottish Public Opinion*.

The Sense of the Nation 215

to women, while conservatives argued that parliament alone expressed a national opinion. Instead of suppressing or ignoring opinion at large, Anne's regime devoted new resources to manage it. By hearing petitions, making concessions in the treaty and reducing the threat of violent resistance, the government reinforced its majority and secured adequate acquiescence out of doors. The union debates thus confirmed the salience and stature of Scottish national opinion at the same time as the nation's constitutional framework was being dissolved.

6.1 The Sense of the Nation, 1689–1701

To maintain the stability of the Revolution monarchy, William's ministries needed to retain the goodwill of the presbyterian majority in the Revolution parliament (which continued with no new elections until 1702) while protecting William's reputation as the saviour of the kingdom and its liberties. This proved difficult as rivalries between presbyterian and episcopalian interests and economic competition intensified Anglo–Scottish tensions in the absentee monarchy. Jacobites, Anglican Tories and Country party leaders stood ready to wring propaganda value from governmental gaffes.

As David Onnekink has shown, William delegated much of the management of Scotland to his favourite, William Bentinck, first earl of Portland. His Scottish ministers struggled to capture the king's attention and William never visited Scotland to soothe unhappy adherents despite repeated invitations.[17] When William and Portland were preoccupied or away on campaign, the Scottish secretaries and privy council acted with minimal oversight, allowing disasters to mushroom unexpectedly. When the Scottish secretary Sir John Dalrymple of Stair ordered the massacre of a small Jacobite clan in 1692, printed and oral reports stirred up an alarm that was only partially assuaged by a 1695 parliamentary inquiry. In the same parliament, acts against blasphemy and profanity played to presbyterian worries but, to the dismay of English commentators, allowed the execution of an Edinburgh college student for blasphemy in 1697. The 1695 chartering of the Company of Scotland Trading to Africa and the Indies by an act of parliament created an international incident as fierce rivalry with English traders played out in diplomatic intrigues and the company's South American colony at Darien found itself in open conflict with Spain without the backing of the king. A 1696 association

---

[17] Onnekink, 'The earl of Portland and Scotland (1689–1699): A re-evaluation of Williamite policy'.

216   Public Opinion in Early Modern Scotland, c.1560–1707

oath boosted Williamite sentiments in England but fears of reviving the covenants meant that the association had little impact in Scotland. Instead, William's handling of the Company of Scotland, including an attempt to restrict petitioning in 1699, generated anger at a time of severe economic recession. By 1701, these difficulties led William to recommend closer union to England's House of Lords.

The 1692 Glencoe massacre stimulated a parliamentary inquiry and an address as the king's officers sought to restore William's reputation as the protector of the Scottish commonweal. In late 1691, William was keen to divert troops from a planned winter campaign against Scottish Jacobites to a new continental offensive against France, but Jacobite clan chiefs were stonewalling generous peace terms. When the chief of the MacDonalds of Glencoe sought to accept an indemnity after a deadline of 1 January 1692, the Scottish secretary Sir John Dalrymple of Stair wrote orders, endorsed by William, to 'extirpate' this 'sept of thieves'.[18] Dalrymple had hoped that the submission of the Jacobite clans would win a positive 'reputation through the world' for William's regime, but the attack achieved the opposite. In mid-January 1692, the state-sponsored *London Gazette* announced the apparent pacification of the Highlands, allowing troops to be shipped to Flanders instead of the north.[19] After the subsequent 13 February attack in Glencoe, news spread by word of mouth. By early March there was 'much talk in London, that the Glencoe men were MURDER'D in their beds after they had taken the allegiance'.[20] A report in the Paris *Gazette* in April included incriminating military orders and was followed by the publication of highly critical Jacobite tracts.[21] A pamphlet printed in London and Oxford around September 1692 by the Scottish Whig–Jacobite Sir James Montgomerie of Skelmorlie portrayed William as a grasping conniver who was plundering the British realms for war supplies and betraying the liberties he had promised to preserve, not least by ordering his officers to 'put Glencoe and all the Males of his Clan, under Seventy, to death', 'without any Legal Tryal'.[22] This was followed by the printing in London of a detailed letter from Scotland on the massacre by the high church Tory Charles Leslie early in 1693. Contemporaries were shocked to learn that troops had been quartered on unsuspecting householders, treating them as citizens rather than

[18] Hopkins, *Glencoe and the End of the Highland War,* 309–11, 318, 328. Part of the larger MacDonald name, the clan also was known as the MacIains.
[19] *London Gazette* 2731 (11–4 January 1692), 2732 (15–8 January 1692).
[20] [Ridpath], *The Massacre of Glenco,* 26.   [21] *Ibid.*; Hopkins, *Glencoe,* 337, 354.
[22] [Montgomery of Skelmorlie], *Great Britain's Just Complaint,* 32.

The Sense of the Nation

combatants, before the forces were ordered to take no prisoners in a night attack.[23] Leslie's 'Letter from a Gentleman in Scotland' emphasised the human tragedy in the betrayal of hospitality, the killing of young boys and elderly men, the 'bad Usages' of women and the flight of women and children in their night-clothes into a snowstorm. The attackers were described as 'Hell-hounds, treacherous Murtherers, the Shame of their Country and Disgrace of Mankind' and military orders were reprinted stating that the attack was 'by the King's SPECIAL COMMAND'.[24]

Fearing for William's international reputation, Mary pressed for an inquiry to clear his name in the eyes of the world. During the summer of 1693, a ministerial investigation concluded that 'there was nothing in the king's instructions' to warrant the attack, but no report was printed for fear it would fan rather than quench public interest.[25] Nevertheless, by 1695 the massacre had become notorious and the Scottish parliament demanded an inquiry into this 'national concern' touching the 'honor and justice of the nation'.[26] With William on campaign in Flanders, joint secretary James Johnston allowed a wide-ranging inquiry under the authority of a royal commission. Characterising the killings as murder, the inquiry blamed Dalrymple and some of the officers who implemented his orders while exonerating William.[27] A petition to parliament on behalf of the 'poor Remnant' of the Glencoe MacDonalds praised William for allowing this investigation, which had shown 'the World' the truth and released 'the Publick' from 'the least Imputation' which might be made by 'Foraign Enemies'. Though it was 'evident to the conviction of the Nation' that their families had been 'murdered and butchered' contrary to 'the laws of nature and Nations, the Laws of hospitality and the publick Faith', neither William nor the Scottish nation was responsible.[28] A parliamentary address to William aimed to 'testify to the world' the king's innocence in this 'barbarous slaughter' that had caused 'so much noise both in this kingdom and your majesties' other dominions'.[29] In a report on the inquiry, the *London Gazette* blamed junior officers. While two prints attempted to clear Dalrymple's name without shifting blame to William,

---

[23] Hopkins, *Glencoe*, 335–7.

[24] [Leslie], *Gallienus Redivivus, Or, Murther Will Out &c Being a True Account of the De-Witting of Glencoe, Gaffney, &c*, 9–16 (second pagination).

[25] Hopkins, *Glencoe*, 373–4. The commission's report was printed in 1703 in [Ridpath], *The Massacre of Glenco.*

[26] Hopkins, *Glencoe*, 366–7; RPS 1695/5/25, 23 May 1695.   [27] Hopkins, *Glencoe*, 409.

[28] McDonald, *To His Grace ... The Humble Supplication of John McDonald of Glencoe.*

[29] *RPS* 1695/5/164, 10 July 1695.

218   Public Opinion in Early Modern Scotland, c.1560–1707

the attack on William was renewed with an Edinburgh reprint of the 'Letter from a Gentleman' and another by Leslie in London.[30] Leslie added a commentary on the 1695 parliament, presenting the inquiry as a sordid ploy to discredit Dalrymple and strengthen the presbyterian faction and its kirk, weakly founded on a false representation of the people's inclinations. Leslie placed the blame for the massacre squarely on William and castigated the Scottish parliament for covering up his role, making the massacre a matter of 'National Guilt' for Scotland.[31]

These continuing attacks drained the confidence of Williamite presbyterians, who were also buffeted by the episcopalian polemic seen in Chapter 5 and the activities of covenanting extremists who spurned the restored kirk. The United Societies continued to meet in the southwest and John Hepburn, a presbyterian minister deposed from the parish of Urr in 1696, led a band of hardliners in Kirkcudbrightshire known as the Hebronites.[32] Williamite presbyterians also faced what the judge David Home, Lord Crossrig described as a burgeoning 'Leaven of Scepticism & Immorality'; a series of weather-related harvest failures leading to a severe dearth in many parts of Scotland by the late 1690s; and a constriction of trade with France during the Nine Years' War (1689–97), combined with extraordinary taxation and recruitment for the war and repeated alarms over anticipated French invasions.[33] By 1699, anxious presbyterians were forming voluntary societies for the reformation of manners in Edinburgh and a few other burghs, following the example of similar societies in England.[34]

In this context, the 1695 ministry sought to reinforce presbyterian loyalty and aid the economy by passing parliamentary acts against blasphemy and profaneness and chartering a national joint-stock trading company. William's letter to the 1695 parliament indicated his desire for war supplies, offering in return a blank cheque for 'whatsoever may be for the security of the government, and the satisfaction of our good subjects'.[35] The act against profanity added teeth to earlier 1690 and 1693 acts and

---

[30] [Dalrymple], *Information for the Master of Stair;* Anon, *An Impartial Account;* Anon., *A Letter from a Gentleman in Scotland.*

[31] [Leslie], *Gallienus Redivivus.*

[32] *AGA,* 255–6; McMillan, *John Hepburn and the Hebronites: A Study in the Post-Revolution History of the Church of Scotland;* Kidd, 'Conditional Britons', 1159.

[33] Home, 'A narrative of the rise, progress and success of the societies in Edinburgh for reformation of manners', 125; Cullen, Whatley and Young, 'King William's ill years: New evidence on the impact of scarcity and harvest failure during the crisis of the 1690s on Tayside'; Graham, *The Blasphemies of Thomas Aikenhead: Boundaries of Belief on the Eve of the Enlightenment,* 54–9; Whatley, 'Taking stock: Scotland at the end of the seventeenth century', 107–19; Hopkins, *Glencoe,* 438–9.

[34] Gray, '"A Publick Benefite to the Nation"', ch. 2.   [35] *RPS* 1695/5/8, 9 May 1695.

The Sense of the Nation

followed a 1694 general assembly act urging the prosecution of profanity by civil and ecclesiastical authorities.[36] The blasphemy act made it a capital crime to argue, 'in writing or discourse', against 'the being of God, or any of the persons of the blessed trinity, or the authority of the Holy Scriptures of the Old and New Testaments, or the providence of God in the government of the world'.[37] This was followed in January 1696 with an act of the general assembly urging the pursuit of atheistic deists, to prevent 'the spreading of that gangrene through the land'.[38]

This move against blasphemy created Anglo–Scottish tensions with the execution in January 1697 of an Edinburgh college student, Thomas Aikenhead. As Michael Graham has shown, leading presbyterian officials and clergymen pressed this case in an atmosphere of moral panic. Aikenhead's trial was held in December 1696, two weeks after the privy council had called out the fencible men to meet an anticipated French invasion. His execution was held on 8 January during a meeting of the general assembly at which the 1696 act against deists was renewed.[39] Shortly after, the privy council authorised the trial and execution of seven men and women for witchcraft in Paisley, reversing a thirty-year decline in the staging of witch trials.[40]

As with the Glencoe massacre, the Aikenhead and Paisley trials were featured in public reportage and commentary, aided by an increase in political printing. From 1695, with the lapsing of licensing restrictions in England, more London newspapers provided occasional reports from Edinburgh on Scottish parliamentary proceedings, privy council and general assembly meetings and notable events, including riots, murders and executions. In Scotland, commercial print production increased and pre-publication licensing became more difficult to enforce. Though episcopalian tracts were published in London to reach English audiences and evade Scottish censorship, Scottish parliamentary speeches and minutes were printed in Edinburgh alongside pamphlets on current affairs. In April 1697, the privy council ordered that pamphlets and books 'Relating to the Government or of publict concern' be reviewed by a committee, though a 1699 renewal indicates that this was not always obeyed.[41] In 1696–7, two pamphlets describing Aikenhead's blasphemies were

---

[36] *RPS* 1690/4/116, 19 July 1690, 1693/4/126, 15 June 1693; *AGA*, 241. This was followed by acts against profanity in 1697 and 1699: *AGA*, 261–2, 280–1.

[37] *RPS* 1695/5/117, 28 June 1695. [38] *AGA*, 253.

[39] Graham, *Blasphemies of Thomas Aikenhead*, ch. 5; *London Gazette* 3246 (17–19 December 1696); *AGA*, 267.

[40] Wasser, 'The western witch-hunt of 1697–1700: The last major witch-hunt in Scotland'.

[41] NRS PC 1/52 (27 July 1699).

220   Public Opinion in Early Modern Scotland, c.1560–1707

published in Edinburgh and accounts of the Paisley witchcraft trials by the presbyterian lawyer Francis Grant (later Lord Cullen) were printed in Edinburgh and London.[42] Grant aimed to combat scepticism in both kingdoms by asserting the reality of demonic possession, but differing reportage in Edinburgh and London on the Aikenhead case created conflicting perceptions of this event. While Scottish readers learned of Aikenhead's theological errors, English news reports made the Scottish regime seem bloodthirsty by stressing his youth and the council's apparently callous refusal of two penitent petitions for a reprieve.[43] The king's ministers tried to counter coffee-house talk about Aikenhead in London by securing favourable coverage in the *Flying Post*, a newspaper published by George Ridpath, a Scottish presbyterian who had been driven into English exile in 1680 after his involvement in an Edinburgh pope-burning.[44] Though taking a clearly Whig stance, Ridpath's paper was reported to be widely read 'by all of both sides'.[45] The general assembly also sent a loyal address to William praising him for his pursuit of 'the monsters of profanity and atheism'.[46]

In 1696, prior to the Aikenhead case, Whigs in England expressed enthusiastic loyalty for William with an oath of association, but this had less impact in Scotland. As Rachel Weil has noted, this updated version of the 1584 Elizabethan bond of association 'strove to imbue the English people with a passionate attachment to both the person of the king and his government' after the discovery of an assassination plot.[47] David Cressy and Mark Knights have shown how eagerly Whig-dominated communities embraced the oath, gathering signatures from thousands of ordinary men as well as office-holders and presenting the signed oaths with loyal addresses.[48] The English association was designed to flush out Jacobites by requiring swearers to accept that William ruled by right as well as by default. In Scotland, the 1690 oath of assurance already had demanded this and moderates on the privy council feared that a Scottish association would be co-opted by hardline presbyterians. In March, it was reported that presbyterians in the southwest had created their own oath of

---

[42] Craig, *A Satyr against Atheistical Deism;* Craig, *A Lye Is No Scandal;* Grant, *Sadducimus Debellatus;* Grant, *A True Narrative.*
[43] *Post Boy* 262 (7–9 January 1697); *Post Boy* 266 (16–19 January 1697); *Post Man* 265 (16–19 January 1697). Some sympathy in England for the Scottish campaign against blasphemy was indicated by the passage of a blasphemy act in 1698, though the English act contained much softer penalties.
[44] Graham, *Blasphemies of Thomas Aikenhead*, ch. 6.
[45] McCormick (ed.), *State Papers and Letters*, 310.   [46] *AGA*, 269.
[47] Weil, *A Plague of Informers: Conspiracy and Political Trust in William III's England*, 251.
[48] Cressy, 'Binding the nation', 227–32; Knights, *Representation and Misrepresentation*, 154–9.

The Sense of the Nation

association with an address to the king defending the presbyterian establishment – and had renewed the covenants alongside the new oath. In Edinburgh, leading Whigs devised a blue cockade for Williamites to wear but it was argued that the king would not approve of any 'marks of distinction', as these were 'a means to make divisions, and not heal them'.[49] The privy council refused to create a presbyterian association for Scotland, signing instead on 10 April the English association oath and licensing it to be 'Printed and Publictly sold' for any who wished to emulate them.[50] Members of parliament signed the oath on 10 September and all civil and military office-holders were required to swear it.[51] A broadside notice of the 'English Association' was printed in Edinburgh, but no Scottish author emulated English tracts urging subscription as a duty for all English subjects.[52]

The implementation of the association oath in Scotland was impeded not just by the fear that it would revive a covenanted nation but by an explosion of interest in an alternative vehicle for national commitment: The Company of Scotland Trading to Africa and the Indies. With the backing of a cadre of Edinburgh merchants and English investors, the company was chartered by the 1695 parliament to rival the English and Dutch East India companies.[53] Endorsed by the king's commissioner in parliament, the 1695 act claimed the direct support of 'his majesty'. William was said to understand that 'several persons, as wel forreigners as natives of this kingdom, are willing to engage themselves with great soumes of money in an American, Affrican and Indian trade to be exercised in and from this kingdom if inabled and encouraged thereunto by the concessions, powers and priviledges, needfull and usual in such cases'. The act gave the Company the sole right in Scotland to trade to Africa, Asia and the Americas, lucrative tax exemptions and authority to settle colonies on land 'not possest' by foreign powers. Though Scots were required to hold at least 50 per cent of the shares, the instigators aimed to attract international investors.[54] Subscriptions were taken in London first, quickly achieving a target of £300,000 sterling in November 1695. Despite

---

[49] McCormick (ed.), *State Papers and Letters*, 287–9.
[50] Privy Council of Scotland, *Association Begun to be Subscribed at Edinburgh.*
[51] *RPS* 1696/9/55, 25 September 1696.
[52] House of Commons, *The English Association of the House of Commons*; Atwood, *Reflections on a Treasonable Opinion, Industriously Promoted, Against Signing the National Association.* Further research in burgh records may yield more evidence of the swearing of the association at local levels.
[53] Watt, *The Price of Scotland: Darien, Union and the Wealth of Nations*, 26–9.
[54] *RPS* 1695/5/104, 26 June 1695.

222   Public Opinion in Early Modern Scotland, c.1560–1707

the publication of a pamphlet by the Company urging Anglo–Scottish cooperation, the English East India Company objected strongly, petitioning the king and the House of Lords for protection from this upstart competitor. Pressured by Lords' and Commons' inquiries and a parliamentary address, William distanced himself from the Scottish act.[55]

This stance excited deep resentment in Scotland, stimulating what Douglas Watt has characterised as 'an early example of a financial mania' as £400,000 sterling was pledged between February and July 1696 from socially diverse male and female investors.[56] The English parliament's address was reprinted in Edinburgh and the Company published a range of promotional material, including notices, minutes of meetings, copies of the 1695 parliamentary act, sample contracts for investors and interim lists of subscribers.[57] These were joined by pamphlets and broadside ballads taking a strongly patriotic stance. The author of *Some Seasonable and Modest Thoughts* argued that in 'the Opinion of the Scots', the English had since 1660 treated them worse than the conquered Irish by designating them as aliens in England's colonial trade and betraying the principle of *post-nati* citizenship established in 1608.[58] Consequently, he asked, 'can any that are Masters of common Sense imagine, and believe that a free, unconq[u]ered, and independent People will be contented to be depressed by a neighbouring Nation, without seeking to relieve themselves'? He added that the English parliament's aggression had backfired, for 'the generality of Mankind have conceived a greater esteem for the Scots East-India Company', 'from the Jealousies you have exprest'.[59] The Company, rather than the monarch, now attracted Latin and vernacular praise poetry, including a 1699 poem by a 'Lady of Honour'.[60]

With the Company of Scotland being presented as a national affair, subscription became a way for individuals to express their patriotism. A poet in 1697 imagined Scotland as the nymph Caledonia, wooed by

---

[55] Watt, *Price of Scotland*, ch. 4.   [56] *Ibid.*, 80.

[57] Parliament of England, *The Humble Address of the Right Honourable, the Lords Spiritual and Temporal and Commons in Parliament Assembled Presented to His Majesty.*

[58] By a case known as 'Calvin's case', in 1608 the Court of King's Bench ruled that those born in Scotland after the 1603 regal union were considered citizens of England and could hold property in England.

[59] K., C., *Some Seasonable and Modest Thoughts Partly Occasioned by and Partly Concerning the Scots East-India Company*, 23–5, 35.

[60] Anon, *Insignia Praelustris Societatis Scoticanae ad Africum & Indias*; Anon., *A Poem Upon the Undertaking of the Royal Company of Scotland*; Anon. ('A Lady of Honour'), *The Golden Island or The Darian Song.*

The Sense of the Nation

Neptune to establish a maritime trading empire, and saw subscription in the Company as a statement of national opinion:

> Had not the English Votes, and Noisie Fears,
> Awak'd the Land, and open'd all their Ears,
> Thus as one Man the Nation has combin'd,
> And speedily a mighty Stock is joyn'd.[61]

As Alasdair Macfarlane has concluded, such publications succeeded in 'conflating the nation's interests with the Company's' as Scottish ambitions for a trading empire united subscribers across religious and political divides.[62] Though this poet described the nation as male, W. Douglas Jones' analysis of subscriptions shows that women, as well as men, invested. The national enthusiasm reached from elite to middling ranks with pledges from noblemen and women, state officers, members of parliament, merchants, lawyers and prosperous widows, plus dozens of craftsmen and other burgh householders whose modest contributions were pooled. Jones has identified ninety-one participating women, including Anne, duchess of Hamilton, the first to sign the book in Edinburgh. Books were opened in Glasgow and Ayr as well as Edinburgh to help draw subscriptions from the southwest and Highland regions, with investors appearing from all of Scotland's mainland shires except northerly Caithness. Such was the enthusiasm that the original target of £300,000 was expanded to £400,000 to accommodate subscribers travelling from afar.[63]

When it became known that the English ambassador in Hamburg had advised the city council, in the name of the king of Great Britain, not to recognise the new Scottish Company, the king's officers had to labour to restrain assertive addressing by the Company to William.[64] In July 1697, secretary Sir James Ogilvy reported to the king's chaplain and confidante William Carstares in London that he had succeeded in getting the Company's directors to give him a petition to take quietly to the king, instead of sending it with a delegation to London; and that he and other leading men were 'resolved to do our best to hinder the petitioning of the [privy] council' to avoid a replay of 1637 when dissidents petitioned the privy council asking them to represent their grievances to Charles I. Ogilvy emphasised the extent to which the Company's petitions reflected a sense

---

[61] Anon., *A Poem Upon the Undertaking of the Royal Company of Scotland*, 5, 14, 16.
[62] Macfarlane, '"A Dream of Darien": Scottish Empire and the Evolution of Early Modern Travel', 186, 201–2.
[63] Jones, '"The bold adventurers": A quantitative analysis of the Darien subscription list (1696)'.
[64] Rycaut, *A Memorial Given in to the Senate of the City of Hamburgh*.

224   Public Opinion in Early Modern Scotland, c.1560–1707

of injured national honour and expressed a wish that 'something may be done to quiet the people, who make great noise about it, and other prejudices they think are imposed on them by England'. Those who did not back the Company, he reported, were castigated as 'ill country-men'.[65]

William refused to back the Company and its attempt, from 1698, to establish a trading post in Darien on land that Spain claimed but (as specified by the Company's charter) did not occupy. Support for the Company might have boosted loyalty to William, as suggested by the 1699 *Caledonia Triumphans*, a 'panegyrick to the king', but William found himself enmeshed in negotiations on the Spanish succession and pressured by English trading interests.[66] In April 1699, proclamations were made in English colonies forbidding any dealings with the Scots colony, with which the king was said to be 'unacquainted'.[67] By this time, news of the colony had spread in Scotland by the newly licensed *Edinburgh Gazette* and pamphlets were being published in Edinburgh defending the Scottish plantation, while attacks printed in London were reprinted in Edinburgh.[68] When ministers repulsed in June 1699 another attempt to get the privy council to petition the king on behalf of the Company, the leaders of the 'Country' opposition in the Scottish parliament, the brothers-in-law John Murray, earl of Tullibardine (later duke of Atholl) and James Hamilton, duke of Hamilton, turned instead to extra-parliamentary petitioning supported by pamphleteering.[69] Reaching back to the tactics of the supplicants in 1637, an address from 'Subscribing Noblemen, Barons and Gentlemen' calling for a meeting of parliament was circulated for subscription mostly in the western Lowlands, though it was said to have gone 'unanimously throw the whole nation' with only 'a few' refusing it 'in vain'.[70] A broadside printed in Glasgow urged support for this 'National Address'. Because the king had said, in answer to a petition from the Company, that he would call a parliament when 'the Good of the Nation does require it', it was argued that 'There can be nothing more Natural, than for the Nation themselves to acquaint his Majesty of the urgent Necessity' of a meeting, for 'so Universal a Concern to the whole Nation'.[71] Supporters aided this push by lobbying for a national fast. The kirk had been an enthusiastic supporter of what the commission described as a 'Great, and Generous Undertaking' by 'noble

---

[65] McCormick (ed.), *State Papers and Letters*, 313, 315.   [66] [Pennecuik], *Caledonia Triumphans*.
[67] Beeston and Gray, *By the Honourable William Beeston Kt. . . . A Proclamation*.
[68] Bowie, *Scottish Public Opinion*, 28–31, 58–9.
[69] McCormick (ed.), *State Papers and Letters*, 481.   [70] NRS PC1/52, f.67.
[71] Anon., *Certain Propositions*.

The Sense of the Nation

Patriots', sending ministers with the colonists to form a presbytery there.[72] The resulting proclamation for a day of humiliation on 30 November did not name the Company but acknowledged the failure of 'Indeavours that have been made for advancing the trade of this nation'.[73]

The national address created a face-off, as in 1637, between the monarch and extra-institutional representations of national opinion.[74] As Lord Advocate Sir James Stewart of Goodtrees stated in August 1699, 'the nation is bent one way, and the King is of another persuasion'. Stewart warned Carstares that parliamentarians would have to be wooed before the next session or 'things will go very cross here'.[75] Matters were made worse in December with a proclamation against the national address as it was being circulated for subscription. Though the proclamation acknowledged the right to petition established by the Claim of Right, it condemned the opposition's 'unusuall method' of collective petitioning, being insufficiently 'orderly and dutifull' and tending 'to alienat' the king from 'the hearts of our good subjects'.[76] This suggestion that the national address was seditious was said to have stimulated even more people to sign it. In a deliberate reference to events in 1637–8, a Jacobite observer declared that the address had become 'a nationall covenant'.[77]

This confrontation between king and the apparent views of the nation continued in the May 1700 parliament. The presentation of petitions from five shires and three burghs contributed to a suspension of the meeting after just nine days.[78] The unusual nature and impact of these eight petitions can be seen in the earl of Melville's over-wrought description of them as 'addresses upon addresses, from all parts of the country'. As in October 1689, a substantial body of oppositional members addressed the king demanding the resumption of parliament to deal with 'the pressing concerns of the Nation'.[79] Melville warned Carstares that 'since they look upon themselves as the major part, if they cannot sit here, they will go somewhere else and sit'.[80] Melville's fears of a breakaway assembly were

---

[72] Commission of the General Assembly, *Letter from the Commission*, 1; Stephen, 'The Presbytery of Caledonia'.

[73] McCormick (ed.), *State Papers and Letters*, 499–504; NRS PC 13/3/1699.

[74] For more detailed accounts of this episode, see Bowie, *Scottish Public Opinion*, 30–5, 58–9 and Bowie, 'Publicity, parties and patronage', 79–83.

[75] McCormick (ed.), *State Papers and Letters*, 490.   [76] NRS PC 1/52 (16 December 1699).

[77] NRS PC1/52, f.67.   [78] *RPS* A1700/5/3–10, 27 May 1700.

[79] Members of Parliament, *Coppy of the Addres: Of a Great Number of the Members of the Parliament of Scotland*.

[80] McCormick (ed.), *State Papers and Letters*, 544. The addressers were reported to number 90, or a little less than half of the 189 recorded as attending parliament. *RPS* 1700/5/2, 21 May 1700; Bowie, 'Publicity, parties and patronage', 81.

226   Public Opinion in Early Modern Scotland, c.1560–1707

enhanced by a major riot in Edinburgh on 20 June celebrating a successful skirmish with the Spanish at Darien during which revellers smashed the glass windows of courtiers' homes.[81] The parliamentary opposition gathered signatures on another national address to the king calling for parliament to reconvene. When it did, Ridpath emulated the form of a petition in a broadside tract expressing the grievances of 'the people of Scotland' and urging parliament to ensure that their institutional 'Sentiments' were consonant with 'those of the Nation express'd in Our Petition'.[82] More petitions from localities were submitted to parliament, from eleven shires and seven burghs, including a petition signed by 474 inhabitants of Glasgow without the cooperation of their burgh council. These two rounds of parliamentary petitions penetrated deep into Scotland, reaching west to Dunbartonshire and north to Perthshire, Inverness, Nairnshire, Banffshire and Orkney.[83] Moreover, the practice of collective protestation was revived when a narrow majority voted by 108 to 84 on 14 January 1701 to address William instead of approving an act asserting the Company's rights. Speaking for the dissenting voters, the duke of Hamilton read out reasons for their votes and insisted that their names be recorded.[84] The Company of Scotland sought to publicise this event by funding the engraving of a copperplate poster celebrating the eighty-four members. This unusual and expensive piece of visual propaganda featured a figure of Scotia identifying the opposition with the nation.[85]

In the 1700–1 session, ministers regained a narrow margin of control of the estates by exerting the levers of persuasion and patronage at their disposal, aided by news of the abandonment of the Darien colony under Spanish duress.[86] In August, Ogilvy, now viscount Seafield, wrote that 'since all hopes of success in the affair of Caledonia are lost', some members 'are not willing to push matters any further, but will rest satisfied with what the King has impowered me to grant them'. Seafield noted that 'if money could be had, I would not doubt of success in the King's business', but his resources were limited.[87] William's letter to parliament was crafted to provide a rationale for his position, acknowledging the pressure of national opinion:

> It is truly our regrate that we could not agree to the asserting of the right of the companies colony in Darien and you may be very confident if it had not

---

[81] Bowie, *Scottish Public Opinion*, 34; Watt, *Price of Scotland*, 197–9.
[82] [Ridpath], *The People of Scotland's Groans and Lamentable Complaints.*
[83] *RPS* A1700/10/25–42, 9 January 1701.   [84] *RPS* 1700/10/179, 14 January 1701.
[85] Watt, *Price of Scotland*, 203–4.   [86] Bowie, 'Publicity, parties and patronage', 82–3.
[87] McCormick (ed.), *State Papers and Letters*, 584–5.

been for invincible reasons, the pressing desires of all our ministers, with the inclination of our good subjects therein concerned, had undoubtedly prevailed. But since we were and are fully satisfied that our yeilding in that matter had infallibly disturbed the general peace of Christendom and brought inevitably upon that our ancient kingdom a heavie warr, wherein we could expect no assistance, and that now the state of that affair is quite altered, we doubt not but you will rest satisfied with these plain reasons.[88]

Expressing sorrow for the Company's losses, William promised to support acts for the 'advanceing of trade' and 'more especially for makeing up the losses and promoteing the concerns of the African and Indian Company'. Other desirable legislation was promised and passed, including an act against popery, an act reconfirming the presbyterian kirk and a *habeas corpus* act.[89] In addition, stricter control of print was implemented from the summer of 1700 with the reassertion of licensing requirements, the burning of a Country pamphlet and, in 1701, the bringing of sedition charges against a printer, a pamphlet seller and two Company employees involved in the Scotia engraving.[90] Conversely, censorship was used to salve opinion with the burning of three anti-Darien pamphlets, described as 'scandalous and calumnious libells' injurious to 'the honour of this nation'.[91]

Historians have presented the Union of 1707 as an inevitable outcome of the 'unmanageable' state of Scottish politics after the 1688–90 Revolution, as Scotland's parliament became more difficult for the monarch to control.[92] This section has shown the significance of national opinion in this dynamic. After the Revolution, an overtaxed monarch relied on a few favourites to secure the cooperation of the nation in parliament and at large, but when mistakes were made, opposition could be more easily expressed in the name of the nation through parliamentary and extra-parliamentary addresses and protests and the spreading reach of printed news and polemic in Scotland. Ill-will created by the Glencoe massacre could not be abated by a Scottish association; and the Aikenhead execution may have assuaged presbyterian fears but it exacerbated Anglo–Scottish differences. The widespread investment of emotional and financial resources in the Company of Scotland created a debacle when the king

---

[88] *RPS* 1700/10/10, 29 October 1700; William II, *His Majesties Most Gracious Letter to the Parliament.*
[89] *RPS* 1700/10/72–3, 23 November 1700, 1700/10/234, 31 January 1700; Watt, *Price of Scotland*, 203–5.
[90] Bowie, *Scottish Public Opinion*, 50; *RPS* 1700/10/45, 15 November 1700.
[91] *RPS* 1700/10/52, 16 November 1700.
[92] Riley, *King William*, 160–1; Watt, *Price of Scotland*, 220.

228   Public Opinion in Early Modern Scotland, c.1560–1707

refused to back its Darien venture. Women as well as men bought shares and wrote pamphlets about the Company, while men from burghs and shires as far north as Orkney signed petitions to king and parliament. The next section will show how this experience led reformers to propose that the Scottish parliament take on greater powers to allow it to act with even less crown oversight. But for William and Anne, the answer was more union as they sought to create 'One People, One Civil Government, One Interest'.[93] The embarrassment, disruption and threat of violence posed by Scottish national opinion needed to be contained. Yet as the struggle over incorporating union produced some of the most ambitious expressions of the sense of the Scottish nation since 1637–8, the government only succeeded in passing a treaty of union by engaging with opinion at large.

6.2 The Sense of the Nation, 1702–1707

Memories of the making of the 1707 Union have been shaped by the contentious question of whether the Union parliament represented the sense of the nation. Until recently, many historians felt that the Scottish parliament had acted in the national interest, even if only a minority of Scots felt this at the time. In contrast, the Burnsian notion that Scotland had been 'bought and sold for English gold' emphasised the corruption of members of parliament in the face of extra-parliamentary resistance.[94] But any assessment of the nation's views needs to start with a historicised understanding of public opinion in early eighteenth-century Scottish politics. Contemporary claims about the nation's opinions cannot be accepted at face value nor dismissed as misguided. With this in mind, this section will consider the representation, management and impact of national opinion from Anne's first pursuit of closer union in 1702 to the securing of the Union in 1707. Anne faced an even more difficult situation than William in her management of Scottish affairs. Because she had no surviving children by 1701, her ministers had the added task of securing, by an act of the Scottish parliament or a union of the kingdoms, Scotland's acceptance of England's statutory successor, Sophia of Hanover, a Protestant granddaughter of James VI. Elections in 1702 complicated the parliamentary landscape by adding a tranche of episcopalian Jacobites who were willing to swear allegiance to Anne as a Stuart but

---

[93] Seton of Pitmedden, *A Speech in Parliament*, 8.
[94] Macinnes, *Union and Empire*, ch. 2; Ferguson, 'The making of the treaty of union of 1707'.

The Sense of the Nation

were unwilling to vote for any act excluding the Jacobite successor. The election of these 'Cavaliers', combined with Anne's known sympathy for episcopalian dissenters, destabilised her presbyterian base, splintered the Court party and led to ministerial reshuffles in 1704, 1705 and 1706. Anne's ministries also were shaken by proposals for constitutional reforms countering the queen's 1702 bid for an incorporating union. Anglo–Scottish tensions reached new heights with a tit-for-tat seizure of ships in 1704–5, culminating in the execution of three members of an English East India crew in Scotland for piracy. When an English Whig ultimatum in 1705 led, somewhat unexpectedly, to a treaty of incorporating union in 1706, objections in Scotland were expressed in extensive pamphleteering and petitioning, a public protestation by militant presbyterians in Dumfries, street protests in several burghs and militia musters in disaffected regions. These activities involved women alongside men, where possible, and reached into Perthshire and the northeast. Opponents called for a referendum of freeholders, or even male and female members of the presbyterian nation. While supporters emphasised the authority of parliament, the queen's government acknowledged the practical force of extra-institutional opinion and the need to devote resources to its containment. Petitioning was defused by being heard; customary constraints on unauthorised meetings were exercised; the Scottish treasury was refreshed with English money to provide necessary sweeteners; and pro-union opinion was encouraged by printed speeches and pamphlets, including those of Daniel Defoe, an agent sent to Edinburgh by Anne's English secretary, Robert Harley.

Opposition to Anne in her first 1702 parliament revealed limits to the Country party's ability to generate out-of-doors opposition, showing that expressions of national opinion relied on meaningful public engagement. Because Anne's ministers had ignored a 1696 law requiring a rapid meeting of parliament on William's death, the duke of Hamilton followed the example of the marquis of Argyll in 1648 by making a protestation and leading about one-third of the members out of the chamber. Hamilton and his followers sent a collective address to the monarch in London (as the opposition had in 1689 and 1700), but because the parliament was still in session, the queen was able to evade this by telling its carriers to take it back to her royal commissioner in Edinburgh. They warned Anne that this would 'incense the whole body of her people', yet the Country party struggled to animate support for their legalistic objections. Having failed to publish any pamphlets explaining their cause, they found little enthusiasm for an attempt to boycott the land tax voted by the ostensibly

230   Public Opinion in Early Modern Scotland, c.1560–1707

illegitimate parliament.[95] Meanwhile, a print of Anne's letter to parliament provided an answer to the estates' January 1701 address, stating her intention to be 'equally tender' of the rights of her Scottish and English kingdoms and to 'avoid all occasions of Mis-understanding'. To that end, she proposed an 'intire Union', on 'an equal and just Foundation', promising also to prevent the impressing of Scots into the English navy and support the Company of Scotland and the nation's trade.[96] The Country party's absence smoothed the passage of an act authorising negotiations for a closer union, though two members recorded their dissent because this act did not prevent discussion of prelacy according to the Claim of Right.[97]

Though Anne's union talks in the winter of 1702–3 were stymied by English Tory objections, Scottish pamphlets published in response to the talks attacked incorporating union and offered alternative proposals to reform the regal union by acts of parliament or a treaty with England.[98] A widely read tract by James Hodges, a London expatriate with links to the duke of Hamilton, established the argument that an incorporating union would be inimical to Scotland's unique rights and interests and dishonourable to its ancient sovereignty, with the benefit of free trade providing no compensation for these disadvantages.[99] Ridpath criticised Anne's projected union by pointing to more generous terms offered in 1543 for a marital union between the young Mary I and Edward of England and federal arrangements agreed by treaty after the Bishops' Wars.[100] Ridpath followed this with another tract arguing that before the 1603 union the Scottish parliament had held a 'commanding Share in all the Rights of Sovereignty' and urging the 1703 parliament to reassert their powers by placing limitations on Anne's successor.[101] In parliament and print, a range of limitations was proposed by Andrew Fletcher of Saltoun on behalf of a breakaway Whig cadre. Of these, parliamentary approval for declarations of war and peace was ratified in 1703 as a constraint on Anne's successor.[102] Also in 1703, an 'Act of Security' insisted that the Scottish parliament would not accept the English heir unless 'conditions of government' had been agreed and Scotland received a 'communication of trade' with the right to trade freely in all British

---

[95] Bowie, *Scottish Public Opinion*, 35, 59–60; Bowie, 'Publicity, parties and patronage', 83–4.

[96] Anne, *Her Majesties Most Gracious Letter to the Parliament*; *RPS* 1702/6/21, 11 June 1702.

[97] *RPS* 1702/6/52, 1702/6/54, 25 June 1702.   [98] Bowie, '"A legal limited monarchy"', 149.

[99] Bowie, *Scottish Public Opinion*, 69; [Hodges], *The Rights and Interests of the Two British Monarchies, Inquir'd Into, and Clear'd; With a Special Respect to an United or Separate State. Treatise I.*

[100] [Ridpath], *A Discourse upon the Union of Scotland and England*.

[101] [Ridpath], An *Historical Account of the Antient Rights and Power of the Parliament of Scotland*, vii; Rose, 'Councils, counsel', 289–90.

[102] Fletcher, *Political Works*, 129–73; *RPS* 1703/5/193, 16 September 1703.

The Sense of the Nation 231

territories.[103] This act was not given the royal asset, though Seafield reported to London his view that England would have to concede free trade to get any agreement on union or the succession.[104] Instead, lords from Fletcher's cadre came into office as the 1704 'New party' ministry and gave the queen's assent for a modified act requiring measures to 'secure the honour and sovereignity of this crown and kingdom, the freedom, frequency and power of parliaments, the religion, liberty and trade of the nation from English or any foreigne influence'. This omitted the 1703 clause on the communication of trade because this was offered separately by the duke of Hamilton with a demand for a treaty on trade.[105]

The controversial matters debated in 1703 and 1704 attracted interest, aided by an increase in political printing and the delegation of control of the Edinburgh presses from the privy council to burgh officials in 1704. Large crowds of men and women gathered outside the parliament house for key votes.[106] A poem by an Aberdeenshire Cavalier laird, issued in response to a 1704 resolve demanding conditions of government and a treaty on trade, described the awakening of Scotland's 'genius', or national spirit, imagined as Scotia, a martial female figure who had slumbered through the previous century of regal union.[107] The reawakening of an armed nation at large was implemented with the creation of a new shire and burgh militia authorised by the Act of Security.

The resentment of English hegemony reflected in oppositional demands for limitations was sustained by continuing Anglo–Scottish clashes. In January 1701, a parliamentary resolve described the English parliament's inquiry and address against the Company of Scotland and the Hamburg memorial as 'undue intermeddleing' in sovereign Scottish affairs.[108] When the House of Lords addressed the monarch in March 1704 on the Scottish succession, another resolve and an address to the queen again declared this to be 'undue intermeddleing' in what was 'the concern of the whole nation'.[109] Relations reached a nadir in 1704–5 with a controversial trial that, like the Aikenhead case, was reported differently in London and Edinburgh. After the Company of Scotland's last ship was impounded by English officials, an English East India vessel sheltering in Leith a few months later was seized when rumours spread that the crew had pirated a

---

[103] *RPS* A1703/5/12, 13 August 1703.   [104] Bowie, 'Publicity, parties and patronage', 87.
[105] *RPS* 1704/7/68, 5 August 1704; Bowie, 'Publicity, parties and patronage', 88.
[106] NRS PC 4/3 (17 March 1704); Bowie, *Scottish Public Opinion*, 74.
[107] [Forbes of Disblair], *True Scots Genius Reviving*.
[108] *RPS* 1700/10/166, 10 August 1700; Bowie, 'Publicity, parties and patronage', 83.
[109] *RPS* 1704/7/71, 8 August 1704, 1704/7/169, 18 August 1704.

232   Public Opinion in Early Modern Scotland, c.1560–1707

missing Company ship. Regular reports on the trial and conviction of the crew circulated in Scotland via three periodicals, the *Edinburgh Gazette*, the *Edinburgh Courant* and the *Observator*, and a flurry of pamphlets. Scottish tracts confirmed the guilt of the accused, while English prints questioned the sentence. Scottish prints also advertised a simultaneous English parliamentary act imposing economic sanctions on Scotland if it did not accept the Hanoverian succession or restart union talks. Providing a contemporary illustration of the sense of the nation, the *Observator* presented an imagined dialogue between a country farmer and a schoolmaster discussing pamphlets and news on the piracy trial and the union question. News of the piracy case led thousands to come to Edinburgh to see the executions early in April 1705; and Chancellor Seafield was attacked in his coach when it was rumoured that he might reprieve the condemned men. Though the privy council knew that the conviction was dubious and had been asked by London to delay, New party leaders chose to proceed in order not to risk further violence nor alienate parliamentary opinion.[110]

When the English parliament's ultimatum produced a treaty of incorporating union early in 1706, the New party (now the *squadrone volante*) joined a reconstituted Court majority in 1706 for incorporating union and the Country party turned to public opposition. Mobilising extra-parliamentary resistance was not difficult: the union question had been discussed widely since at least 1700 and a new wave of pamphlets provided arguments against the terms of the new treaty. The policing of the presses by Edinburgh magistrates was contested in parliament, leading to the waiving of any meaningful pre-production censorship, though the estates condemned a 'scurrilous' anti-incorporation title to be burned in December.[111] In Edinburgh, large, aggressive crowds of men and women followed the debates in parliament and erupted into rioting in response to votes on key articles. As Rosalind Carr has shown, Katherine Skene, Lady Murray recorded that men and women alike threw stones at the royal commissioner's coach as he passed between parliament to Holyrood Palace.[112] Organised protests included the staging of a protestation by the Hebronites in Dumfries. This emulated earlier militant Covenanter testimonies by making a declaration against the union and burning the treaty at the market cross. By drawing up in military formation, they

[110] Bowie, 'Newspapers, the early modern public sphere and the 1704–5 Worcester affair'.
[111] Bowie (ed.), *Addresses*, 304; *RPS* M1706/10/49, 12 December 1706.
[112] Carr, 'Gender, national identity and political agency', 121.

The Sense of the Nation 233

invoked a covenanted nation at arms as they protested against any union passed 'over the Belly of the Generality of this Nation.'[113] Country party leaders and some activist clerics encouraged addressing from local and national bodies, producing robust rejections of incorporation from the Convention of Royal Burghs, the Company of Scotland, fifteen shires, twenty-one royal burghs, nine baronial burghs, fifty-one parishes, three presbyteries and a body of southwestern dissenters. The commission of the general assembly expressed concerns in four addresses, with their second address providing sharp objections to elements of incorporation, including the presence of bishops in the British House of Lords.[114] Anti-treaty officials sought to prime the nation at arms with regular musters of the newly created militia. In Lanarkshire, the duchess of Hamilton encouraged parish militias to muster and in Stirling, the provost called out the burgh militia to sign an address.[115]

Addresses, pamphlets and protestations urged parliament to listen to the opinions of the nation. The presbytery of Hamilton asked parliament to attend to the 'distracted State' of their parishioners and 'prevent the dreadfull confusions' that would result from incorporation.[116] Like many parish petitions, a pamphlet by Hodges emphasised that 'a great multitude of the Scots Nation' felt themselves to be bound by their covenants and therefore were unable to accept the treaty because it was inconsistent with their sworn obligation to maintain a Scottish parliament and confederal British union.[117] While some writers argued for a parliamentary recess to allow members to consult their constituents, Hodges in 1706 went further in demanding the unanimous consent of all Scottish freeholders in a special 'National Assembly'. In elaborating this, he proposed the inclusion not just of nobles, heritors, burgesses and their freeborn children but 'All the Freeborn Fair Sex', 'All the Noble Ladies, and All the Boanie Lasses'. These female spouses and children, he argued, were 'Freed from the Trouble of Government, and Reserv'd for Better Uses, Yet have as good a Title to all the Benefits of the mention'd Fundamental National Rights, as the Men can Pretend to'. Like Sage's proposals for a poll on church government, Hodges' suggestion was unusual, but shows how the pressure of events stimulated thinking on the extra-institutional nation. Hodges' strong presbyterian sentiments suggest that the creation of a covenanted

---

[113] Anon., *An Account of the Burning of the Articles.*   [114] Bowie (ed.), *Addresses*, 16–7.
[115] Bowie, *Scottish Public Opinion*, 139–46; Bowie, 'A 1706 manifesto', 251–2.
[116] Bowie (ed.), *Addresses*, 269–70.
[117] Hodges, *Rights and Interests of the Two British Monarchies*, 56–8.

234   Public Opinion in Early Modern Scotland, c.1560–1707

nation made it possible for him to imagine women as part of the Scottish political community. He even expressed a hope, possibly informed by the tenacity of female dissenters, that these women would continue to defend Scottish rights when the men flagged.[118] In November 1706, a manifesto for collective action by 'the free people of Scotland' was penned by the minister Robert Wylie, though never used. This distanced the nation from the proposed union by blaming the treaty on English influence and a traitorous faction that had pursued incorporation in defiance of 'the known mind of the nation' and the people's covenanted obligations. The paper demanded a national address to the queen and the nullification of votes passed 'contrary to the publickly expressed mind of the nation'.[119] Jacobite opponents employed similar rhetoric, as seen in a draft text for an address to the queen citing 'almost universal aversion to this treaty' and asking the queen to authorise elections for a new parliament. In January, the duke of Atholl made a protestation in parliament calling for the queen to be informed of the 'inclinations of her people' so she could be served by a new parliament more in touch with the 'sentiments of the nation'.[120] A walk-out of members led by the duke of Hamilton, as in 1702, was planned for January with a collective protestation that emphasised the 'unprecedented' number of addresses presented from 'the subjects of this nation of all ranks and qualities'. The protestation proposed elections for a convention of estates, 'instructed with a more immediate sense of the nation'.[121]

Some on the queen's side responded by characterising popular opinion as misguided, trying to block petitions or arguing that parliament had ample authority to approve the treaty without recourse to its constituents. The duke of Argyll showed disdain for opinion at large by suggesting in parliament that the long scrolls of addresses should be used to make paper kites.[122] For the earl of Cromarty, the idea that members of parliament were mere delegates implied mob rule; if freeholders had to provide unanimous consent, then sovereignty remained with them and 'the Whole are still in Anarchy' with no true government. Instead, Scottish sovereignty had, in the distant past, been passed to the monarch and consequently, the queen's parliament had full powers to vote for incorporating union.[123]

---

[118] [Hodges], *Rights and Interests of the Two British Monarchies*, 69–74.
[119] Bowie, 'A 1706 manifesto for an armed rising against incorporating union', 262–7.
[120] *RPS* 1706/10/212, 7 January 1707.
[121] Szechi (ed.), *'Scotland's Ruine'*, 187, 190–1; Bowie (ed.), *Addresses*, 30–1.
[122] Szechi (ed.), *'Scotland's Ruine'*, 150.   [123] [Mackenzie], *A Friendly Return to a Letter*, 6–9.

The Sense of the Nation

Cromarty also warned that union dissidents and the threat of violent resistance needed to be brought to heel, whether 'by Force or Perswasion'.[124] As in previous reigns, unauthorised assemblies were banned to quell crowds in Edinburgh; in addition, the recent law authorising militia musters was suspended. Blackmail also came into play as the duke of Hamilton was warned that he would have no political future if he were to cause the treaty to fail. This led him to discourage armed action and refuse to lead the planned January walkout. Armed action also was discouraged by the recruitment of double agents in the southwest and the transfer of troops to the border.[125]

Alongside these efforts to diffuse extra-parliamentary pressure, opinion was courted with pro-union propaganda, treaty concessions and enhanced patronage resources. This included the prolific printed output and impassioned personal advocacy of Defoe, sent up from London to act as a spin doctor and spy. More than a paid hack, Defoe's fervency reflected his sympathy with presbyterian co-religionists and his desire for unity among Revolution supporters. His pamphlets joined other tracts, printed speeches and periodical dialogues that aimed to amplify Scottish unionism, building support among moderate presbyterians, who feared Catholic France and the Jacobites more than the Anglicans, and among 'men of business' who hoped to benefit from the promised colonial trade.[126] Anxieties in the kirk and the trading community were addressed with targeted pamphlets and concessions, including an act promising the perpetual establishment of the presbyterian church and treaty amendments giving tax exemptions and the promise that Company of Scotland shares would be bought out at face value plus 5 per cent interest.[127] Money was committed to the wooing of votes with the secret disbursement of £20,000 sterling from the English treasury to selected members, largely to pay arrears of salary and provide an entertainment fund for the queen's commissioner, the duke of Queensberry.[128]

From 1702 to 1707, the queen contended with opinion at large and an uncooperative parliament. As tensions in the union of crowns stimulated

---

[124] *Ibid.*, 29.

[125] Bowie, 'Popular resistance and the ratification of the Anglo–Scottish treaty of union'.

[126] Kidd, *Union and Unionism*, ch. 2; Bowie, *Scottish Public Opinion*, 103–14; Bowie, 'Popular resistance, religion and the Union of 1707', 41–5; Duncan (trans. and ed.), *History of the Union*, 137.

[127] Bowie, *Scottish Public Opinion*, 103–14, 131–7, 150–7; Bowie, 'Popular resistance and the ratification of the Anglo-Scottish treaty of union', 23–5.

[128] Szechi (ed.), *'Scotland's Ruine'*, appendix A.

236   Public Opinion in Early Modern Scotland, c.1560–1707

attempts to reform the union by devolving more powers to the Scottish parliament, the queen pursued an incorporating union in 1702–3 and 1706–7. Opinion at large, already primed by public disputes with William, remained visible through petitions, crowds and patriotic pamphleteering. In the final struggle over incorporation, the opposition sought to reject the queen's policy with representations of national opinion, returning to earlier practices of adversarial petitioning and protestation. Instead of rejecting these out of hand, as Charles I did in 1637, or trying to constrain petitioning, as William had done in 1699, Anne's government allowed public opinion to be expressed while taking steps to minimise its impact. Acknowledging the force but not the validity of anti-incorporation opinion, the queen's government deployed old laws and new resources to manage parliament and defuse the risk of violent resistance.

6.3 Conclusions

In anti-incorporation prints, the 1704 figure of Scotia was joined by other allegorical representations of the realm. These included the elaborately imagined Fergusia, a 'Lady of Venerable Antiquity' with a small but honourable estate worked by 'Bold and Hardy People', whose neighbour, a greedy and violent younger man with a rich estate, was pressing her to marry him; and 'Scotland' as a mother who chided her sons for leaving her 'strip naked' of her 'Ancient Honour' before England, her 'Proud and Potent Sister'.[129] With the realm itself under threat of incorporation, writers deployed this imagery to inspire patriotic fervour for the ancient kingdom of Scotland. But alongside these abstractions, the actual opinions of freeholders and subjects were invoked in tracts, speeches and protestations, displayed in militia musters, protests and crowds and evidenced in thousands of signatures on petitions from national bodies, shires, burghs and parishes. These representations directly challenged the capacity of the Scottish parliament to speak for the nation at large.

From 1689, the Revolution monarchy had relied on the backing of the Scottish parliament, embodying a presbyterian Williamite consensus. But loyalty towards William was shaken by the Glencoe massacre and the disavowal of the Company of Scotland, advertised by word of mouth and rising volumes of political print in a context of war, dearth and moral panic. By 1699, the king's apparent disregard for Scottish interests fuelled

---

[129] [Wright], *The Comical History of the Mariage betwixt Fergusia and Heptarchus*, 3; [Clark], *Scotland's Speech to Her Sons.*

The Sense of the Nation

Country opposition in parliament, leading to the collapse of the Court party's majority in May 1700. Anne struggled to regain control of the estates as constitutional reforms were demanded and crowds closely followed events in Edinburgh. Her push in 1706 for closer union divided opinion. Closer union was seen by some as the best means of protecting Scottish interests in an unequal regal union and, with the help of sweeteners, a modest majority in parliament was willing to accept the treaty. But the Convention of Royal Burghs, the commission of the general assembly, half of the shires and about one-third of the burghs expressed concern with the treaty in the largest petitioning campaign seen in Scotland since 1637. In his unionist account of these events, Sir John Clerk of Penicuik acknowledged 'how widely parliament and people had diverged, for not even one per cent approved what the former was doing'.[130] Faced with assertive representations of national sentiments, the government did not choose to mobilise extra-parliamentary support for the treaty. One such attempt showed the difficulties: a lukewarm address from the burgh council in Ayr endorsing incorporation with amendments was countered by a fervent petition from the burgh at large signed by over 1,000 hands.[131] Anne's government focused instead on containing anti-treaty opinion and averting out-of-doors resistance. Though 'the nation' commanded more respect than 'the people', being rooted more in the estates than the commons, the influence of national opinion in early modern Scotland still relied on an implicit threat of popular violence.

Studies of the Union have emphasised the stark contrast between parliamentary and extra-parliamentary opinions on the treaty. This chapter has shown how the stimulation and representation of 'the sense of the nation' on this scale depended on post-Revolution conditions of free petitioning and parliamentary debate, loosening controls on Scottish political printing and the engagement of ordinary men and women in national affairs not just through literacy but also taxation, military service, the covenants and the Company of Scotland. These modes of participation stretched down the social scale, across genders and throughout the land. Though anti-incorporation petitions, protests and pamphleteering were concentrated in the Lowlands, new research has confirmed the engagement of Mackenzie clan gentry in the union question, indicating a need for further research on opinion politics in the Highlands.[132] When the relative

[130] Duncan (trans. and ed.), *History of the Union*, 118.   [131] Bowie (ed.), *Addresses*, 119–23.
[132] Sheffield, 'Clan Mackenzie, the Act of Union and a Chief Abroad'.

independence of the post-Revolution parliament and nation at large caused problems for the monarch and England, Anne's union sought to resolve this, and the open succession, by removing the Scottish parliament and its noisy Country activists. The Revolution thus helped to embed national opinion as an intrinsic part of Scottish political culture while creating conditions that encouraged the monarch to subsume the Scottish nation into a new entity, the United Kingdom of Great Britain.

Conclusions

On 7 January 1707, John Murray, first duke of Atholl, made a protestation in the Scottish parliament against the ratification of the treaty of Anglo–Scottish union. The terms of his protestation reveal how much the language and standing of public opinion had changed over the preceding 150 years.

> And since it evidently appears, not only from the many protests of the honourable and worthie members of this house, but also from the multitudes of addresses and petitions from the severall parts of this kingdome, of the barons, freeholders, heritors, burrows and commons and from the commission of the generall assemblie, that ther is a generall dislike and aversion to the incorporating union as contained in these articles, and that ther is not one address from any part of the kingdome in favours of this union, I do therfor further protest against concluding this and the following articles of this treaty untill her majestie shall be fully informed of the inclinations of her people, that, if her majestie think fitt, she may call a new parliament to have the immediat sentiments of the nation, since these articles have been made publick, where it is hoped they may fall on such methods as may allay the ferment of the nation, satisfie the minds of the people, and creat a good understanding betwixt the two kingdoms by an union upon honourable, just and equall terms.[1]

Atholl invoked 'the inclinations of the people' to indicate the opinions of individuals outside parliament holding meaningful views on political questions, especially questions of church government. He used the 'sentiments of the nation' to indicate the collective opinions of the community of the realm, normally represented by the estates assembled in parliament. He deployed these constructs to suggest that parliament's approval of the treaty of union was out of step with public opinion and he called on

---

[1] *RPS* 1706/10/212, 7 January 1707.

239

240   Public Opinion in Early Modern Scotland, c.1560–1707

Queen Anne to authorise new elections to constitute an assembly imbued with a better idea of what their constituents wanted.

The actual balance of opinion across Scotland on the question of union will never be known and can only be the subject of informed speculation. Instead of pursuing this, the preceding chapters have aimed to show how public opinion came to feature in Atholl's final attempt to stop the Union. Looking back at the sixteenth century, Atholl's formulations bear little resemblance to allegorical representations of the nation and people imagined by Sir David Lindsay in his 1552 play *Ane Satyre of the Thrie Estaitis*. In this courtly drama, the character John the Commonweil was portrayed as a poorly dressed, disabled figure, much reduced by neglect and corruption. John used a petition to bring complaints to the parliamentary estates, speaking as a personification of the common good.[2] Separately, a Pauper character emitted complaints in an amusingly disruptive manner suggestive of popular revolt.[3] A tenant farmer impoverished by clerical exactions, the Pauper can be seen as a version of the contemporaneous stock character Jock Upaland. This straight-talking man of the soil could speak truth to power as an embodiment of *vox populi*.[4] When Lindsay and his contemporaries imagined public opinion, they reached for abstract or stock figures; by contrast, Atholl made claims about the actual sentiments of the nation and inclinations of the people. This book has identified and explained this long-term shift by investigating opinion politics; that is, the formation, expression and political impact of public opinion.

Over the past several decades, scholars have elaborated detailed accounts of the public sphere as an extra-institutional space, typically urban, for the rational discussion of printed news and commentary, mostly by middling men; and have shown how a public (or publics and counter-publics) formed around these discourses. The rise of the public sphere in realms with large and sophisticated urban print markets like England and France has been correlated with the increasing authority of public opinion. Scotland does not present an obvious fit with this scenario. Before the mid-eighteenth century, Scotland had a relatively small print market, constrained by costs and censorship. Though the market expanded slowly, with print outputs spiking in the 1640s and rising again from the 1670s,

---

[2] Lyall (ed.), *Ane Satyre of the Thrie Estaitis*; Withington, *Society in Early Modern England*, 138–40; Early Modern Research Group, 'Commonwealth'.

[3] Lyall (ed.), *Ane Satyre of the Thrie Estaitis*, 69–70, 82–3, 101, 106–7.

[4] Edington, *Court and Culture in Renaissance Scotland*, 115–6, 127–9; Milligan, '"To ding thir mony kingis doun": Jock Upaland and the Scottish labourer stereotype'; Cowan, 'Scotching the beggars: John the Commonweal and Scottish history'.

Conclusions 241

Scotland did not experience the explosive growth in printed news, dialogic pamphleteering and petitioning seen in the neighbouring realm of England. Prior research has shown that the model of the public sphere only begins to fit Scotland in the early eighteenth century and a public can only be said to exist in seventeenth-century Scotland if more than print communications are included in its constitutive discourse. While a rhetoric of public reason can be discerned in Scottish political culture, especially by the later seventeenth century, God's truth remained an essential benchmark for the rightness of opinions and a threat of popular violence continued to lend weight to invocations of opinion at large.

Similar caveats in other national contexts have led scholars to identify an evanescent or episodic public sphere. But historians find what they look for, and by looking for the public sphere, other dynamics contributing to the formation or expression of public opinion can be missed. Some scholars have explored alternative paradigms, including Raffe's 'culture of controversy' and Lake's 'politics of publicity'. Complemented by studies of print and manuscript culture, these have produced more historicised accounts of extra-institutional debate in early modern Scotland and England. This book has taken a further step by shifting attention to the formation and expression of extra-institutional opinions for political ends. Reinstating public opinion as a topic of analysis, this study has evaluated the engagement, shaping and representation of collective opinions in protestations, petitions, oaths and public communications, integrating rising print publication with the continuing influence of oral and manuscript communications. It has identified the changing language and underlying conceptualisation of extra-institutional opinion in early modern Scotland and considered how claims about collective opinion affected the flow of political events. This has revealed important innovations, including collective protestation, adversarial petitioning, inclusive covenanting and the intensification of public propaganda. Together these produced a distinctive communications context that achieved unusual levels of social participation in political episodes despite geographical and linguistic constraints.

These creative responses were stimulated by intense anxieties about backsliding and counter-reformation after Scotland's 1560 Reformation and the constitutional challenge of the 1603 regal union, which attenuated communications and encouraged stricter crown management of national assemblies. This context fuelled escalating efforts to weaponise and regulate opinion at large, making public opinion more salient in political culture. Public opinion also became more inclusive as women swore confessional oaths, heard, wrote or read political communications and

242   Public Opinion in Early Modern Scotland, c.1560–1707

joined the presentation of protestations and petitions. Though their distance from Edinburgh produced diminishing opportunities for engagement, Gaelic speakers swore oaths and heard translated communications and vernacular political poetry.

This formulation of early modern public opinion bears only a passing resemblance to the Habermasian ideal of a bloodless urban field of discourse created by the consumption and discussion of news and tracts by a male bourgeoisie. This suggests a new research agenda for countries like Scotland that do not fit this structural model. Even where this model fits more comfortably, this approach can help to expand current narratives on the public sphere and integrate these with the separate pursuit of popular politics. Differing scholarly perspectives have tended to produce a split between the study of popular politics from below and the more elite public sphere, with composite activities like collective petitioning (involving elite organisers, a range of signatories and mixed crowds) only recently attracting close attention. This bifurcation can create a misleading contrast between violent plebeian action (despite scholarly stress on the internal logic of the crowd) and rational elite discourse. By focusing on public opinion, the investigation of crowds and public discourse can be brought together. This follows Tim Harris's recommendation that, instead of investigating 'popular' activities defined by social participation, historians should 'instead start with the particular cultural phenomenon that interests us – say, a particular belief, ritual, or text (or set of texts) – and ask questions about social penetration and appropriation'.[5] Public opinion offers a lens through which social participation in extra-institutional politics can be examined, integrating a range of activities beyond written discourse.

Across this study, public opinion has been accompanied by a threat of violence, signalled from the first page by the 'convulsions' predicted by Robert Wylie. Collective opinions could be manifested through crowds, and gatherings of supporters often accompanied petitions, protestations, oath-takings or public communications. When balladeers called for the defence of the reformed church in early Jacobean Scotland, they emphasised the leadership of nobles, signalling their fear of the many-headed monster. But over the next century, ongoing religious conflict encouraged leaders to create more active forms of engagement, and the ensuing swearing, signing, presenting, protesting, and dissenting activity transformed the social basis of public opinion. The minds, consciences and

[5] Harris, 'Popular, plebeian, culture: Historical definitions', 58.

Conclusions 243

emotions of many ordinary men and women were stimulated, leading them to hold opinions, convictions and feelings on current affairs. In exploring the historical construction of the 'inclinations of the people' and the 'sense of the nation', this study has emphasised the conscientious and emotional, as well as rational, makeup of early modern public opinion, and its many manifestations from public argument to peaceful protest to violent resistance.

By emphasising this historicisation of early modernity, this book confirms that the study of public opinion need not be a search for the origins of modern public opinion. While this study's findings may help to show how public opinion came to be considered authoritative in the modern Western world, this has not been its purpose. Instead, the aim has been to explore what public opinion meant in Scotland from the Reformation to the Union and what role it played in national politics. It has examined manifestations of public opinion to understand their formation, language, credibility and impact. This has provided an approach that can be applied to other national contexts or periods, facilitating comparative analysis. Indeed, this method encourages the study of individual polities by asking how a given institutional and cultural context shaped the appearance of public opinion and how this changed over time.

This approach also has yielded a fresh perspective on the political history of early modern Scotland. In recent years, the Scottish Reformation has been re-examined through a cultural lens; the historical function and power of the Scottish parliament have been re-evaluated in an international comparative context; and state formation in the early modern kingdom has been acknowledged and outlined.[6] This book cuts across these topics by identifying an essential yet unrecognised cultural dynamic. It shows that public opinion mattered in early modern Scotland as religious and constitutional conflicts stimulated the formation, regulation and expression of opinions. Dissidents reworked old methods of protestation and petition into new tools for the public presentation of collective opinions. They merged bands and confessions into national covenants, harnessing men and women to the defence of political and religious constitutional principles with the support of oral, written and printed communications. Rulers found it necessary to pay more attention to the management of opinions, producing books, proclamations and oaths designed to correct misapprehensions and maintain consensus. Each regime struggled to master these

---

[6] Brown, 'Early modern Scottish history'; Stewart, 'Power and faith in early modern Scotland'; Bowie, 'Cultural, British and global turns in the history of early modern Scotland'.

244   Public Opinion in Early Modern Scotland, c.1560–1707

challenging circumstances: James VI tried to persuade his people but fell out of touch after 1603; Charles told his people what they should think and would not listen to their concerns; the Covenanters' innovative efforts triumphed for a time, then lost coherence under the pressure of war; Charles II stored up discontent by combining proactive publicity with the repression of grievances; and James VII paid this debt when, like his father, he lost the good opinion of his people by appearing to threaten the Reformation.

The instrumental nature of these activities, and their unintended consequences, should be emphasised. Histories of the Scottish presbyterian church have tended to portray the kirk as a democratic force, forged in a reformation from below, reasserted in a grassroots revolution through the covenants, defended after the Restoration by freedom fighters and reinstated by a grassroots revolution in 1688–90. In this populist view, the kirk was governed by a democratic general assembly that rivalled the Scottish parliament. This book has shown how clerics marshalled lay support and made populist arguments, but only as far as was convenient. When the majority was not in their favour, they justified a minority position by pointing to weightier parts and true remnants. Still, the turn towards popular participation facilitated by Scottish clerics could not be unmade. Women and men had sworn oaths and signed petitions and protestations; poets, proclamations and pamphleteers had called on the people to defend the covenants and the king. When James Hodges proposed in 1706 that women should join a political assembly to vote on the union, he may have done this for pragmatic reasons, but his capacity to imagine such a radical step relied on the participation of women in religious politics since the Reformation.

This highlights the conceptual tensions at the heart of early modern public opinion. Were the people simple and easily misled, or able to form thoughtful views that should influence decision-making? Did public opinion reflect spiritual commitments or rational and informed opinions and did these views deserve satisfaction? Who constituted the nation, an educated, propertied elite or the subjects at large? To what extent did this include women as well as men? A separate study would be required to trace the changing shape and conceptions of the political nation in this period as men and women, to varying degrees across Scotland, became more engaged in public affairs not just through the communicative forms examined here but also the experience of national dynamics including military service, taxation and colonial enterprises. Further study also could tease out connections between ideas about public opinion and popular

Conclusions 245

sovereignty.[7] This book has noted the occasional appearance of radical thinking about the nation and its political powers, from the claim that the covenant could not be unmade without the consent of all swearers to the suggestion that the people could take up arms against a king who had broken his covenanted compact. Claims about public opinion also rested on older ideas about good kingship, by which kings were expected to listen to their people's grievances and preserve the commonweal. Increasingly, early modern Scots disagreed on who should judge the people's best interest: the monarch, the parliament or the people at large? Though only a handful of thinkers articulated controversial principles of ascending political power, the rhetoric of public opinion, in which the judgement of the king or parliament was countered with the views of subjects at large, facilitated the exploration of more populist philosophies.

Finally, consideration should be given to the implications of this study for the period after 1707. The model of the public sphere has been applied to Scotland's flourishing Enlightenment culture and book trade, focusing on urban male clubs, universities and book-based discourse, while the thematic study of the first half-century after the Union has centred on Jacobitism, party politics and national identity.[8] Though Raffe's study of the 'culture of controversy' extended to 1714, further work is needed to investigate opinion politics in Scotland's new British context, especially as the flow of printed material increased between England and Scotland. Adam Fox has noted that many songs considered indigenous to eighteenth-century Scotland had their origins in pirated prints of 'Scotch' airs composed for England's Restoration stage, suggesting that Scotland's print culture became more intertwined with England while remaining distinctly Scottish.[9] Initial research indicates that the expression of Scottish collective opinions before 1707 through petitions and pamphlets facilitated British petitioning campaigns and contributed to the growing stature of extra-parliamentary opinion in eighteenth-century British political culture. Petitioning privileges in Scotland did not mirror England's exactly, but were close enough to encourage shared practices and

---

[7] David Coast has made a recent contribution to this question for England in his 'Speaking for the people'.

[8] Benchimol, 'Cultural historiography and the Scottish Enlightenment public sphere: placing Habermas in eighteenth-century Edinburgh'; Benchimol, 'Periodicals and public culture'; Wood, 'Science, the universities and the public sphere in eighteenth-century Scotland'; Mellor, 'Joanna Baillie and the counter-public sphere'; Carr, *Gender and Enlightenment Culture in Eighteenth-Century Scotland*; Towsey, *Reading the Scottish Enlightenment: Books and Their Readers in Provincial Scotland, 1750–1820*.

[9] Fox, 'Jockey and Jenny: English broadside ballads and the invention of Scottishness'.

a common political culture.[10] At the same time, however, the formation and expression of a distinct sense of Scottish national opinion before the 1707 Union contributed to the survival of Scottish national identity within the United Kingdom, limiting British integration and sustaining demands for home rule, devolution and independence to the present day.[11]

[10] Bowie, 'From customary to constitutional right: The right to petition in Scotland before the 1707 Act of Union'.

[11] Bowie, 'National opinion and the press in Scotland before the union of 1707'.

Bibliography

Manuscript Primary Sources

National Library of Scotland

Adv. MS. 22.2.11, 'Jok up Landis Newes and Dreame'

MS Grey 753

MS 34.5.15

Wodrow Quarto 16, Alexander Shields, To Sir R[obert] H[amilton] the answer of his protestation, c.1690

Wodrow Quarto 98, John Brown, Whether or not it be lawfull for the people of God in Scotland to subscribe a bond wherein they oblige themselves to live peaceablie and not to lift armes etc under a pecuniall penalty, 1668

Wodrow Quarto 99, A testimony against the embracing of the liberty granted to some ministers in Scotland, 3 Sept 1672

Wodrow Folio 28, vol 2, Act of the Presbyterie of Hamilton appointing a day of solemn humiliation and prayer, 30 July 1700

National Records of Scotland

CH2/472/1, Kinghorn Kirk Session Records, ff. 249–258

CH8/184, Copy instructions given to commissioner of noblemen, to address Queene Anne, re episcopalians in Scotland, 1703

GD3/10/3/10, Copy of an address from Glasgow to the Prince, 1688

GD3/10/22, Barony Court Book of Ardrossan

GD16/57/31, Copy of Glenisla King's Covenant, 1638

GD157/1349, Copy of protestation by synod of Merse and Teviotdale, 1651

GD406/1/450, [Marquis of Huntly] to [Marquis of Hamilton], [Oct. 1638]

GD406/1/674, Bishops of Ross and Brechin to Marquis of Hamilton, 21 Nov. 1638

GD406/1/966, Earl of Traquair to Marquis of Hamilton, 20 July 1638

GD406/1/5294, James duke of Hamilton to Anne duchess of Hamilton, 22 Oct. 1706

RH1/2/427, Copy Confession of Faith 25 Feb. 1587/88

248 *Bibliography*

PA7/17/1/38, The petition of the magistrates of Edinburgh in behalf of their poor, 1700

PC1/52-3, Privy Council Register of Acta, 13 July 1699–30 April 1707

PC4/3 Privy Council Minute Books, 2 Jan 1700–25 Jan 1707

Printed Primary Sources

Abercromby, Patrick, *The Martial Atchievements of the Scots Nation*, 2 vols (Edinburgh: Robert Fairbairn, 1711–15)

[Adamson, Patrick], *A Declaratioun of the Kingis Maiestes Intentioun and Meaning Toward the Last Actis of Parliament* (Edinburgh: Vautrollier and London: R. Field, 1585)

Adamson, Patrick, *The Recantation of Maister Patrik Adamsone* ([Middleberg: R. Schilders], 1598)

Anne, *Her Majesties Most Gracious Letter to the Parliament* (Edinburgh: Heirs of Andrew Anderson, 1702)

    Her Majesties Most Gracious Letter to the Privy Council of Scotland (Edinburgh: Heirs of Andrew Anderson, 1703)

Anon., *A Brief Account of his Sacred Majestie's Descent in a True Line Male* (Edinburgh: Heirs of Andrew Anderson, 1681)

    A Briefe and Plaine Narration of Proceedings at an Assemblie at Glasco 8 Iune 1610 ([Middelberg: R. Schilders], 1610)

    A Civil Correction of a Sawcy Impudent Pamphlet (Edinburgh: Heirs of Andrew Anderson, 1681)

    A Cloud of Witnesses for the Prerogatives of Jesus Christ, or the Last Speeches and Testimonies of Those Who Have Suffered for the Truth, in Scotland, since the Year 1680 ([Edinburgh]: n.p., 1714)

    A Faithfull Report of Proceedings Anent the Assemblie of Ministers at Aberdein vpon Tuesday 2 Iuly 1605 ([Middelberg: R. Schilders], 1606)

    A Letter from a Gentleman in Scotland to His Friend at London, Who Desired a Particular Account of the Business of Glenco ([Edinburgh]: n.p., 1695)

    A Letter from a Presbyterian Minister to a Member of Parliament ([Edinburgh]: n.p. [1693])

    A Letter from the Nobility, Barons & Commons of Scotland in the Year 1320 ([Edinburgh]: n.p., 1689)

    A Letter from the West to a Member of the Meeting of the Estates of Scotland ([Edinburgh]: n.p., 1689)

    A Modest Apology for the Students of Edenburgh Burning a Pope 25 December 1680 (London: Richard Janeway, 1681)

    A Poem Upon the Undertaking of the Royal Company of Scotland Trading to Africa and the Indies (Edinburgh: James Wardlaw, 1697)

    A Short and General Confessioun of the Trew Christian Faith according to Goddis Word, and Actis of our Parliamentis, Subscryuit be the Kingis Majestie, his Houshald, his Nobilitie and Haill Estaitis of this Realme, to the Glorie of God,

Bibliography
249

and Gude Exampill of All Men, at Edinburgh the 20. Day of Ianuarie, 1580 [1581] (Edinburgh: Henry Charteris, 1596)

A Solemn League and Covenant for Reformation and Defence of Religion (Edinburgh: Society of Stationers, 1660)

A True Account of the Trial, Condemnation and Burning of the Pope at Aberdene in Scotland ([London, 1689])

An Account of the Affairs of Scotland, In Answer to a Letter Written upon the Occasion of the Address Lately Presented to His Majesty by Some Members of the Parliament of that Kingdom ([London]: n.p., 1689)

An Account of the Burning of the Articles at Dumfries ([Edinburgh]: n.p., 1706])

An Address Sign'd by the Greatest Part of the Members of the Parliament of Scotland ([Edinburgh]: n.p., 1689)

An Answer to the Declaration of the Pretended Assembly at Dundee and to a Printed Paper, Intituled, the Protestation Given in by the Dissenting Brethren to the General Assembly, July 21 1652, Reviewed and Refuted ([Leith: Evan Tyler], 1653)

Ane Humble Remonstrance of the Citizens of Edenburgh to the Convention of Estates of Scotland (Edinburgh: Evan Tyler, 1648 [1647])

An Impartial Account of Some of the Transactions in Scotland (London: Booksellers of London and Westminster, 1695)

Ane Information of the Publick Proceedings of the Kingdom of Scotland ([Edinburgh: Evan Tyler], 1648)

Allegiance and Prerogative Considered in a Letter from a Gentleman to His Friend on Being Chosen a Member of the Meeting of States in Scotland ([Edinburgh]: n.p., 1689)

Certain Propositions Relating to the Scots Plantation of Caledonia, and the National Address ([Glasgow]: n.p., 1700)

Draught of an Act for Toleration with a Few Short Remarks Thereupon ([Edinburgh]: n.p., [1703])

Insignia Praelustris Societatis Scoticanae ad Africum & Indias, Mercaturam Facientis, Explicata ([Edinburgh]: n.p., [1696])

Laetitiae Caledonicae or Scotland's Raptures ([Edinburgh]: n.p., [1660])

Newes from Scotland, Declaring the Damnable Life and Death of Doctor Fian (London: William Wright, [1591])

Reasons Why the Ministers, Elders, and Professors, Who Protested against the Pretended Assemblies at St. Andrews, Dundee and Edinburgh Cannot Agree to the Overtures Made Unto Them at the Conference upon the 28 and 29 of July 1652 (Leith: Evan Tyler, 1652)

Salus Populi Suprema Lex Or, The Free Thoughts of a Well-Wisher, for a Good Settlement ([Edinburgh]: n.p., 1689)

Some Reflections Upon His Highness the Prince of Oranges Declaration (Holyrood: P. B. Enginier, 1688)

Some Sober Animadversions ... Upon a Testimony and Warning Emitted by the Presbytery of Edinburgh, against a Petition Lately Presented to the Parliament, in Defence of the Said Petition ([London]: n.p., 1659)

250 *Bibliography*

The Battell of Bodwell-Bridge (n.p., [1679])

The Copie of a Letter, Showing the True Relation, of the Late and Happie Victorie ... at Alfoord ([Aberdeen?: J. Brown?], 1645)

The Declaration of the Rebels in Scotland (n.p., [1679])

The Entertainment of the High and Mighty Monarch, Charles, King of Great Britaine, France and Ireland, into His Auncient and Royall City of Edinburgh (Edinburgh: John Wreitton, 1633)

The National Covenant of the Kirk of Scotland and the Solemn League and Covenant of the Three Kingdoms (Edinburgh: Society of Stationers, 1660)

The Petition of the Kingdome of Scotland (London: E.G. for Henry Overton, 1642)

The Petition of the Nobilitie, Gentrie, Burrows, Ministers and Commons of the Kingdom of Scotland (London: Robert Barker, 1642)

The Profession of the True Protestant Religion, or the Protestation of the Kirk of Scotland (1642)

The Remonstrance of the Nobility, Barons, Ministers, Burgesses and Commons Within the Kingdome of Scotland (Edinburgh: James Bryson, 1639)

The Representation, Propositions, and Protestation of Divers Ministers, Elders and Professors for Themselves, and in Name of Many Others (Leith: Evan Tyler, 1652)

The Scots Demonstration of Their Abhorrence of Popery, with All Its Adherents ([Edinburgh]: n.p., 1681)

The True Petition of the Entire Body of the Kingdome of Scotland (London: George Lindesay, 1642)

The True Relation of the Late and Happie Victorie Obtained by the Marquess of Montrose ... at Kilsyth ([Aberdeen?: J. Brown?], 1645)

To His Grace, His Majesties High Commissioner; And to the Right Honourable, the Estates of Parliament. The Address of the Presbyterian Ministers and Professors of the Church of Scotland ([Edinburgh]: n.p., 1689)

To the Queen's Most Excellent Majestie, the Humble Address and Supplication of the Suffering Episcopal Clergy in the Kingdom of Scotland ([Edinburgh]: n.p., 1703)

('A Lady of Honour'), *The Golden Island or The Darian Song* (Edinburgh: John Reid, 1699)

('Member of the General Assembly'), *The Protestation Given in by the Dissenting Brethren to the General Assembly, July 21 1652, Reviewed and Refuted* (Leith: Evan Tyler: 1652)

('Some Witnesses to the Way of Protestation'), *Protesters No Subverters and Presbyterie no Papacie* (Edinburgh, n.p., 1658)

('Sundry Ministers in the Gospel in the Provinces of Perth and Fife'), *A Testimony to the Truth of Jesus Christ* (Edinburgh: Heirs of Andrew Anderson, 1703)

Archbishops and bishops of Scotland, *The Declinator and Protestation, of the Archbishops, and Bishops, of the Church of Scotland, and Others Their Adherents within that Kingdome agaynst the Pretended Generall Assemblie, Holden at Glasgow, Novemb. 21. 1638* (Aberdene: Edward Raban, 1639)

Army of England, *A Declaration of the Army of England, Upon Their March into Scotland* (Edinburgh: Evan Tyler, 1650)

Bibliography

Atwood, William, *Reflections on a Treasonable Opinion, Industriously Promoted, Against Signing the National Association* (London: E. Whitlock, 1696)

[Balcanquhall, Walter], *A Large Declaration Concerning the Late Tumults in Scotland* (London: Robert Young, 1639)

[Bannatyne, John], *A Letter from a Presbyterian Minister in the Countrey to a Member of Parliament and also the Commission of the Church Concerning Toleration and Patronages* ([Edinburgh]: n.p., 1703)

Beeston, William and R. Gray, *By the Honourable William Beeston Kt. . . . A Proclamation* ([Edinburgh]: n.p., 1699]

[Brown, John], *An Apologeticall Relation of the Particular Sufferings of the Faithfull Ministers and Professors of the Church of Scotland since August 1660* ([Rotterdam]: n.p., 1665)

The History of the Indulgence ([Rotterdam]: n.p., 1678)

[Burnet, Gilbert], *A Modest and Free Conference betwixt a Conformist and Non-Conformist, about the Present Distempers of Scotland* ([Edinburgh]: n.p., 1669)

[Calder, Robert], *Reasons for a Toleration to the Episcopal Clergy* (Edinburgh: n.p., 1703)

[Calderwood, David], *Perth Assembly* ([Leiden: William Brewster], 1619)

A Defence of our Arguments against Kneeling in the Act of Receiving the Sacramentall elements of bread and Wine impugned by Mr. Michelsone ([Amsterdam: Giles Thorpe], 1620)

A Solution of Doctor Resolutus, His Resolutions for Kneeling ([Amsterdam: G. Veseler], 1620)

The Speach of the Kirk of Scotland to Her Beloved Children ([Amsterdam: Giles Thorp], 1620)

Quaeres Concerning the State of the Church of Scotland ([Amsterdam: Giles Thorpe], 1621)

A Dispute vpon Communicating at our Confused Communions, ([Amsterdam: Successors to Giles Thorpe], 1624)

An Answere to M. I. Forbes of Corse His Peaceable Warning ([Edinburgh: n.p.], 1638)

Campbell, Archibald, earl of Argyll, *A Declaration and Apology of the Protestant People* (Campbeltown: n.p., 1685)

Canaries, James, *A Sermon Preacht at Selkirk Upon the 29th of May 1685* (Edinburgh: Heirs of Andrew Anderson, 1685)

Charles I, *A Declaration of his M. Pleasure Anent Religion & Present Government* (Edinburgh: Thomas Finlason, 1625)

Charles by the Grace of God, King of great Britaine, France and Ireland . . . One Taxation (Edinburgh: R. Young, 1633)

Charles by the Grace of God, King of great Britaine, France and Ireland . . . One Yearly Extraordinary Taxation (Edinburgh: R. Young, 1633)

Charles by the Grace of God King of Scotland . . . Whairas We Have by Many Fair and Calm Waies (London: R. Young, 1639)

The Kings Majesties Speech in the Parliament at Edinburgh the Seventeenth Day of August 1641 (Edinburgh: James Bryson, 1641)

252   *Bibliography*

Charles II, *His Majesties Gracious Proclamation Concerning the Government of his Ancient Kingdom of Scotland* (Edinburgh: Society of Stationers, 1660)

A Proclamation against all Seditious Railers and Slanderers, Whether Civil or Ecclesiastick, of the Kings Majestie and His Government (Edinburgh: Society of Stationers, 1660)

A Proclamation . . . against Unlawfull Meetings and Seditious Papers (Edinburgh: Society of Stationers, 1660)

A Proclamation, Allowing a Further Diet to the Commons for Taking the Test (Edinburgh: Heir of Andrew Anderson, 1683)

A Proclamation Anent Jus Populi (Edinburgh: Evan Tyler, 1671)

A Proclamation Anent the Murtherers of the Late Archbishop of St Andrews, and Appointing Magistrates and Councils of Burghs Royal to Sign the Declaration at Michaelmas Next (Edinburgh: Heir of Andrew Anderson, 1679)

A Proclamation, Appointing the Magistrates of Burghs of Regality and Barony, and their Clerks, to Take the Oath of Alleadgeance, and Signe the Declaration (Edinburgh: Heir of Andrew Anderson, 1678)

A Proclamation. Containing His Majesties Gracious Pardon and Indemnity (Edinburgh: Heir of Andrew Anderson, 1679)

A Proclamation Declaring Mr. Richard Cameron, and Others, Rebels and Traitors (Edinburgh: Heir of Andrew Anderson, 1680)

A Proclamation for Discovering Such as Own, or Will Not Disown a Late Treasonable Declaration of War against His Majesty, and the Horrid Principle of Assassination (Edinburgh: Heir of Andrew Anderson, 1685)

A Proclamation, for Offering the Band Obliging Heretors and Masters for their Tenents and Servants, in Some Shires (Edinburgh: Heir of Andrew Anderson, 1678)

A Proclamation, Oblidging Heritors and Masters, for their Tennants and Servants (Edinburgh: Andrew Anderson, 1674, 1677)

A Proclamation Prohibiting the Nobility, and Others to Withdraw from this Kingdom without Licence (Edinburgh: Heir of Andrew Anderson, 1678)

Church of Scotland, *In the National Assemblie at Edinburgh the Fourth Day of August 1641* (Edinburgh: Robert Bryson, 1641)

[Clark, James], *Scotland's Speech to her Sons* ([Edinburgh]: n.p., [1706])

[Cockburn, John], *A Continuation of the Historical Relation of the Late General Assembly in Scotland* (London: B. Griffin, 1691)

Cockburn of Langtoun, Sir William, *Respublica De Decimis* (Edinburgh: John Wreitton, 1627)

Commission of the General Assembly, *A Declaration against a Crosse Petition* (London: I.B., 1642 [1643])

A Declaration against a Late Dangerous and Seditious Band, Under the Name of an Humble Remonstrance (Edinburgh: Evan Tyler, 1646)

A Declaration of the Commissioners of the Kirk and Kingdom of Scotland, to the Whole Kirk and Kingdome of Scotland (Edinburgh: Evan Tyler and London: Robert Bostock, 1648)

A Necessary Warning to the Ministerie of the Kirk of Scotland (Edinburgh: Evan Tyler, 1643)

Bibliography

A Short Declaration to the Whole Kirk and Kingdom Concerning Present Duties (Edinburgh: Evan Tyler, 1648)

A Short Exhortation and Warning to the Ministers and Professours of this Kirk (Aberdeen: James Brown, 1651)

A Short Information from the Commission of the General Assembly, Concerning the Declaration of the Honourable Court of Parliament ([Edinburgh]: np, 1648)

A Solemn Acknowledgement of Public Sins and Breaches of the Covenant (Edinburgh: Evan Tyler, 1648)

A Solemne and Seasonable Warning to All Estates and Degrees of Persons Throughout the Land (Edinburgh: Evan Tyler, 1646)

A Solemn League and Covenant (Edinburgh: Robert Bryson and Evan Tyler, 1643)

A Solemn Warning to All the Members of this Kirk (Aberdeen: James Brown, 1651)

A True Copy of the Humble Desires of the Commissioners of the General Assembly 22 March. Presented by Them to the Parliament with their Answer (London: Robert Bostock, 1648)

An Information of the Present Condition of Affairs, and Declaration Concerning Present Duties (Edinburgh: Evan Tyler, 1648)

Answer of the Commissioners of the General Assembly unto the Observations of the Honourable Committee of Estates upon the Declaration of the Late General Assembly (Edinburgh: Evan Tyler, 1648)

For the Under-Officers and Souldiers of the English Army, from the People of Scotland ([Edinburgh]: Evan Tyler, 1650)

Letter from the Commission of the General Assembly of the Church of Scotland to the Honourable Council and Inhabitants of the Scots Colony of Caledonia in America (Glasgow: Robert Sanders, 1700)

The Answer of the Commission of the Generall Assemblie to the Quaeries Propounded to Them, from the Parliament, with an Answer, from the Commission of the Generall Assemblie, to a Letter, Sent to Them, by the Presbyterie of Sterline (Aberdeen: James Brown, 1651)

The Humble Remonstrance of the Commission of the General Assembly to the Honourable and High Court of Parliament (Edinburgh: Evan Tyler, 1647)

To the Right Honourable Committee of Estates, the Humble Remonstrance of the Commissioners of the General Assembly (Edinburgh: Evan Tyler, 1647)

Unto His Grace, Her Majesties High Commissioner, and the Most Honourable Estates of Parliament, The Humble Representation of the Commission of the Late General Assembly ([Edinburgh]; n.p., 1703)

Commissioners for Regulating the Judicatories, *Articles for Regulating of the Judicatories* (Edinburgh: Evan Tyler, 1670)

Committee of Estates and the Commission of the General Assembly, *A Declaration of the Committee of Estates ... Together with a Declaration and Warning unto All the Members of this Kirk and Kingdom* (Edinburgh: Evan Tyler, 1650)

[Cowper, William], *The Bishop of Galloway His Dikaiologie: Contayning a Just Defence of His Former Apologie Against the Unjust Imputations of Mr. David Hume* (London: Thomas Snodham for John Budge, 1614)

Bibliography

Craig, Mungo, *A Lye Is No Scandal, Or a Vindication of Mr. Mungo Craig* ([Edinburgh]: [Robert Hutchison], 1697)

    A Satyr against Atheistical Deism (Edinburgh: Robert Hutchison, 1696)

[Crokatt, Gilbert and John Monro], *The Scotch Presbyterian Eloquence, or The Foolishness of Their Teaching Discovered* (London: Randal Taylor, 1692)

[Dalrymple, Hew], *Information for the Master of Stair* ([Edinburgh]: n.p., [1695])

Dalrymple of Stair, Sir James, *The Institutions of the Law of Scotland* (Edinburgh: Heirs of Andrew Anderson, 1681)

    Modus Litigandi, or, Form of Process, Observed before the Lords of Council and Session in Scotland (Edinburgh, 1681)

Douglas, Robert, *The Form and Order of the Coronation of Charles the Second* (Aberdeen: James Brown, 1651)

Drummond of Hawthornden, William, *The Works of William Drummond of Hawthornden* (Edinburgh: James Watson, 1711)

[Ferguson, Robert], *The Late Proceedings and Votes of the Parliament of Scotland Contained in An Address Delivered to the King Signed by the Plurality of the Members Thereof, Stated and Vindicated* (Glasgow: Andrew Hepburn, 1689)

Forbes of Corse, John, *A Peaceable Warning to the Subjects of Scotland* (Aberdeen: Edward Raban, 1638)

[Forbes of Disblair, William], *True Scots Genius Reviving: A Poem Written upon Occasion of the Resolve Past in Parliament, the 17th of July 1704* ([Edinburgh]: n.p., 1704)

Forrester, Henry, 'The Paithe Way to Salvatione, 1615', ed. John McCallum in *Miscellany of the Scottish History Society* xiv (Woodbridge, 2013), 61–85

[G., A.], *The Speech Which Was to Have Been Delivered to the Kings Majestie* (Edinburgh: Robert Bryson, 1641)

[Garden, George], *The Case of the Episcopal Clergy and Those of the Episcopal Perswasion Considered* ([Edinburgh]: n.p., 1703).

General Assembly of the Church of Scotland, *A Necessary Warning to the Ministerie of the Kirk of Scotland* (Edinburgh: Evan Tyler, 1643)

    A Solemne and Seasonable Warning to the Noble-Men, Barons, Gentlemen, Burrows, Ministers and Commons of Scotland (Edinburgh: Evan Tyler, 1645)

    An Information to all Good Christians in the Kingdome of England (Edinburgh: James Bryson, 1639)

    A Remonstrance and Declaration of the General Assembly of the Church of Scotland (Edinburgh: Evan Tyler and London: Robert Bostock, 1649)

    A Declaration of the General Assembly of the Kirk of Scotland (Edinburgh: Evan Tyler, 1650)

    A Short Reply to a Declaration Intituled, the Declaration of the Army of England (n.p., 1650)

    The Protestation of the Generall Assemblie of the Church of Scotland, and of the Noblemen, Barons, Gentlemen, Borrows, Ministers and Commons; Subscribers

Bibliography

of the Covenant, Lately Renewed, Made in the High Kirk, and at the Mercate Crosse of Glasgow, the 28 and 29 of November 1638 (Glasgow: George Anderson, 1638)

The Protestation of the Generall Assembly of the Kirk of Scotland, and of the Noble-men, Barrons, Gentlemen, Burrowes, Ministers and Commons. Subscribers of the Covenant Lately Made at the Mercat Crosse of Edinburgh the 18. of December 1638 (Edinburgh: James Bryson, 1639)

[Gillespie, George], *A Dispute against the English-Popish Ceremonies, Obtruded upon the Church of Scotland* ([Leiden: Willem Christiaenez van der Boxe and Amsterdam: John Canne], 1637)

Gillespie, George, *An Usefull Case of Conscience Discussed and Resolved* (Edinburgh: Heirs of George Anderson, 1649)

[Gillespie, George], *Reasons for which the Service Booke, Urged upon Scotland Ought to Bee Refused* ([Edinburgh: G. Anderson], 1638)

Gordon, James, *History of Scots Affairs, from MDCXXXVII to MDCXLI* (Aberdeen: Spalding Club, 1841)

[Gordon, John], *Plain Dealing: Being a Moderate General Review of the Scots Prelatical Clergies Proceedings in the Latter Reigns* (London: Richard Baldwin, 1689),

Graham, James, marquis of Montrose, *Declaration of His Excellency James Marques of Montrose* (Gothenburg: n.p., 1649; [London]: n.p, 1650; [Edinburgh?]: n.p., 1650)

[Grant, Francis], *A True Narrative of the Sufferings and Relief of a Young Girle; Strangely Molested, by Evil Spirits* (Edinburgh: James Watson, 1698)

[Grant, Francis], *Sadducimus Debellatus, or a True Narrative of the Sorceries and Witchcraft Exercis'd by the Devil and His Instruments upon Mrs. Christian Shaw* (London: H. Newman and A. Bell, 1698)

[Guthrie, James], *The Nullity of the Pretended Assembly at St. Andrews & Dundee* ([Leith: Evan Tyler], 1652)

[Guthrie, James], *A Vindication of the Freedome and Lawfullnesse, and so of the Authority of the Late General Assembly...Together with a Review of the said Vindication* ([Leith: Evan Tyler], 1652)

[Guthrie, James], *The Causes of the Lord's Wrath Against Scotland* (Edinburgh: Heirs of George Anderson], 1653)

[Hadow, James], *A Survey of the Case of the Episcopal Clergy, and of Those of the Episcopal Perswasion* (Edinburgh: George Mosman, 1703)

Hamilton, James, earl of Arran, *A Speech Made by the Right Honourable the Earl of Arran to the Scotish Nobility and Gentry* (Edinburgh: John Reid, 1689)

Hay of Naughton, Peter, *An Aduertisement to the Subjects of Scotland* (Aberdeen: Edward Raban, 1627)

[Henderson, Alexander], *The Protestation of the Noblemen, Barrons, Gentlemen, Borrowes, Ministers, and Commons, Subscribers of the Confession of Faith and Covenant, Lately Renewed within the Kingdome of Scotland, Made at the Mercate Crosse of Edinburgh, the 4. of Iulij Immediatly after the Reading of the Proclamation, Dated 28. Iune. 1638*, [Edinburgh]: n.p., 1638)

256 *Bibliography*

[Hodges, James], *The Rights and Interests of the Two British Monarchies Inquir'd into and Clear'd, with a Special Respect to an United or Separate State, Treatise I* (Edinburgh: John Reid, 1703)

The Rights and Interests of the Two British Monarchies (London: n.p., 1706)

Hope, Sir Thomas, *Minor Practicks, or, A Treatise of the Scottish Law* (Edinburgh: Thomas Ruddiman, 1726)

[Honyman, Andrew], *Survey of Naphtali Part II* (Edinburgh: Evan Tyler, 1669)

James VI, *Ane Shorte and General Confession of the Trewe Christiane Fayth and Religion According to Godis Word* (Edinburgh: Robert Lekprevike, 1581)

Basilikon Doron (Edinburgh: Robert Waldegrave, 1599)

The Confession of Faith, Subscrived by the Kingis Maiestie and his Houshold Togither with the Copie of the Bande, Maid Touching the Maintenance of the True Religion, the Kingis Majesties Person and Estate, &c: Seuerally to be Subscriued by all Noblemen, Barrons, Gentlemen and Otheris (Edinburgh: Robert Waldegrave, 1590)

James VII, *Act for Security of the Protestant Religion* (Edinburgh: Heir of Andrew Anderson, 1685)

A Proclamation against Slanderers and Leesing-Makers (Edinburgh: Heir of Andrew Anderson, 1686)

A Proclamation Containing His Majesties Gracious and Ample Indemnity (Edinburgh: Heir of Andrew Anderson, 1688)

This Day Being the Festival of St George, The Coronation of Their Sacred Majesties King James the Second and Queen Mary Was Performed at Westminster (London: Thomas Newcomb; Edinburgh: Heir of Andrew Anderson, 1685)

[Johnston of Wariston, Archibald], *A Short Relation of the State of the Kirk of Scotland* ([Edinburgh]; n.p., 1638)

Reasons Against the Rendering of our Sworne and Subscribed Confession of Faith ([Edinburgh: G. Anderson?], [1639])

The Declinatour and Protestation of the Some-times Pretended Bishops, Presented in Face of the Last Assembly, Refuted and Found Futile (Edinburgh: James Bryson, 1639)

K., C., *Some Seasonable and Modest Thoughts Partly Occasioned by and Partly Concerning the Scots East-India Company* ([Edinburgh]: n.p., 1696)

King, John and John Kid, *The Last Speeches of the Two Ministers Mr. John King and Mr. John Kid at the Place of Execution at Edinburgh* ([Edinburgh]: n.p., 1680)

L., M., *Albion's Elegie, or a Poem upon the High and Mighty Prince James* (Edinburgh: Heir of Andrew Anderson, 1680)

L[aurie], R[obert], *God Save the King, or the Loyal and Joyful Acclamation of Subjects to their King* (Edinburgh: Christopher Higgins, 1660)

[Leslie, Charles], *Gallienus Redivivus, or Murder Will Out &c Being a True Account of the De-Witting of Glencoe, Gaffney, &c* (Edinburgh: n.p., 1695)

Leslie, John, 6th earl of Rothes, *A Relation of Proceedings Concerning the Affairs of the Kirk of Scotland, from August 1637 to July 1638* (Edinburgh: Bannatyne Club, 1830)

Bibliography

Lindsay, Colin, *earl of Balcarres, Memoirs touching the Revolution, M.DC.LXXXVIII-M.DC.XC* (Edinburgh: Bannatyne Club, 1841)

Lithgow, William, *Scotland's Welcome to Her Native Sonne* (Edinburgh: John Wreitton, 1633)

L[auder], G[eorge], *Caledonias Covenant, or Ane Panegyrick to the World* ([Edinburgh?: Robert Bryson?], 1641)

London Gazette (to 1707)

[M., P.], *King Charles His Birthright* (Edinburgh: John Wreitton, 1633)

M[a]cdonald of Glencoe, John, *To His Grace, His Majesties High Commissioner and the Right Honourable Estates of Parliament, The Humble Supplication of John Mcdonald of Glencoe* ([Edinburgh: n.p., 1695])

[Mackenzie, George, earl of Cromarty], *A Few Brief and Modest Reflexions Perswading a Just Indulgence to be Granted to the Episcopal Clergy and People in Scotland* ([Edinburgh]: n.p., 1703)

[Mackenzie, George, earl of Cromarty], *A Continuation of a Few Brief and Modest Reflexions* ([Edinburgh]: n.p., 1703)

[Mackenzie, George, earl of Cromarty], *A Friendly Return to a Letter Concerning Sir George Mackenzie's and Sir John Nisbet's Observation and Response, on the Matter of the Union* ([Edinburgh]: n.p., 1706)

Mackenzie of Rosehaugh, Sir George, *A Vindication of the Government of Scotland during the Reign of Charles II* (London: J. Hindmarsh, 1691)

Mackenzie of Rosehaugh, Sir George and George Mackenzie, viscount Tarbat, *A Memorial to His Highness the Prince of Orange, In Relation to the Affairs of Scotland* (London: Randal Taylor, 1689)

[McWard, Robert], *The Banders Disbanded or An Accurat Discourse* (n.p., 1681)

The Case of the Accommodation (n.p., 1671)

The True Non-Conformist in Answere to the Modest and Free Conference ([Amsterdam?]: n.p., 1671)

The Poor Man's Cup of Cold Water, Ministered to the Saints and Sufferers for Christ in Scotland, Who Are Amidst the Scorching Flames of Fiery Trial ([Amsterdam]: n.p., 1678)

Members of Parliament, *Coppy of the Addres: Of a Great Number of the Members of the Parliament of Scotland* (Edinburgh: John Reid, 1700)

[Mocket, Richard], *God and the King* (London: for James Primrose in Scotland, 1616)

Monck, George, *A Declaration of the Commander in Chief of the Forces in Scotland* (Edinburgh: Christopher Higgins, 1659)

[Monro, Alexander], 'The fourth letter', in *An Account of the Present Persecution of the Church of Scotland in Several Letters* (London: S. Cook, 1690), 63–8

Presbyterian Inquisition as It Was Lately Practiced Against the Professors of the Colledge of Edinburgh (London: J. Hindmarsh, 1691)

[Montgomery of Skelmorlie, Sir James], *Great Britain's Just Complaint* (Oxford: n.p., 1692)

[Morer, Thomas], 'The first letter' in *An Account of the Present Persecution of the Church of Scotland in Several Letters* (London: S. Cook, 1690), 1–6

258   *Bibliography*

[Murray, John], *A Dialogue betwixt Cosmophilus and Theophilus anent the Urging of New Ceremonies upon the Kirke of Scotland* (Amsterdam, 1620 [1621])

[Nalson, John], *The True Protestants Appeal to the City and Countrey* (Edinburgh: n.p., 1681)

Officers of the Scottish Army, *To the Right Honourable the Lords and Others of the Committee of Estates, the Humble Remonstrance and Supplication of the Officers of the Army* (Edinburgh: Evan Tyler, 1650)

Officers of the Army in Scotland, *A Declaration of the Officers of the Army in Scotland to the Churches of Christ in the Three Nations* (Edinburgh: Christopher Higgins, 1659)

Parliament of Scotland, *Questions Exhibited by the Parliament Now in Scotland Assembled* ([Edinburgh]: n.p., 1641)

Parliament of England, *The Humble Address of the Right Honourable, the Lords Spiritual and Temporal and Commons in Parliament Assembled Presented to His Majesty* (Edinburgh: n.p., 1696)

[Pennecuik, Alexander], *Caledonia Triumphans: A Panegyrick to the King* (Edinburgh: Heirs of Andrew Anderson, 1699)

Privy Council of Scotland, *Association Begun to be Subscribed at Edinburgh, April 10, 1696* (Edinburgh: n.p., 1696)

   A Letter Directed from the Council of Scotland to the King ([Edinburgh: Heir of Andrew Anderson], 1680)

   A Letter to His Majesty from His Privy Council in Scotland ([Edinburgh]: n.p., 1680)

   A True and Exact Copy of a Treasonable and Bloody Paper, Called the Fanaticks New Covenant (Dublin: n.p., 1680)

   A True Narrative of the Reception of their Royal Highnesses at Their Arrival in Scotland (Edinburgh: Heirs of Andrew Anderson, 1680)

Presbytery of Edinburgh, *A Testimony and Warning of the Presbytery of Edinburgh, against a Late Petition* ([Edinburgh?]: n.p., 1659)

Presbytery of Stirling, *The Remonstrance of the Presbyterie of Sterling against the Present Conjunction with the Malignant Party* (Edinburgh: Evan Tyler, 1651)

R[amsay], J[ames], *Moses Returned from Midian, or Gods Kindnesse to a Banished King; His Office, and His Subjects Duty* (Edinburgh: Gedeon Lithgow, 1660)

[Renwick, James], *The Testimony of Some Persecuted Presbyterian Ministers of the Gospel* ([Edinburgh?]: n.p., 1688)

[Renwick, James and Alexander Shields], *An Informatory Vindication of a Poor, Wasted, Misrepresented, Remnant of the Suffering, Anti-Prelatick, Anti-Erastian, Anti-Sectarian, True Presbyterian Church of Christ in Scotland, United Together in a Generall Correspondence* ([Edinburgh?]: n.p., orig. pub. 1687; 1707 edition)

[Ridpath, George], *A Continuation of the Answer to the Scotch Presbyterian Eloquence* (London: n.p., 1693)

Bibliography

[Ridpath, George], *A Discourse upon the Union of Scotland and England* ([Edinburgh]: n.p., 1702)

[Ridpath, George], *An Answer to the Scotch Presbyterian Eloquence in Three Parts* (London: Thomas Anderson, 1693)

[Ridpath, George], *An Historical Account of the Antient Rights and Power of the Parliament of Scotland* ([Edinburgh]: n.p., 1703)

[Ridpath, George], *The Massacre of Glenco* (London: B. Bragg, 1703)

[Ridpath, George], *The People of Scotland's Groans and Lamentable Complaints, Pour'd Out Before the Honourable Court of Parliament* (n.p., [1700])

[Ridpath, George], *The Queries and Protestation of the Scots Episcopal Clergy* (London: n.p., 1694)

[Ridpath, George], *The Scots Episcopal Innocence or The Juggling of That Party* (London: n.p., 1694)

Row, John, *The History of the Kirk of Scotland from the Year 1558 to August 1637* (Edinburgh: Wodrow Society, 1842)

Russell, James, *A True and Exact Copy of a Prodigious and Traiterous Libel* (Edinburgh: n.p., 1681)

Rycaut, Sir Paul, *A Memorial Given in to the Senate of the City of Hamburgh* (Edinburgh: n.p., 1697)

[Sage, John], *Fundamental Charter of Presbytery, as It Hath Been Lately Established in the Kingdom of Scotland, Examin'd and Disprov'd* (London: C. Brome, 1695)

[Sage, John], 'The second letter' and 'The third letter' *An Account of the Present Persecution of the Church of Scotland in Several Letters* (London: S. Cook, 1690), 6–51 and 52–63

Seton of Pitmedden, William, *A Speech in Parliament on the Second Day of November* (Edinburgh: n.p., 1706)

The Interest of Scotland in Three Essays ([Edinburgh]: n.p., 1700)

Scrougie, Alexander, *Mirabilia Dei, or Britannia Gaudia Exultans* (Edinburgh: Society of Stationers, 1660)

Settle, Elkanah, *An Heroic Poem on the Coronation of the High and Mighty Monarch James II* (Edinburgh: Heir of Andrew Anderson, 1685)

[Sharp, James], *A True Representation of the Rise, Progresse and Present State of the Divisions in the Church of Scotland* (London: n.p., 1657)

Skene, Sir John, *De Verborum Significatione: The Exposition of the Termes and Difficill Wordes, Conteined in the Foure Buikes of Regiam Majestatem* (Edinburgh: David Lindsay, 1681)

Spalding, John, *The History of the Troubles and Memorable Transactions in the Reign of Charles I* (Aberdeen: George King, 1829)

Spottiswood, John, *History of the Church of Scotland*, 3 vols (Edinburgh: Oliver & Boyd, 1851)

[Stewart of Goodtrees, James], *An Accompt of Scotlands Grievances by Reason of the D. of Lauderdales Ministry, Humbly Tendred to his Sacred Majesty* ([Edinburgh]: n.p., 1675)

[Stewart of Goodtrees, James], *Jus Populi Vindicatum* ([Rotterdam]: n.p., 1669)

260   *Bibliography*

[Stewart of Goodtrees, James and James Stirling], *Napthali, Or the Wrestlings of the Church of Scotland for the Kingdom of Christ* ([Rotterdam]: n.p, 1667)

[Sydserf, Thomas], *Edinburghs Joy at His Majesties Coronation in England* ([Edinburgh]: n.p., 1661)

[Sydserf, Thomas], *Mercurius Caledonius* (Edinburgh: Society of Stationers and London, 8 Jan. 1661)

[Sydserf, Thomas], *The Work Goes Bonnely On* ([Edinburgh]: n.p., 1661)

Symson, Matthias, *Mephibosheth, or The Lively Picture of a Loyal Subject* (Edinburgh: Gedeon Lithgow, 1660)

Turner, Francis, *A Sermon Preached before Their Majesties K James II and Q Mary at Their Coronation* (London: Robert Clavel; Edinburgh: Heir of Andrew Anderson, 1685)

University of St. Andrews, *The Addres of the University of St. Andrews to the King* (London: J. R., 1689)

[Webster, James], *An Essay upon Toleration by a Sincere Lover of the Church and State* ([Edinburgh]: n.p., 1703)

[Wedderburn, Robert], *The Complaynt of Scotland* (Paris: n.p., 1550)

[William of Orange and others], *His Highness the Prince of Orange His Speech to the Scots Lords and Gentlemen with Their Address and His Highness His Answer* ([London]: R. Janeway, 1689)

William of Orange, *The Declaration of His Highness William Henry by the Grace of God Prince of Orange &c, of the Reasons Inducing Him to Appear in Arms for Preserving of the Protestant Religion and Restoring the Laws and Liberties of the Ancient Kingdom of Scotland* (The Hague: Arnout Leers, 1688; Edinburgh: n.p., 1689)

William II, *His Majesties Most Gracious Letter to the Parliament of Scotland* (Edinburgh: Heirs of Andrew Anderson, 1700)

Williamson, David, *A Sermon Preached Before His Grace, the King's Commissioner and the Three Estates of Parliament June the 15th 1690* (Edinburgh: John Reid, 1690)

[Wishart, George], *The History of the Kings Majesties Affairs in Scotland* (The Hague: Samuel Browne, 1647)

Wodrow, Robert, *The History of the Sufferings of the Church of Scotland from the Restauration to the Revolution*, 2 vols (Edinburgh: James Watson, 1721–22)

[Wood, James], *A Vindication of the Freedom & Lawfulnes of the Late Generall Assembly* (London: n.p, 1652)

A Declaration of the Brethren Who Are for the Established Government and Judicatories of this Church (Edinburgh: n.p., 1658)

[Wright, William], *The Comical History of the Mariage betwixt Fergusia and Heptarchus* ([Edinburgh]: n.p., 1706)

[Wylie, Robert], *A Speech Without Doors, Concerning Toleration* ([Edinburgh]: n. p., [1703])

Letter from a Gentleman in the City to a Minister in the Country ([Edinburgh]: n. p., [1703])

The Insecurity of a Printed Overture for an Act for the Church's Security ([Edinburgh]: n.p., [1706])

Bibliography

Edited and Collected Primary Sources

1599 Geneva Bible, *Bible Gateway*, www.biblegateway.com

Airy, Osmund (ed.), *Burnet's History of My Own Time*, 2 vols (Oxford: 1898–1900; Burlington: Tanner-Ritchie, 2016)

The Lauderdale Papers, 3 vols (Westminster: Camden Society, 1884–5; Burlington: Tanner-Ritchie, 2015)

Anderson, Henry, 'Ecloga I' and 'Ecloga II' (1617) in Reid, Steven and David McOmish (eds), *Bridging the Continental Divide: Neo-Latin and Its Cultural Role in Jacobean Scotland, as seen in the* Delitiae Poetarum Scotorum (1637), www.dps.gla.ac.uk

Bain, Joseph et al. (eds), *Calendar of State Papers relating to Scotland and Mary Queen of Scots, 1542–1560*, 12 vols (Edinburgh: General Register House, 1898–1969; Burlington: Tanner-Ritchie, 2005–08)

Balfour, Sir James (ed.), *Letters and State Papers During the Reign of James VI* (Edinburgh: Abbotsford Club, 1838)

Balfour-Melville, E. W. M. (ed.), *An Account of the Proceedings of the Estates in Scotland, 1689–90*, 2 vols (Edinburgh: Scottish History Society, 1954–5)

'Banishment from Scotland, 1685', *Journal of Presbyterian History (1962–1985)* 40:2 (June 1962), 121–125

Baxter, Jamie Reid (ed.), 'Jok up Landis Newes and Dreame', unpublished transcription and notes, NLS Adv.MS. 22.2.11

Bowie, Karin (ed.), *Addresses Against Incorporating Union, 1706–1707* (Woodbridge: Scottish History Society, 2018)

Brown, Keith M. (gen. ed.), *Records of the Parliament of Scotland* (St. Andrews, 2007–2018), www.rps.ac.uk

Calderwood, David, *The History of the Kirk of Scotland*, ed. T. Thomson, 8 vols (Edinburgh: Wodrow Society, 1842–49; Burlington: Tanner-Ritchie, 2006)

Cowan, Ian B., Annie I. (Cameron) Dunlop, James Kirk, E. R. Lindsay, David MacLauchlan, Alan Macquarrie and Roland J. Tanner (eds), *Calendar of Scottish Supplications to Rome, 1417–1492*, 6 vols (Edinburgh and Glasgow, 1934–2017)

Cranstoun, James (ed.), *Satirical Poems of the Time of the Reformation*, 2 vols (Edinburgh: Scottish Text Society, 1893)

Doak, Laura (ed.), 'Robert Garnock's protestation against the parlimenters (1681)' in *Miscellany of the Scottish History Society* (Woodbridge: Boydell, forthcoming)

Duncan, Douglas (trans. and ed.), *History of the Union of Scotland and England by Sir John Clerk of Penicuik* (Edinburgh: Scottish History Society, 1993)

Fleming, David Hay (ed.), *Register of the Minister Elders and Deacons of the Christian Congregation of St. Andrews*, 2 vols (Edinburgh: Scottish History Society, 1889–90)

Fleming, David H. (ed.), *Scotland's Supplication and Complaint against the Book of Common Prayer (Otherwise Laud's Liturgy), the Book of Canons, and the Prelates, 18th October 1637* (Edinburgh: Society of Antiquaries of Scotland, 1927)

Bibliography

[Fleming, David Hay and James D. Ogilvie, (eds)], 'The National Petition to the Scottish Privy Council, October 18, 1637', *Scottish Historical Review* 22:88 (July 1925), 241–8

Fletcher, Andrew, *Political Works*, ed. John Robertson (Cambridge, 1997)

Gardiner, S. R. (ed.), *The Constitutional Documents of the Puritan Revolution, 1625–1660*, 3rd edition (Oxford: Clarendon Press, 1958)

General Assembly of the Church of Scotland, *Acts and Proceedings of the General Assemblies of the Kirk of Scotland*, ed. T. Thomson, 3 vols (Edinburgh: Bannatyne Club, 1839–45)

General Assembly of the Church of Scotland, *Acts of the General Assembly of the Church of Scotland, 1638–1642* (Edinburgh: Church Law Society, 1843)

Goodare, Julian (ed.), 'Diary of the convention of estates, 1630', *Miscellany of the Scottish Historical Society XIV* (2010), 86–110

Gordon, George, second marquis of Huntly, 'Oath to the Covenanters (c.1639)', *Manuscript Pamphleteering in Early Stuart England*, www.mpese.ac.uk

Haig, James (ed.), *The Historical Works of Sir James Balfour of Denmylne and Kinnaird, Knight and Baronet, Lord Lyon King of Arms to Charles the First and Charles the Second*, 4 vols (Edinburgh: Constable, 1824–5)

Home, Sir David, Lord Crossrigg, 'A narrative of the rise, progress and success of the societies of Edinburgh for reformation of manners, 1701', ed. Nathan Gray, *Miscellany of the Scottish History Society XIV* (Woodbridge: Boydell, 2013), 111–38

Hopper, Andrew, David J. Appleby, Mark Stoyle and Lloyd Bowen (eds.), *Civil War Petitions: Conflict, Welfare and Memory During and After the English Civil Wars, 1642–1710*, www.civilwarpetitions.ac.uk

House of Commons of England, *Journals of the House of Commons*, 22 vols (Burlington: Tanner Ritchie, 2011–15)

House of Commons of England, *The English Association of the House of Commons* (Edinburgh: Heirs to Andrew Anderson, 1696)

Howell, T. B. (ed.), *A Complete Collection of State Trials, Vol. III* (London: T. C. Hansard, 1816)

James VI and I, *Political Writings*, ed. Johan P. Sommerville (Cambridge, 1994, 2001)

Jardine, Mark, 'The "Petitione for Margaret Lachlisone" of 18 April 1685', 'The first post-martyrdom sources of 1687', 'The "Galloway" memorandum of the Killing Times', 'The woman who never was', 'Declarations–1680 Sanquhar', 'Table: Judicial executions of militant Presbyterians', *Jardine's Book of Martyrs*, www.drmarkjardine.wordpress.com

King, Adam, 'Επιβατήριον ad Regem in Scotiam Redeuntem' (1617) in Reid, Steven and David McOmish (eds), *Bridging the Continental divide: Neo-Latin and its Cultural Role in Jacobean Scotland, as Seen in the* Delitiae Poetarum Scotorum (1637), www.dps.gla.ac.uk

Kinloch, G. R. (ed.), *The Diary of Mr. James Melville 1556–1601* (Edinburgh: Bannatyne Club, 1829)

Kirkton, James, *The Secret and True History of the Church of Scotland from the Restoration to the Year 1678*, ed. Charles K. Sharp (Edinburgh: Longman, Hurst, Rees, Orme and Brown and John Ballantyne, 1817)

Bibliography

Laing, David (ed.), *Letters and Journals of Robert Baillie*, 3 vols (Edinburgh: Bannatyne Club, 1841–42)

Original Letters Relating to the Ecclesiastical Affairs of Scotland, 2 vols (Edinburgh: Bannatyne Club, 1851)

The Miscellany of the Wodrow Society (Edinburgh: Wodrow Society, 1844)

The Works of John Knox, 6 vols (Edinburgh: Wodrow Society, 1895; Burlington: Tanner-Ritchie, 2010)

Lauder of Fountainhall, Sir John, *Historical Notices of Scotish Affairs*, 2 vols (Edinburgh: Bannatyne Club, 1848)

Historical Observes of Memorable Occurents in Church and State from October 1680 to April 1686 (Edinburgh: Bannatyne Club, 1837)

Lyall, Roderick (ed.), *Ane Satyre of the Thrie Estaitis* (Edinburgh: Canongate, 1994)

MacKenzie, Annie M. (ed.), *Orain Iain Luim: Songs of John MacDonald, Bard of Keppoch* (Edinburgh: Scottish Gaelic Texts Society, 1964)

Marwick, Sir J. D., *Extracts from the Records of the Convention of Royal Burghs*, 5 vols (Edinburgh: Convention of Royal Burghs, 1866–85)

Marwick, Sir J. D. and Robert Renwick, *Extracts from the Records of the Burgh of Glasgow*, 5 vols (Glasgow: Scottish Burgh Records Society, 1876–1916)

Mason, Roger A. and Martin S. Smith (trans and eds), *A Dialogue on the Law of Kingship among the Scots: A Critical Edition and Translation of George Buchanan's De Jure Regni apud Scotos Dialogus* (Aldershot: Ashgate, 2004)

Mason, Roger (ed.), *On Rebellion* (Cambridge, 1994; repr. 1996)

McCrie, Thomas (ed.), *The Life of Mr. Robert Blair, Minister of St. Andrews, Containing his Autobiography, from 1593 to 1636* (Edinburgh: Wodrow Society, 1848)

McCormick, Joseph (ed.), *State-papers and Letters Addressed to William Carstares* (Edinburgh: John Balfour, 1774)

McGinnis, Paul J. and Arthur H. Williamson (trans and eds), *The British Union: A Critical Edition and Translation of David Hume of Godscroft's De Unione Insulae Britannicae* (Aldershot: Ashgate, 2002)

McMaster, Jane H. and Marguerite Wood (eds), *Supplementary Report on the Manuscripts of the Duke of Hamilton K.T., Vol. 2* (London: HMSO, 1932; Burlington: Tanner-Ritchie, 2009)

Melville, William Henry Leslie (ed.), *Letters and State Papers Chiefly Addressed to George Earl of Melville Secretary of State for Scotland 1689–1694* (Edinburgh: Bannatyne Club, 1843)

Mitchell, Alexander P. and James Christie (eds), *The Records of the Commissions of the General Assemblies of the Church of Scotland*, 2 vols (Edinburgh: Scottish History Society, 1892–6)

Napier, Mark (ed.), *Memorials of Montrose and His Times*, 2 vols (Edinburgh: Maitland Club, 1810)

Normand, Lawrence and Gareth Roberts, *Witchcraft in Early Modern Scotland: James VI's Demonology and the North Berwick Witches* (Exeter, 2000)

264   *Bibliography*

'Oath Offered to the Scots in London' (1639), *Manuscript Pamphlets in Early Stuart England*, www.mpese.ac.uk

Parliament of Ireland, *A Collection of the Protests of the Lords of Ireland, from 1634 to 1770* (London: J. Almon, 1771)

Paton, Henry (ed.), *Report on the Laing Manuscripts*, 2 vols (London, 1914–25; Burlington: Tanner-Ritchie, 2013)

Paul, George M., David Hay Fleming and James D. Ogilvie (eds), *The Diary of Sir Archibald Johnston of Wariston*, 3 vols (Edinburgh: Scottish History Society, 1911–40)

Paul, J. Balfour, 'Scottish emigrants in the seventeenth century', *Scottish Historical Review* 19:75 (April 1922), 239–40

Pitcairn, Robert (ed.), *Ancient Criminal Trials in Scotland*, 3 vols (Edinburgh: Maitland Club, 1833)

Privy Council of Scotland, *Register of the Privy Council of Scotland*, 36 vols, ed. John Hill Burton, David Masson, P. Hume Brown, Henry Paton and Robert Kerr Hannay (Edinburgh: HM General Register House, 1877–1933; Burlington: Tanner Ritchie, 2004)

Rogers, Charles (ed.), *The Earl of Stirling's Register of Royal Letters*, 2 vols (Edinburgh: n.p., 1885)

Routh, M. J. (ed.), *Bishop Burnet's* History of His Own Time, 6 vols (Oxford: Clarendon Press, 1823)

Steele, Robert, *Tudor and Stuart Proclamations, 1485–1714, Vol. II Scotland and Ireland* (Oxford: Clarendon Press, 1910)

Stephen, William (ed.), *Register of the Consultations of the Ministers of Edinburgh and Some Other Brethren of the Ministry, 1652–1660*, 2 vols (Edinburgh: Scottish History Society, 1921–30)

Stuart, John (ed.), *The Miscellany of the Spalding Club*, 5 vols (Aberdeen: Spalding Club, 1841–52)

Szechi, Daniel (ed.), *'Scotland's Ruine': Lockhart of Carnwath's Memoirs of the Union* (Aberdeen: Association for Scottish Literary Studies, 1995)

Terry, Charles Sanford (ed.), *The Cromwellian Union: Papers Relating to the Negotiations for an Incorporating Union between England and Scotland 1651–1652* (Edinburgh: Scottish History Society, 1902)

Thomson, T. (ed.), *Memoirs of His Own Life by Sir James Melville of Halhill, M.D.XLIX.-M.D.XCIII* (Edinburgh: Bannatyne Club, 1827)

Tweedie, W. K. (ed.), *Select Biographies*, 2 vols (Edinburgh: Wodrow Society, 1845–47)

Wallace, James, 'Narrative of the Rising at Pentland' in Thomas McCrie (ed.), *Memoirs of Mr. William Veitch and George Brysson* (Edinburgh: William Blackwood and London: T. Cadell, 1825), 388–432

Watson, George (ed.), *Bell's Dictionary and Digest of the Law of Scotland*, 7th edition (Edinburgh: Edinburgh Legal Education Trust, 2012)

Bibliography

Secondary Sources

Reference Websites

'Dictionary of the Older Scottish Tongue' in *Dictionary of the Scots Language* (Glasgow, 2018), www.dsl.ac.uk

Houston, Robert A., *Peasant Petitions: Social Relations and Economic Life on Landed Estates, 1600–1850* (Basingstoke: Palgrave Macmillan, 2014)

Oxford English Dictionary (Oxford, 2020), www.oed.com

Logeion (Chicago, 2011), www.logeion.uchicago.edu

'Scottish National Dictionary' in *Dictionary of the Scots Language* (Glasgow, 2018), www.dsl.ac.uk

Books, Chapters and Articles

Adams, Sharon, 'The making of the radical south-west: Charles I and his Scottish kingdoms, 1625–1649' in John R. Young (ed.), *Celtic Dimensions of the British Civil Wars* (Edinburgh: John Donald, 1997), 53–74

Adams, Sharon and Julian Goodare, 'Scotland and its seventeenth-century revolutions' in Sharon Adams and Julian Goodare (eds), *Scotland in the Age of Two Revolutions* (Woodbridge: Boydell Press, 2014), 1–22

Allan, David, *Philosophy and Politics in Later Stuart Scotland: Neo-Stoicism, Culture and Ideology in Crisis, 1540–1690* (East Linton: Tuckwell, 2000)

Anderson, James, *The Ladies of the Covenant* (Edinburgh: Blackie & Son, 1857)

Baker, Keith Michael, 'Politics and public opinion under the Old Regime: some reflections' in Jack R. Censer and Jeremy D. Popkin (eds), *Press and Politics in Pre-Revolutionary France* (Berkeley, Los Angeles and London: Univ. of California Press, 1987), 204–46

Baldwin, Geoff, 'The 'public' as a rhetorical community in early modern England' in A. Shepard and P. Withrington (eds), *Communities in Early Modern England* (Manchester University Press, 2000), 199–215

Bambery, Chris, 'Terrorism and fanaticism: were the early Calvinists Scotland's Daesh?', *The National* (8 Dec. 2015)

Bardgett, Frank D. '"Foure Parische Kirkis to Ane Preicheir"', *Records of the Scottish Church History Society* 22 (1986), 195–209

Barrett, John and Alastair Mitchell, 'Plunder in the north: the Elgin depositions of 1646', *History Scotland* (July/Aug. 2008), 19–25

Baxter, Jamie Reid, 'Elizabeth Melville, Lady Culross: new light from Fife', *Innes Review* 68:1 (2017), 38–77

Benchimol, Alex, 'Cultural historiography and the Scottish Enlightenment public sphere: placing Habermas in eighteenth-century Edinburgh' in Alex Benchimol and Willy Maley (eds.), *Spheres of Influence: Intellectual and Cultural Publics from Shakespeare to Habermas* (Oxford: Peter Lang, 2007), 105–150

'Periodicals and public culture' in Murray Pittock (ed.), *The Edinburgh Companion to Scottish Romanticism* (Edinburgh, 2011), 84–99

Bevan, Jonquil, 'Scotland' in *Cambridge History of the Book in Britain 1557–1695* (Cambridge, 2002), 687–700

Black, Joseph, 'The Martin Marprelate tracts (1588–89) and the popular voice', *History Compass* 6:4 (2008), 1091–1106

Blanning, T. C. W., *The Culture of Power and the Power of Culture: Old Regime Europe 1660–1789* (Oxford, 2002)

Bowie, Karin, 'A 1706 manifesto for an armed rising against incorporating union', *Scottish Historical Review* 94, 2: 239 (Oct. 2015), 237–67

'"A legal limited monarchy": Scottish constitutionalism in the Union of Crowns, 1603–1707', *Journal of Scottish Historical Studies* 35:2 (2015), 131–54

'Cultural, British and global turns in the history of early modern Scotland' in Andrew Mackillop (ed.), *The State of Early Modern and Modern Scottish Histories, Scottish Historical Review* 92, supplement: 234 (April 2013), 38–48

'From customary to constitutional right: the right to petition in Scotland before the 1707 Act of Union', in Karin Bowie and Thomas Munck (eds), *Early Modern Petitioning and Public Engagement in Scotland, Britain and Scandinavia, c.1550–1795, Parliaments, Estates and Representation* 38:3 (2018), 279–92

'National opinion and the press in Scotland before the Union of 1707', *Scottish Affairs* 21:1 (2018), 13–19

'Newspapers, the early modern public sphere and the 1704–05 *Worcester* affair' in Alex Benchimol, Rhona Brown and David Shuttleston (eds), *Before Blackwood's: Scottish Journalism in the Age of Enlightenment*, (London: Pickering & Chatto, 2015)

'Popular resistance and the ratification of the Anglo-Scottish treaty of union', *Scottish Archives* 14 (2008), 10–26

'Popular resistance, religion and the Union of 1707' in T. M. Devine (ed.), *Scotland and the Union 1707–2007* (Edinburgh, 2008), 39–53

'Publicity, parties and patronage: parliamentary management and the ratification of the Anglo-Scottish Union' *Scottish Historical Review* 87: supplement (2008), 78–93

Scottish Public Opinion and the Anglo-Scottish Union (Woodbridge: Royal Historical Society, 2007)

Bowie, Karin and Alasdair Raffe, 'Politics, the people and extra-institutional participation in Scotland', *Journal of British Studies* 56:4 (Oct. 2017), 797–815

Braddick, Michael, 'Prayer book and protestation: anti-popery, anti-Puritanism and the outbreak of the English civil war' in C. W. A. Prior and G. Burgess (eds), *England's Wars of Religion, Revisited* (Farnham: Ashgate, 2011), 125–46

Bibliography

Brock, Michelle D., 'Plague, covenants, and confession: the strange case of Ayr, 1647–8', *Scottish Historical Review* 97, 2 (Sept. 2018), 129–52

Brodie-Innes, J. W., *Comparative Principles of the Courts and Procedure of England and Scotland* (Edinburgh: Green, 1903)

Brown, Keith M., 'Early modern Scottish history – a survey' in Andrew Mackillop (ed.), *The State of Early Modern and Modern Scottish Histories, Scottish Historical Review* 92, supplement: 234 (April 2013), 5–24

Noble Power from the Reformation to the Revolution (Edinburgh: Edinburgh University Press, 2011)

'Party politics and parliament: Scotland's last election and its aftermath, 1702–3', in Keith M. Brown and Alistair J. Mann (eds), *Parliaments and Politics in Scotland, 1567–1707* (Edinburgh, 2005), 245–86

'The second estate: parliament and the nobility' in Keith M. Brown and Alan R. Macdonald (eds), *Parliament in Context, 1235–1707* (Edinburgh, 2011), 67–94

Brown, Keith Mark, 'Toward political participation and capacity: elections, voting, and representation in early modern Scotland', *Journal of Modern History* (2016), 1–33

Buckroyd, Julia, *Church and State in Scotland, 1660–1681* (Edinburgh: John Donald, 1980)

'Bridging the gap: Scotland 1659–60', *Scottish Historical Review* 66 (1987), 1–25

Buckroyd, Julia M., '*Mercurius Caledonius* and its immediate successors, 1661', *Scottish Historical Review* 54 (1975), 1–21

Burns, J. H., *The True Law of Kingship: Concepts of Monarchy in Early Modern Scotland* (Oxford, 1996)

Burrell, S. A., 'The apocalyptic vision of the early Covenanters', *Scottish Historical Review* 43 (1964), 1–24

Callow, John, 'Cargill, Donald [Daniel]', *Oxford Dictionary of National Biography* (2004)

Carr, Rosalind, *Gender and Enlightenment Culture in Eighteenth-Century Scotland* (Edinburgh, 2014)

Cipriano, Salvatore, 'The Scottish universities and opposition to the National Covenant, 1638', *Scottish Historical Review* 97, 1: 244 (April 2018), 12–37

Clarke, Tristram, '"Nurseries of sedition?": The episcopal congregations after the Revolution of 1689' in James Porter (ed.), *After Columba, After Calvin: Religious Community in North-East Scotland* (Aberdeen: Elphinstone Institute, 1999), 63–9

Coast, David, *News and Rumour in Jacobean England: Information, Court Politics and Diplomacy, 1618–25* (Manchester, 2014)

'Speaking for the people in early modern England', *Past & Present* 244 (Aug. 2019), 51–88

Coffey, John, *Politics, Religion and the British Revolutions: The Mind of Samuel Rutherford* (Cambridge, 1997)

Bibliography

Cohn, Samuel K., *Creating the Florentine State: Peasants and Rebellion, 1348–1434* (Cambridge, 1999)

Lust for Liberty: The Politics of Social Revolt in Medieval Europe, 1200–1425: Italy, France, and Flanders (Boston, MA: Harvard University Press, 2008)

Collinson, Patrick, *Richard Bancroft and Elizabethan Anti-Puritanism* (Cambridge, 2013)

Condren, Conal, *Argument and Authority in Early Modern England: The Presupposition of Oaths and Offices* (Cambridge, 2006)

Cowan, Brian, 'Geoffrey Holmes and the public sphere: Augustan historiography from post-Namierite to post-Habermasian', *Parliamentary History* 28:1 (Feb. 2009), 166–178

Cowan, Edward J., 'Scotching the beggars: John the Commonweal and Scottish history' in A. Murdoch with E. J. Cowan and R. J. Finlay (eds), *The Scottish Nation: Identity and History* (Edinburgh: John Donald, 2007), 1–17

'The Covenanting tradition in Scottish history' in *Scottish History: The Power of the Past*, ed. Edward J. Cowan and Richard J. Finlay (Edinburgh University Press, 2002), 121–45

'The making of the National Covenant' in John Morrill (ed.), *The Scottish National Covenant in its British Context, 1638–51* (Edinburgh University Press, 1990), 68–89

'The political ideas of a Covenanting leader: Archibald Campbell, marquis of Argyll, 1607–1661' in Roger A. Mason (ed.), *Scots and Britons: Scottish Political Thought and the Union of 1603* (Cambridge, 1994), 241–62

'The Solemn League and Covenant' in Roger A. Mason (ed.), *Scotland and England 1286–1815* (Edinburgh: John Donald, 1987), 182–202

Cowan, Ian, 'Church and state reformed? The Revolution of 1688–1689 in Scotland' in Jonathan Israel (ed.), *The Anglo-Dutch Moment* (Cambridge, 1991), 163–83

The Scottish Covenanters 1660–88 (London: Victor Gollanz, 1976)

Cowans, Jon, *To Speak for the People: Public Opinion and the Problem of Legitimacy in the French Revolution* (New York and London: Routledge, 2001)

Cressy, David, 'Binding the nation: the bonds of association, 1584 and 1696' in DeLloyd J. Guth and John W. McKenna (eds), *Tudor Rule and Revolution* (Cambridge, 1982), 217–34

Dangerous Talk: Scandalous, Seditious, and Treasonable Speech in Pre-Modern England (Oxford, 2010)

'The Protestation protested, 1641 and 1642', *Historical Journal* 45:2 (June 2002), 251–79

Cullen, Karen J., Christopher A. Whatley and Mary Young, 'King William's Ill Years: new evidence on the impact of scarcity and harvest failure during the crisis of the 1690s on Tayside', *Scottish Historical Review* 85, 2: 220 (Oct. 2006), 250–76

Cust, Richard, 'Charles I and popularity' in *Politics, Religion and Popularity in Early Modern Britain*, eds Thomas Cogswell, Richard Cust and Peter Lake (Cambridge, 2002), 235–258

'News and politics in early seventeenth-century England', *Past & Present* 112 (1986), 60–90

Darcy, Eamon, 'Political participation in Early Stuart Ireland', *Journal of British Studies* 56:4 (Oct. 2017), 773–796

Dawson, Jane, 'Bonding, religious alliance and covenanting' in Stephen Boardman and Julian Goodare (eds), *Kings, Lords and Men in Scotland and Britain, 1300–1625*, (Edinburgh, 2014), 155–72

'Calvinism and the *Gàidhealtachd* in Scotland' in Andrew Pettegree, Alasdair Duke and Gillian Lewis (eds), *Calvinism in Europe, 1540–1620* (Cambridge, 1994), 231–53

'The *Gàidhealtachd* and the emergence of the Scottish Highlands' in Brendan Bradshaw and Peter Roberts (eds), *British Consciousness and Identity: The Making of Britain, 1533–1707* (Cambridge, 1998), 259–300

Scotland Re-Formed, 1488–1587 (Edinburgh, 2007)

Der Weduwen, Arthur, '"Everyone has hereby been warned": the structure and typography of broadsheet ordinances and the communication of governance in the early 17C Dutch Republic', in Andrew Pettegree (ed.), *Broadsheets: Single-Sheet Publishing in the First Age of Print* (Leiden: Brill, 2017), 240–67

Doak, Laura, 'The "vanishing of a fantosme"? The 1685 Argyll Rising and the 'Covenanting' opposition', *Scottish Historical Review* (forthcoming)

'Militant women: the execution of Isabel Alison and Marion Harvie, 1681', *Journal of the Northern Renaissance* (forthcoming)

Dodd, Gwilym, *Justice and Grace: Private Petitioning and the English Parliament in the Late Middle Ages* (Oxford, 2007)

'Kingship, Parliament and the court: the emergence of 'high style' in petitions to the English crown, c.1350–1405', *English Historical Review* 129:538 (June 2014), 515–48

Donald, Peter, *An Uncounselled King: Charles I and the Scottish Troubles* (Cambridge, 1990)

Donegan, Barbara, 'Casuistry and allegiance in the English civil war' in Derek Hirst and Richard Strier (eds), *Writing and Political Engagement in Seventeenth-Century England* (Cambridge, 1999), 89–111

Downie, J. A., *Robert Harley and the Press: Propaganda and Public Opinion in the Age of Swift and Defoe* (Cambridge, 1979)

Drummond, Andrew L. and James Bulloch, *The Scottish Church 1688–1843: The Age of the Moderates* (Edinburgh: St. Andrew Press, 1973)

Early Modern Research Group, 'Commonwealth: the social, cultural and conceptual contexts of an early modern keyword', *Historical Journal* 54:3 (2011), 659–687

Edington, Carol, *Court and Culture in Renaissance Scotland: Sir David Lindsay of the Mount* (Amherst: University of Massachusetts Press, 1994)

Farge, Arlette, *Subversive Words: Public Opinion in Eighteenth-Century France*, trans. Rosemary Morris (Cambridge: Polity Press, 1994)

Farr, James, 'Understanding conceptual change politically' in Terence Ball, James Farr and Russell L. Hanson (eds), *Political Innovation and Conceptual Change* (Cambridge, 1989), 24–49

Ferguson, William, 'The making of the treaty of union of 1707', *Scottish Historical Review* XLIII:136 (October 1964)

Bibliography

Finlay, John, 'The petition in the Court of Session in early modern Scotland' in Karin Bowie and Thomas Munck (eds), *Early Modern Petitioning and Public Engagement in Scotland, Britain and Scandinavia, c.1550–1795, Parliaments, Estates and Representation* 38:3 (2018), 337–349

Fleming, David Hay, *The Subscribing of the National Covenant in 1638* (Edinburgh and London: William Green & Sons, 1912)

Fletcher, Anthony, *The Outbreak of the English Civil War* (London: Edward Arnold, 1980),

Ford, John D., 'Conformity in conscience: the structure of the Perth Articles debate in Scotland, 1618–1638', *Journal of Ecclesiastical History* 46:2 (April 1995), 256–77

   'Epistolary control of the College of Justice in Scotland' in Ignacio Czeghun, Jóse Antonio López Nevot and Antonio Sánchez Aranda (eds), *Control of Supreme Courts in Early Modern Europe* (Berlin: Duncker & Humblot, 2018)

   'Protestations to parliament for remeid of law', *Scottish Historical Review* 88:1 (2009), 57–107

   'The lawful bonds of Scottish society: the five Articles of Perth, the Negative Confession and the National Covenant', *The Historical Journal* 37:1 (1994), 45–64

   Law and Opinion in Scotland in the Seventeenth Century (Oxford: Hart, 2007)

Foster, Elizabeth Read, 'Petitions and the Petition of Right', *Journal of British Studies* 14:1 (Nov. 1974), 21–45

Fox, Adam, 'Jockey and Jenny: English broadside ballads and the invention of Scottishness', *Huntington Library Quarterly* 79:2 (Summer 2016), 201–20

   '"Little story books" and "small pamphlets" in Edinburgh: the making of the Scottish chapbook', *Scottish Historical Review* 92,2:235 (Oct. 2013), 207–30

   Oral and Literate Culture in England, 1500–1700 (Oxford, 2000)

Fraser, Sir William, *The Melvilles Earls of Melville and Leslies Earls of Leven*, 3 vols (Edinburgh: n.p., 1890)

Furgol, Edward, 'Scotland turned Sweden: the Covenanters and the military revolution, 1638–51' in John Morrill (ed.), *The Scottish National Covenant in Its British Context, 1638–1651* (Edinburgh 1990), 134–54

Galloway, Bruce, *The Union of England and Scotland, 1603–1608* (Edinburgh: John Donald, 1986)

Gardner, Ginny, 'McWard [Macward], Robert (c.1625–1681)', *Oxford Dictionary of National Biography* (2004)

   The Scottish Exile Community in the Netherlands 1660–1690 (East Linton: Tuckwell Press, 2004)

Glynn, Carroll J., Susan Herbst, Mark Lindeman, Garrett J. O'Keefe and Robert Y. Shapiro, *Public Opinion*, 3rd edition (New York: Routledge, 2018)

Godfrey, Mark, *Civil Justice in Renaissance Scotland* (Leiden: Brill, 2009)

Goldie, Mark, 'Divergence and Union: Scotland and England, 1660–1707', in *The British Problem c.1534–1707: State Formation in the Atlantic Archipelago*, ed. Brendan Bradshaw and John Morrill (Basingstoke: Palgrave Macmillan, 1996)

Bibliography

Goodare, Julian, 'Parliament and politics' in Keith M. Brown and Alan Macdonald (eds), *Parliament in Context, 1235–1707* (Edinburgh, 2010), 216–43

'Parliamentary taxation in Scotland, 1560–1603', *Scottish Historical Review* 68, 1: 185 (Apr. 1989), 23–52

'The attempted Scottish *coup* of 1596' in J. Goodare and A. A. Macdonald (eds), *Sixteenth-Century Scotland* (Leiden, 2008), 311–36

'The Scottish convention of estates of 1630', *SHR* 93, part 2, 237 (Oct. 2014), 217–239

'The Scottish Parliament of 1621', *Historical Journal* 38, 1 (March 1995), 29–51

Graham, Michael F., *The Blasphemies of Thomas Aikenhead: Boundaries of Belief on the Eve of the Enlightenment* (Edinburgh, 2008)

Gray, Jonathan M., *Oaths and the English Reformation* (Cambridge, 2012)

Greaves, Richard L., *Secrets of the Kingdom: British Radicals from the Popish Plot to the Revolution of 1688–89* (Stanford, 1992)

Green, Roger P.H., 'The king returns: *The Muses Welcome* (1618)' in Reid, Steven J. and David McOmish (eds), *NeoLatin Literature and Literary Culture in Early Modern Scotland* (Leiden: Brill, 2017), 126–62

Gribben, Crawford, *The Puritan Millennium: Literature & Theology, 1550–1682* (Dublin: Four Courts Press, 2000)

Gunn, J. A. W., 'Public interest' in Terence Ball, James Farr and Russell L. Hanson (eds), *Political Innovation and Conceptual Change* (Cambridge, 1989), 194–210

'Public opinion' in Terence Ball, James Farr and Russell K. Hanson (eds), *Political Innovation and Conceptual Change* (Cambridge, 1989), 247–65

Queen of the World: Opinion in the Public Life of France from the Renaissance to the Revolution (Oxford: Voltaire Foundation, 1995)

Habermas, Jürgen, *The Structural Transformation of the Public Sphere*, trans. T. Burger with F. Lawrence (Cambridge: Polity Press, 1989, 1999)

Hadfield, Andrew, *Lying in Early Modern English Culture: From the Oath of Supremacy to the Oath of Allegiance* (Oxford, 2017)

Halliday, James, 'The Club and the Revolution in Scotland 1689–90', *Scottish Historical Review* 45:140, 2 (Oct. 1966), 143–159

Hamrick, Wes, 'The public sphere and eighteenth-century Ireland', *New Hibernia Review/Iris Éireannach Nua* 18:4 (Geimhreadh/Winter 2014), 87–100

Harris, Bob, 'The Anglo-Scottish treaty of union, 1707 in 2007: defending the Revolution, defeating the Jacobites', *Journal of British Studies* 49:1 (Jan 2010), 28–46

Harris, Tim, 'Popular, plebian, culture: Historical definitions' in Joad Raymond (ed.), *The Oxford History of Popular Print Culture: Cheap Print in Britain and Ireland to 1660* (Oxford, 2011), 50–58

'Publics and participation in the three kingdoms: was there such a thing as "British public opinion" in the seventeenth century?' *Journal of British Studies* 56:4 (Oct. 2017), 731–53

Bibliography

'The people, the law, and the constitution in Scotland and England: a comparative approach to the Glorious Revolution', *Journal of British Studies* 38 (1999), 28–58

Restoration: Charles II and His Kingdoms, 1660–1685 (London: Allen Lane, 2005)

Revolution: The Great Crisis of the British Monarchy, 1685–1720 (London: Allen Lane, 2006)

Hasler, Antony J., *Court Poetry in Late Medieval England and Scotland: Allegories of Authority* (Cambridge, 2011)

Hay, Richard, *Genealogie of the Hayes of Tweeedale* (Edinburgh: T. G. Stevenson, 1835)

Henderson, G. D., *Religious Life in Seventeenth-Century Scotland* (Cambridge, 1937)

Henderson, T. F., rev. Martin Holt Dotterweich, 'Lekpreuik [Lekprevick], Robert', *Oxford Dictionary of National Biography* (2004)

Hewison, James King, *The Covenanters*, 2 vols (Glasgow: John Smith, 1908)

Hill, Alexandra, 'The lamentable tale of lost ballads in England, 1557–1640' in Andrew Pettegree (ed.), *Broadsheets: Single-Sheet Publishing in the First Age of Print* (Leiden: Brill, 2017), 442–458

Holfelder, K. D. 'Dickson [Dick], David (c. 1583–1662), Church of Scotland minister and theologian', *Oxford Dictionary of National Biography* (2004)

Holfeder, K. D., 'James Guthrie (c.1612–1661), *Oxford Dictionary of National Biography* (2004)

Hopkins, Paul, *Glencoe and the End of the Highland War* (Edinburgh: John Donald, 1986)

Houston, Robert A., 'The literacy myth? Illiteracy in Scotland, 1630–1760', *Past & Present* 96 (1982), 81–102

Hoyle, Richard W., 'Petitioning as popular politics in early sixteenth-century England', *Historical Research* 75:190 (Nov. 2002), 365–89

Hyman, Elizabeth Hannan, 'A church militant: Scotland, 1661–1690', *The Sixteenth Century Journal*, 26:1 (Spring, 1995), 49–74.

Imrie, John D., 'The Carrick covenant of 1638', *Ayrshire Archaeological and Natural History Society Collections*, second series, iii (1955), 107–18.

Jackson, Clare, *Restoration Scotland 1660–1690: Royalist Politics, Religion and Ideas* (Woodbridge: Boydell, 2003)

Jackson, Clare and Pamela Glennie, 'Restoration politics and the advocates' secession, 1674–1676', *Scottish Historical Review* 91, 1: 231, (2012), 76–105

Johnston, John C., *Treasury of the Scottish Covenant* (Edinburgh: Andrew Elliot, 1887)

Jones, David Martin, *Conscience and Allegiance in Seventeenth Century England: The Political Significance of Oaths and Engagements* (Rochester, 1999)

Jones, W. Douglas, '"The bold adventurers": A quantitative analysis of the Darien subscription list (1696)', *Scottish Economic and Social History* 21: 1 (May 2001), 22–42

Bibliography

Kennedy, Allan, "'A heavy yock uppon their necks": Covenanting government in the northern Highlands, 1638–1651', *Journal of Scottish Historical Studies* 30:2 (2010), 93–122

'The Covenanters of the northern Highlands: politics, war and ideology', *History Scotland* (Jan./Feb. 2010), 22–29

'The Covenanters of the northern Highlands: the Covenanted kirk', *History Scotland* (Mar./Apr. 2010), 15–22

'Rebellion, government and the Scottish response to Argyll's rising of 1685', *Journal of Scottish Historical Studies* 36:1 (2016), 40–59.

Kidd, Colin, 'Conditional Britons: the formation of confessional cultures in Scotland, 1660–1715', *English Historical Review* 117:474 (Nov. 2002), 1147–76

'Identity before identities: ethnicity, nationalism and the historian' in Julia Rudolph (ed.), *History and Nation* (Lewisburg: Bucknell University Press, 2006), 9–44

'Religious realignment between the Restoration and the Union' in John Robertson (ed.), *A Union for Empire: Political Thought and the British Union of 1707* (Cambridge, 1995)

Union and Unionism: Political Thought in Scotland, 1500–2000 (Cambridge, 2008)

Kirk, James, *Patterns of Reform: Continuity and Change in the Reformation Kirk* (Edinburgh: T&T Clark, 1989)

Koziol, Geoffrey, *Begging Pardon and Favor: Ritual and Political Order in Early Medieval France* (Ithaca: Cornell University Press, 1992)

Knights, Mark, 'London's "monster" petition of 1680', *Historical Journal* 36:1 (Mar. 1993), 39–67

Politics and Opinion in Crisis, 1678–81 (Cambridge, 1994)

Representation and Misrepresentation in Later Stuart Britain: Partisanship and Political Culture (Oxford, 2005)

'"The lowest degree of freedom": The right to petition parliament, 1640–1800' in Richard Huzzey (ed.), *Parliamentary History* 37:S1 (July 2018), 18–34

Koenigsberger, H. G., 'The power of deputies in sixteenth-century assemblies' in *Estates and Revolutions: Essays in Early Modern European History* (Ithaca: Cornell University Press, 1971), 176–210

Kümin, Beat and Andreas Würgler, 'Petitions, *gravamina* and the early modern state: local influence on central legislation in England and Germany (Hesse)', *Parliaments, Estates and Representation* 17:1 (2010), 38–60

Lacey, Helen, '"Grace for the rebels": the role of the royal pardon in the Peasants' Revolt of 1381', *Journal of Medieval History* 34:1, 36–63

Lake, Peter, *Bad Queen Bess? Libels, Secret Histories and the Politics of Publicity in the Reign of Elizabeth I* (Oxford, 2016)

'Puritans, popularity and petitions: local politics in national context, Cheshire, 1641', in Thomas Cogswell, Richard Cust and Peter Lake (eds), *Politics, Religion and Popularity in Early Stuart Britain* (Cambridge, 2002), 259–89

'The king (the queen) and the Jesuit: James Stuart's *True Law of Free Monarchies* in context/s', *Transactions of the Royal Historical Society* 14 (2004), 243–60

'Publics and participation: England, Britain and Europe in the "post-Reformation"', *Journal of British Studies* 56:4 (Oct. 2017), 836–54

Lake, Peter and Steve Pincus, 'Rethinking the public sphere in early modern England,' *Journal of British Studies* 45:2 (April 2006), 270–92

Lee, Maurice, 'Graham, William, first earl of Airth and seventh earl of Menteith', *Oxford Dictionary of National Biography* (2004)

Lenman, Bruce, 'Militia, fencible men and the home defence, 1660–1797' in Norman MacDougall (ed.), *Scotland and War, AD 79–1918* (Edinburgh: John Donald, 1991), 170–92

'Scottish episcopal clergy and the ideology of Jacobitism' in Eveline Cruickshanks (ed.), *Ideology and Conspiracy: Aspects of Jacobitism, 1689–1759* (Edinburgh: John Donald, 1982), 36–48

Leighton, C. D. A, 'Scottish Jacobitism, episcopacy and counter-Enlightenment', *History of European Ideas* 35 (2009), 1–10

Lind, Andrew, 'Battle in the burgh: Glasgow during the British civil wars, c.1638–1651', *Journal of the Northern Renaissance* (forthcoming)

Love, Harold, *Scribal Publication in Seventeenth-Century England* (Oxford, 1993)

MacDonald, Alan R., 'Consultation and consent under James VI', *Historical Journal* 54:2 (June 2011), 287–306

'Consultation, counsel and the "early Stuart period" in Scotland', in Jacqueline Rose (ed.), *The Politics of Counsel in England and Scotland 1286–1707* (Oxford: British Academy, 2016), 193–210

'Deliberative processes in parliament c. 1567–1639: multicameralism and the lords of the articles', *Scottish Historical Review* 81:211 (April 2002), 23–51

'Neither inside nor outside the corridors of power: prosaic petitioning and the royal burghs in early modern Scotland' in Karin Bowie and Thomas Munck (eds), *Early Modern Petitioning and Public Engagement in Scotland, Britain and Scandinavia, c.155–1795, Parliaments, Estates and Representation* 38:3 (2018), 293–306

The Jacobean Kirk, 1567–1625: Sovereignty, Polity and Liturgy (Aldershot: Ashgate, 1998)

'The Subscription Crisis and church-state relations 1584–86', *Records of the Scottish Church History Society* 25 (1994), 222–55

'Voting in the Scottish parliament before 1639', *Parliaments, Estates and Representation* 30:2, 145–161

'Uncovering the legislative process in the parliaments of James VI' *Historical Research* 84:226 (Nov 2011), 601–17

MacDonald, Alasdair A., *George Lauder (1603–1670): Life and Writings* (Cambridge: D.S. Brewer, 2018)

MacGregor, Martin, 'The Statutes of Iona: text and context', *Innes Review* 57:2 (Autumn 2006), 111–81

Bibliography

'Gaelic barbarity and Scottish identity in the later Middle Ages' in Dauvit Broun and Martin MacGregor (eds), *Mìorun Mòr nan Gall, 'The Great Ill-Will of the Lowlander'? Lowland Perceptions of the Highlands, Medieval and Modern* (Glasgow: Centre for Scottish and Celtic Studies, 2007), 7–48

Maclean, Donald, *Typographia Scoto-Gadelica Or Books Printed in the Gaelic of Scotland from the Year 1567 to 1914* (Edinburgh: John Grant, 1915)

Macinnes, Allan I., 'Crowns, clan and fine: the 'civilising' of Scottish Gaeldom, 1568–1637', *Northern Scotland* 13 (1993), 31–55

Charles I and the Making of the Covenanting Movement 1625–1641 (Edinburgh: John Donald, 1991)

'Scottish Gaeldom, 1638–1651: the vernacular response to the Covenanting dynamic' in John Dwyer, Roger A. Mason and Alexander Murdoch (eds), *New Perspectives on the Politics and Culture of Early Modern Scotland* (Edinburgh: John Donald, 1982), 59–94

The British Revolution, 1629–1660 (Basingstoke: Palgrave Macmillan, 2005)

Union and Empire: The Making of the United Kingdom in 1707 (Cambridge, 2007)

MacIntosh, Gillian, *The Scottish Parliament Under Charles II, 1660–1685* (Edinburgh, 2007)

MacKenzie, Kirsteen, *The Solemn League and Covenant of the Three Kingdoms and the Cromwellian Union, 1643–1663* (Routledge: Abingdon, 2018)

Maltby, Judith, *Prayer Book and People in Elizabethan and Early Stuart England* (Cambridge, 1998)

Mann, Alastair J., 'Embroidery to enterprise: the role of women in the book trade of early modern Scotland' in *Women in Scotland, c.1100–c.1750*, ed. Elizabeth Ewan and Maureen M. Meikle (East Linton: Tuckwell, 1999), 136–45

'House rules: parliamentary procedures' in Keith M. Brown (ed.), *Parliament in Context, 1235–1707* (Edinburgh, 2010), 122–56

James VII: Duke and King of Scots, 1633–1701 (Edinburgh: John Donald, 2014)

'Parliaments, princes and presses: voices of tradition and protest in early modern Scotland' in Uwe Böker and Julie A. Hibbard (eds), *Sites of Discourse-Public and Private Spheres-Legal Culture*, December 2001 (Amsterdam: Rodopi, 2002), 79–91

The Scottish Book Trade 1500–1720: Print Commerce and Print Control in Early Modern Scotland (East Linton: Tuckwell, 2000)

Mason, Roger A., 'Chivalry and citizenship: aspects of national identity in Renaissance Scotland' in *Kingship and Commonweal: Political Thought in Renaissance and Reformation Scotland* (East Linton: Tuckwell Press, 1998)

'Counsel and covenant: aristocratic conciliarism and the Scottish Revolution' in Jacqueline Rose (ed.), *The Politics of Counsel in England and Scotland 1286–1707* (Oxford: Oxford University Press for the British Academy, 2016), 229–48

'People power? George Buchanan on resistance and the common man' in Robert von Fredeberg (ed.), *Widerstandsrecht in der Fruhen Neuzeit* (Berlin: Duncker & Humblot, 2001), 163–181

'The aristocracy, episcopacy and the revolution of 1638' in Terry Brotherstone (ed.), *Covenant, Charter and Party: Traditions of Revolt and Protest in Modern Scottish History* (Aberdeen: Aberdeen University Press, 1989), 7–24

'This realm of Scotland is an empire? Imperial ideas and iconography in Early Renaissance Scotland', in B. Crawford (ed.), *Church, Chronicle and Learning in Medieval and Early Renaissance Scotland* (Edinburgh: Mercat Press, 1999), 73–91

Mathison, Hamish, 'Scotland' in Joad Raymond (ed.), *The Oxford History of Popular Print Culture, Volume One: Cheap Print in Britain and Ireland to 1600* (Oxford, 2011), 31–8

May, Thomas Erskine, *A Treatise upon the Law, Proceedings and Usage of Parliament* (London, 1844)

Maxwell, Rev. Thomas, 'Presbyterian and Episcopalian in 1688', *Records of the Scottish Church History Society* 13 (1959), 25–37

McAlister, Kirsty and Roland Tanner, 'The first estate: parliament and the church' in Keith M. Brown and Alan Macdonald (eds), *Parliament in Context, 1235–1707* (Edinburgh, 2010), 31–66

McDougall, Jamie, 'The reception of the 1643 Solemn League and Covenant', *Scottish Church History* 45:1 (June 2016), 49–65

McElligott, Jason, 'Atlantic royalism? Polemic, censorship and the 'Declaration and Protestation of the Governour and Inhabitants of Virginia' in J. McElligott and D. L. Smith (eds), *Royalists and Royalism during the Interregnum*, (Manchester, 2010), 214–34

McElroy, Tricia A., 'Imagining the "Scottis natioun"': populism and propaganda in Scottish satirical broadsides', *Texas Studies in Literature and Language* 49:4 (Winter 2007), 319–39

McIntyre, Neil, 'Presbyterian conventicles in the Restoration era', *Scottish Church History* 45:1 (June 2016), 66–81

'Representation and resistance in Restoration Scotland: the political thought of James Stewart of Goodtrees (1635–1713)', *Parliaments, Estates and Representation* 38:2 (2018), 161–74

McMillan, William, *John Hepburn and the Hebronites* (London: James Clarke, 1934)

McNeill, Peter G.B. and Hector L. MacQueen (eds.), *An Atlas of Scottish History* (Edinburgh: University of Edinburgh, 2000)

McNeill, William A. and Peter G.B. McNeill, 'The Scottish progress of James VI, 1617', *SHR* 75: 199, 1 (Apr. 1996), 38–51

Meek, Donald, 'The Reformation and Gaelic culture: perspectives on patronage, language and literature in John Carswell's translation of "The Book of Common Order"' in James Kirk (ed.), *The Church in the Highlands* (Edinburgh: Scottish Church History Society, 1998), 37–62

Bibliography

Mellor, Anne K., 'Joanna Baillie and the counter-public sphere', *Studies in Romanticism* 33:4 (1994), 559–67

Melton, James van Horn, *The Rise of the Public in Enlightenment Europe* (Cambridge, 2004)

Milligan, Tony '"To ding thir mony kingis doun": Jock Upaland and the Scottish labourer stereotype', *Scottish Literary Journal* 25:1 (May 1998), 26–36

Millstone, Noah, *Manuscript Circulation and the Invention of Politics in Early Stuart England* (Cambridge, 2016)

Monahan, Arthur P., *Consent, Coercion and Limit: The Medieval Origins of Parliamentary Democracy* (Kingston and Montreal: McGill-Queen's University Press, 1987)

Morrill, John S., 'An Irish Protestation? Oaths and the Confederation of Kilkenny' in Michael J. Braddick and Phil Withington (eds.), *Popular Culture and Political Agency in Early Modern England and Ireland* (Woodbridge: Boydell, 2017), 243–65

The Nature of the English Revolution: Essays (London: Longman, 1993)

Mullan, David G., *Narratives of the Religious Self in Early-Modern Scotland* (Farnham: Ashgate, 2010)

Mullen, David G., *Scottish Puritanism, 1590–1638* (Oxford, 2000)

Nubola, Cecilia, 'Supplications between politics and justice: the northern and central Italian states in the early modern age', *International Review of Social History* 46:supplement (2001), 35–56

Onnekink, David, 'The earl of Portland and Scotland (1689–1699): a re-evaluation of Williamite policy', *Scottish Historical Review* 85,2: 220 (Oct. 2006), 231–49

Ormrod, W. Mark, 'Murmur, clamour and noise: voicing complaint and remedy in petitions to the English Crown, c.1300–c.1460', in W. Mark Ormrod, Gwilym Dodd and Anthony Mussen (eds), *Medieval Petitions: Grace and Grievance* (Woodbridge: York Medieval Press, 2009), 135–55

Patrick, Derek J., 'Unconventional procedure: Scottish electoral politics after the Revolution' in *Parliament and Politics in Scotland, 1567–1707*, K.M. Brown and A.J. Mann, (eds) (Edinburgh, 2005), 208–44

Peacey, Jason, *Print and Public Politics in the English Revolution* (Cambridge, 2015)
'The print culture of Parliament, 1600–1800', *Parliamentary History* 26:1 (March 2007), 1–16

Pearce, A.S. Wayne, 'Cameron, Richard', *Oxford Dictionary of National Biography* (2004)

Pettegree, Andrew, *Reformation and the Culture of Persuasion* (Cambridge, 2005)

Pollmann, Judith and Andrew Spicer (eds.), *Public Opinion and Changing Identities in the Early Modern Netherlands* (Leiden: Brill, 2007)

Porter, Bertha, rev. Glenn Burgess, 'Mocket, Richard', *Oxford Dictionary of National Biography* (2004)

Raffe, Alasdair, 'Petitioning in the Scottish church courts, 1638–1707', in Karin Bowie and Thomas Munck (eds), *Early Modern Petitioning and Public*

278   *Bibliography*

Engagement in Scotland, Britain and Scandinavia, c.1550–1795, Parliaments, Estates and Representation 38:3 (2018), 323–336

'Confessions, covenants and continuous reformation in early modern Scotland', *Études Épistémè* 32 (2017), http://journals.openedition.org/episteme/1836

The Culture of Controversy: Religious Arguments in Scotland, 1660–1714 (Woodbridge: Boydell, 2012)

'Episcopalian polemic, the London printing press and Anglo-Scottish divergence in the 1690s', *Journal of Scottish Historical Studies* 26 (2006), 23–41

'Female authority and lay activism in Scottish Presbyterianism, 1660–1714' in *Religion and Women in Britain, 1660–1760*, ed. Sarah Apatrei and Hannah Smith (Farnham: Ashgate, 2014), 61–78

'James VII's multi-confessional experiment and the Scottish Revolution of 1688–90', *History* 100:341 (2015), 354–373

'Presbyterians and Episcopalians: the formation of confessional cultures in Scotland, 1660–1715', *English Historical Review* 125:514 (June 2010), 570–598

'Propaganda, religious controversy and the Williamite Revolution in Scotland' *Dutch Crossing* 25:1 (2005), 21–42

'Scottish state oaths and the Revolution of 1688–90' in Sharon Adams and Julian Goodare (eds), *Scotland in the Age of Two Revolutions* (Woodbridge: Boydell Press, 2014), 173–91

Scotland in Revolution, 1685–1690 (Edinburgh, 2018)

Rait, Robert S., *The Parliaments of Scotland* (Glasgow: Maclehose, Jackson & Co, 1924)

Raven, James, 'New reading histories, print culture and the identification of change: the case of eighteenth-century England', *Social History* 23:3 (Oct. 1998), 268–289

'"Print culture" and the perils of practice' in Eve Patten and Jason McElligott (eds), *Book, Print and Publishing History in Theory and Practice* (Houndmills: Palgrave Macmillan, 2014), 218–237

Raymond, Joad, *Pamphlets and Pamphleteering in Early Modern Britain* (Cambridge, 2003)

'Perfect speech: the public sphere and communication in seventeenth-century England' in A. Benchimol and W. Maley (eds), *Spheres of Influence: Intellectual and Cultural Publics from Shakespeare to Habermas* (Oxford: Peter Lang, 2007), 43–70

The Invention of the Newspaper: English Newsbooks, 1641–49 (Oxford: Clarendon, 1996)

Reid, David, 'Hume of Godscroft on parity', in Crawford Gribben and David George Mullen (eds), *Literature and the Scottish Reformation* (Abingdon: Routledge, 2009), 191–209

Reid, Steven J., *Bridging the Continental Divide: Neo-Latin and Its Cultural Role in Jacobean Scotland, as seen in the* Delitiae Poetarum Scotorum (1637), www.dps.gla.ac.uk

Bibliography

'Of bairns and bearded men: James VI and the Ruthven Raid' in Miles Kerr-Peterson and Steven J. Reid (eds), *James VI and Noble Power in Scotland, 1578–1603* (Abingdon: Routledge, 2017), 32–56

Reid, Steven J. and David McOmish (eds), *Neo-Latin Literature and Literary Culture in Early Modern Scotland* (Leiden: Brill, 2017)

Reid, Steven J. and Roger A. Mason (eds), *Andrew Melville (1545–1622): Writings, Reception, and Reputation* (Farnham: Ashgate, 2014)

Richards, Judith, '"His nowe majestie" and the English monarchy: The kingship of Charles I before 1640', *Past & Present* 113 (Nov. 1986), 77–81

Rickard, Jane, *Authorship and Authority: The Writings of James VI and I* (Manchester, 2007)

Riley, P.W.J., *King William and the Scottish Politicians* (Edinburgh: John Donald, 1979)

Roberts, John L., *Clan, King and Covenant: History of the Highland Clans from the Civil War to the Glencoe Massacre* (Edinburgh: Edinburgh University Press, 2000)

Robertson, Barry, 'The Covenanting north of Scotland, 1638–1647', *Innes Review* 61:1 (2010), 24–51

'The House of Huntly and the First Bishops' War', *Northern Scotland* 24 (2004), 1–15

Rock, Joe, 'Richard Cooper Sr. and Scottish book illustration' in Stephen W. Brown and Warren McDougall (eds), *The Edinburgh History of the Book in Scotland, Volume 2: Enlightenment and Expansion, 1707–1800,* (Edinburgh, 2012)

Rollinson, David, *The Commonwealth of the People: Popular Politics and England's Long Social Revolution, 1066–1649* (Cambridge, 2010)

Rose, Jacqueline, 'Councils, counsel and the seventeenth-century composite state' in Jacqueline Rose (ed.), *The Politics of Counsel in England and Scotland 1286–1707* (Oxford: British Academy, 2016), 271–94

Rospocher, Massimo and Rosa Salzberg, 'An evanescent public sphere: voices, spaces and publics in Venice during the Italian wars', in Massimo Rospocher (ed.), *Beyond the Public Sphere: Opinions, Publics, Spaces in Early Modern Europe* (Bologna: Il Molino; Berlin: Duncker & Humbolt, 2012), 93–114

Rospocher, Massimo, 'Beyond the public sphere: a historiographical transition' in Massimo Rospocher (ed.), *Beyond the Public Sphere: Opinions, Publics, Spaces in Early Modern Europe* (Bologna: Il Molino; Berlin: Duncker & Humbolt, 2012), 9–28

Sanderson, Margaret H. B., *A Kindly Place? Living in Sixteenth-Century Scotland* (East Linton: Tuckwell, 2002)

Sawyer, Jeffrey K., *Printed Poison: Pamphlet Propaganda, Faction Politics and the Public Sphere in Early Seventeenth-Century France* (Berkeley and Los Angeles: University of California Press, 1990)

Schmidt, Leigh Eric, *Holy Fairs: Scotland and the Making of American Revivalism*, 2nd ed. (Grand Rapids, Mich: William B. Eerdman Publishing, 2001)

280 *Bibliography*

Schwoerer, Lois, *The Declaration of Rights, 1689* (Baltimore and London: Johns Hopkins Press, 1981)

Shagan, Ethan, *Popular Politics and the English Reformation* (Cambridge, 2003)

Sillitoe, Peter, '"And afterward to his pallace of Westminster, there to solace himself": rediscovering the progresses of Charles I', *Yearbook of English Studies* 44 (2014), 87–102

Smout, T. C., 'Born again at Cambuslang: new evidence on popular religion and literacy in eighteenth-century Scotland', *Past & Present* 97 (1982), 114–27

Somerset, Douglas W. B., 'Walter Ker and the "Sweet Singers"', *Scottish Reformation Society Historical Journal* 2 (2012), 85–108

Spencer, Andrew M., 'The coronation oath in English politics' in Benjamin Thompson and John Watts (eds), *Political Society in Later Medieval England* (Woodbridge: Boydell Press, 2015), 38–54

Speier, Hans, 'The rise of public opinion' in Robert Jackall (ed), *Propaganda* (Basingstoke: Macmillan, 1995), 26–46

Spiller, Michael R. G., 'Drummond, William of Hawthornden', *Oxford Dictionary of National Biography* (2004; rev. 2007)

Spurlock, Scott, 'Cromwell's Edinburgh press and the development of print culture in Scotland', *Scottish Historical Review* 90, 2: 230 (Oct. 2011), 179–203

  Cromwell and Scotland: Conquest and Religion 1650–1660 (Edinburgh: John Donald, 2007)

  'Social order and social ordering in Stuart Ireland and Scotland', *Journal of Irish and Scottish Studies* 6:2 (Spring 2013), 1–29

Spurr, John, '"The strongest bond of conscience": oaths and the limits of tolerance in early modern England' in Harald E. Braun and Edward Vallance (eds), *Contexts of Conscience in Early Modern Europe, 1500–1700* (Basingstoke, 2004), 151–65

Steele, Margaret, 'The 'politick Christian': the theological background to the National Covenant' in John Morrill (ed.), *The Scottish National Covenant in its British Context, 1638–51* (Edinburgh, 1990), 31–67

Stephen, Jeffrey, 'Defending the Revolution: The Church of Scotland and the Scottish parliament, 1689-95', *Scottish Historical Review* 89, 1:227 (April 2010) 19–53

  'The presbytery of Caledonia: an early Scottish mission', *History Scotland* 9:1 (2009), 14–19

Stevenson, David, 'A revolutionary regime and the press: the Scottish Covenanters and their press, 1638–51', *The Library* ser 6, 7:4 (1985), 315–37

  'Conventicles in the kirk, 1619–37: the emergence of a radical party', *Records of the Scottish Church History Society* 18 (1972–4), 99–114

  'Deposition of ministers in the Church of Scotland under the Covenanters, 1638–1651', *Church History* 44 (1975), 321–55

  'Reactions to ruin, 1648–51: *A Declaration and Vindication of the Poore Opprest Commons of Scotland*, and other pamphlets', *Scottish Historical Review* 84:218, 2 (Oct. 2005), 257–65

Revolution and Counter-Revolution in Scotland, 1644–1651 (Edinburgh: John Donald, 2003)

'Scotland's first newspaper', *The Bibliotheck* 10:5 (Jan. 1981), 123–6

Scotland's Last Royal Wedding: the Marriage of James VI and Anne of Denmark (Edinburgh: John Donald, 1997)

'The early covenanters and the federal union of Britain' in Roger A. Mason (ed.), *Scotland and England 1286–1815* (Edinburgh: John Donald, 1987), 163–181

'The English devil of keeping state: elite manners and the downfall of Charles I in Scotland' in Roger A. Mason and Norman MacDougall (eds), *People and Power in Scotland* (Edinburgh: John Donald, 1992), 126–44

'The "Letter on Sovereign Power" and the influence of Jean Bodin on political thought in Scotland', *Scottish Historical Review* 61:171, 1 (April 1982), 25–43.

'The National Covenant: a list of known copies', *Records of the Scottish Church History Society* 23:2 (1988), 255–99

'The Solemn League and Covenant: a list of known copies', *Records of the Scottish Church History Society* 25:3 (1995), 154–87

'Wishart, George (1599–1671)', *Oxford Dictionary of National Biography* (2004)

Stevenson, Jane, 'Reading, writing and gender in early modern Scotland', *The Seventeenth Century* 27:3 (2012), 335–374

Stevenson, Katie, *Power and Propaganda: Scotland 1306–1488* (Edinburgh, 2014)

Stewart, David, 'The "Aberdeen Doctors" and the Covenanters', *Records of the Scottish Church History Society* 22 (1984), 35–44

Stewart, Laura A. M., 'Authority, agency and the reception of the Scottish National Covenant of 1638' in Robert Armstrong and Tadhg Ó hAnnracháin (eds), *Insular Christianity: Alternative Models of the Church in Britain and Ireland, c.1570–c.1700* (Manchester, 2013), 88–106

'"Brothers in treuth": propaganda, public opinion and the Perth article debate' in R. Houlbrooke (ed.) *James VI and I: Ideas, Authority and Government* (Aldershot: Ashgate, 2006), 151–68

'Petitioning in early seventeenth-century Scotland, 1625–51' in Karin Bowie and Thomas Munck (eds), *Early Modern Petitioning and Public Engagement in Scotland, Britain and Scandinavia, c.1550–1795, Parliaments, Estates and Representation* 38:3 (2018), 307–22

'Power and faith in early modern Scotland' in Andrew Mackillop (ed.), *The State of Early Modern and Modern Scottish Histories, Scottish Historical Review* 92, supplement: 234 (April 2013), 25–37

Stewart, Laura A.M. (ed.), *Publics and Participation in Early Modern Britain, Journal of British Studies* 56:4 (Oct. 2017)

Rethinking the Scottish Revolution: Covenanted Scotland 1637–1651 (Oxford, 2016)

'The political repercussions of the Five Articles of Perth: A reassessment of James VI and I's religious policy in Scotland', *The Sixteenth Century Journal* 38:4 (Winter 2008), 1013–36

282   *Bibliography*

Urban Politics and British Civil Wars: Edinburgh, 1617–1653 (Leiden: Brill, 2006)

Sowerby, Scott, *Making Toleration: The Repealers and the Glorious Revolution* (Cambridge, MA: Harvard University Press, 2013)

Tanner, Roland, 'The Lords of the Articles before 1540: a reassessment', *Scottish Historical Review* 79,2:208 (Oct. 2000), 189–212

Terry, Charles Sanford, *A History of Scotland: From the Roman Evacuation to the Disruption, 1843* (Cambridge, 1920)

Todd, Margo, *The Culture of Protestantism in Early Modern Scotland* (New Haven: Yale University Press, 2004)

Towsey, Mark, *Reading the Scottish Enlightenment: Books and their Readers in Provincial Scotland, 1750–1820* (Leiden: Brill, 2010)

Tully, James, 'The pen is a mighty sword: Quentin Skinner's analysis of politics' in James Tully (ed.), *Meaning and Context: Quentin Skinner and His Critics* (Cambridge: Polity Press, 1988), 7–25

Vallance, Edward, '"From the hearts of the people": loyalty, addresses and the public sphere in the Exclusion Crisis' in Tony Claydon and Thomas N. Corns (eds), *Religion, Culture and National Community in the 1670s* (Cardiff, 2011), 127–47

'Oaths, casuistry and equivocation: Anglican responses to the Engagement controversy', *Historical Journal* 44:1 (2001), 59–77

'Protestation, vow, covenant and engagement: swearing allegiance in the English civil war', *Historical Research* 75:190 (Nov 2002), 408–24

Revolutionary England and the National Covenant: State Oaths, Protestantism and the Political Nation, 1553–1682 (Woodbridge: Boydell, 2005)

'Women, politics and the 1723 oaths of allegiance to George I', *Historical Journal* 59:4 (2016), 975–99

Van Nierop, Henk, 'A beggars' banquet: The compromise of the nobility and the politics of inversion', *European History Quarterly* 21:419 (1991), 419–443

Van Voss, Lex Heerma, 'Introduction', *International Review of Social History* 46: supplement (2001), 1–10

Verweij, Sebastiaan, *The Literary Culture of Early Modern Scotland: Manuscript Production and Transmission, 1560–1625* (Oxford, 2016)

Walsby, Malcolm, 'Cheap print and the academic market: the printing of dissertations in 16C Louvain' in Andrew Pettegree (ed.), *Broadsheets: Single-Sheet Publishing in the First Age of Print* (Leiden: Brill, 2017), 355–75

Walter, John, 'Confessional politics in pre-civil war Essex: prayer books, profanations and petitions', *The Historical Journal* 44:3 (2001), 677–701

Understanding Popular Violence in the English Revolution: The Colchester Plunderers (Cambridge, 1999)

Covenanting Citizens: The Protestation Oath and Popular Political Culture in the English Revolution (Oxford, 2016)

Warfield, Abaigéal, 'Witchcraft illustrated: the crime of witchcraft in early modern German news broadsheets', in Andrew Pettegree (ed.), *Broadsheets: Single-Sheet Publishing in the First Age of Print*, (Leiden: Brill, 2017), 459–87

Bibliography

Warner, Michael, 'Publics and counterpublics', *Public Culture* 14:1 (Winter 2002), 49–90
   The Letters of the Republic: Publication and the Public Sphere in Eighteenth-Century America (Cambridge, MA: Harvard University Press, 1990)
Wasser, Michael B., 'The western witch-hunt of 1697–1700: the last major witch-hunt in Scotland' in Julian Goodare (ed.), *The Scottish Witch-Hunt in Context* (Manchester, 2002), 146–65
Watt, Douglas, *The Price of Scotland: Darien, Union and the Wealth of Nations* (Edinburgh: Luath Press, 2007)
Watts, John, 'Public or plebs: the changing meaning of "commons", 1381–1549' in H. Pryce and J. Watts (eds), *Power and Identity in the Middle Ages* (Oxford, 2007), 242–60
Waurechen, Sarah, 'Covenanter propaganda and conceptualisations of the public during the Bishops' Wars, 1638–40', *The Historical Journal* 52:1 (2009), 63–86
Weil, Rachel, *A Plague of Informers: Conspiracy and Political Trust in William III's England* (New Haven: Yale, 2014)
Weiser, Brian, 'Access and petitioning during the reign of Charles II' in E. Cruickshanks (ed.), *The Stuart Courts* (Stroud: Sutton, 2000), 203–13
Wells, V. T., 'Constitutional conflict after the Union of Crowns: contention and continuity in the parliaments of 1612 and 1621' in Keith M. Brown and Alistair J. Mann (eds), *Parliaments and Politics in Scotland, 1567–1707* (Edinburgh, 2005), 82–100
Whatley, Christopher A., 'Taking stock: Scotland at the end of the seventeenth century' in T. C. Smout (ed.), *Anglo-Scottish Relations from 1603 to 1900* (Oxford: British Academy, 2005), 103–125
Whatley, Christopher and Derek Patrick, 'Persistence, principle and patriotism in the making of the Union of 1707: The Revolution, Scottish parliament and *squadrone volante*', *History* 92:306 (Apr. 2007), 162–86
Whyte, Ian D. and Kathleen A. Whyte, 'Married to the manse: The wives of Scottish ministers, c. 1560–c.1800' in Elizabeth Ewan and Maureen M. Meikle (eds), *Women in Scotland, c.1100–c.1750*, (East Linton: Tuckwell, 1999), 221–32
Whytock, Jack C., *"An Educated Clergy": Scottish Theological Education and Training in the Kirk and Secession, 1560–1850* (Milton Keynes: Paternoster, 2007)
Williamson, Arthur, 'Scotland and the rise of civic culture, 1550–1650', *History Compass* 4:1 (2006), 91–123
   Scottish National Consciousness in the Age of James VI: The Apocalypse, the Union and the Shaping of Scotland's Public Culture (Edinburgh, 1979)
Wilson, Bronwen and Paul Yachnin, 'Introduction', in Bronwen Wilson and Paul Yachnin (eds), *Making Publics in Early Modern Europe: People, Things, Forms of Knowledge* (Abingdon: Routledge, 2010), 1–21
Wilson, Kathleen, *The Sense of the People: Politics, Culture and Imperialism in England, 1715–1785* (Cambridge, 1995)
Withington, Phil, *Society in Early Modern England: The Vernacular Origins of Some Powerful Ideas* (Cambridge: Polity Press, 2010)

284   *Bibliography*

Wolgast, Eike, 'Speyer, Protestation of', trans. Susan M. Sisler, *Oxford Encyclopedia of the Reformation* (2005)

Wormald, Jenny, 'Bloodfeud, kindred and government in early modern Scotland', *Past & Present* 87 (May 1980), 54–97

    Lords and Men in Scotland: Bonds of Manrent, 1442–1603 (Edinburgh University Press, 1985)

    'The headaches of monarchy: kingship and the kirk in the early seventeenth century' in J. Goodare and A. Macdonald (eds), *Sixteenth-Century Scotland* (Leiden: Brill, 2008), 367–393

Wood, Paul, 'Science, the universities and the public sphere in eighteenth-century Scotland', *History of Universities* 13 (1994), 99–135

Wood, Andy, *Riot, Rebellion and Popular Politics in Early Modern England* (Houndmills: Palgrave, 2002)

Würgler, Andreas, 'Voices from among the "silent masses": humble petitions and social conflicts in early modern central Europe', *International Review of Social History* 46 (2001), supplement, 11–34

Yeoman, Louise, 'James Melville and the Covenant of Grace' Sally Mapstone (ed.), in *Older Scots Literature*, (Edinburgh: John Donald, 2005), 574–83

Young, John R., 'Charles I and the 1633 Parliament' in Keith M. Brown and Alastair J. Mann (eds), *Parliament and Politics in Scotland, 1567–1707* (Edinburgh, 2005), 101–37

    'The Scottish parliament and the politics of empire: Parliament and the Darien project, 1695–1707', *Parliaments, Estates and Representation* 27:1 (2007), 175–90

Zaret, David, *Origins of Democratic Culture: Printing, Petitions and the Public Sphere in Early-Modern England* (Princeton, 2000)

    'Petitions and the 'invention' of public opinion in the English Revolution', *The American Journal of Sociology* 101:6 (May 1996), 1497–555

Unpublished Theses and Papers

Beckett, Margaret J., 'Political Works of John Lesley, Bishop of Ross (1527–96)' unpublished PhD thesis, University of St. Andrews (2002)

Carr, Rosalind, 'Gender, National Identity and Political Agency in Eighteenth-century Scotland', unpublished PhD thesis, University of Glasgow (2008)

Clarke, Tristram N., 'The Scottish Episcopalians, 1688–1720', unpublished PhD thesis, University of Edinburgh (1987)

Doak, Laura Isobel, 'On Street and Scaffold: The People and Political Culture in Restoration Scotland, c.1678–1685', unpublished PhD thesis, University of Glasgow (2020)

Gray, Nathan Phillip, '"A Publick Benefite to the Nation": The Charitable and Religious Origins of the SSPCK, 1690–1715', unpublished PhD thesis, University of Glasgow (2011)

Bibliography

Jardine, Mark, 'The United Societies: Militancy, Martyrdom and the Presbyterian Movement in Late-Restoration Scotland, 1679–88', unpublished PhD thesis, University of Edinburgh (2009)

Lind, Andrew, '"Bad and Evill Patriotts"? Royalism in Scotland during the British Civil Wars, c.1638–1651', unpublished PhD thesis, University of Glasgow (2020)

Mason, Rebecca, '"With Hir Gudis & Geir": Married Women Negotiating the Law of Property in the Courts of Seventeenth-Century Glasgow', unpublished PhD thesis, University of Glasgow (2020)

Macfarlane, Cameron Alasdair, '"A Dream of Darien": Scottish Empire and the Evolution of Early Modern Travel Writing', unpublished PhD thesis, University of Durham (2018)

McDougall, Jamie, 'Covenants and Covenanters in Scotland, 1638–1679', unpublished PhD thesis, University of Glasgow (2017)

McIntyre, Neil, 'Saints and Subverters: The Later Covenanters in Scotland, c.1648–1679', unpublished PhD thesis, University of Strathclyde (2016)

'Re-framing the Covenant: The Reception and Legacy of *A Solemn Acknowledgement* (1648) in Scotland and Beyond', *Humanities Lecture Series*, University of Glasgow (20 March 2019)

McSeveney, Alan James, 'Non-Conforming Presbyterian Women in Scotland, 1660–1679', unpublished PhD thesis, University of Strathclyde (2005)

Sheffield, Edwin, 'Clan MacKenzie, the Act of Union, and a Chief Abroad', North American Conference on British Studies, Providence R.I. (Oct. 27, 2018)

Murdoch, Steve, 'Preparation and propaganda: building the army of the Covenant, 1633–39', Centre for Scottish and Celtic Studies seminar series, University of Glasgow (5 March 2019)

Tapscott, Elizabeth Leona, 'Propaganda and Persuasion in the Early Scottish Reformation, c. 1527–57', unpublished PhD thesis, University of St. Andrews (2013)

Index

Aberdeen, 33, 39, 41, 83, 98, 107, 111, 160, 163, 168, 173, 189, 193, 202, 206
Aberdeen Doctors, 160
Aberdeenshire, 109, 206–7, 231
Aberlady, 114
academics, 107, 110–11, 139, 157–8, 160, 188, 200, 202, 204, 206, 245
accommodation, 123–7, 195
Act anent war and peace (1703), 230
Act of classes, 115, 118
Act of security (1704), 230–1
Act recissory (1661), 122, 174
Adamson, Patrick, archbishop of St Andrews, 139, 151
admonition, 33, 35, 55, 61, 64, 102
Aikenhead, Thomas, 218–20
Ainslie bond, 95
Aliens act (1705), 232
Alison, Isabel, 128
allegorical figures, 146–7, 153–5, 159, 161, 170, 203, 222, 231, 236, 240
Amsterdam, 142, 181
ancient monarchy, 168, 172, 179, 227, 230, 236
Anderson, George, 158
Angus, 42, 109
Anne, 15, 18, 205, 207, 228–30
Antwerp, 142
Apologetical Declaration (1684), 47, 130
Argyll's rising (1685), 132, 181
Articles of Grievances (1689), 185–6, 192
Articles of Perth (1618), 63, 66–8, 72, 91, 102–3, 106, 109–10, 152–4, 158
Ayr, 41, 92, 97, 110, 123, 150, 188, 223
Ayrshire, 31, 71–2, 77, 86, 108, 116–17, 123, 127

Baillie, Robert, 196
Balcanquhall, Walter, 161
band, 89, 94, 113, 129
 caution, 94, 127, 131
 collective, 94–5, 98–9, 128–9
 friendship, 94

maintenance, 94
 manrent, 94
Banffshire, 109, 226
Bannatyne, John, 208
Bassandyne, Thomas, 142
Battle of Bothwell Bridge (1679), 46, 85, 127–8
birthday of monarch, 46, 174
Bishops' Wars (1639-40), 75, 112, 158, 162, 230
Black Acts (1584), 97, 101, 149
 subscription, 97, 101, 113
Black, David, 60–1
Blackadder, John, 45
blasphemy, 218–20
Bo'ness, 128
Bond of Association (1584), 90, 98, 102, 220
Bothwell, 46, 127
Brown, John, 176, 198
Bruce, Peter, 182
Bryson, James, 158
Bryson, Robert, 158
Buchanan, George, 143, 147, 172, 176
Burnet, Alexander, archbishop of Glasgow, 84
Burnet, Gilbert, bishop of Salisbury, 177, 187
Burntisland, 111

Caithness, 115
Calder, Robert, 206
Calderwood, David, 16, 31, 34, 151–4, 158, 160
Caledonia, 162, 173, 180, 222
Cambuslang, 151
Cameron, Richard, 128
Cameronians, 45, 128, 190, 201
Campbell, Archibald, eighth earl and first marquis of Argyll, 41, 117, 174, 229
Campbell, Archibald, ninth earl of Argyll, 132, 181
Campbell, Archibald, second duke of Argyll, 207, 221, 234
Canaries, James, 182
Cargill, Donald, 128
Cargill's covenant (1680), 128, 179, 208

Index

287

Carmichael, James, 97, 99
Carrick, 108, 111
Carstares, William, 192, 223, 225
Cathkin, James, 152
Catholicism, fear of, 61, 86, 96, 98–9, 106, 129, 132, 134, 160, 168, 181–2, 227
Catholics, 61, 86, 98, 101–2, 133–4, 180–1, 188, 203
censorship, 38, 132, 137–8, 142–3, 148–9, 151–3, 157, 169, 177, 181–2, 231, 240
  England, 142
  licensing, 142, 149, 152, 158, 164–6, 174–5, 219, 221, 224, 227, 232
  public burning, 113, 152, 174–5, 177, 179, 227, 232
Chanonry, 42
chaplains, 130, 164, 192, 223
Charles I, 36, 38, 41, 64–70, 78, 103–4, 113, 115, 118, 121, 154–6, 159–61, 164, 166, 204, 244
Charles II, 41, 45, 78, 85, 118–19, 128, 166, 168, 172, 174, 179, 188, 204, 244
Claim of Right (1689), 18, 185–6, 192–3, 207–8, 225, 230
Clerk of Penicuik, Sir John, 237
Cockburn, John, 202
coffeehouses, 19, 181, 220
commission of the general assembly, 76, 154
  1643, 76, 113–14
  1648, 76, 116–17, 165–6
  1649, 167
  1650, 41, 78
  1651, 168
  1703, 207
  1706, 233
commission on grievances, 65
commons, 11, 14, 40, 71, 76, 81, 105–6, 146–8, 153–5, 159, 170, 176, 181, 184, 197–8, 201–3, 213, 244
commonweal, 39, 59, 155, 192–3, 240, 245
Commonwealth, Cromwellian, 44, 120, 133, 170
Company of Scotland, 221–7, 230–1, 233, 235, 237
  Darien colony, 224, 226
  investment, 221, 223
comprehension, 186, 193–5, 200, 203
Confession of faith (1560), 28, 60, 97, 129–30
Confession, King's or Negative (1581), 28, 49, 91, 95–8, 101, 110, 129, 160
  printing, 100
  renewal, 44, 74, 98, 100–1, 105–6, 109
conscience, 27–30, 34, 44, 78, 86, 90, 94, 97, 101, 103, 105, 115–16, 119, 123, 126, 129, 135, 153–4, 159–60, 163, 170–2, 176, 189, 243

exoneration, 47, 158
satisfaction, 42, 77, 121, 167–8, 181, 198
tender, 69, 128, 133, 159
consent, 7, 49, 119, 160, 189, 193, 195, 233–4, 245
  national, 44
constitution, 101, 104, 135, 199, 208
consultation, 13, 233
contractual monarchy, 46, 98, 119, 124, 128, 160, 164, 192, 198, 201, 245
conventicles. *see* dissenting worship
Convention of Royal Burghs, 58, 84, 188, 233
coronation, 89, 133, 198
  1567, 95, 148
  1633, 67, 155
  1651, 11, 47, 119, 124, 128, 168, 172, 174, 201
  1660, 174
  1685, 182
  1689, 192
Country party, 18, 213, 224, 229, 232–3
Court of Session, 24, 54, 57, 66
Court party, 232
covenant, Old Testament, 90, 98–100, 105, 119
Covenanting Revolution (1637–41), 13, 19, 52, 140, 244
Cowper, William, bishop of Galloway, 151–2
Cromwell, Oliver, 78–9, 118, 157
Cromwell, Richard, 80
crowds, 4, 60, 70, 108, 111, 174, 190, 206, 208, 242
  Edinburgh, 37–9, 61, 72–3, 77, 116, 185, 190, 204, 226, 231–2, 235
  women, 231
culture of controversy, 8, 172, 241, 245
Cumbernauld band (1640), 113
Cunningham, William, eighth earl of Glencairn, 121

Dalkeith, 120
Dalrymple of Stair, Sir James, 24–5, 31
Dalrymple of Stair, Sir John, 194, 216
declaration, 47, 55, 76, 85, 120, 165–7, 171, 181, 188
Declaration (1662), 122–3, 125–6, 129
  printing, 122
Declaration and Acknowledgement (1649), 118
Declaration of Arbroath (1320), 201
Declaration of Rights (1689), 187, 192
Deer, 41
Defoe, Daniel, 229
deposition, 110–11, 115, 118, 124, 130, 195, 218
dialogue text, 147, 149, 153–4, 177, 232

288 *Index*

Dickson, David, 72
dissenting worship, 45, 47, 85, 124–5, 127–8, 132–3, 178, 195, 202, 206, 208
Douglas, 103, 111, 172, 201
Douglas, James, fourth earl of Morton, 148
Douglas, James, second duke of Queensberry, 207, 232, 235
Drummond of Hawthornden, William, 70, 156, 163
Dumbarton, 42
Dumbartonshire, 226
Dumfries, 41, 117, 150, 189, 232
Dumfriesshire, 124
Dunbar, 78, 118
Dunbar, William, 56
Dundee, 170, 206
dying speech, 175–6

East India Company, 221, 231
Edinburgh, 39, 72, 95, 98, 100, 108, 124, 128–9, 139, 151, 155, 164, 171, 173–5, 180–1, 185, 188–91, 200, 204, 208, 218, 220, 223, 226, 232, 235
    mercat cross, 32, 97, 152, 177
    town council, 71, 123
elections, 82, 84, 123, 191, 202, 204, 207, 215, 229, 240, 267
elective monarchy, 147, 172, 201
Elgin, 107, 114, 206
Elphinstone, John, second Lord Balmerino, 50, 67–70, 156
Engagement (1647), 41, 76, 115, 117, 165, 167
Enlightenment, 5, 245
evil counsellors, 56, 61, 154
Exclusion (1679-81), 179–80
excommunication, 117, 128, 169
execution, 41, 47, 78, 81–2, 118, 127–8, 131, 142, 166, 172, 174–5, 219
exiles, 60, 132, 151, 175, 177, 185, 187–8, 192, 194, 196, 220

false news, 143, 174, 188
famine, 218
fasting, 61, 100, 106–7, 117, 129, 162, 178, 224
federal theology, 105
Fergusia, 236
Ferguson, Robert, 194
Fife, 42, 71, 96, 100, 109, 116, 118, 123, 150, 178, 206
First Band of the Lords of the Congregation (1560), 94
First Book of Discipline, 95
Flanders, 216–17
Fletcher of Saltoun, Andrew, 230
Forbes of Corse, John, 160, 177, 197

Forbes, Patrick, bishop of Aberdeen, 160
France, 216, 235
free trade, 230–1, 235

Gaelic language, 4, 16–17, 19, 103, 112, 138–40, 144, 164, 166, 212, 242
Galloway, 26, 116, 123, 127, 131
Garden, George, 206
Garnock, Robert, 47
general assembly, 28, 194, 244
    1566, 59
    1570, 28
    1572, 29
    1578, 30
    1581, 96, 99
    1588, 98
    1590, 99
    1596, 60, 100
    1606, 151
    1610, 102, 151
    1618, 35, 63, 68, 102, 152, 161
    1638, 39, 75, 110, 158–9
    1639, 112
    1640, 112
    1641, 113
    1642, 76
    1643, 112, 114
    1644, 112
    1645, 115
    1649, 118, 166
    1651, 42
    1652, 43, 170
    1697, 219–20
    management, 14, 33, 35, 39, 62, 101, 154, 241
    petitioning, 59–60, 63
    protestation, 26–7, 31, 39, 42
    right to meet, 33, 68
General Band (1590), 98, 101, 105, 108–9, 160
genius, 189, 191, 196, 209, 231
Gibb, John, 129
Gibbites, 129, 179
Gillespie, George, 135, 157–8
Glasgow, 40–1, 46, 77, 79, 81, 107, 110–11, 116, 121, 130, 139–40, 150, 160, 188–90, 200, 202, 208, 223, 226
Glen, James, 182
Glencairn rising (1653), 121
Glencoe massacre (1692), 216–18
Glenisla, 110
Gordon, George, second marquis of Huntly, 109, 113, 166
Gordon, John, 203
Gothenburg, 167
Graham, James, fifth earl and first marquis of Montrose, 113, 115, 118, 163, 167, 174

Index

Graham, John, first viscount Dundee, 191, 199, 203
Graham, William, seventh earl of Menteith, 67
Grant, Francis, Lord Cullen, 220
Guthrie, James, 48, 82
Guthrie, Jonet, 151
Guthrie, Samuel, 169–70
Guthrie, Sophia, 177

Habermas, Jürgen. *See* public sphere, Habermasian
Haddingtonshire, 114
Hadow, James, 206–7
Haig, William, 68, 103
Hamburg, 223, 231
Hamilton, 41, 46, 85, 127, 198, 208, 233
Hamilton of Whitelaw, Sir William, 208
Hamilton, Anne, duchess of Hamilton, 223, 233
Hamilton, James, fourth duke of Hamilton, 187, 189, 224, 229–30, 234–5
Hamilton, James, third marquis and first duke of Hamilton, 39, 74, 107–8
Hamilton, Jean, countess of Cassillis, 108
Hamilton, William, third duke of Hamilton, 85, 190
Hampton Court Conference (1606), 101
Harvie, Marion, 48–9, 128
Hay, Father Thomas, 200
Hebronites, 218, 232
Hepburn, James, fourth earl of Bothwell, 95
Hepburn, John, 218
Hewat, Peter, 34
Highland Host (1678), 126
Highlands, 16, 112, 121, 139, 203–4, 212, 216, 223, 237
Hodges, James, 230, 233–4, 244
Hogg, Thomas, 68
Holyrood Palace, 182, 188, 232
Home, David, Lord Crossrigg, 218
Honyman, Andrew, bishop of Orkney, 177
Howieson, John, 151
Humble Remonstrance (1646), 115, 163
Hume of Godscroft, David, 28, 151
Hume, Alexander, 101, 152
humours, 177, 196, 200

images, 142, 146, 150, 226
inclinations, 83, 192, 194, 196–8, 227, 234, 239
indemnity, 86, 125, 132, 216
indifferency, 117, 172
indulgence, 83–4, 126–8, 133, 177, 182
information, 35, 40, 55, 64, 71, 159, 165–6
instructions, 7, 204
instrument, 22, 25, 32, 37–8, 45, 68
instrument of government, 44, 192

Inverlochy, 212
Inverness, 107, 166, 226
Irvine, 41, 72, 123, 188

Jacobites, 189, 191, 193, 199–201, 203, 212, 216–18, 220, 225, 231, 234–5, 245
James VI, 13, 27, 31–2, 87, 95, 100–1, 145, 149, 152, 193, 204, 244
   Basilikon Doron, 27, 34, 62, 149, 159
James VII, 47, 131–2, 181, 185, 188, 191–2, 205, 244
James, duke of Albany, 46, 129, 172, 179
Jock Upaland, 154, 170, 197, 203, 240
John the Commonweil, 148, 240
Johnston of Wariston, Archibald, 37, 39–40, 42, 104, 106–7, 121, 160, 176
Johnston, James, 217

Keppoch, 164
Kilcumin Band (1645), 115
Killing Times (1679–85), 128
Kilsyth, 163
King's Covenant (1638), 109–11, 122, 160
Kinghorn, 96, 109
Kintyre, 181
Kirk party, 78, 117–18, 166
Kirkaldy, 103
Kirkcudbright, 130–1
Kirkton, James, 119
kneeling, 35–6, 66, 152, 158
Knox, Andrew, bishop of the Isles, 103
Knox, John, 26, 28, 37

Lady Scotland, 148
Lanark, 41, 47, 79, 108, 121, 130, 208
Lanarkshire, 71, 116–17, 123, 127, 233
Latin, 138–9, 150–1, 155, 164, 176, 222
Lauder of Fountainhall, Sir John, 128, 179–80
Lauder, George, 161
Law, James, bishop of Orkney, 151
leasing-making, 82, 133, 162
Leith, 95, 109
Lekpreuik, Robert, 147
Leslie, Charles, 216, 218
Leslie, John, sixth earl of Rothes, 39, 41, 68, 196
Lesmahagow, 190
levy, 41, 75–8, 115–17, 165–6, 168–70
libel, 69, 143, 148, 151–2, 175, 179–80, 227
liberties, 27, 32, 40, 60, 91, 97, 105, 113–14, 121, 128, 192–3, 201, 215–16, 260
limitations, 13, 185, 192, 197, 230–1
Lindsay of the Mount, Sir David, 21, 240
Lindsay, Colin, third earl of Balcarres, 188, 190, 201
Lindsay, David, bishop of Brechin, 152

Index

Linlithgow, 173
literacy, 139–41
Livingston, John, 106, 108, 112, 118
Logie, 210
Lom, Iain, 164, 166, 173, 181, 212
London, 13, 142, 171, 174, 189, 194, 214, 216,
  220–1, 223, 235
Lothians, 116

Mackays, 115
Mackenzie of Rosehaugh, Sir George, 184, 191,
  199
Mackenzie, George, second earl of Seaforth, 115,
  163
Mackenzie, George, viscount Tarbat and first earl
  of Cromarty, 191, 199, 205, 234
Maddie, 147, 197
Maitland, John, first duke of Lauderdale, 84–5
majority, 25, 30, 35, 199, 203, 206, 208, 225
  generality, 10, 43, 85, 170, 180, 187, 194,
    196–7, 199–200, 202–4, 206, 208, 222, 233
  greater part, 30, 36, 59, 83, 95, 106, 110, 176,
    194, 202, 206
malignants, 41, 78, 111, 115, 117, 167–8
manuscript publication, 6–7, 11, 16, 28, 33, 44,
  52, 79, 96, 101, 106, 138–9, 142–4, 150–1,
  154, 160, 169–70, 177, 182, 197, 213
Majoribanks, Margaret, 151
Marprelate press, 143
Mary I, 95, 146, 230
Mary II, 185, 192, 194, 217
Mary of Guise, 26, 59
Mauchline Moor, 77, 116, 118
Maybole, 108
McLachlan, Margaret, 131
Mein, Robert, 174
Melville of Halhill, Sir James, 87
Melville, Andrew, 145
Melville, George, first earl of Melville, 187,
  191–2, 199, 225
Melville, James, 101
memorial, 191
Michaelson, John, 153
Midlothian, 114
militia, 85, 100, 125–7, 188, 212, 219, 231, 233,
  235
millenarianism, 106
minority dissent, 25, 192, 199, 202, 226, 230,
  234, 244
  schismatic, 29, 43, 179–80
  weightier part, 30, 36, 42, 45–8
Montgomerie of Skelmorlie, Sir James, 216
Montrose, 147
Moray, 42, 107, 114, 121

More of Stonywood, James, 207
Morer, Thomas, 201–2
multitude, 42, 77, 148, 152–3, 161, 164, 177,
  187, 194, 196–7, 199–200, 233, 242
Munro, Alexander, 200, 202
Murray, John, first duke of Atholl, 224, 234, 239
Musselburgh, 109
muster, 147, 178, 233, 235

Nairnshire, 226
National Covenant (1638), 29, 38, 44, 74, 91–3,
  104–6, 119–20, 160, 194, 198
  legality, 105–6
  printing, 112, 173
  renewal, 93, 112, 132, 190, 197, 221
  subscription, 108, 111–12, 114
  swearing, 92, 106–8, 111–12, 204
New party, 231–2
Newbattle, 114
newspapers, 142, 166, 174, 181, 219
  Edinburgh Courant, 232
  Edinburgh Gazette, 224, 232
  Flying Post, 220
  London Gazette, 180, 188, 216–17
  Mercurius Caledonius, 174
  Observator, 232
  Paris *Gazette*, 216
Nine Years' War (1689-97), 218
northern band (1650), 118

oath
  abjuration, 131–2
  allegiance, 92, 97, 101–2, 121–3, 125–6, 129,
    132–3, 150, 195
  assertory, 23, 27, 96, 122
  association, 90, 98, 220–1
  assurance, 195, 220
  confessional, 28, 74, 96, 129
  coronation, 89, 95, 128, 133, 192
  engagement, 117, 120
  explanations, 97, 107, 112, 122, 130, 195
  new entrants, 63, 67–8, 97, 101–3, 109, 112
  non-resistance, 122, 125, 127, 129, 133
  obedience, 61, 95, 97, 100, 103, 106, 113,
    116, 118, 121–4, 126, 129, 131–3
  promissory, 23, 96
  subscription, 90, 94–5, 99, 109–11, 117, 131,
    140, 220
  swearing, 38, 41, 92, 100, 106–8, 112, 114,
    117–18, 131, 153
  test, 111, 114, 119, 121–2, 129, 195
Oath of Association (1696), 220–1
Ogilvy, James, first earl of Seafield, 223, 226,
  231–2

Index

291

opinion at large, 1, 3–4, 15, 17, 19, 23, 41, 69, 104, 120, 138, 154, 160, 174, 176, 190, 234–5
opinion politics, 3, 16, 138, 172, 228, 237, 240, 245
Orkney, 80, 123, 226

pageantry, 72, 102, 150, 155, 174, 180
Paisley, 130
Paris, 142, 164, 216
parliament, 14, 25, 244
  1561 convention, 95
  1612, 102
  1621, 35, 63, 68, 102
  1625 convention, 54, 64, 69
  1630 convention, 55, 66–9, 103
  1633, 69, 103, 155
  1640, 113
  1641, 113
  1643, 114
  1648, 116
  1649, 118, 212
  1661, 174, 176
  1685, 132
  1686, 133
  1689, 194
  1689 convention, 187, 190–3, 202, 204–5
  1690, 194
  1695, 217–18, 221
  1700, 225
  1700–01, 226
  1702, 207, 229
  1703, 206–8, 230
  1706–07, 232–5
  committee of estates, 41, 115–16, 118, 164, 166–7
  Lords of the Articles, 14, 58, 68, 83, 213
  management, 35, 39, 58, 63–4, 67–8, 83, 213, 225–7, 232, 235, 241
  petitioning, 57–8, 63, 67–8, 75, 83, 86, 98, 190, 193–4, 204, 217, 225–6, 233, 240
  protestation, 25–6, 32–4, 40–1, 226, 229, 234, 239
  remeid of law, 57
  separate meetings of estates, 33
  walk-out, 213, 229, 234–5
parliament of England, 22, 51, 57, 76, 81, 162, 167, 180, 187, 222, 231, 233
pasquil, 143, 146, 149, 180
Paterson, John, archbishop of Glasgow, 205
Penninghame, 131
Pentland rising (1666), 83, 124, 176
Perth, 42, 95, 128, 150, 152
Perthshire, 226

petition, 44–5, 63, 124, 126, 156, 190, 200, 203, 208, 220, 222–3, 240
  address, 52, 55, 84, 134, 188, 191, 193–4, 205–7, 217, 224–5, 229, 231, 233–4
  answers, 53, 60–3, 66, 72–4, 76–7, 163, 224, 230
  counter-petition, 51, 75–7, 113
  England, 51–2, 57, 81
  humility, 50, 53, 55, 66, 69, 82, 85
  loyal address, 52, 55, 81, 86, 188, 220
  right to, 52, 67, 213, 225, 245
  serial, 61
  subscription, 60, 72, 76–7, 80, 189, 193, 205, 209, 224
  tumultuous, 37, 45, 73, 83
poetry, 140, 143, 150, 155, 158, 164, 166, 173, 180, 182, 212, 222, 242
polling, 3, 16, 202, 204–5, 233
popular politics, 7, 242
popular resistance, 46–7, 77, 83, 116, 124, 176, 190, 201, 208, 212, 226, 232, 234–5, 240–2, 245
popular sovereignty, 54, 147, 164, 176, 179, 198, 201, 234, 245
populism, 43, 176, 201, 244
postmaster, 174
prayer book (1637), 52, 70, 74, 104, 109, 111, 159, 161
Preston, 166
Primrose, James, 150
print culture, 6, 245
  England, 6, 137
print market, 8, 19, 138, 141–2, 219, 240
printing, 8, 235
  Aberdeen, 40, 141, 157–8, 160, 163, 168
  committee of estates, 162, 167
  Cromwellian, 167, 169
  crown, 96, 99, 109, 141, 149–51, 158, 161–2, 179–82, 188, 217, 226, 230
  Edinburgh, 1, 141–2, 157–9, 165, 169–71, 180, 182, 203, 219, 222, 224, 231–2
  Glasgow, 141, 158, 194, 224
  kirk, 100, 114, 117, 141, 158, 163–4, 166–8
  London, 40, 143, 152, 158, 167, 169, 171, 181, 194, 200, 202–3, 216, 219, 224, 230, 232, 241
  Netherlands, 151–3, 157, 159, 164, 175–7, 188
  parliament, 165
  Protesters, 169–71
  Resolutioners, 169–71
  royalist, 160, 163
  St Andrews, 153

proclamation, 144, 208
  Charles I, 37–8, 73–4, 109, 155, 159, 162
  Charles II, 82, 85, 173, 178–9
  James VI, 12, 61, 94, 96, 148, 153
  James VII, 182, 188
  Mary I, 146
  William II, 224–5
Protectorate (1653-9), 43–4, 121, 173
protest
  armed, 46–7, 83, 85, 116–17, 124, 232
  burning, 46–7, 129–30, 181, 189, 220, 232
protestation, 23–9, 39, 77, 101, 103, 110, 203
  out of doors, 32, 35, 37, 39–40, 97, 232
  power to nullify, 24, 34, 38–40, 43
  printing, 43, 169
  remeid of law, 24
  serial, 35, 46
  subscription, 22, 31, 33, 35, 43
Protestation (1641), 22, 91
Protesters, 23–9, 45, 79, 82, 119, 121, 127, 157,
  168–70, 174
public opinion, 71, 118, 244
  authority, 1, 11, 43, 160, 164, 172, 186, 200,
    240, 243
  clerical, 35–6, 61, 63, 68, 86, 167, 170, 194,
    203, 205
  covenanted nation, 38, 40, 44–8, 102, 105–6,
    117, 128, 176, 233–4
  definition, 2, 10–13
  freeholders, 59, 233
  godly, 42–3, 80, 115, 153, 167, 170–1, 175,
    197, 203
  historicisation, 2, 4, 9, 19, 241, 243
  kingdom, 39–40, 78, 159, 166, 199
  kirk, 153, 155, 159, 193
  laity, 36, 43, 61, 112, 163, 193–4, 201–8, 233
  lay patrons, 67
  nation, 76, 79, 83, 193, 202–3, 217, 222–4,
    226, 231, 233–4, 239
  nobles, 155
  origins of, 2, 4
  people, 63, 69, 71, 75, 78–9, 109, 161, 167,
    176, 189, 191, 224, 226, 234, 239
  subjects, 59, 61, 71, 73, 112, 155, 173, 194,
    227
  true remnant, 46–7, 178
public sphere, 51, 138, 183, 240
  England, 5, 7, 137, 240
  episodic, 6, 241
  Habermasian, 1, 4–8, 52, 242
  Ireland, 17
publics, 6, 8, 10, 52, 157, 240
  counter-publics, 6
  the publick, 11–12, 69, 217

Quakers, 133
quartering, 57, 75, 124–6, 216

Ramsay of Shielhill, Jane, 177
reasons, 33, 38, 42, 71, 227
rebellion, 74, 85–6, 133, 176, 181, 189–91, 199
referendum, 10, 233
Reformation (1560), 4, 53, 58, 94–5, 103, 133,
  241, 243–4
reformation of manners, 218
Reformation rebellion (1559-60), 94
remonstrance, 13, 40–1, 55, 69, 74, 78, 82, 84,
  115, 118–19, 159, 163–4, 170
Renfrew, 130
Renfrewshire, 123, 127, 130
representation, 40, 42, 52, 74, 76, 112, 153, 161,
  164, 176, 202
republicanism, 128, 167, 179
res publica, 154
Resolutioners, 42–3, 79, 119, 121, 127, 168–70,
  174
Restoration (1660), 45, 81–3, 91–2, 121, 123,
  173–5, 197
Revolution of 1688-90, 58, 91, 93, 185–7, 197,
  201–2, 211, 213, 215, 227, 237
ribbons, 181, 221
Ridpath, George, 203, 220, 226, 230
Ross, 42
Rotterdam, 176
Row, John, 35, 38, 68, 96, 154
royal supremacy, 14, 63, 67, 83, 86, 97, 100,
  102–3, 122–3, 129, 134, 149, 152, 197
royalism, 105, 110–11, 113, 118, 150, 160–1,
  163, 180–1
  rising, 115, 118, 121, 163, 166–7, 203, 212
Rule, Gilbert, 204
Russell, James, 179
Rutherford, Samuel, 121, 156, 175–6
Rutherglen, 46, 85

Sage, John, 200–1, 204, 233
salvo jure cujuslibet, 26
Sanquhar, 46–7, 128, 132
Sanquhar declaration (1680), 46, 128
Sanquhar protestation (1685), 47, 132
schoolmasters, 112, 123, 126, 130, 150, 232
Scotia, 197, 226, 231, 236
Scots language, 4, 16, 19, 138–9, 150, 155
Scott, James, first duke of Monmouth, 86
Second Book of Discipline, 101
  subscription, 99
sedition, 48, 74, 82, 152, 154, 159, 161, 174–5,
  194, 198, 225
  assembly, 33–4, 40, 62–3, 82

Index

leasing-making, 69, 143
petition, 50, 74, 82–4
protestation, 35, 45
regulation, 65, 77, 83, 97, 100–1, 122, 127, 133, 143, 149, 162, 174–5, 182, 227
sense, 1, 41, 44, 77–8, 115, 129, 176, 189, 202–3, 211, 222, 234
sentiments, 4, 23, 128, 211, 226, 234, 239
sermons, 11, 60–1, 100–1, 134, 144, 149, 173, 175, 182, 202–3
Seton of Pitmedden, William, 196
Sharp, James, archbishop of St. Andrews, 85, 171, 174
Shetland, 177
silence, 25, 35, 60–1
Skene, Katherine, Lady Murray, 232
Solemn Acknowledgement (1648), 117–18, 167, 169, 176
renewal, 190
Solemn Engagement (1648), 117
Solemn League and Covenant (1643), 44, 76, 91–3, 114–16, 120–1, 194, 198
burning, 174, 179
printing, 114, 117, 158, 173
renewal, 93, 117–18, 124, 132, 167, 190, 197, 221
subscription, 114
swearing, 114
Spain, 224
Spottiswood, John, archbishop of St Andrews, 34, 62, 69, 102
squadrone volante, 232
St Andrews, 42, 95, 101, 107, 111, 175, 188, 206
state formation, 100, 124–5, 127, 135, 212, 231, 243
Statutes of Iona (1609), 103
Stewart of Goodtrees, Sir James, 85, 176–7, 182, 198, 201, 225
Stewart, Henry, Lord Darnley, 146
Stewart, James, first earl of Moray, 148
Stewart, James, fourth duke of Lennox, 72
Stewart, John, first earl of Traquair, 71
Stirling, 37, 41–2, 82, 95, 98, 150, 173, 210, 233
Stirlingshire, 128
Strang, William, 160
Stranraer, 112, 123
Stuart, Esmé, first duke of Lennox, 95, 148
students, 96, 129, 181
subscription, 25, 28–9, 108
notary public, 25, 73, 96, 108, 110, 114
supplication. *See* petition
Sydserf, Thomas, 174

taxes, 55, 57, 155, 204, 212, 218, 229
tender of union (1652), 120, 170
Test (1681), 129–32, 191, 194
testimony, 17, 22, 28, 30, 33, 41, 44–8, 79, 118, 133, 135, 171, 176, 178–9, 181, 189–90, 192, 217
war by testimony, 47–8
The Hague, 164
toleration, 44, 79–80, 86, 121, 132–4, 169, 171, 182, 189, 193, 200, 205–8
Torwood excommunication (1680), 128
transportation, 125, 132
treason, 13, 16, 35, 37, 48, 62, 82, 115, 122, 127–8, 131–2, 151, 179, 188, 207
Treaty of London (1641), 75, 112–14
Twyne, John, 165
Tyler, Evan, 158

union negotiations, 32–3, 207, 230, 232
Union of 1707, 18–19, 53, 93, 187, 227–8, 237, 245–6
Union of Crowns (1603), 4, 13–14, 53, 62, 138, 150, 155, 214, 230–1, 241
United Societies, 92, 132–3, 190, 218
Urr, 218

vox populi, 240

Waldegrave, Robert, 151
Watson, James, 182
Webster, James, 208
western association, 118
Western Remonstrance (1650), 41, 78, 82, 119
Westminster confession (1647), 115, 195, 198
Westminster directory (1645), 115, 193
Whiggamore Raid (1648), 77, 117
Wigtown, 131
William II, 15, 192–4, 215–18, 221, 224
William of Orange, 134, 185, 188, 191, 196, 199
Williamites, episcopalian, 191, 193
Williamson, David, 203
Wilson, Margaret, 131
witch trials, 142, 149, 219
witness, 22, 27–8, 36, 44, 46
women, 16, 45, 48, 71, 108–9, 118, 123, 125, 132, 138, 147, 154, 177, 180, 212, 233–4, 241, 244
consent, 233
crowds, 16, 60, 70, 84, 109, 111, 190, 226, 232
execution, 128, 131
investors, 223
literacy, 16, 85, 140

women (cont.)
oaths, 16, 91–2, 97, 131–2
petitioning, 51, 57, 73, 75, 80, 84
preaching, 129
protestation, 48
subscription, 16, 97, 99, 108, 114

taxation, 213
writing, 16, 151, 222
Wood, James, 169, 171
Wylie, Robert, 1, 208, 234

Young, Robert, 158

Lightning Source UK Ltd.
Milton Keynes UK
UKHW021446091220
374873UK00003B/53